The Senses Considered as Perceptual Systems

The Senses Considered as Perceptual Systems

James J. Gibson / *Cornell University*

GREENWOOD PRESS, PUBLISHERS
WESTPORT, CONNECTICUT

Library of Congress Cataloging in Publication Data

Gibson, James Jerome, 1904-
    The senses considered as perceptual systems.

    Reprint. Originally published: Boston : Houghton
Mifflin, 1966.
    Bibliography: p.
    Includes index.
    1. Perception. 2. Senses and sensation. I. Title.
BF311.G52 1983   152.1   83-1716
ISBN 0-313-23961-4 (lib. bdg.)

Reprinted with the permission of Houghton Mifflin Company

Reprinted in 1983 by Greenwood Press
An imprint of Greenwood Publishing Group, Inc.
88 Post Road West, Westport, Connecticut 06881

Printed in the United States of America

10

Editor's Foreword

How do animals, including human beings, secure the information from the world about them that is essential to their adaptation to it and their survival in it? Since ancient times this all-important question has been asked in many ways and a great variety of answers have been proposed. In this book the basic problem is analyzed anew and solutions are suggested which are both scientifically satisfying and almost startlingly novel.

Dr. Gibson does not treat of the different senses as mere producers of visual, auditory, tactual, or other sensations. Rather, he regards them as active seeking mechanisms for looking, listening, touching, and the like. This means that the emphasis is on explanations of how we are able to have the constant perceptions that we need for effective action and avoidance of physical harm in our everyday lives. The author clearly supports his view that the perception of reality is not something assembled or computed by the brain from an ever-varying kaleidoscope of sensations.

Dr. Gibson emphasizes the importance of regarding the different perceptual systems not only as active, but also interrelated. He points out that visual perception, for example, is frequently a seeking of information by head and eye movements coordinated in the so-called eye-head system. Similar active adjustments take place as the organism secures information with its ear-head system. The same can be said of the seeking and searching of the hand-body system. These out-reaching mechanisms search out for the organism the required perceptual information about the world in which it exists.

This dynamic perception is contrasted with the quite different sensory experience that results from the activation of essentially passive receptors. As the author notes, sensory experiences resulting from passive stimulation, that is, simple receptor activation, have been very widely studied in laboratories of physiology and psychology, with rigorous control of both the stimulus energies presented to the organism and the receptor cells that are acted upon. Dr. Gibson acknowledges these sensory experiences as facts, but he treats them as by-products of perception rather than building blocks.

In other words, this book is not just another treatise on the anatomy and physiology of receptors. It is not a new report on quantitative experimental findings of sensory thresholds. It is not an essay on psychophysics. It is even not directly concerned with the sensory projection areas of the brain or with the coding of impulses in afferent peripheral nerves. Rather, it has quite another mission, all too often neglected or forgotten. It explains how our senses, as active interrelated systems, provide continuous, stable information that alone makes adaptive living possible.

Successive chapters embrace the contribution made by each of the main receptor systems that are basic to the adjustment of the organism to its world. To me, the author's thesis seems most arresting in his daring, yet convincing new look at the psychological functions of the total visual mechanism. He introduces the concept of "ecological optics." This new treatment is not mentalistic; it is not traditionally physiological or physical; but it is still rigorously scientific. In terms of this novel point of view, the book examines some fundamental questions in psychology: What is innate and what is acquired in perception? What is the role of learning in establishing adult perception? How is perceiving related to expectancy? What is the effect of language on perceiving? What are perceptual illusions?

All in all, the editor considers this novel and challenging book a most important contribution to the assumptions underlying all scientific concern with living animals, especially human beings. In some respects it amplifies and develops ideas that were first presented in the author's earlier book, *The Perception of the Visual World* (Houghton Mifflin, 1950). That book has received wide acceptance and has sparked many continuing fruitful experimental programs. An acquaintance of the editor, one of England's ablest psychologists, said of that earlier book that it seemed to him the most insightful volume to come from American psychology for decades. Certainly this new book merits similar praise. I have no doubt it will be forthcoming. It is refreshingly novel in the solutions it proposes for some of the oldest and most fundamental problems.

Certainly not all professional students of mental life will agree with all the conclusions of this book. But it will be a brave psychologist indeed who feels he can afford to be ignorant of what is said in it.

Leonard Carmichael

Preface

This book has had to be written twice — once in 1958–59 and again in 1963–64. The second draft is more explicit and coherent than the first, for a good deal of experimenting, teaching, arguing, reading, and reformulating came in between. I needed to restudy the theories of perception handed down from the philosophers of the seventeenth and eighteenth centuries — theories that were only slightly modified by the experimental psychologists of the nineteenth and twentieth centuries. I also had to survey the whole area of the anatomy and physiology of the senses. It was difficult to shake off the traditional explanations of the facts while keeping hold of the facts themselves.

I am very grateful to the Institute for Advanced Study in Princeton for taking me in and then leaving me alone while the first draft was being written. The Center for Advanced Study in the Behavioral Sciences sheltered me during the second draft, and that year was a real pleasure. These admirable establishments have made this book possible. And if the National Institutes of Health had not granted Cornell one of their career research awards on my behalf, the book would not be finished yet.

A series of experiments lies behind the writing of this book. These studies, published and unpublished, have been supported for many years by the Physiological Psychology Branch of the Office of Naval Research under a contract with Cornell (Nonr 401-14). This agreement is for work on the perception of "motion" and of "space." The justification for such support has been that clarification of these ancient puzzles might contribute to aviation — and so it will someday.

These chapters have been read in various versions and parts by a considerable number of knowledgeable persons, and to them I am indebted. The ones who gave the greatest help in revision were Leonard Carmichael, Wendell Garner, Lloyd Kaufman, and T. A. Ryan. In formulation there are many others who helped, especially Julian Hochberg, who helped by arguing with me (or sometimes even agreeing) and thereby lessened the obscurity that the reader must face.

The three experimental investigators in the field of perception who seem to be working closest to the vein of evidence that I am trying to mine are all from outside this country. They are Ivo Kohler of Innsbruck, Gunnar Johansson of Uppsala, and the late Albert Michotte of Louvain.

Their discoveries are invaluable and, however the facts are interpreted, crucial for any theory of sense perception.

Psychologists of the previous generation to whom I owe the greatest intellectual debt are E. B. Holt, Kurt Koffka, L. T. Troland, and E. G. Boring. This is a mixed group, but the fact is that I am attempting to reformulate stimulus-response theory, Gestalt phenomenology, and psychophysics so as to extract new theorems from these old theories.

Above all, I am indebted to my students. A teacher depends on his students as much as they do on him. The young psychologists to whom I owe most are John Hay, Jacob Beck, Howard Flock, William Schiff, Horace Reynolds, Anne Danielson Pick, and Herbert Pick.

This whole inquiry has been shared for years with Eleanor J. Gibson, my wife. In 1963, however, we divided the problems between us, and she has concentrated on perceptual learning and development while I concentrated on the senses. Her forthcoming book will take up the story where mine leaves off.

Ithaca, New York   J. J. G.
April 1966

Contents

of Mechanoreceptors in the Body **106**/ Perceptual Subsystems **109**/ The Difference between Muscle Sensitivity
and Joint Sensitivity **109**/ The Use of the Term
"Kinesthesis" **111**/ The Covariation of Skin Sensitivity and
Joint Sensitivity **111**/ The Differentiated Skin **114**/

Any appearances whatever present themselves, not only when its object stimulates a sense, but also when the sense by itself alone is stimulated, provided only it be stimulated in the same manner as it is by the object.

ARISTOTLE, 330 B.C.

Upon every great agitation or concussion of the brain whereby the optic nerve suffereth any great violence, there appeareth before the eye a certain light, which light is nothing without, but an apparition only, all that is real being the concussion. THOMAS HOBBES, 1651

That which through the medium of our senses is actually perceived by the sensorium is indeed merely a property or change of condition of our nerves; but the imagination and reason are ready to interpret the modification in the state of the nerves as properties of the external bodies themselves.

JOHANNES MÜLLER, 1838

Such objects are always imagined as being present in the field of vision as would have to be there in order to produce the same effect on the nervous mechanism.

HERMANN VON HELMHOLTZ, 1867

There is nothing so plain boring as the constant repetition of assertions that are not true.

J. L. AUSTIN, 1962

INTRODUCTION

What are the senses?

It has always been assumed that the senses were channels of sensation. To consider them as systems for perception, as this book proposes to do, may sound strange. But the fact is that there are two different meanings of the verb *to sense*, first, *to detect something,* and second, *to have a sensation.* When the senses are considered as perceptual systems the first meaning of the term is being used.

In the second meaning of the term there is a vast difference between sensations and perceptions. In 1785, Thomas Reid wrote:

> The external senses have a double province; to make us feel, and to make us perceive. They furnish us with a variety of sensations, some pleasant, others painful, and others indifferent; at the same time they give us a conception, and an invincible belief of the existence of external objects. This conception of external objects is the work of nature. The belief of their existence, which our senses give, is the work of nature; so likewise is the sensation that accompanies it. This conception and belief which nature produces by means of the senses, we call perception. The feeling which goes along with the perception, we call sensation. The perception and its corresponding sensation are produced at the same time. In our experience we never find them disjoined. Hence we are led to consider them as one thing, to give them one name, and to confound their different attributes. It becomes very difficult to separate them in thought, to attend to each by itself, and to attribute nothing to it which belongs to the other (*Essays on the Intellectual Powers of Man,* II, p. 17).

That province of the senses which is to "furnish us with a variety of sensations" is by no means the same as that which is to "make us perceive." Reid was right. The part of this passage that might be objected

1

to is the suggestion that perception of objects must depend on "conception and belief." It will here be suggested that the senses can obtain information about objects in the world without the intervention of an intellectual process — or at least that they can do so when they operate as perceptual systems.

In this book I will distinguish the input to the nervous system that evokes conscious sensation from the input that evokes perception. I will not even speak of the ingoing impulses in nerves as "sensory," so as not to imply that all inputs arouse sense impressions. For it is surely a fact that *detecting* something can sometimes occur without the accompaniment of sense impressions. An example is the visual detection of one thing behind another, which is described in Chapter 10. There will be many examples of the principle that stimulus information can determine perception without having to enter consciousness in the form of sensation.

The reader should make allowance for the double meaning of the verb *to sense*. The detecting of stimulus information without any awareness of what sense organ has been excited, or of the quality of the receptor, can be described as "sensationless perception." But this does not mean that perception can occur without stimulation of receptors; it only means that organs of perception are sometimes stimulated in such a way that they are not specified in consciousness. Perception cannot be "extra-sensory," if that means without any input; it can only be so if that means without awareness of the visual, auditory, or other quality of the input. An example of this is the "obstacle sense" of the blind, which is felt as "facial vision" but is actually auditory echo detection. The blind man "senses" the wall in front of him without realizing what sense has been stimulated. In short, there can be sensationless perception, but not informationless perception.

The seemingly paradoxical assertion will be made that perception is not based on sensation. That is, it is not based on having sensations, as in the second meaning, but it is surely based on detecting information, as in the first meaning.

There are two different levels of sensitivity. It will be evident in Chapter 2 that the so-called sense organs are of at least two different sorts: the passive receptors that respond each to its appropriate form of energy, and the active perceptual organs, better called systems, that can search out the information in stimulus energy. The receptors have measurable thresholds below which they are not excited; the organs and systems do not have fixed thresholds except as they depend on receptors.

Similarly, there are different levels of stimulation. The stimulus energy of optics, mechanics, and chemistry is coordinate with receptors, but the stimulus information to be described is coordinate with perceptual systems. Stimulus energy varies along simple dimensions like intensity and frequency, but stimulus information varies along innumerable complex dimensions, not all amenable to physical measurement.

When the senses are considered as channels of sensation (and this is how the physiologist, the psychologist, and the philosopher have considered them), one is thinking of the passive receptors and the energies that stimulate them, the sensitive elements in the eyes, ears, nose, mouth, and skin. The experimenters in physiology and psychology have been establishing the conditions and limits at this level of stimulation for more than a century. A vast literature of sensory physiology has developed and a great deal is known about the receptors. It is a highly respected branch of science. But all this exact knowledge of sensation is vaguely unsatisfactory since it does not explain how animals and men accomplish sense perception.

It can be shown that the easily measured variables of stimulus energy, the intensity of light, sound, odor, and touch, for example, vary from place to place and from time to time as the individual goes about his business in the environment. The stimulation of receptors and the presumed sensations, therefore, are variable and changing in the extreme, unless they are experimentally controlled in a laboratory. The unanswered question of sense perception is how an observer, animal or human, can obtain constant perceptions in everyday life on the basis of these continually changing sensations. For the fact is that animals and men do perceive and respond to the permanent properties of the environment as well as to the changes in it.

Besides the changes in stimuli from place to place and from time to time, it can also be shown that certain higher-order variables — stimulus energy, ratios, and proportions, for example — do *not* change. They remain invariant with movements of the observer and with changes in the intensity of stimulation. The description of such stimulus invariants is a main concern of the chapters to follow. And it will be shown that these invariants of the energy flux at the receptors of an organism correspond to the permanent properties of the environment. They constitute, therefore, information about the permanent environment.

The active observer gets invariant perceptions despite varying sensations. He perceives a constant object by vision despite changing sensations of light; he perceives a constant object by feel despite changing sensations of pressure; he perceives the same source of sound despite changing sensations of loudness in his ears. The hypothesis is that constant perception depends on the ability of the individual to detect the invariants, and that he ordinarily pays no attention whatever to the flux of changing sensations.

The ways in which animals and men pick up information by looking, listening, sniffing, tasting, and touching are the subject of this book.

These five perceptual systems overlap one another; they are not mutually exclusive. They often focus on the same information — that is, the same information can be picked up by a combination of perceptual systems working together as well as by one perceptual system working alone. The eyes, ears, nose, mouth, and skin can orient, explore, and investigate. When thus active they are neither passive senses nor channels of sensory quality, but ways of paying attention to whatever is constant in the changing stimulation. In exploratory looking, tasting, and touching the sense impressions are incidental symptoms of the exploration, and what gets isolated is information about the object looked at, tasted, or touched. The movements of the eyes, the mouth, and the hands, in fact, seem to keep changing the input at the receptive level, the input of sensation, just so as to isolate over time the invariants of the input at the level of the perceptual system.

The Senses and the Sensory Nerves

What about the input of the sensory nerves? We have been taught that the impulses in these fiber bundles comprised the messages of sense and that they were the only possible basis for perception. This doctrine is so generally accepted that to challenge it seems to fly in the face of physiology. There is said to be a receptor mosaic for each sense connecting with the central nervous system and projecting the pattern of excited receptors to the brain. But let us note that if the perceptual organs are normally exploratory, as they are, this anatomical projection of receptors is quite simply irrelevant for the process of normal perception. It is not false, for it explains after-images, as well as many of the curiosities of subjective sensory experience that occur when stimuli are imposed on a passive observer by an experimenter. Experiments on sensation are usually of this sort. But the neural input of the mobile eyes in the mobile head of a mobile animal, for example, cannot be thought of as the anatomical pattern of the nerve cells that are excited in the fiber bundle. This anatomical pattern changes from moment to moment. Neurophysiologists in the past have been reluctant to face up to this difficulty in explaining perception, for they know more about the anatomy of the eyes, ears, and skin than they do about the physiology of looking, listening, and touching.

What might be a physiological or functional equivalent of the external information, if it cannot be anatomical? How could invariants get into the nervous system? The same incoming nerve fiber makes a different contribution to the pickup of information from one moment to the next. The pattern of the excited receptors is of no account; what counts is the external pattern that is temporarily occupied by excited receptors as the eyes roam over the world, or as the skin moves over an object. The individual sensory units have to function *vicariously,* to borrow a term from Lashley, a neuropsychologist.

The answers to these questions are not yet clear, but I am suggesting new directions in which we may look for them. Instead of looking to the brain alone for an explanation of constant perception, it should be sought in the neural loops of an active perceptual system that includes the adjustments of the perceptual organ. Instead of supposing that the brain constructs or computes the objective information from a kaleidoscopic inflow of sensations, we may suppose that the orienting of the organs of perception is governed by the brain so that the whole system of input and output resonates to the external information.

If this formula is correct, the input of the sensory nerves is not the basis of perception as we have been taught for centuries, but only half of it. It is only the basis for passive sense impressions. These are not the data of perception, not the raw material out of which perception is fashioned by the brain. The active senses cannot be simply the initiators of *signals* in nerve fibers or *messages* to the brain; instead they are analogous to tentacles and feelers. And the function of the brain when looped with its perceptual organs is not to decode signals, nor to interpret messages, nor to accept images. These old analogies no longer apply. The function of the brain is not even to *organize* the sensory input or to *process* the data, in modern terminology. The perceptual systems, including the nerve centers at various levels up to the brain, are ways of seeking and extracting information about the environment from the flowing array of ambient energy.

The Improvement of Perception with Learning

The elementary colors, sounds, smells, tastes, and pressures that were supposed to be the only data of sense (and that are indeed obtained when a passive observer is stimulated by carefully measured applications of energy in a laboratory) have been thought of as an inborn repertory of experience on which a baby's later perception is founded. Learning to perceive, then, had to be some such process as the associating of memories with these bare impressions, or the interpreting of them, or the classifying of them, or the organizing of them. Theories of perception have been concerned with operations of this sort.

If the senses are perceptual systems, however, the infant does not have sensations at birth but starts at once to pick up information from the world. His detection equipment cannot be exactly oriented at first, and his attention is imprecise; nevertheless, he looks at things, and touches and mouths them, and listens to events. As he grows, he learns to use his perceptual systems more skillfully, and his attention becomes educated to the subtleties of stimulus information. He does learn to perceive but he does *not* have to learn to convert sense data into perception.

On the assumption that the senses are channels of sensation, the process of learning has been thought of by stimulus-response psychologists as an attaching of new responses to a fixed set of possible inputs. On the assumption that the senses are perceptual systems, however, the emphasis is shifted to the discovery of new stimulus invariants, new properties of the world, to which the child's repertory of responses can be applied. This is perceptual learning as distinguished from performatory learning. Both kinds of learning occur in the child, but perceptual learning is the more in need of study because it is the more neglected. In Chapter 3, and especially in Chapter 12, this idea will be followed up.

The Facts to be Surveyed

The plan of this book is to put together the existing knowledge of the senses in the framework of the theory that has just been outlined — to survey the senses in the interest of understanding perception. Sensory physiology and psychology are factual disciplines, not theoretical ones, and the solid body of facts written down in journals and books would fill a large library. It is hard for the curious student of perception to weigh this mass of evidence, for it is highly specialized and much of it makes dull reading.

Few modern attempts have been made to integrate all this information within the covers of a book. The only two are Piéron, *The Sensations* (1952), and Geldard, *The Human Senses* (1953). The handbooks of physiology and experimental psychology do not attempt an overview, and the popularizations that have been written are misleading. The investigators of the senses tend to stay close to that sense in which they specialize.

As to the books on perception, there are many, by psychologists and philosophers, but they are not much grounded in the biology of sensitivity. They take sensations for granted, leaving them to the specialists, and are mainly concerned with theories of perception, the problem of perceptual constancy, the ways in which perceiving depends on the personality of the perceiver, and the reasons we have such an invincible belief in external objects when we have no right to it.

The question, then, is, how do the senses work? Since the senses are being considered as perceptual systems, the question is not how the receptors work, or how the nerve cells work, or where the impulses go, but how the systems work as a whole. We are interested in the useful senses, the organs by which an organism can take account of its environment and cope with objective facts.

1 / The Environment as a Source of Stimulation

In considering the problem of perception in man and animals the first question to ask should be, what is there to be perceived? And the preliminary answer would be, the environment that is common to man and animals. The senses convey information about the world, and therefore we ought to review what is known about the world that the senses detect. The senses of an individual only work when they are stimulated, and the environment of the individual is the source of all stimulation. Let us begin by describing the general environment of all animals and then describing the ambient stimulus environment of a single animal at a given place and time in relation to the first.

The habitat of all animals, as far as we now know, is the planet earth. In the most general terms this is a sphere composed of land, water, and air. There is in fact a lithosphere, a hydrosphere, and an atmosphere, the last being a sort of shell or envelope surrounding the spherical surface of earth and sea. Animals live fairly close to this surface, although some are aquatic and some are terrestrial. Land, water, and air are the main components of the environment, and we should keep this fact in mind when we consider the sources and causes of stimulation.

To say that these are *components* reminds us of the ancient belief in the "elements," earth, air, and water, and a mysterious one named fire. In our sophistication about physical science we now reserve the term *element* for the chemical substances of the periodic table and assert that only these are truly elementary. But the Greek observers of the world were not wrong, and their elements do not really contradict modern physical knowledge. We now say that matter can exist in one of three states, solid, liquid, or gas, and that all are somehow manifestations of energy. The principal solid is the earth and its furniture, the principal liquid is the waters of the earth, the principal gas is the air, and the most obvious example of energy is fire. The Greeks were quite right about the overall composition of the world, although they had not analyzed its components as finely as we have. What science takes as an element depends on the level of the particular science, and we are here concerned with ecology, not with chemistry and physics. The bodies of animals, their behavior, and their organs for receiving stimulation depend profoundly on elements in the Greek sense — on whether they live *in* the water or *on* the land, or fly in the air.

The Terrestrial Environment

The face of the earth consists of wrinkled surfaces of rock and soil along with smooth surfaces of water. The liquid surface is everywhere exactly perpendicular to the line of gravity; the solid surface is on the average perpendicular to it.

The curvature of these surfaces is so small that it approaches the zero curvature of a plane. The size of the planet, in other words, is so vast in comparison to the size of any animal that for ordinary purposes the substratum is flat. The ancient men who assumed that the *world* was flat were thus not mistaken in this observation either; they were only limited in their conception of the size of the world. The measurement of this substratum conformed to the plane geometry of Euclid, and its geography was, and still is, excellently represented by a plane map.

The environment of a terrestrial animal, then, during the millions of years of evolutionary history, had certain simple invariants. They were the earth "below," the air "above," and the "waters under the earth." The ground was level and rigid, a surface of support. The air was unresistant — a space for locomotion, open to the daily cycles of warmth and light from the sky, penetrating everywhere among the furniture of the earth. The air was always and everywhere a medium for breathing, the occasional bearer of odors and sounds, and transparent to the shapes of things by day.

The solid terrestrial environment, we noted, is wrinkled. It is structured by mountains and hills on the scale of kilometers. It is structured by trees and other vegetation on the scale of meters. It is further structured into all sorts of things like stones and sticks on the scale of centimeters. And it is still further textured by such things as crystals and plant cells on the scale of millimeters. In short, it has structure at all levels of size. The layout or arrangement of these solid surfaces relative to the medium of the air has determined the behavior and the very life of terrestrial animals.

The Consequences of Rigidity

Since an important part of the environment consists of matter in the solid state, it would be useful to review the simpler physical facts of solidity. A solid substance is one that has a high resistance to any change of its shape, and this resistance can be measured. A liquid is one that has little resistance to change of shape. A gas cannot even be said to have a shape. The explanation of these facts is to be found in molecular forces within the substance.

It is well to remember also that the solid, liquid, or gaseous state of anything depends on its temperature. Earth, water, and air keep their state only at the moderate range of temperature which holds for this planet in its present era of cosmic evolution. Solids have a very high boiling point; gases have a very low freezing point. For millions of years the temperatures on the face of the earth have not gone far beyond the limits within which water is liquid — zero degrees to 100 degrees on the Centigrade scale. The choice of this rather than some other scale of numbers for measuring temperature is a practical one. Animals and men cannot live beyond these limits; they die when the water in their tissues either freezes or boils. The world would not be what it is if its water were either ice or steam. The evolution of life depended on the present level of temperature. The vicissitudes of life included the variations of this level, the climatic changes over time during the ice ages, and the climatic differences between equatorial and polar zones of the earth.

So the solid environment is a "support" for behavior. It is rigid. Unlike the viscous or liquid environment of mud, lava, slough, or water, it permits the animal to stand and walk upon legs, and to find his way about from place to place. This rigidity of layout puts him in danger of collision, to be sure, either with an obstacle or by falling off a cliff, but it does afford surfaces which keep the same arrangement. Rigidity gives geometrical permanence to places and constancy of shape and size to things. It therefore "supports" not only the upright stance but also locomotion, orientation, and manipulation.

The airspaces between connected solids are also permanent in shape, although not themselves solid. It is this fact, perhaps, that has led abstract thinkers to extend the concept of rigidity and apply it to so-called empty space, to assume that even the outer space between the stars is like the airspace of Euclidean geometry. However dubious this may be, it is certain at least that terrestrial space is rigid. The measuring stick of the earthbound surveyor is rigid, and the distances and angles of the terrain conform to the laws of Euclid.

A fair part of the habitat of animals, however, is not rigid. The swamp and the stream will not support locomotion. Water flows and falls. The surfaces of the cloud and the fire change. Mud and clay, being viscous, can be formed or transformed by the hands of men — into pots, for example. But the most notable non-rigid substances of one organism's environment are the bodies of other organisms. They grow in size and alter in shape. Plants and animals are flexible. The part of an individual's environment that consists of the squirming and moving bodies of other animals is at a special level, which will be considered later.

The Consequences of Gravity

Any substance, whatever its state, is attracted toward the center of the earth by a force proportional to its own mass, as Newton discovered. This law explains why the planet is round and at the same time why the earth tends everywhere toward the horizontal. A horizontal plane is simply a plane perpendicular to the line of force of gravity. This law explains not only "falling bodies" but also "sinking substances" — that is, the general layout of earth, water, and air. Considering their mass relative to their volume, a solid, a liquid, and a gas will tend to form layers, in that order.

Animals no less than other bodies are pressed downward upon the substratum by gravity. They touch the earth's surface and are touched by it. Land animals would in fact be flattened out on the ground like stranded jellyfish if they did not have rigid skeletons to prevent it. None of us, animals or men, can long avoid contact with the earth, and only upon it can we come to rest. Gravity is a universal and continuous constant. All organisms, even the plants, respond in some sense to gravity. The most primitive kind of responsiveness, accordingly, is that to gravity.

Although the gravitational fields known to astronomy surround the heavenly bodies, extending outward through other bodies and explaining their mutual attraction, the gravitational field of the earth as a habitat is simpler, for it is on a much smaller scale. Terrestrial gravity is a downward force coming from the substratum. It constantly pulls the animal toward its surface of support. The lines of force of the field are stationary, parallel, and vertical. The field brings about two major kinds of stimulation in animals.

The first effect is to produce stresses inside the body of an animal, causing heavier organs to press upon lighter tissues and putting tension on the skeleton and muscles. The second effect is to produce mechanical deformation of the underside of the body in contact with the ground. As we shall see, animals have developed special receptors for both the internal and the superficial kinds of stimulation.

Animals are generally mobile, and the higher animals go through periodic cycles of sleep and wakefulness in which their muscles are in a relatively low or a relatively high state of tension. Only in the latter state can they maintain postural equilibrium with respect to gravity. Only then can they move about. The limp animal is asleep and relatively unreceptive — or dead. The animal in an upright posture is awake, receptive, and prepared to behave. It is balanced, but in a different way from the balance of a rock on its base. It can move, but in a way different from the movement of a falling body. It obeys Newton's laws of gravity and motion, but it transcends them by resisting gravity and by initiating its own motion.

The Consequences of Electromagnetic Radiation

Considered as a planet, the earth rotates with reference to the sun and accordingly a given region is periodically exposed to the sun's radiation. When such a region is considered as a habitat, however, the environment consists of two halves, the ground and the sky, separated by a horizon, and thus the sun moves with reference to the environment. From sunrise to sunset a region is exposed to the direct radiation of the sun, to diffused radiation from the sky, and to reflected radiation from the surfaces of the terrain itself.

The sun's radiation, as we know, covers a wide band of wavelengths, from short to long, from ultraviolet to infrared, although what reaches the earth is by no means the whole electromagnetic spectrum. The "far" ultraviolet is absorbed by the atmosphere. The waves of intermediate length are called light. The longer waves are called radiant heat. A great deal of energy is carried by the longer waves.

This radiation keeps the plants alive, by virtue of photosynthesis and the carbon dioxide cycle, and the plant's food keeps the animals alive. The energy flow from the sun and the energy exchanges involving plants, soil, water, atmosphere, and animals make life possible and constitute a sort of nutritional economy. But the sun's heat also affects animals directly. The daily fluctuations of temperature (due to the planet's axial rotation) and the seasonal fluctuations of the northern and southern hemispheres (due to the planet's tilted axis and its orbit around the sun) are cycles to which every animal must adapt its behavior. It must act in one way when the temperature goes up and in another way when the temperature goes down — during day and night, during summer and winter. These cycles determine corresponding cycles of its activity, for all levels of activity from chemistry to consciousness.

The birds and the mammals especially, having developed a way of keeping their internal temperature constant, must be sensitive to the rate at which their bodies are losing heat to the environment or gaining it. If the surrounding medium is too cold, or too hot, the outflow may exceed the capacity for physiological compensation, and a behavioral adjustment is required. An increase or a decrease in the temperature of the air and ground, then, is a cause of stimulation. We say loosely that animals "feel the cold" or "feel the heat."

The Special Consequences of Light

The limits of the special band of radiation we call light are difficult to define objectively except in terms of the photochemistry of certain organic substances. "Light" is not quite the same thing for plants as it is for animals, and it has different limits for invertebrate animals like bees than for vertebrate animals like birds. Nevertheless, energy of wavelengths somewhere between a thousandth of a millimeter (a micron) and a millionth of a millimeter (a millimicron) has special characteristics that make it a unique stimulating agency for animals. For our purposes, this is light.

The physics of light, disregarding bioluminescence, is described in many textbooks. As a kind of radiation, light is propagated outward from an incandescent substance (sun, fire) with enormous velocity. It is transmitted through a gas with little interference, through a liquid with somewhat more interference, and through a solid usually not at all, being reflected or absorbed instead. A certain proportion of light is reflected at a surface, the remainder being either absorbed (by an opaque surface) or transmitted with refraction (by a transparent surface). An opaque solid surface of low reflectance (called "black") reflects little and absorbs much of the light; a surface of high reflectance (called "white") reflects much and absorbs little of the light. Although light travels through air in straight lines, a certain amount is diffused or scattered by fine particles such as dust or liquid droplets. All of these facts about the physics of light must be combined in order to understand the ecology of light — that is, the illumination of an environment.

The only terrestrial surfaces on which light falls exclusively from the sun are planes that face the sun's rays at a given time of the day. Other surfaces may be partly or wholly illuminated by light but not exposed to the sun. They receive diffused light from the sky and reflected light from other surfaces. A "ceiling," for example, is illuminated wholly by reflected light. Terrestrial airspaces are thus "filled" with light; they contain a flux of interlocking reflected rays in all directions at all points. This dense reverberating network of rays is an important but neglected fact of optics, to which we will refer in elaborating what may be called *ecological* optics.

As a consequence of this arrangement, only a part of the light falling on a terrestrial animal comes *directly* from the sun, usually a small part and sometimes none. Most of it is either diffused light from the sky or light scattered and reflected from other terrestrial surfaces. *All* of it is the latter if the animal is under a shelter. *Ambient* light, therefore, is quite a different thing from *radiant* light, having been modified in the ways mentioned above (see Figure 1.1). It is the light that surrounds an observer.

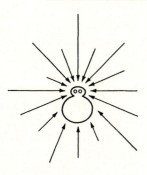

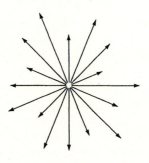

Ambient light to an organism   Radiant light from an energy source

Figure 1.1   Ambient and Radiant Light

Ambient light is recurrent, in accordance with the cycle of day and night, and it tends to establish the sleeping-waking rhythms of animals. The upper and lower hemispheres of ambient light are anchored to gravity, in that the intensity of light from the sky is always greater than the intensity of light from the earth. A negative geotropism therefore usually coincides with a positive phototropism. On a level terrain, the two hemispheres of ambient light are exactly divided by the meridian of the horizon, the plane of this meridian being exactly perpendicular to gravity. The ambient light in this lower hemisphere is structured and textured in a way that corresponds to the structure and texture of the earth.

These facts of ecological optics are not usually described in physical optics. Ambient light is taken with reference to an organism; radiant light is taken with reference to the source of energy. Abstractly, ambient rays converge to a point in space, whereas radiant rays diverge from a point in space. Ambient energy has reference to an environment; radiant energy has reference to the universe.

The essential feature of ambient light as a potential stimulus for an organism is that intensities are different in different directions. Even in the simplest organisms there seems to be an ability to respond to a difference of intensity in the light falling on one half of its body and that falling on the other. This is the basis of phototropism. The animal that orients to "light" is actually responding to the uneven distribution of ambient light on its skin. The coarsest and crudest intensity difference in ambient light is caused by the difference between sky and substratum. The finer and more elaborate differences involve the pattern and texture of ambient light. How animals come to evolve the ability to respond to these finer differences will be the subject of a later chapter. It may be noted here that the great majority of animals adapted to ambient light with a pair of lateral eyes permitting panoramic vision, not forward-pointing eyes of the human type which both fix on the same object.

The Air as a Medium

The emergence of life from the sea was surely one of the greatest strides in evolution. Animals had to acquire not only air-breathing but a new mode of locomotion. They were no longer buoyed up by water but pulled down upon the ground. A fish-like creature could only writhe, squirm, or glide. Later, animals developed more elaborate and faster ways of getting around by means of limbs — ways like hopping, walking, running, and even flying. Much later, certain mammals became adept at moving among tree branches. All these divergent adaptations, exploiting the various possible ways of getting from one place to another, began with the original adaptation to a solid surface with airspace above it. The feet of animals depended on the footing afforded.

Air is an excellent medium for terrestrial locomotion. Being unresistant compared to water, it does not require the streamlined anatomy needed by fish for rapid movement, and therefore makes possible various evolutionary experiments with the anatomy of limbs. A most successful adaptation of locomotor organs was that of the primates, who evolved hands instead of forepaws, providing a basis for the still more complex behavior of manipulating objects.

The atmosphere, then, is a medium. A medium permits more or less unhindered movements of animals and displacements of objects. Fundamentally, I suggest, this is what is meant by "space." But a medium has other equally important properties. It also permits the *flow of information*. It permits the flux of light, it transmits vibration, and it mediates the diffusion of volatile substances. Only by illumination do animals "see" things, only by vibration do they "hear" things, and only by diffusion do they "smell" things. I shall argue that in these three ways various properties of a thing are broadcast, as it were, when it is illuminated, or vibrating, or chemically volatile.

We need to examine the physical basis of these types of flow of stimulus information from a source in the distant environment to the position of a sentient animal. How an individual *picks up* the information in light, sound, and odor is a question for later chapters. Most of what is broadcast by a light-emitting or light-reflecting source, or a noisy or an odorous source, is never picked up at all; it is wasted for purposes of stimulation. But a set of perspective projections, or a field of sound waves, or the diffusion field of a volatile substance is a perfectly objective physical fact. It is *potentially* stimulating, and whether or not it actually excites receptors need not here concern us.

Ambient Information

Perspective Projections of an Object

A habitat consists of an arrangement of surfaces, that is, a layout of planes at various angles to one another. Call them *faces* or *facets*, depending on whether they are large or small. If this layout is illuminated, the reflecting planes will generate the dense interlocking network of rays mentioned earlier. At every point in the illuminated medium there will be a sheaf or "pencil" of rays converging from all directions. This ray-sheaf is simply an abstract mathematical statement of what is meant by ambient light. The fact to be noted here is that there is no limit to the number of possible convergence points in the medium. Each of these can be called a *station-point.*

Consider now not one station-point and many surrounding surfaces but one object and many surrounding station-points. The faces and facets of the object will be "projected" to all of these station-points in accordance with certain laws of projective geometry. An "aspect" of each face is obtainable anywhere in the medium. In effect, aspects of the shape and texture of the object are projected outward from it in all directions. Herein lies the truth of the figurative assertion that aspects of an object are "broadcast." Only an emitting body truly radiates energy, but a reflecting body can be said to radiate *structure* or *information* by virtue of the reverberating flux of reflected light in a medium.

This account of the projective capacities of illumination is incomplete. A fuller description of the information in light will be deferred until we are ready to consider the various kinds of ocular systems possessed by animals. Meanwhile it is important to note that nothing whatever has been said about the *image* of an object, or a *replica,* or a *picture* of it, and nothing about projection on a hypothetical picture-plane. I am describing the preconditions for vision, not vision as such.

Compression Waves from a Vibratory Event

A mechanical disturbance or dislocation is propagated outward from a source in accordance with the laws of wave action. Many different types of mechanical disturbance are possible: a solid may undergo shear, rupture, frictional movement, collision, or even explosion; a liquid may undergo turbulence, splashing, or even boiling; a gas may undergo vibratory flow in crevices or pipes. All of these, as described in the textbooks, involve some back-and-forth movement. And this vibration is propagated throughout the solid and thence into the adjacent medium of air, or into a medium of water for that matter.

The waves of compression pass outward with a velocity which depends on the density of the medium and on its temperature. The amplitude of the waves depends on the violence of the event. Their amplitude at a given distance depends on the inverse-square law. When the event is very intense, the field of vibration is very large. But these mechanical waves, unlike electromagnetic waves, are not transmitted in a vacuum or through outer space. The explosions and vibrations of the sun do not reach the earth. Fields of terrestrial vibration, however, are common.

The earth "quakes," for example, whenever the underlying rock ruptures under strain, and these waves may travel for hundreds of miles. On a smaller scale the earth vibrates from a rockfall, and on a minute scale from even the slightest footfall. The water vibrates in surface and subsurface waves. But the vibrations in air are our main concern, since the shaking of a medium progressively outward from the original disturbance will also, to put it simply, shake any animal that happens to be there. An avalanche will shake the air for many miles and even a breaking twig for many yards.

Whether this vibration is to be called *sound,* with subjective connotations, or merely *shaking,* with physical connotations need not confuse us if we keep in mind that vibration is only *potentially* stimulating for an organism. Whether or not it is effective depends on the receptive equipment of the animal. Mechanical vibration has a whole spectrum of frequencies mixed together, like electromagnetic vibration, and different portions of this total spectrum are sent out by different events. Moreover, different portions of the spectrum are picked up by different animals. For our species, the very low frequencies, less than about 20 cycles per second, are called "subsonic" and this shaking can only be "felt," not "heard." The very high frequencies, over about 20,000 cycles per second, are called "supersonic." Man is not sensitive to these, but some other animals are.

In any given airspace, then, there will ordinarily be a number of long-lasting or short-lasting fields of airborne compression waves, each emanating from the locus of a mechanical disturbance. In one place a waterfall will be continuously broadcasting. In another the friction of wind in a crevice may be sounding. In still another the fall of an acorn, or a dead tree or a whole cliffside, will send out an expanding hemisphere of aerial disturbance, but a transistory one. Or a thunderclap in the upper atmosphere will yield an expanding sphere, not a hemisphere, of vibration, the whole event being over in an instant. In all of these cases, the kind of wave train is specific to the kind of mechanical event at the source of the field; that is, the sequence and composition of pressure changes at a point in the air correspond to what happened mechanically at the center of the sphere. This correspondence is the physical justification for our metaphorical assertions that the waterfall "splashes," the wind "whistles," and the thunder "cracks."

The correspondence of sound waves to their source, in this sense, means that information about an event is physically present in the air around the event. The shape and size of this field of specification depends, of course, on the variables described by physical acoustics. It is not a *radiant* field, composed of rays, for sound does not travel in straight lines, and it is not occluded at solid edges. Sound passes around obstacles, is slower than light, and drifts with the wind. It echoes somewhat in enclosed spaces, but does not even approach the reverberation of reflected light, and its echoes carry little information about the objects from which they are reflected. But the information about the temporal structure of the event that caused it and the vibratory frequency of this event are given with great precision.

No mention has been made of the animals themselves as sources of sound. Those that are vocal emit sounds during a good part of the day, and the primates, including man, are noisy creatures. This means that each animal is often surrounded by a vibratory field and that the waves specify a great deal about the animal. To this we shall return later. Over and above vocalization, moreover, each animal makes sounds that are specific to its locomotion and other behavior. No footfall is wholly silent. The scratching or digging of earth, the brushing of leaves, the pecking of bark, all make sounds indicative of the activity in question, not to mention the enormous repertory of pounding, splitting, rumbling, and chugging noises that characterize a civilized environment. Man likes to make sounds and to hear them, even beyond vocalization, using instruments for the purpose. The man-made environment also includes a whole gamut of vibrations derived from sound recording and sound reproduction. This ultimate complexity of sound sources which merely represent other sound sources we do not now consider.

Sound fields originating from events at different places will overlap one another in the air. Thus, wave fronts may reach a given station-point from different directions. The events may be separately listened to, in some degree. But ambient sound is not even comparable to ambient light in the degree of differentiation of the directions from which it may come. The direction of a sound source is detectable, as we shall see, and several directions may even be detectable at once, but there is no parallel to the uncountable facets of an array of ambient light.

The Diffusion of Volatile Substances

The air, as we have already noted, is a constant component of the world of animals, a fixed fact of life. It has had the same properties for millions of years. It is a mixture of gases, chemically speaking — not a simple element as the Greeks thought, but a mixture whose proportions remain remarkably constant. The nitrogen, oxygen, carbon dioxide, and water vapor (with traces of other gases) exist in nearly the same amounts at all times and in all places. Over time, this balance is maintained by cyclic action. The plants take carbon dioxide from the air and give back oxygen; the animals take oxygen from the air and give back carbon dioxide. Evaporation converts water into vapor and precipitation converts vapor into water. Over space, the balance is maintained by diffusion and wind. Any chemical added to the atmosphere is therefore soon distributed uniformly.

This composition is not, of course, perfectly uniform. Organisms not only take in parts of the immediate environment but give off parts of themselves. Plants and animals emit not only oxygen and carbon dioxide, respectively, but also volatile parts of their own substance. The emission of volatile substances to the air, in fact, accompanies most of the chemical events of the world, such as oxidation and organic decomposition. A fire gives off smoke and a dead organism returns its substance to the air — on the forest floor, in the swamp, or on the seashore. The earth itself sometimes yields emanations from sources like volcanoes and sulphur springs. The atmosphere thus contains overlapping islands of slightly abnormal composition. Each is a cloud of some diffusing substance that originates in a chemical event. Such a diffusion field is hemisperical in still air, but only in still air; it will be elongated by a breeze or streamed out by a wind. It will be dissipated by rain, but re-established if the original chemical event persists. It is a source of potential stimulation for animals.

The application of the term "odor" to an unusual volatile substance in the air is like the application of the term "sound" to a vibratory disturbance of the air; it seems to have a subjective reference. But, again, there is no need for confusion if we remember that a diffusion field, like a vibration field, is only potentially stimulating. In the whole manifold of gaseous chemicals, some are "odorous" and some are not. Moreover, some animals respond to one set and others to a different set. Whether or not a gas is effectively stimulating depends on the biological relevance of the gas and on the receptive equipment of the animal.

But let us note that a diffusion field in the air carries information about its source, and does so in a wholly objective or physical way. The volatile substance is specific to its source. Just as smoke corresponds to fire, so does a musky aroma correspond to a skunk. Every animal is the origin of a cloud of vapor which was originally part of the animal. Some animals have special glands for exuding substances unique each to its own kind. Plants also broadcast their identity — their flowers and fruits often have extremely volatile "essential oils" unique to the species. The sexual receptivity of a female animal, as well as its identity, may thus be advertised, and the state of flowering of a plant as well as its species. We are accustomed to saying that animals "smell things." They smell fire or food, predator or prey, another species or their own, same sex or opposite sex, danger or safety. We say that they are attracted or repelled by odors, for we can observe that they seem to orient their behavior to the sources of the corresponding diffusion fields. But literally all an individual can do is breathe the air immediately surrounding him. He may detect a foreign substance in its composition, but this is only a proximal stimulus, not the source. How he identifies the source and orients his behavior to it requires explanation. A physical foundation for this explanation has been provided but the question itself remains for a later chapter.

Chemical Contacts with the Environment

Terrestrial animals must breathe, drink, and eat, which is to say they take into their bodies air, fluids, and certain solid parts of the environment. The selective ingestion of nutritive substances — liquid, solid, or intermediate — involves complex behavior. Animals must find, choose, and eat food, and keep the water balance of their tissues normal.

Abstractly, every organism is in one sense continuous with its environment across the boundary of its skin, exchanging matter and energy. But in a very important sense it is discontinuous with the environment. It is highly selective in what it will take in, and, of that, what it will assimilate. For example, the land animal breathes air but assimilates only oxygen; it ingests plants or other animals but assimilates only some of their chemical components. These are two of the ways in which it maintains its *separation* from the environment. In the modern term, it is a homeostatic system.

Eating is selective ingestion. For each kind of animal there is a set of natural substances in the world which will nourish it and a remainder which will not. Out of the whole array of biochemical entities, those which are nutritive must be chosen. Some animals are strictly herbivorous, some carnivorous, some both. The set of edible things may be scarce or plentiful, special or general, but it exists. A few things are biochemically edible for all animals, some for most animals; some things are not edible by any animal, and a few are toxic. "Food" is a relative term. But the nutritive potential of a substance is a fact of life which the animal needs to detect.

The food value of a substance may be fairly well specified at the periphery of its diffusion field, but it is even better specified by chemical contact with the substance. A combination of licking and sniffing a thing yields more information about it than merely sniffing the air, for the stimulus and its source then are not separated. The stimulus is more concentrated, and its chemistry is more nearly the same as the chemistry of the object. Contact with an object is in many ways the best and final test of the properties of the object.

Nothing has yet been said about the "taste" or "smell" of a substance, although we shall have to come to a consideration of these facts. Different animals have developed rather different ways of registering chemical information. The fact to be noted here is that the natural materials of the world, especially as they are nutritive or toxic, are important sources of stimulation for animals.

Mechanical Contacts with the Environment

A main branch of classical physics is mechanics, and part of this is what might be called contact mechanics — the study of collision, friction, the elastic deformation of bodies, and the like. The mechanical consequences for animal bodies of the force of gravity and contact with the earth were described at the beginning of this chapter. Let us consider now the mechanical consequences of contacts with objects — the "furniture" of the earth.

A solid object colliding with an animal, or pushing it even slightly, deforms the surface of the animal. So does the animal colliding with the object or pushing it; the deformation is the same whether the object or the animal has moved. This rule holds even when the deformation of the skin is mediated by the motion of hairs or feathers. A medium such as air or water, on the other hand, does not deform the surface of the animal, except in the special case of a *flow* of the medium over it. Consequently a deformation of the skin specifies the presence of something substantial and non-deformation of the skin specifies the presence of the insubstantial medium only.

It is important to avoid misunderstanding here about the physical concept of pressure. The air pressure on an organism is 15 pounds per square inch — an "atmosphere" of pressure — and the water pressure increases drastically with depth below sea level, but such uniform pressure is not deforming and not mechanically stimulating. It is only *differential* pressure that counts. Deformation of tissue is the stimulus. As we have already noted, one surface of a resting creature is deformed by the substratum while the opposite surface remains undeformed. This enables the animal to locate the ground in any posture, and to orient itself — that is, to cause its *ventral* surface to be stimulated and its *dorsal* surface not. In principle, the same thing happens in any encounter with another body; the site of the deformation enables the animal to locate the encounter and then to orient appropriately to the object.

Many types of physical events besides the simple collision of elastic bodies could be described by contact mechanics. There may occur rolling, sliding, friction, vibration, bending, torsion, stretching, and others.

**Figure 1.2   The Bottom of a Resting Creature
Deformed by the Substratum**

The same types apply to the mechanical encounters of animals with external bodies. Since animals are viscous, or visco-elastic, what happens to the animal is best described as a *temporary deformation*. In the last analysis, work has to be done, or energy expended. The word "touch" is not adequate to cover all these encounters. Neither is "pressure," or "impression." Touch is not a simple fact, as we tend to assume.

Does a deformation always specify the presence of a solid *object?* No, for a flow of water or air can stimulate the skin on one side of the body. Animals can, in fact, orient themselves to a flow of the medium, as a blind man can walk with the wind in his face. But the touch of the wind has a different pattern from the touch of an object. They are probably never confused.

The World of Physics and the Sources of Stimulation

The world described so far in this chapter is the physical world. But it may seem to the reader rather different from the world of physics as this is pictured in textbooks. Modern physics often gives the impression of being concerned mainly with the atomic and the cosmic level of things and leaving out everything in between.

In one sense, however, physics can encompass everything that exists — the whole of physical science, including chemistry and biochemistry, geology and geophysics, geography and paleontology. When physical sciences are considered in relation to organisms they become ecology, the study of the environment. We have been considering the world of animals, especially the surroundings of terrestrial animals, and particularly the sources of stimulation for these animals. Ultimately we are interested in the stimulus environment of human animals.

The *ecology* of stimulation, as a basis for the behavioral sciences and psychology, is an undeveloped discipline. These sciences have had to depend on the *physics* of stimulation, in the narrow sense. I believe that this situation has led to serious misunderstandings.

For example, some thinkers, impressed by the success of atomic physics, have concluded that the terrestrial world of surfaces, objects, places, and events is a fiction. They say that only the particles and their fields are "real." The very ground under one's feet is said to be "merely" the bombardment of molecules. An object is "actually" a swarm of atoms. The physicist, Eddington, in *The Nature of the Physical World,* made these assertions (1929), and this kind of reasoning has persisted. If it is correct, the sources of stimulation can only be the ultimate particles, for they are all that exist in the world of physics.

But these inferences from microphysics to the perception of reality are thoroughly misleading. The world can be analyzed at many levels, from atomic through terrestrial to cosmic. There is physical structure on the scale of millimicrons at one extreme and on the scale of light years at another. But surely the appropriate scale for animals is the intermediate one of millimeters to kilometers, and it is appropriate because the world and the animal are then comparable. As we noted at the beginning of the chapter, the terrestrial world is itself differently structured at various levels from that of crystals and grains to that of hills and mountains, and the behavior of animals is coordinated to these levels.

Eddington's paradox is attractive and the fallacy is not always evident. The reader who is still tempted by it should read an explicit criticism by Stebbing in *Philosophy and the Physicists* (1937).

The Animate Environment

The environment of animals contains other animals. It is time to include living matter in our account of the material world: the substances of greater chemical complexity, partly solid and partly liquid; the bodies which move spontaneously; the objects which are *animate.* These substances, bodies, or objects are sources of stimulation like the others so far described — similar in some ways, but of an entirely different order.

Animals can be sources of all the kinds of energy that physics lists — mechanical, thermal, chemical, sound, even radiant light (as in fireflies) and current (as in electric eels). One and the same creature can at the same time reflect light, emit sound, give off odor, and radiate warmth. It can also afford a variety of mechanical encounters, being furred or prickly or sharp-toothed, and being above all motile. The "other animal," then, is likely to be a source of *multiple* stimuli. Multiple stimuli from the same source are likely to be concurrent in time, i.e., to begin and end together, and to be covariant, i.e., to change together. The possibility of different stimuli being invariably *associated* (or dissociated) is a matter to which we will have to return more than once. We note now that different stimuli may be specific to the same animal. That is, the kind of light it reflects, the kind of sound it makes, and the kind of chemical it diffuses will all specify the sort of animal it is — carnivore or herbivore, male or female, young or adult. Light, sound, odor, and a mechanical encounter ("touch") may all thus carry the same *information*, in a sense, inasmuch as they are all specific to the same living thing.

It is clearly of biological importance for a sentient individual to be able to distinguish or discriminate plant from animal, prey from predator, own species from other species, and mate from rival. He can hardly afford to react in the same way to these different biological classes. The fact is that the stimuli from these sources provide multiple opportunities for distinguishing them.

The environment consists of *opportunities* for perception, of *available* information, of *potential* stimuli. Not all opportunities are grasped, not all information is registered, not all stimuli excite receptors. But what the environment *affords* an individual in the way of discrimination is enormous, and this should be our first consideration. The animate environment affords even more than the physical environment does since animals have more characteristics than things and are more changeable.

Social Stimulation

For millions of years, reptiles, birds, and mammals evolved on the face of the earth, reproducing, dividing and subdividing into new species, specializing, finding new niches in the environment, and exploiting the possibilities of terrestrial, aerial, and arboreal life. The diverging adaptations were governed by variation and natural selection. The adaptations were at once both anatomical and behavioral. Modified limbs and specialized sense organs went along with new styles of motor action and new modes of stimulus discrimination. Anatomical, behavioral, and sensory development were interdependent, and therefore correlated. The development of *general sensitivity* will be traced in later chapters, but let us note here that animals had to be sensitive to each other as well as to the physical environment. If the response of one animal to another is considered a "social" response, then the stimulus from the other animal is a "social" stimulus, and we therefore need to consider the nature of this stimulation.

A fundamental kind of social stimulation is that which brings together the egg and the sperm for reproduction. In the higher animals, this requires intricate mating and copulatory behavior. It is therefore necessary that the sex of an individual and its state of readiness for mating be broadcast as potential stimulation for a mate. This can be done by odor, by optical display (form, color, or movement), or by vocalization. The advertisements of a dog in heat, of a peacock, and of songbirds, are familiar examples. Tinbergen, in *The Study of Instinct* (1951), has described many forms of stimuli for sexual reactions, calling them "releasers."

Another kind of social stimulation is that which specifies the infancy of an animal and the nurturance requirements of the infant or, reciprocally, the parenthood of an animal and the nurturing capacity of the parent. Again, the information can be given by chemical, optical, or acoustic stimulation. A whiff of odor can mean precisely the lamb to the ewe. A gaping movement can denote the nestling to the mother bird, and a flash of color can denote the mother to the nestling (thereby producing the gaping response). Sounds do the same; the cries of both young and old carry simple but definite information.

Social Interaction

Certain stimuli from animate sources are themselves responses. Animals, that is, create stimuli by reacting as well as by merely existing, and by reacting *so as to stimulate* another animal. The resulting response of the other can in turn create a stimulus, and so on. At least two animals are involved, each related to the other by mutual or reciprocal stimuli. The male-female, the parent-offspring, and the predator-prey are examples of such "dyadic" groups. The sexual pair is the most universal, from the conjugation of one-celled creatures to the mating of men. This involves mutual mechanical and chemical contacts. If the movement of the first partner stimulates the second, the resulting movement of the second stimulates the first, and a *behavioral loop* is established.

The loop of social interaction between two animals can become extremely diversified and elaborated in higher species. Beyond the sexual, maternal, and predatory interactions are those of territorial behavior, fighting and sham-fighting, social play, grooming, and various sorts of cooperation. These loops are possible, however, only within the limits of the existing channels of physical stimulation.

The movements of one individual are projected to the eyes of another by the flux of daylight illumination and in straight lines. The vocalizations of an individual are transmitted to the ears of another during night or day and not necessarily by linear projection. Sound goes around corners. It is an excellent channel for communication, and it has been fully exploited by animals in the evolution of social interaction by cries, calls, growls, and grunts. There has been a parallel development of displays, including movements of the face, especially in primates.

The Environment of Emerging Man

Some time around the beginning of the Pleistocene age, a million or so years ago by some modern estimates, there began to appear primates called hominids, or man-like apes. The archeological traces of these proto-men are now being actively sought and studied; the origin of the genus *homo* is still obscure, and the number of species that may have existed is unknown, but a few facts are certain. Primordial men were of various sorts, but all of them were slow to mature, with long-dependent offspring and hence grouped in families, omnivorous in diet, highly vocal, upright in posture, flat of face, and with frontal eyes that could fixate on the hands. Their ancestors, the hominoids, had long since come down from the trees and they could *use* their hands and eyes in various ways. A million years permitted a great deal of mutation and adaptation of these characteristics.

The environment during this era put many pressures on these primates, but it also afforded many opportunities. It included the so-called Ice Ages. There were four glacial and three interglacial periods with resulting extremes and changes of climate. However, there were plenty of food sources, including other mammals to be hunted. There was opportunity and need for weapons and for hunting cooperatively. The climate required migration, but also encouraged the special use of shelters, and the invention of clothing and food-storing. The control of fire, when it was learned, must have had a whole set of consequences: for warming cave shelters, for cooking, for campfires during hunting expeditions, and for frightening away predators. But this required the skills of *making* fire (as with a fire-drill), of *tending* fire (finding and storing fuel), and *preserving* fire (with coals or the slow match).

Skills and techniques of the eye and the hand transfer from one to the other. The missile and the axe, the club and the spear, the chopper and the knife, are interrelated objects with interrelated uses. Tools led to new tools, both in the making and the using. The properties of stone and wood, once observed and manipulated, opened up whole realms for new discriminations and new habits.

Above all, the vocal-auditory communication of these hominid animals took a great leap forward. Suddenly or gradually, the voice itself came to be used as a sort of tool. Instead of advertising merely the species, identity, and state of an animal, its vocal cry came to specify also something external to the animal and in the common environment of both animals. This was the beginning of speech. It is easy to see how vast the consequences were for man, and how hard it is to describe them.

Quite possibly other kinds of motor expression besides the vocal one participated in this radical development. Gestures of the hands, such as pointing, could easily come to have an external reference. Movements of the head and eyes, or the face, could come to indicate something in the world as well as to express emotion. The mimicking of things may have accompanied or even preceded the development of speech. The essence of the matter was that the expression, vocal or gestural, came to have a further meaning.

In one formula, vocal sounds made up another and more powerful "signalling system" (Pavlov, 1927). In other words, they became "coded." If words are used specifically and conventionally for external events, they can *substitute* for the visual, tactual, or other stimuli from these sources. They become equivalent to things as stimulus sources. Words, like gestures, can then be used to direct the sense organs of the hearer toward parts of the environment he would not otherwise perceive, and to induce a second-hand perception of parts of the larger environment that the speaker has perceived but the hearer has not.

The making and hearing of speech sounds had to be contrived or developed and, accordingly, the uttering and understanding of speech had to be learned, by each generation of human offspring, and learned anew. But speech, once learned, makes the learning of everything else easier. Learning can *accumulate*, both in the life-span of an individual and over successive generations of individuals by means of oral instruction. There is more to the birth of language than the above account suggests, notably the rise of the capacity for predication — the making of statements about things (Hockett and Ascher, 1964) — but this will suffice for the present.

The Cultural Environment

In the study of anthropology and ecology, the "natural" environment is often distinguished from the "cultural" environment. As described here, there is no sharp division between them. Culture evolved out of natural opportunities. The cultural environment, however, is often divided into two parts, "material" culture and "non-material" culture. This is a seriously misleading distinction, for it seems to imply that language, tradition, art, music, law, and religion are immaterial, insubstantial, or intangible, whereas tools, shelters, clothing, vehicles, and books are not. Symbols are taken to be profoundly different from things. But let us be clear about this. There have to be modes of stimulation, or ways of conveying information, for any individual to perceive anything, however abstract. He must be sensitive to stimuli no matter how universal or fine-spun the thing he apprehends. No symbol exists except as it is realized in sound, projected light, mechanical contact, or the like. All knowledge rests on sensitivity.

In speaking, painting, sculpting, and writing, the human animal learned to *make* sources of stimulation for his fellows, and to stimulate himself in doing so. These sources, admittedly, are of a special sort, unlike the sources in the "natural" environment. They are "artificial" sources. They generate a new kind of perception in man, which might be called knowledge, or perception at second hand. The so-called accumulation of knowledge in a society of men, however, depends wholly on communication, on ways of getting stimuli to the sense organs of individuals. We will consider these sources now, although the question of how they mediate knowledge remains to be examined.

Man is known by his artifacts. He is an artisan, an artificer, an employer of the arts, an artist, and a creator of art. Beginning with tools and fire and speech, the "tripod of culture," he went on to making pictures and images, then to the exploitation of plants and animals, then to the exchange of goods for money, and finally to the invention of writing. The important items on this list for our purposes are the ones that mediate communication: vocal expression, gestural and facial expression, the making of images and pictures, and writing.

The advent of speech, as of conventional gesturing, cannot be dated with any certainty. Anthropologists seem to agree that it marked the beginning of man, although several groups of hominids barely removed from man may have developed it independently and later vanished. The origin of pictures and sculpture can be dated with some confidence. It was achieved by the human species some twenty to thirty thousand years ago. Scratchings and paintings on the walls of caves went along with the making of images by modeling and carving. Writing can be dated even more exactly, since history began with written records. It began around four or five thousand years ago with alphabets that froze speech sounds into tracings (Moorhouse, 1953). First speaking and hearing, then making and looking at images, then writing and reading — these were the steps in the evolution of the transmission of information.

The cultural environment of today contains an enormous amount of potential stimulation from these "media of communication." As for sounds, besides all the talk of flesh-and-blood persons, and all the "live" music they make, we are surrounded by sound-reproducing sources, the vibrating diaphragms or "loudspeakers" of transmitted and recorded sounds. As for images, sculptured images and models have proliferated. But pictorial images have had an accelerated recent development. For thousands of years pictures have been made by hand, but photographic pictures were contrived only a hundred years ago, cinematography was invented only fifty years ago, vacuum-tube images quite recently, and the end is not yet. As for writing, it has exploded in the modern world. A book must still begin as a manuscript, but the invention of printing enabled one writer to have millions of readers, and now books threaten to fill the oceans.

There is a bewildering variety of ways in which men can *communicate* with other men. Besides speech, there are laughing, crying, singing, chanting, and instrumental music. Besides gestures, there are facial expressions, dancing, mimicry, theatrical acting, and making "signs" or "signals." Besides replicative images there are all sorts of non-replicative models, and besides faithful pictures there are many kinds of non-representative but "graphic" tracings. Writing itself can be either ideographic (semipictorial) or phonemic (alphabetic). It seems difficult to classify this chaos of communication. But a start can be made by first noting that some communication *conveys information about the world* and some does not. One can then note that information about the world can be conveyed by words on the one hand or by pictures on the other.

Words, spoken or written, and images, solid or flat, are components of the environment and sources of stimulation, I repeat. But they are the most difficult of all components or stimuli to define in scientific terms. They are facts of such high order that it is easy to be confused about them. They are so familiar to us, we fail to understand their complexity. We tend to think of direct stimuli from the terrestrial environment as being like words and pictures instead of realizing that words and pictures are at best man-made substitutes for these direct stimuli. Language and art yield perceptions at second hand. This second-hand perception no doubt works backward on direct perception, but knowledge *about* the world rests on *acquaintance* with the world, in the last analysis, and this is our first problem.

The Meaning of the Term "Stimulus"

The word *stimulus* is widely used in psychology, in physiology, and in everyday speech, but with a variety of meanings (Gibson, 1960). It is perhaps most commonly used in psychology to signify an object of some sort that is *presented* to or *applied* to an individual, rat or human, in a psychological experiment. A stimulus in this sense is a red circle or a gray square, a thousand-cycle tone or a spoken word, a prod pushed into the skin, or an odorous substance. It is whatever the investigator of behavior has arranged to control, while keeping everything else in the situation constant.

This use of the term to mean an object is emphatically not the meaning employed in this chapter or in the remainder of this book. A clear distinction has been made between things that are *sources* of stimulation, either in the environment or in a laboratory, and the stimuli themselves. The former are objects, events, surfaces, places, substances, pictures, and other animals. The latter are *patterns and transformations of energy at receptors*. A stimulus may specify its source, but it is clearly not the same thing as its source.

In this chapter a further distinction has been made between a stimulus proper and the field of potential stimulation emanating from the source. A field of reflected illumination around an object, a field of air vibration from an event, and a field of chemical diffusion from a substance, all carry stimulus information. But whether the stimulus is effective or not depends on the presence of an observer, his receptive equipment, and his acts of looking, listening, or sniffing. The use of the term *stimulus* in sensory physiology to mean light, sound, or odor is close to the present one. Nevertheless, it fails to distinguish between an available stimulus and an effective one, and this difference is important. It also fails to distinguish between stimulus *energy* and stimulus *information,* and this difference is crucial. The energy that activates a single living cell so as to modify its metabolism is properly considered a stimulus, but combinations of energy at combinations of cells are a different matter.

Summary

For millions of years our animal ancestors lived with the earth, the sun, the sky, gravity, solid bodies, volatile and chemically reactive bodies, vibratory events, and with the squirming, moving, warm, odorous, light-reflecting, and noisy bodies of their fellow animals. For thousands of years — relatively few — men have been living in a physical environment having the same constants and the same cycles, but which they have profoundly modified. They have paved and straightened the solid surfaces, altered the vegetation, regulated the paths, subdivided the places, eliminated dangers, provided islands of light during the night, and of comfort during the cold. They have subordinated the lives of all other animals to their own social life without limit. Most strikingly, they have flooded the environment with shapes, sounds, and visible patterns which have meaning only to themselves.

All these things, the oldest and the newest, are sources of stimulation. All beings, animal or human, detect them by sensitivity to such stimulation. How they do so is the problem of perception.

The environment described in this chapter is that defined by ecology. Ecology is a blend of physics, geology, biology, archeology, and anthropology, but with an attempt at unification. The unifying principle has been the question of what can stimulate a sentient organism.

References for a Stimulus Ecology

This chapter is put together with evidence drawn from many disciplines. Much of it comes from ecology, but the boundaries of this new biological science are not established, and there are bits of physics, chemistry, astronomy, geology, anthropology, and philosophy, along with architecture, engineering, and nutrition.

The reader who wants to go deeper into the ways in which the environment is a source of stimulation will not find any treatises on the problem. But he might read ecology in general, especially Allee, *et al.*, *Principles of Animal Ecology*, 1949, Le Barre, *The Human Animal*, 1954; parts of Singer, *et al.*, *A History of Technology*, 1954; and Clifford, *The Common Sense of the Exact Sciences*, 1946.

The living animal is stimulated not only from sources in the environment but also by itself. Its internal organs provide stimulation, and so do the movements of its extremities and sense organs or feelers, and the locomotor movements of its whole body through space.

Sensitivity to action or behavior is clearly of a special kind, unlike the more familiar sensitivity to the prods and pushes of the external world or the pangs and pressures of the internal environment. The stimuli are self-produced, and the causal link is from response to stimulus as much as from stimulus to response. The classical stimulus-response formula, therefore, is no longer adequate; for there is a loop from response to stimulus to response again, and the result may be a continuous flow of activity rather than a chain of distinct reflexes.

Action-produced stimulation is *obtained*, not *imposed* — that is, obtained *by* the individual not imposed *on* him. It is intrinsic to the flow of activity, not extrinsic to it; dependent on it, not independent of it. Instead of entering the nervous system through receptors it re-enters. The input is not merely afferent, in the terminology of the neurologist, but *re-afferent* — that is, contingent upon efferent output. The favorite modern term for this action-produced input is one borrowed from electronic circuitry, namely, *feedback*.

The ordinary idea of a stimulus is taken from the Latin meaning of the term — a goad or sting — which implies, first, that a stimulus is imposed on a passive organism and, second, that it comes from outside. But this original meaning is inadequate, and it gets in the way of our thinking. First, an organism is seldom passive and a stimulus is often obtained by its activity. Second, a stimulus can be imposed from *inside* the skin of an organism as well as from outside. It can arise from an empty stomach, a distended bladder, a bending of its joints by another agent, or from the pull of gravity on the weights of its inner ear.

Imposed stimulation is produced by some state of affairs (outside or

31

inside the individual) that does not depend on the individual's own action. The event intrudes upon the course of action. Obtained stimulation is produced (inside or outside the individual) by his own action or in the course of action. A pure case of imposed stimulation would occur when a wholly relaxed and passive individual is aroused by a prodding with an object, by a light, a sound, an odor, or a draft of cold air; or when he is aroused by a bellyache, an acceleration, loss of support, or being flexed or pushed about. A pure case of obtained stimulation would occur when an active individual moves his limbs or head, stretches his muscles, or scratches himself; or when, on the other hand, he pushes into the prod, looks at the light, listens to the sound, sniffs the odor, or seeks the draft of air. Imposed stimulation occurs with a passive observer. Obtained stimulation occurs with an active observer.

Two Ways of Obtaining Stimulation

The higher animals have evolved both mobile extremities and adjustable sense organs. Hence they can modify the stimulus input in two ways: by moving the organs of the body that are called "motor" and by moving the organs of the body that are called "sensory." Confusion arises because some organs — the hand, for example — are both motor and sensory, but the fact remains that some movements accomplish behavior in the usual meaning of the term and other movements accomplish the pickup of stimulus information. The former will be called performatory or executive, the latter exploratory or investigative. The individual can obtain stimulation for the steering and control of performance, on the one hand, or he can obtain stimulation for the perception of the world on the other. The potential or available stimulation provided by the world was described in the last chapter. It is not simply forced on the individual. Animals and men can select or enhance the stimuli they receive from the world, or even exclude certain kinds, by orienting and adjusting their sense organs.

The observer who is awake and alert does not wait passively for stimuli to impinge on his receptors; he seeks them. He explores the available fields of light, sound, odor, and contact, selecting what is relevant and extracting the information. Even for an imposed stimulus, the observer begins to modify it after the first moment. He turns toward or away from a shaft of light. He turns toward a sound, balancing the stimuli in the two ears. He sniffs the odor. He moves away from the goad or toward the soft pressure. The passive detection of an impinging stimulus soon gives way to active perception.

Active perception thus entails not only stimulation from the environment but also stimulation from the attentive actions and reactions of the observer. The input to the nervous system has two components, one that is independent of the observer and another that depends upon movements of the eyes, head, hands, or body.

The classical concept of a sense organ is of a passive receiver, and it is called a receptor. But the eyes, ears, nose, mouth, and skin are in fact mobile, exploratory, orienting. Their input to the nervous system will normally have a component produced by their own activity. The photographic camera is an analogue to a passive receptor. But the eye is not a camera; it is a self-focusing, self-setting, and self-orienting camera whose image becomes optimal because the system compensates for blur, for extremes of illumination, and for being aimed at something uninteresting. This fact might seem to complicate hopelessly an understanding of how the senses work, but the intermixture of externally-produced and activity-produced stimulation promises to be the clue to an understanding of how the perceptual systems work.

The Fallacy of Ascribing Proprioception to Proprioceptors

For half a century — since Sherrington (1906) — the eyes, ears, nose, mouth, and skin have been classified as exteroceptors; the end organs in muscles, joints, and the inner ear have been called proprioceptors; and the presumed nerve endings in the visceral organs have been called interoceptors. It seemed very plausible that three types of sensation should correspond to these three types of receptors, (a) sensations of external origin, (b) sensations of movement, and (c) vague sensations of the internal organs. These were considered, respectively, the bases for (a) perception, (b) kinesthesis, or the awareness of movement, and perhaps (c) feeling and emotion, although this last idea was debateable.

In Sherrington's time it was taken for granted that there had to be a certain number of senses and that each sense had to have its specialized receptors that could excite the corresponding sensory nerves. It was taken for granted because it had become accepted doctrine that the impulses in sensory nerves could not specify the stimuli that had excited the receptors but only the special receptors that had been excited. This was the doctrine of the specific sensory qualities of the nerves, or the doctrine of "specific nerve energies," formulated earlier by Johannes Müller. Consequently, it was believed, if the individual had a sense of his own movements it was only because he had a set of receptors specialized for signalling his movements, just as he had eyes for indicating light, ears for indicating sound, and receptors in the skin for indicating touch.

Proprioception, or kinesthesis, could only be another sense, supplementing the classical senses.

We now realize that action sensitivity or movement sensitivity does not depend on specialized receptors. The eyes, ears, and skin can register the behavior of the individual as well as external events. The eyes, for example, register the movements of the head — forward, backward, or rotary — by way of the motions of ambient light (Figure 2.1 and Chapter 10). The ears register the sounds of locomotion, and of vocalization. The skin registers manipulation. Conversely, the motions of the joints and of the inner ear can register passively imposed movements of the body as well as movements initiated by the individual. Proprioception considered as the obtaining of information about one's own action does not necessarily depend on proprioceptors, and exteroception considered as the obtaining of information about extrinsic events does not necessarily depend on exteroceptors. Evidently something is wrong with the whole theory of the special senses, and with the doctrine of specific nerve energies. More precisely, something is wrong with the theory that all experience is correlated with activation of specific receptors and their nerves.

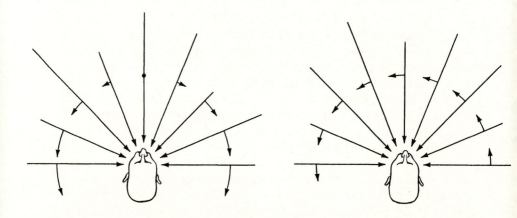

This motion of a hemisphere of the ambient optic array specifies a forward movement of the observer relative to the environment. When this is simulated on a panoramic motion-picture screen, he experiences a movement in space toward the center of the expanding array.

This motion of a hemisphere of the ambient optic array specifies a rotation of the observer to the right relative to the environment. When this is simulated by rotating a striped cylinder to the left around the observer, he experiences himself being turned to the right.

Figure 2.1 Two Examples of Visual Kinesthesis

The Lower Proprioceptive Systems: Posture and Equilibrium

Sherrington's contribution to the study of behavior was to show experimentally how the posture and locomotion of animals was governed by autostimulation, or the circular action of the nervous system. He demonstrated it at the level of reflexes, the actions necessary for resisting gravity, for maintaining equilibrium, and for walking, although in 1900 he probably failed to realize that the same circular action also operates at higher levels, as in the visual guidance of locomotion, the control of skilled manipulation, and the auditory control of speech.

The tension or tonus of the extensor muscles — i.e., the antigravity muscles — depends on stretch receptors imbedded in the muscles themselves. Roughly speaking, when a muscle is stretched, a reflex circle arises so as to contract the muscle and compensate for the pull. The delicate play of this tonus in all muscles is what enables the animal to keep its balance. Equilibrium is a process of continuous compensation.

Note that the stable orienting of the head depends on a stable body posture (supported by the legs), and that the orienting of the nose, ears, and eyes depends in turn on the stability of the head, so that there is a hierarchy of postures from the head to the body to the legs to the ground. As Sherrington and others showed, there is another supplementary effect on muscular tonus and equilibrium coming from the gravity receptors of the inner ear. This effect is also circular and continuous. Upright posture, and a sense of the postural vertical, are thus assured by at least two concurrent kinds of information.

Locomotion obviously depends on postural equilibrium; in order to walk one must stand. There are *phasic* reflexes as well as *tonic* ones. In a quadruped, the opposing muscles of each leg must work reciprocally by alternately contracting and relaxing, extending and flexing, and the bilaterally opposite muscles of the legs must work reciprocally in order to walk with alternate steps. As Sherrington proved by nerve-cutting experiments, the whole system of coordination is circular and depends on continuous registration of the positions of the parts of the body. Position registration seems to depend on the sensitivity of the joints of the skeleton, not on the sensitivity of muscles.

. . . .

The Concept of Equilibrium

The term equilibrium originally referred to a lever balanced by weights, or an egg balanced on one end ("unstable" equilibrium). It has come to mean also the balanced posture of a terrestrial animal on its feet ("maintained" equilibrium). Currently the word is being used to refer to the balancing of forces or processes other than those of gravity. There are many ways in which a living system can achieve and maintain some kind of optimal state. There are other and higher kinds of stability than being in balance. Some of them are called "homeostasis" by physiologists but there are others, like the focussing of the lens of an eye, that would appear to optimize perception.

. . . .

The Higher Proprioceptive Systems: Purposive Action

It has long been known that if the incoming sensory pathways from the muscles and joints of a human limb are interrupted at the dorsal spinal root, the limb is still mobile, for the outgoing motor pathways are intact, although uncontrollable. However, the movements of the limb *can* be voluntarily controlled by looking at the limb. Evidently the movement sensitivity of the visual system can be substituted for the movement sensitivity of the muscular and articular systems.

It seems to be true also that the action sensitivity of the visual system *dominates* the action sensitivity of the muscular and articular systems, at least in manipulation and locomotion. This is what happens when a tool is used in place of the hand itself for manipulating an object, as when grasping it with pliers instead of with the fingers, or striking it with a hammer instead of with a fist. The felt action of muscles, joints, and skin is then rather different, but the visible action is essentially the same and the visual system can easily control the motor output. The situation is similar when one uses the steering-wheel of a vehicle instead of one's legs to guide the direction of one's locomotion (Gibson, 1958). The muscles used are entirely different but the lower level of kinesthesis is entirely subservient to the higher, visual level of kinesthesis.

Similarly, the speech movements of man are controlled at one level by the feedback from the lips, tongue, palate, and jaw, but at another level by the feedback from the ears — that is, by hearing one's own speech as it occurs. It is known that if the auditory feedback is artificially delayed by a fraction of a second, speech itself is disrupted, although the lower-level proprioception remains unaltered.

Evidently there are many concurrent loops available for the propriocep-tive control of action. They seem to be at different levels; some of the loops remain inside the body, some pass outside. A list of the kinds of action reception is given below, from lower to higher, and from more automatic to less automatic. The list is provisional, for new evidence is accumulating and much more will probably be known in the future.

Muscular proprioception. The receptors are in the muscles. They are probably excited by tension of the muscle, not by shortening of it. So they probably register effort, not movement. This is the traditional "muscle sense," but it is doubtful that there are sensations to correspond.

Articular proprioception. The receptors are in the joints of the skeleton and perhaps the tendons. They probably register the angle made by the joined bones, and the change of this angle. This is kinesthesis, defined narrowly as sensitivity to skeletal movement. A joint can register both active and passive movement, whether the information is obtained by muscular effort or imposed by an extraneous force. There seems to be conscious awareness of the joints, that is, one can feel the angles which the bones make to one another.

Vestibular proprioception. The receptors are in the vestibule of the inner ear and they are known to be excited by linear or angular forces, that is to say, by acceleration but not by a constant speed. The organ thus registers the starting and stopping of a head movement obtained by muscular effort. It does the same if the head is moved by an external force. A part of this organ, the "statocyst," continuously registers the external force of gravity.

Cutaneous proprioception. The receptors are in the skin but perhaps also in most of the body tissue. They are excited mechanically by any deformation obtained by pushing against the adjacent environment, including the ground, or by pushing against another part of the skin. So the skin is action-sensitive whenever the individual makes contact with something, or grasps or clings to it, or makes contact with himself. It also, of course, registers a deformation imposed by an external object, and the hand can explore external objects.

Auditory proprioception. The receptors are in the cochlea of the inner ear. The organ registers any sounds made by action, as in walking, eating, vocalizing, or speaking, and by tool-using, as in hammering, typing, or music-making. The ears also, of course register external sounds, and the ear-head system can localize sounds.

Visual proprioception. The receptors are in the eyes. The single receptor cells are excited by light but the larger receptive units of the retina seem to be excited by margins and motions of the light. The eye registers (a) any shift of the retinal image over the retina obtained by a fast eye-movement (but without any visual sensation to correspond), (b) any transformation of the retinal image obtained by a movement of the head in space (with a sensation to correspond), and (c) any retinal motion obtained by a movement of a visible part of the body (with a corresponding sensation). The eye also, of course, registers all the external motions, colors, and shapes that are imposed on it, and it can explore the external array.

Visual proprioception, more than any other kind, is important for the guidance of purposive actions in the surrounding world. In an habitual motor skill one can fall back on the feeling of movement for guidance but in any new task one needs visual control. Herein lies the handicap of the blind. One can go from place to place in a familiar room without light, trusting to the joints, inner ear, and skin, but in order to get to a new place one needs to steer by vision (see Figure 2.1).

Theories of Action Sensitivity

The foregoing account of proprioception contradicts the fundamental doctrine of how the senses work. This doctrine asserts that no information whatever about the *cause* of a receptor's arousal can get past the receptor and into the nervous system. A receptor fires nervous impulses; to the receptor it makes no difference whether the cause is an action or a stimulus intruding on the course of action. An example of long standing is the puzzle of how the eye could tell the difference between a turning of the eye itself and a turning of the world outside the eye. This doctrine, and the puzzle that goes with it, is fundamental to the theory of sensations. It assumes that a sensation is the "awareness of the state of a nerve," and that the qualities of sensations are the qualities of the specific receptors excited, not of the stimuli that excited them. The causes of the excitations of our nerves, according to Johannes Müller, are forever hidden from us. We have only the deliverances of sense to go by, and we are imprisoned within the limitations of the senses. We have to *deduce* the causes of our sensations, as Helmholtz put it, for we cannot *detect* them. The elaboration of this doctrine and the contributions of Charles Bell, Johannes Müller, and Herman von Helmholtz are described by Boring (1942, Ch. 2).

Wherein lies the truth of this famous doctrine and wherein is it false? I suggest that it holds for the senses considered as channels of sensation but not for the senses considered as detection-systems. Information about the cause of arousal may not get into a nervous system through a single receptor but it may well get into the nervous system through a combination of receptors. We may sometimes be "aware of the state of a nerve," as Müller put it, but we are more likely to be aware of patterns and transformations of input that specify the causes of arousal quite independently of the specific nerves that are firing.

Animals and men do in fact distinguish between the results of their own actions and the results of events other than their actions—between intrinsic and extrinsic stimulation. The question is *how* they distinguish them. Two kinds of answers are available, although both are speculative. We have little evidence available at present about the physiology of information pickup as contrasted with the physiology of receptor excitation.

One theory suggests that whenever the brain sends out a command for a certain movement it stores a copy. When the input of any receptor reaches the brain it is automatically compared with the current stored copy. If it matches, the input is taken to be a case of proprioception—a feedback. If it does not match, the input is taken to be a case of extero-ception — a feed-in. In this theory, the input does not itself specify its cause; the cause must be deduced (von Holst and Mittelstädt 1950).

An alternative theory assumes that the neural input caused by self-produced action is simply different from the neural input caused by an intruding stimulus. The two kinds of input are different in their sequential properties, they are different kinds of transformation or change, and the simultaneous pattern of nerve fibers might be widely dispersed. In the long run, this second hypothesis may prove to be the simpler of the two, for it does not presuppose a brain that copies, stores, compares, matches, and decides. This is the kind of hypothesis favored here. And some evidence will be given to show that the two kinds of input, self-produced and externally produced, *are* different.

There is an old question as to why the motion of the retinal image over the retina caused by the rapid eye movement from one fixation to another does not cause any sensation of motion (Helmholtz, 1925, pp. 242ff.). Other displacements of the image relative to the retina do; why should this one not? Physiologists have inferred, as noted above, that the sensation is somehow cancelled in the brain by the fact that the brain *commanded* the eye movement. A simpler explanation would be that just this retinal motion and no other specifies a saccadic eye movement and no other, and that the brain so distinguishes it. This feedback is marked as a feedback, not as a visual motion sensation. The retinal quality of the input is not experienced but the eye-movement specification is registered. We shall return to this problem in Chapter 12.

The Characteristics of a Natural Stimulus

It was noted earlier in the chapter that the Latin word *stimulus* meant a goad or sting, hence a spur to action. In ordinary English the term still has this meaning. In physiology it means an application of energy to a receptor, and this implies something *punctate* and *momentary* (i.e., instantaneous). In experimental psychology it seems to mean whatever can be applied or presented to a whole individual, animal or human, not just to a receptor. But the original implication of something punctate and momentary still remains, and this leads to confusion. For the stimuli that occur when an individual is active and immersed in a natural environment are typically *not* punctate and momentary. I have discussed the problem elsewhere at greater length (Gibson, 1960).

A natural stimulus for proprioception or perception has the following characteristics. First, it always has some degree of adjacent order. Second, it always has some degree of successive order. And third, it always therefore has some component of non-change and some component of change.

1. A stimulus always has some adjacent order. It has a simultaneous structure or pattern in "space." Even the sharp stick on the skin or the narrow beam of light on the retina yields a border or transition, not a mathematical point. To say that a stimulus has "pattern" or "form" is an effort to express this fact.

2. A stimulus always has some successive order. It has some structure in "time." At the very least there is a transition at the beginning and another at the end, so that the stimulus is never a mathematical instant. It has sequential structure just as inevitably as it has simultaneous structure.

3. Consequently a stimulus always has some component of nonchange and some component of change. The spatial pattern may either continue for a long time or may change promptly, but the change is part of the stimulus. It is a mistake to conceive each persisting pattern as a separate stimulus, as we are tempted to do. Transformations of pattern are just as stimulating as patterns are. This fact is sometimes expressed by saying that motion is immediately detected by animals, not secondarily deduced from change of position, but the fact applies to other kinds of stimulation as well as to visual.

These three postulates are intended to apply to all kinds of physical stimulation, light, sound, mechanical, or chemical, and to whatever sensitive part of the body is stimulated, interior or exterior. A stimulus can be small or large, from a single finger joint or from the whole skeleton, from a star or from the whole sky. It can be brief or prolonged, from a twitch or a skilled act, from a single note or a whole melody. There are stimuli at low and high levels of spatial order, and at low and high levels of temporal order. The size of the unit of stimulation we choose to consider depends on the level of sensitivity we are concerned with.

Receptors, Organs, and Systems

The term *receptor* is ambiguous. It implies on the one hand a passive mechanism that starts nerve impulses when touched off by a stimulus. But it also is used in reference to an organ like the eye, an active mechanism that accommodates itself to the possibilities of stimulation, that adjusts and explores. The two meanings ought to have different terms. Here and throughout this book, "receptor" will be used only for the immobile parts of the input system and the word "organ" will be used for the mobile parts.

• RECEPTORS: CELLS AND UNITS. At the lowest anatomical level a receptor is a single cell that responds to mechanical energy, chemical energy, or light. Receptor cells are microscopic structures. The most familiar kind are the photosensitive rods and cones of the retina. The cell is sometimes called an energy transducer by physiologists who think in terms of engineering. When energy is applied, it responds.

Receptors of this kind are probably always grouped into receptive units. A group of cells is connected to the branches of a single ingoing nerve fiber, the "primary afferent neuron" (Gray, 1959, Ch. 4), and this is the smallest single pathway into the central nervous system. Receptive units are now being actively studied with new techniques, and new discoveries are being made, but certain facts about them are already clear. A receptive unit may set off a train of impulses in its fiber but more often it *modulates* an already existing train of impulses when energy is applied to it. An "off" unit, for example, stops its spontaneous firing when excited. "On-off" units fire bursts of impulses at the beginning and end of excitation. Moreover, there are units of visual reception that fire only when a sharp border of the retinal image falls on them, and others that fire only when a *moving* border occurs, and still others that respond to the *inclination* of a border, or its *curvature*. To say more about them would be premature, and the reader should follow the experimental literature for new results.

One thing is certain. The generally accepted picture of a sense organ as a mosaic of energy transducers each connected to a distinct nerve fiber and thereby to a distinct cell in the brain is quite wrong. In the skin, the retina, and other organs, the receptive units constitute overlapping fields of cells, the peripheral beginnings of the afferent neurons being intermingled like the roots of trees in a dense forest. They are functional, not anatomical, units.

These units seem to modify their input as a function of a change of energy (sequential order) or a relation of energy (adjacent order), not as a function of the application of energy. What they register is not the energy of stimulation, but the sequence or arrangement of stimulation, that is, information.

• ORGANS. An organ of sensitivity is a structure containing many energy receptors and many receptive units that can adjust so as to modify the input from cells and units. An organ must therefore have muscles, and they must be supplied with efferent fibers from the central nervous system. The afferent and efferent fibers, incoming and outgoing, may be gathered in a single bundle, a nerve, like the nerve from each eye, or they may be distributed in many bundles, like the fibers from the skin. The so-called sensory nerves are anatomical expedients; there is not a specific nerve for each sense despite a popular idea to the contrary.

. . . .

The Failure of Correspondence Between
Nerves and Senses

Anatomy is an ancient discipline. When the first anatomists discovered fiber bundles leading inward from each eye, each ear, and the olfactory membrane, they called them the optic nerves, the auditory nerves, and the olfactory nerve. It was then assumed that each nerve transmitted special messages from its sense organ to the brain—that is, that each was a channel for a special mode of sensation. But actually, the correspondence between nerves and senses is more false than true. There is no distinct nerve for taste. There is certainly none for touch. The twelve bilateral pairs of cranial nerves have mixed functions. There are not twelve corresponding modes of sensation, and surely not one mode for each side of a pair. Incoming and outgoing fibers are often found in each bundle, so that the concept of "sensory" and "motor" nerves is a myth. The thirty-one pairs of spinal nerves are even less in correspondence with types of sensation, that is, with qualities of experience.

. . . .

The organs of sensitivity, like other organs of the body, exist in a hierarchy of *organization*. Lower organs are subordinated to higher. Smaller structures serve larger structures, and they overlap. The eyeball is "all of a piece," but it is an unusual sense organ. The ear, the functional auditory organ, is not a single piece of tissue, and the organ of touch is dispersed over the whole body. The receptive and the adjustive parts of an organ need not be in the same place. The olfactory organ that we call the nose, that is, the functional nose, has its receptive part deep in the facial bones but its motor part in the chest muscles for breathing and sniffing. The receptive and the adjustive part can only be understood in relation to one another.

• SYSTEMS. The real organs of sensitivity are evidently not parts of the body, and the units of anatomy are not the units of function. The organs fall into systems. The proprioceptive systems were described earlier in this chapter; the perceptual systems will be described in the next, but it should be remembered that they overlap one another. Consider the main perceptual system, the visual one, and note its various levels of function. The single eye is a system of low order, although it is already an organ with an adjustable lens for sharpening the retinal image and a pupil for normalizing its intensity. The eye with its attached muscles is a system of higher order; it is stabilized in the head relative to the environment with the help of the inner ear, and it can scan the environment. The two eyes together make a dual system of still higher order; the eyes converge for near objects and diverge for far ones. And the two-eyes-with-head-and-body system, in cooperation with postural equilibrium and locomotion, can get around in the world and look at everything.

It is reasonable to suppose that the higher-order systems of sensitivity correspond to higher orders of stimuli, or of stimulus-information. It is surely true, at least, that the stimulus for an organ is not the same as the stimulus for a cell.

Mechanoreceptors, Chemoreceptors, and Photoreceptors

Consider the lowest level of receptors, the so-called transducers of energy. As noted in the first chapter, the types of energy that carry stimulus information are (1) mechanical energy in all its manifestations, including vibration, (2) chemical energy or particle exchanges of certain substances, and (3) the energy that goes in "rays," radiation, including the band called photic and the band called thermal. It cannot be questioned that animal sensitivity depends on contact mechanics, contact chemistry, and the absorption of radiation. Physiologists assume three corresponding kinds of receptor cells in the bodies of animals: mechanoreceptors, chemoreceptors, and photoreceptors. Some progress is being made in finding out just how they are excited in terms of the cell membrane. But this progress has mostly been made in the past by trying such means as applying a needle to a mechanoreceptor, a drop of liquid to a chemoreceptor, and a beam of light to a photoreceptor, or by applying an electric current to any of them. This gives only a distorted picture of how groups of receptors are excited by natural stimuli when they are incorporated in organs. The applying of current to receptors, as physiologists do, is quite unnatural, for throughout the history of the environment this kind of energy — static electricity or lightning — has never carried information about anything.

All animals, even a single-celled creature like the *ameba*, respond to contact mechanics, contact chemistry, and light-heat. The *ameba* makes only a few crude responses like approach or avoidance to such energy applications (Jennings, 1906), for the whole animal is all one receptor, while higher animals make more elaborate responses to finer differences. The latter have specialized receptors for the types of energy. Sherrington's formula for designating the specialization of a receptor is that it has a low threshold for a particular kind of energy and a high threshold for all other kinds. In the course of evolution this kind of specialization has increased demonstrably. The ears and noses and eyes of animals got progressively more sensitive to faint sounds, diffused odors, and weak lights, respectively, in terms of the amount of physical energy required for their mechanoreceptors, chemoreceptors, and photoreceptors. The absolute lower thresholds for sound, odor, and light in man are about as low as they can be. But it should not be forgotten that this kind of sensitivity is useful to animals only insofar as faint sounds, odors, and lights carry information. Receptive cells, units, organs, and systems all evolved together, and the specializing of receptors for transducing energy went hand in hand with the elaboration of systems for obtaining information.

Mechanoreceptive cells and units are found all over the body and within it — in the skin, the underlying tissue, the muscles, and the skeletal joints. The nerve endings, under the microscope, are of great variety — "branches," "sprays," "baskets," and "encapsulated" endings. The hairs of mammals and the feathers of birds are each wrapped with nerve fibrils at their base; so too are nails, claws, horns, teeth, and the special hairs called vibrissae. It is reasonable to guess that these terminal structures are units that when squeezed, stretched, or bent in certain ways specify certain events. Other mechanoreceptive units with ciliated cells are found in the two parts of the inner ear, one specialized for forces and the other for vibrations.

Chemoreceptive cells and units are found in the skin of fish but are concentrated mostly in the nose and mouth regions of land animals. The latter have an area that reacts to volatile substances and another that reacts to soluble substances, the substances being brought into contact with the receptors by breathing or sniffing and by eating or licking.

Photoreceptive cells and units are incorporated in the eyespots of simple animals and in the compound eyes of crustacea and the chambered eyes of mollusks and vertebrates. The evolution of ocular systems will be considered in Chapter 9. In vertebrates, the photosensitive cells are of two types only, rods and cones, but the structures and mechanisms into which they are built are astonishingly complex.

Summary

This chapter has been concerned with the reception of stimuli but two theses have been advanced; first, that perception is to be distinguished from proprioception and, second, that imposed stimulation is not to be confused with obtained stimulation. Perception has to do with the environment; proprioception with the body. Imposed stimulation is forced on a passive organism; obtained stimulation comes with activity. We must consider, therefore, (1) imposed perception, (2) imposed proprioception, (3) obtained perception, and (4) obtained proprioception.

Imposed perception arises from the skin, nose, mouth, ears, or eyes when these organs are passive and the stimulation impinges on them, or is applied to them. This is exteroception, in Sherrington's term, by the classical five senses. This is what has generally been studied experimentally in the past by physiologists and psychologists.

Imposed proprioception occurs when members of the body are moved and the joints are thereby stimulated, when the head is accelerated or turned and the vestibular organs are stimulated, and when the whole individual is passively transported and the eyes are stimulated by motion perspective. The muscles do not participate.

Obtained perception arises from the classical sense organs when they are oriented to the environment by way of the body and when they are active, that is, when they adjust and explore so as to obtain information. This is the main topic of this book. The active senses are called perceptual systems and they will be further considered in the next chapter and taken up singly in the following chapters.

Obtained proprioception occurs when the individual behaves, or performs with any of the motor systems of the body. Executive behavior of this sort requires control. Six kinds of proprioception were listed, with six corresponding types of feedback loops. They work at different levels, from reflex to voluntary, and in various combinations. These proprioceptive systems overlap with the perceptual systems but do not correspond with them. Muscle sensitivity was not listed as a perceptual system, and smelling and tasting do not seem to be proprioceptive, or not obviously so. Obtained proprioception and the control of purposive behavior, the study of what has been called "cybernetics," is a new and important field of psychology and it is reasonable to expect that a great deal more will be known in the future about the "steering" of voluntary actions and the execution of intentions than is known at present.

What is the relation between obtained perception and obtained proprioception, that is, between active perception and the control of action? Some psychologists, in the tradition of behaviorism, would answer that perceptual activity is only a special form of behavioral activity, that perceiving is a "response" of the organism, and that consequently it is fundamentally a "motor" act. They would argue that knowing is simply an attenuated kind of behaving. In this book, however, admitting that behaving and perceiving usually go together in life, I shall assume that they must be separately considered and separately explained. A man may sit and contemplate the world without behaving. He may simply look at the scenery. He is not passive; as he would be if asleep; he is active, but this activity is *attentive*, not *executive*; *investigatory*, not *performatory*.

If we adopt this formula, the simple, neat easily-remembered contrast between *receptors* and *effectors*, between *sensory* and *motor*, will have to be abandoned. It is a pity, but the facts are not that simple. The notion of receptors that receive stimuli from the world and effectors that have effects on the world leaves too much out of account.

The input of the nervous system is of several types, not just one, and so is the output of the nervous system. Following von Holst, many physiologists have already classified the inputs, the *afferent* impulses, into two types, the *exafferent* (mainly exteroceptive) and the *reafferent* (mainly proprioceptive). I have suggested that inputs should be even further classified into *imposed* and *obtained*. And I have further argued that the output of the nervous system, the *efferent* impulses, should be classified into those that cause *exploratory* action and those that cause *performatory* action.

The result of this classification is diagrammed below.

Input
(afferent
impulses)

- Exteroceptive
  - Imposed (with sense organs passive)
  - Obtained (with sense organs active)
- Proprioceptive
  - Imposed (on passive organs or limbs)
  - Obtained
    - (by mobile organs)
    - (by mobile limbs and body)

Output
(efferent
impulses)

- Exploratory activity (of perceptual systems)
- Performatory activity (of executive systems)

]]] / *The Perceptual Systems*

We shall have to conceive the external senses in a new way, as active rather than passive, as systems rather than channels, and as interrelated rather than mutually exclusive. If they function to pick up information, not simply to arouse sensations, this function should be denoted by a different term. They will here be called *perceptual systems.*

For a long time, two assumptions have been made about the senses, first that they are the only sources of knowledge about the world and second that they are the channels for special qualities of experience. John Locke formulated the first position in 1690 with the doctrine of the *tabula rasa* — the "blank tablet" of the mind at birth. Johannes Müller crystallized the second position in 1826 with the doctrine of the *specific qualities of nerves.* These two positions have long been accepted together, but they do not necessarily go together. The need to reconcile them has always been troublesome, for in fact they are inconsistent with one another. If the senses are instruments through which knowledge is obtained they cannot be conveyers of mere sensory quality; if they are conveyers of sensory quality they cannot be instruments for obtaining knowledge. How to resolve this contradiction? If we distinguish between information and qualities of experience and denote them by different terms, we can separate the two positions. We can say that perceptual systems are the sources of knowledge and admit that the channels of sensation are the sources of conscious qualities. There is reason to believe that the inflow of information does not coincide with the inflow of sensation; they are at least semi-independent.

The receptors of man *can* be stimulated in such a way as to yield little or no information and the resulting experiences can justly be called sensations. The input of a whole perceptual system can theoretically be analyzed by an introspectively trained human observer into mere sensory impressions. The study of sensation is a perfectly valid branch of psychology and a vast body of knowledge has resulted from it. But the pickup

47

of stimulus information, I will argue, does not entail having sensations. Sensation is not a prerequisite of perception, and sense impressions are not the "raw data" of perception — that is, they are not all that is given for perception.

This theory of the non-relation of sensation to perception has radical and far-reaching implications. For one thing, it means that we do not have to catalog the sensations as a preliminary to studying perception. In this book they will be considered only incidentally, as occasional accompaniments of perception. But it might be well to consider here why the catalog of sensations, necessary as it was, could never be made.

The Historical Difficulty of Cataloging the Sensations

The naive list of senses is familiar to everyone. Stimulation of the eye or the optic nerve evokes visual sensation; stimulation of the ear or the auditory nerve evokes auditory sensations; stimulation of the nose and mouth, or of the olfactory and gustatory nerves, evokes sensations of smell and taste respectively; and stimulation of the skin evokes sensations of touch, although by no single nerve, and by what set of nerves has never been clear. (Neither is there a single gustatory nerve, for that matter.) This list of five senses is learned by every child and was stated by Aristotle, but it is inadequate. It fails, first, to include many other kinds of experience that are now called proprioceptive in origin; it fails second, to include certain experiences obtained by these five organs when they are active instead of passive. So the search began for additional qualities of sensation.

The effort to inventory sensations is implicit in the doctrine of John Locke. Empiricism asserts that sensations are the sole basis of knowledge and the elements of all awareness. The best account of this effort is given by Boring's *Sensation and Perception in the History of Experimental Psychology* (1942). The great contributors were Helmholtz, Wundt, and Titchener, upholders of the conviction that sensations are converted into perceptions by past experience or memory, not by innate powers of the mind. They had to make an inventory because the inputs of the receptors were the sole raw data for any process of perception they could conceive other than a mysterious one.

It is fair to say that the effort failed. No inventory was exhaustive. The qualities of sensation within the five modalities of exteroception faded off into unreportable vagueness, and even the five modalities were compromised. There is today no accepted list of modalities and the number of senses given in textbooks varies from six to a dozen or more. The reason for the persistent naive belief in five senses is another matter entirely. There are five familiar modes of external attention.

A Classification of the Perceptual Systems

When the "senses" are considered as active systems they are classified by modes of activity not by modes of conscious quality. And within each exploratory system no exhaustive inventory of perceptions can be expected, since the potential stimulus information is unlimited and the pickup of information has no definite bounds. Some of the systems, moreover, will pick up the same information as others, redundant information, while some will not, and they will cooperate in varying combinations.

A classification of the perceptual systems is offered in Table 1. They are the *orienting system*, which is basic to all the others, the *auditory system*, the *haptic system*, the *taste-smell system*, and the *visual system*. The order is arbitrary; it is simply the order in which they will be considered in the chapters to follow.

The modes of attention are listed in the second column, the types of energy receptors incorporated in the organ are listed in the third column, the names of the organs of perception are in the fourth column (and these are not simple), the typical activities of the organs are in the fifth column, the available stimuli in the sixth column, and the kind of external information obtained in the seventh column.

This table of perceptual systems is intended to apply to man and all mammals, and most of it holds for all vertebrates. It would have to be somewhat modified for invertebrates and insects, for their systems, although analogous, are different, not only in anatomy but also in the range of information detected. The table is at least much more adequate than the usual treatments of the "senses" of animals (e.g., Milne and Milne, 1962), for such treatments take it for granted that since animals have senses they must also have sensations.

The list may be usefully compared with the list of proprioceptive systems in the last chapter. Many of the perceptual systems provide feedback for the steering of behavior, but perception is not the same thing as proprioception.

The Five Modes of External Attention

The suggestion is that the higher animals have five principal ways of orienting the perceptual apparatus of the body, *listening, touching, smelling, tasting,* and *looking.* They are not to be confused with the human

TABLE 1: THE PERCEPTUAL SYSTEMS

Name	Mode of Attention	Receptive Units	Anatomy of the Organ	Activity of the Organ	Stimuli Available	External Information Obtained
The Basic Orienting System	General orientation	Mechano-receptors	Vestibular organs	Body equilibrium	Forces of gravity and acceleration	Direction of gravity, being pushed
The Auditory System	Listening	Mechano-receptors	Cochlear organs with middle ear and auricle	Orienting to sounds	Vibration in the air	Nature and location of vibratory events
The Haptic System	Touching	Mechano-receptors and possibly Thermo-receptors	Skin (including attachments and openings) Joints (including ligaments) Muscles (including tendons)	Exploration of many kinds	Deformations of tissues Configuration of joints Stretching of muscle fibers	Contact with the earth Mechanical encounters Object shapes Material states Solidity or viscosity
The Taste-Smell System	Smelling	Chemo-receptors	Nasal cavity (nose)	Sniffing	Composition of the medium	Nature of volatile sources
	Tasting	Chemo- and mechano-receptors	Oral cavity (mouth)	Savoring	Composition of ingested objects	Nutritive and biochemical values
The Visual System	Looking	Photo-receptors	Ocular mechanism (eyes, with intrinsic and extrinsic eye muscles, as related to the vestibular organs, the head and the whole body)	Accommodation, Pupillary adjustment, Fixation, convergence Exploration	The variables of structure in ambient light	Everything that can be specified by the variables of optical structure (information about objects, animals, motions, events, and places)

capacities to *hear*, to feel *touches*, to experience *smells* and *tastes*, and to *see*, respectively. The latter are passive abilities.

These kinds of attention involve adjustments and exploratory movements of the *eye-head* system, the *ear-head* system, the *hand-body* system, the *nose-head* system, and the *mouth-head* system. The orientation of the head and body is presupposed. The movements of the eyes, ears, hands, nose, and mouth can be observed, and they will be described in the following chapters. Pavlov called such movements "investigatory responses." The adjustments are made so as to enhance the input of information and clarify perception (Chapter 13). They are kinds of overt or external attention, not of internal attention conceived as a filtering of the ingoing impulses at centers of the nervous system (Broadbent, 1958). A man can appear to be looking, listening, or savoring his food and actually be thinking of something else. But this is not the kind of attention here considered.

Henri Piéron was probably the greatest authority of modern times on general sense physiology. He never thought of questioning the primacy of sensations for psychology. Nevertheless he asserted that "there are five senses because there are five modalities of reactions aiming at a better knowledge of an interesting object or event, five modalities of sensory attention: looking, listening, touching, smelling, and tasting" (Piéron, 1952, p. 29).

The basic orienting system does not have a specific mode of attention, but it might be said to have a general one — being awake, alert, and upright. The postures of the sensitive organs in the head depend on the posture of the head, and the postures of the extremities depend on the posture of the body. Hence the exploratory searching of the eyes, ears, nose, mouth, and hands depends on an upright body, and the orienting of these organs rests on orientation to gravity.

The Education of Attention in Perceptual Systems

We can now suppose that the perceptual systems develop perceptual skills, with some analogy to the way in which the behavioral systems develop performatory skills. The analogy should not be carried too far, since the clarification of perception is not the same as the execution of intention, but both are kinds of learning.

Note that the substitution of perceptual systems for the classical senses is required for the above hypothesis. The channels of sense are not subject to modification by learning. The data of sense are *given*, by definition. The perceptual systems, however, are clearly amenable to learning. It would be expected that an individual, after practice, could orient more exactly, listen more carefully, touch more acutely, smell and taste more precisely, and look more perceptively than he could before practice.

The "education of the senses" has often been the aim of those concerned with child development (Montessori, 1912). They have asserted that it is possible, despite the fact that it involves a contradiction in terms—the sensations being supposedly innate and perceptions being the products of learning. These educators have been less interested in logic than in the improvement of discriminative capacity or sensitivity. They note the almost inexhaustible curiosity of children in looking, listening, touching, poking, prying, feeling, and sniffing, and they argue that a rich environment should be provided the child with opportunity for obtaining stimulation of all sorts. By the education of the "senses" they mean what would here be called the education of perceptual systems.

The improvement of perceptual skill with training can be demonstrated experimentally in children, but it is hard to separate this improvement from the improvement in motor skill, and from growth or maturation of the perceptual apparatus with age. In adults, it is undeniable. Experimental evidence for increasing accuracy of discriminative judgments in psychological experiments is abundant, as E. Gibson (1953) has shown. It holds for all the "departments of sense" that have been studied. But the alteration can hardly be one of sensations. These experiments involved comparing, matching, or distinguishing instances of stimulation provided by an experimenter. Any change from the beginning to the end of these experiments seemed to be a change of attention. There was a greater *noticing* of the critical differences with less noticing of irrelevancies. In all the experiments surveyed the process could be interpreted as the progressive focusing or centering of a perceptual system on the information provided by the experimenter.

According to the traditional theory of the senses, in which they are considered to provide the requisite data for perception but no more, perceptual learning can only be an associative enrichment of these bare impressions, or else an attachment of particular responses to them (Gibson and Gibson, 1955). But according to the theory of perceptual systems, perceptual learning can be a process of detection and differentiation (Chapter 13).

The Pickup of Information by the Perceptual Systems

The question, of course, is *how* the information in the available stimulation is picked up, supposing it to be present. In the following chapters the groundwork will be laid for an answer to this question. The anatomy and physiology of each system will first be described, but from a *molar*, not a *molecular* point of view. How the receptive units combine and their inputs covary in systems and subsystems will be emphasized. The main interest will be in the human apparatus, but comparisons with that of other animals will often be made. The capabilities of each system for useful perception and adaptive behavior will be stressed. The limitations of each will be noted, however, and the illusions to which it may be subject will be recognized. The evidence for its capabilities will be experimental when this exists, but much of it will come from outside the laboratory.

• THE BASIC ORIENTING SYSTEM. The apparatus of the inner ear picks up forces of acceleration. These specify the direction of gravity, an incessant force, and also the beginnings and endings of movements of the body, which are transient forces. The gravitational input covaries with that of touch, which is part of the haptic system, so that a double registration of the ground is possible. This system cooperates, in fact, with all the other perceptual systems since it provides a frame of reference for them.

• THE AUDITORY SYSTEM. This apparatus evolved from the primitive statocyst, and it responds to being shaken, although the shaking is only the minute vibrations of the air. The input specifies the nature of vibratory events in the world and, when both ears are used to explore, specifies the direction of the event. Both of the above systems have a dual bilateral apparatus.

• THE HAPTIC SYSTEM. This apparatus consists of a complex of subsystems. It has no "sense organs" in the conventional meaning of the term, but the receptors in tissue are nearly everywhere and the receptors in the joints cooperate with them. Hence the hands and other body members are, in effect, active organs of perception. The inputs in combination and covariation can specify a variety of facts about the adjacent world which is astonishing to most of us who depend on vision for our conscious contacts with things. Touch and vision in combination often yield a redundant, doubly guaranteed input of information.

• THE TASTE-SMELL SYSTEM. The nose and mouth may be justly regarded as distinct organs, but they enter into combinations to make a superordinate system. Food can be merely sniffed, but when it is tasted the receptors of the mouth and nose work together. Eating also includes *feeling* the food, so that a special part of the haptic system combines with tasting. A substance is generally given a thoroughgoing set of tests, chemical and physical, before it is finally swallowed—tests involving its volatility, solubility, chemical composition, and physical consistency. How the chemoreceptors and mechanoreceptors in the nose and mouth work is imperfectly understood, but information about the food value of a substance, its edibility, is picked up in these several ways.

• THE VISUAL SYSTEM. This apparatus combines with all the others and overlaps with all of them in registering objective facts. The available information in the structure of ambient light is enormous. The ground and the horizon of the earth are "in" the light. The environmental motions that occur are "in" the light. Even the locomotions and manipulations of the individual are specified by optical transformations in the light. The visual system has its limitations, to be sure, but its capabilities outweigh them. It registers some kinds of information that no other system can, such as the pigment color of surfaces. Above all, it makes possible a kind of perceptual contact with stimulus sources at a great distance, as long as they are illuminated.

The problem of how the eyes pick up information about objects is the oldest and most controversial problem in the study of perception. Our consideration of it comes last. All I suggest now is that the traditional theory of visual perception based on a retinal picture or image of each object is profoundly misleading. I will treat the eyes of insects, animals, and men not as a pair of cameras at the ends of a pair of nerves but as an apparatus for detecting the variables of contour, texture, spectral composition, and transformation in light.

The Partial Equivalence of Perceptual Systems

Hornbostel once remarked that "it matters little through which sense I realize that in the dark I have blundered into a pigsty" (1927, p. 83). He was arguing for a sort of "unity of the senses," a paradoxical equivalence of supposedly different modalities of sensation. On the theory of perceptual systems this equivalence is not a paradox at all.

Consider a fire — that is, a terrestrial event with flames and fuel. It is a source of four kinds of stimulation, since it gives off sound, odor, heat, and light. It crackles, smokes, radiates in the infrared band, and radiates or reflects in the visible band. Accordingly, it provides information for the ears, the nose, the skin, and the eyes. The crackling sound, the smoky odor, the projected heat, and the projected dance of the colored flames all specify the same event, and each alone specifies the event. One can hear it, smell it, feel it, and see it, or get any combination of these detections, and thereby perceive a fire. Vision provides the most detailed information, with unique colors, shapes, textures, and transformations, but any one of the others will also serve. For this event, the four kinds of stimulus information and the four perceptual systems are *equivalent*.

If the perception of fire were a compound of separate sensations of sound, smell, warmth, and color, they would have had to be associated in past experience in order to explain how any one of them could evoke memories of all the others. But if the perception of fire is simply the pickup of information the *perception* will be the same whatever system is activated, although, of course, the conscious sensations will not be the same. If all perceptual systems are activated, the information is redundant.

In this theory the problem of perception is not how sensations get associated; it is *how the sound, the odor, the warmth, or the light that specifies fire gets discriminated from all the other sounds, odors, warmths, and lights that do not specify fire.*

Different stimulus energies — acoustical, chemical, and radiant — can all carry the same stimulus information. The equivalence of different "stimuli" for perception and behavior has long been a puzzle, but it ceases to be puzzling if we suppose that it results from equivalent stimulus information being carried by different forms of stimulus energy. Examples of this equivalence will be met repeatedly in the chapters to follow. If the visible patterns of written speech are equivalent to the audible patterns of vocal speech by the laws of alphabetic writing, it is not surprising that patterns in the flux of sound, touch, and light from the environment may be equivalent to one another by invariant laws of nature.

. . . .

The Equivalence of Different Stimuli

The concept of stimulus equivalence — the fact that different objects and different energies may elicit the same response — was emphasized by Klüver (1933). If responses depend on stimuli, as they surely do in some sense, this is a paradox. As Klüver realized, it is one of the most challenging problems in psychology.

The formula here proposed is not that stimuli are equivalent when they are different but that stimulus *information* may be identical when stimuli are different.

. . . .

On this theory, information about the world can be obtained with any perceptual system alone or with any combination of perceptual systems working together. It is not required that one sense be *validated* by another, as vision is supposed to require confirmation by touch. It is not required that one sense get meaning from another, as visual sensations are supposed to get objective meaning by having been associated with tactual sensations. It is not implied that one channel of information is intrinsically more trustworthy than another. To kick a stone is no better guarantee of its presence than to see it, actually, for both depend on the energizing of receptors whether in the toe or the eye. Mechanical impact is one thing and photochemical reaction is another, but either one can be an informative stimulus.

The Irrelevance of Sensations to the Perceptual Systems

I have suggested that Johannes Müller's law of "specific nerve energies" applies to the channels of sensation but not to the perceptual systems. The law asserts that unique conscious qualities correspond to the different bundles of sensory neurons, and it is taken for granted that conscious sensory qualities are the basis of all awareness. As extended by Helmholtz, it even asserts that a unique sensation corresponds to each single neuron in a bundle and that this is the ultimate element of awareness. Until quite recently, this law has seemed to be the unassailable basis for any theory of perception, for animals and men are only acquainted with the qualities of their nerves, and neurons, not with the properties of the external world. They can become imperfectly acquainted with the world, presumably, because different receptors are specialized for different external stimuli.

Now it is true that human observers, if they introspect in a certain way, can have a sort of acquaintance with the quality of the nerve bundle that has been stimulated (although it is very doubtful that they can become aware of the particular neuron stimulated), but this fact need not have anything to do with awareness of the environment — that is, with perception. For the active perceptual systems cut across the channels of passive conscious quality and do not consist of a specific set of nerves and neurons, as we observed in the last chapter.

The anatomical aspect of a perceptual apparatus is only one of several; it also has various functional aspects. The same anatomy can be used on different occasions in different ways. Just as the hand can be used for grasping and carrying or for exploring, for pointing, and for drawing pictures, so also the eyes, with the optic nerves and their internal connections, can be employed in a number of ways. The individual nerve or neuron changes function completely when incorporated in a different system or subsystem. And consequently the human awareness of the sensation corresponding to the nerve or neuron excited (when this is noticeable) is the merest incidental symptom of the perceptual activity, not the element out of which it is compounded. Moreover, if such sensations are not elements of perception, the perceptual process need not be one of putting them together by any process of organization in the brain.

The Relation of Muscle Systems to Perceptual Systems

It was pointed out in the last chapter that an individual can move both the organs of the body that are called "motor" and the organs of the body that are called "sensory." The neat and simple contrast between sense organs and motor organs is incorrect, and the convenient formula of the sensory-motor arc to represent the action of the nervous system is inadequate. There is an output to perceptual systems and an input from motor systems. The physiologist can properly distinguish between afferent and efferent, ingoing and outgoing pathways, but he really ought not to speak of "sensory" and "motor" pathways. Nevertheless there are muscles, and they combine in complex combinations to make muscle systems. What is the relation of the perceptual systems that have been described to these muscle systems?

Movement, is was suggested, is of two general types, exploratory and performatory, the first serving perception and the second behavior as usually conceived. In order to clarify matters, it might be well to consider all the systems that involve muscles. The following classification is tentatively proposed.

1. *The postural system.* The body need not "move" at all, except for small compensatory movements to preserve equilibrium. There is orientation to the earth. This system is fundamental to all the others.

2. *The orienting-investigating system.* Movements occur, turning movements, but also mere postures of pointing and fixating. These are adjustments of the head, eyes, mouth, hands, and other organs for obtaining external stimulus information. There is orientation to special features of the earth, not just to gravity.

3. *The locomotor system.* Movements occur that put the animal in a more favorable place in the environment, such as approaching, pursuing, avoiding, escaping.

4. *The appetitive system.* Movements occur that take from or give to the environment, such as breathing, eating, eliminating, and sexual interaction.

5. *The performatory system.* Movements occur that alter the environment in ways beneficial to the organism, such as displacing things, storing food, constructing shelter, fighting, and using tools.

6. *The expressive system.* Postural, facial, and vocal movements occur that specify emotional states and that identify the individual.

7. *The semantic system.* Signalling movements of all sorts occur, especially coded speech.

Note that proprioceptive feedback at various levels is characteristic of all these systems. But perception considered as observation of the environment does not accompany all of them. The second system is the one that mainly serves the activity of observing. Some kind of *awareness* goes along with all of them, but not always *perceptual* awareness.

Note also that the movements made do not always depend on the particular muscles at work. The movement systems are characterized by "vicarious action" of different muscles. The classification above is not based primarily on the anatomy of body members but on purposes. This is especially true of the performatory system. Just as perceptions do not depend on specific sensations, so motor actions do not depend on specific muscles.

Summary

It is argued that the sensing in *sense perception* is not the same as the sensing in *having sensations*. The former is sensitivity to information while the latter is sensitivity to something else — energy, or the receptors excited by energy, or the nervous pathways transmitting the excitation by energy, but in any event a kind of sensitivity to be considered separately. Hence we can proceed to a description of the perceptual systems without having to make an inventory of the channels of qualitative sensory impressions.

The perceptual systems, as it turns out, correspond to the organs of active attention with which the organism is equipped. These bear some resemblance to the commonly recognized sense organs, but they differ in not being anatomical units capable of being dissected out of the body. Each perceptual system orients itself in appropriate ways for the pickup of environmental information, and depends on the general orienting system of the whole body. Head movements, ear movements, hand movements, nose and mouth movements, and eye movements are part and parcel of the perceptual systems they serve. These adjustments constitute modes of attention, it is argued, and they are senses only as the man in the street uses the term, not as the psychologist does. They serve to explore the information available in sound, mechanical contact, chemical contact, and light.

IV / The Basic Orienting System

A living animal can orient itself in many ways. All of these are orientations to the environment, but to different features of the environment, such as gravity, or the sun in the sky, or a sudden noise, or a mate. We may conceive of orientation at different levels, the higher depending on the lower. The following levels can be distinguished.

First, the terrestrial animal maintains permanent orientation to the earth — that is, to gravity and the surface of support, these being the chief constants of the environment. Second, the animal adopts temporary orientations to events and objects whenever he attends to them. The orientation of the head, ears, eyes, mouth, nose, and hands depends, however, on the orientation of the body as a whole to the earth as a whole. Third, the animal exhibits from time to time oriented locomotion. This may be a simple tropism to a source of light or it may be an elaborate making of one's way to a goal. In the latter case the directing of locomotion may depend on the orienting of the organs in the head to the source of stimulation, as in listening and looking. Finally, there can occur the remarkable kind of oriented locomotion shown in homing and migration where animals and men find their way to a goal over long distances. This is geographical orientation, the kind we ourselves are aware of when we become "lost."

In this chapter, we will consider the simplest kind of orientation, to the direction up-down and to the plane of the ground. Along with this goes a basic type of perception on which other perceptions depend, that is, the detection of the stable permanent *framework* of the environment. This is sometimes called the perception of "space," but that term implies something abstract and intellectual, whereas what is meant is something concrete and primitive — a dim, underlying, and ceaseless awareness of what is permanent in the world.

The Statocyst Organ

The primary kind of orientation is to gravity. In the water or on the land all animals respond to the pull of the earth, and most of the multi-cellular animals have developed a special organ for detecting the direction of gravity when resting. In its simplest form it is called a statocyst. The way it works, or a prototype of how it works, is shown in Figure 4.1. At the top of this highly simplified animal is a sac filled with fluid and lined with mechanoreceptors of the ciliated type, the hairs being stimulated by a weight which can be displaced relative to the sac. The receptors discharge when the hairs are bent. In some organs they may fire in different ways when the hairs are bent in different directions, but in any case there is an unceasing pattern of nervous input which is very useful to the animal. The statocyst of the invertebrate is perhaps the earliest clearly specialized sense organ to appear in the whole animal kingdom.

This organ yields its possessor an index of the direction "down" — that is, it yields information in terms of the possible range of patterns of

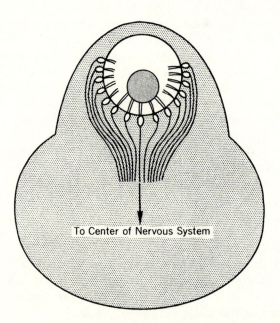

To Center of Nervous System

Figure 4.1   A schematic statocyst. The diagram is highly simplified. The fluid-filled cyst (sac), the statolith (weight), the receptive hair cells, and a theoretical set of nerve fibers are shown. This arrangement for the arousal of hair cells by a weight is only one of many that are possible.

hairs excited. If the animal happens to be tilted to the right, the stimulation makes one pattern; if to the left, another. The neural input is specific to the posture of the animal's body. If different patterns of input cause different patterns of output to motor organs of the animal, compensatory movements can occur which will keep the animal upright. The movements are such as to *normalize* the pattern of input. The statocyst thus permits the animal to maintain postural orientation, in the sea or on the land. The statolith is literally a stone, being composed of calcium carbonate, and is quite heavy relative to the fluid and tissue around it.

The organ also yields other information. It specifies temporary accelerations as well as the permanent acceleration of gravity. If the animal is pushed forward (by a current, say), the hairs are bent backward; if backward, forward. So also for a push to the right or left; the statolith lags behind. If a terrestrial animal falls, if it undergoes loss of support, the bending of the hairs is eliminated; if it is borne upward, the bending is increased. In short, the organ is a "dynamocyst" as well as a statocyst and, in fact, its effective stimulus is force, or acceleration. As will be evident later, this fact puts certain limitations on the organ as a gravity detector.

One might wonder whether the simple organ diagrammed would be able to specify a *rotary* acceleration, a turning as distinct from a displacement. The directions of hair-bending would then make a much more complex pattern to be registered. In some invertebrate animals it is known from electrophysiological experiments that the organ can do so, but the vertebrate animals, from fish upward, have developed a more elaborate organ with specialized semicircular canals so as to clearly separate rotations from displacements, and to distinguish rotations from one another.

• PASSIVE AND ACTIVE AROUSAL OF THE STATOCYST. The organ incessantly registers gravity and occasionally picks up external pushes. But it also picks up the *self-pushes* of the animal — that is, the starting and stopping of spontaneous locomotion. The feedback through the hair cells from any such movement means that the organ is proprioceptive as well as exteroceptive. Note that it is not sensitive to muscular action directly but to a displacement of the whole animal resulting from muscular action. Displacement in space is a higher order of information than contraction of a muscle.

Any higher animal, of course, has a specialized *head* containing the organs of orientation and the center of the nervous system. It is the locomotion of the head that counts, since the body follows along. The abstract animal being considered has no head to speak of, only a top and bottom.

The Statocyst in Relation to Other Organs

All animals orient to gravity but terrestrial animals also orient to the surface of support. These are closely related, but not necessarily the same. Response to the solid environment is mediated by the skin. A simplified terrestrial animal resting on the ground is shown in the diagram on the left. The skin, like the statocyst, contains receptors and is deformed by the ground. The area of contact, if it is differentiated from other possible areas of contact, specifies the location of the ground relative to the organism. It also enables the organism to right itself relative to the substratum by keeping its ventral area stimulated and its dorsal area not. This "ventral earth reaction" ordinarily combines with the statolith-normalizing reaction to maintain the upright posture.

If the ground is level, its force against the skin will be in the opposite direction to the force of the statolith on the lining of the statocyst, as shown in Figure 4.2. No matter what posture the animal adopts, even if it rolls over, the force of gravity and the counterforce of the substratum coincide. The two will necessarily vary together. They yield both *coincident* and *covariant* information.

What if the substratum is *not* horizontal? The counterforce of the substratum (the resultant of two components) is no longer parallel to gravity, as shown in Figure 4.3. The angle of this discrepancy is the slope of the ground. The concurrent inputs from the skin and the statocyst are still *covariant* in time but there is a shift or discrepancy in the

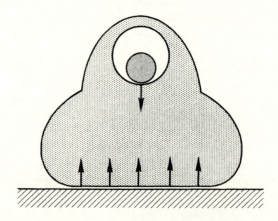

Figure 4.2   The statocyst of an animal resting on a substratum.
The pull of gravity and the push of the surface of support are represented by arrows. If the ground is horizontal, the directions coincide.

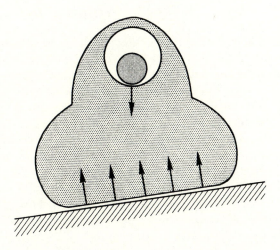

Figure 4.3   The statocyst of an animal resting on a sloping substratum. The directions of the pull of gravity and the push of the surface of support do not coincide.

simultaneous correspondence between them so that they are no longer *coincident.* In this case the discrepancy is information, however, and it will be constant over time, for any posture of the animal. If it can be registered, the organism will be able to detect the slope of the ground.

The implications of covariant stimulus information, with and without coincidence between the different inputs, will be followed up in later chapters. One further example may be given. If our simplified organism were granted eye-spots for detecting the incidence on its body of the light from the sky, it would have a third kind of information about the permanent environment. It could orient by a "dorsal light reaction" as well as by the ventral earth reaction and the statolith-normalizing reaction already described. If it possessed an eye that could detect the horizon, this information about the sky would be very precise. If an eye were added to the diagram above there would be a number of possible combinations of these three inputs. The reader is invited to imagine experiments with this simple animal in which these inputs are modified artificially. There are experiments in psychology of this sort. They are said to involve *conflicting cues* for the perception of the horizontal and vertical axes of space. Anomalies of posture, of orientation, and of perception, arise in human observers when these three types of information do not all coincide (Gibson, 1952).

The Evolution of the Vestibular Organ

The animal pictured above never existed; it is too simple even for a jellyfish. Worms, some of them at least, have a pair of statocysts at the head end. Vertebrates have skulls with elaborate bilateral statocysts. Each of these organs has two sacs containing weighted hair cells, one (the utricle) with semicircular canals connecting into it, and another (the saccule) from which a still more elaborate organ (the cochlea) grew. The whole structure is called the labyrinth because it is a maze of interconnected chambers and tubes. The labyrinth of man is shown in Figure 4.4. Another name for it is the inner ear.

The "vestibule" of the inner ear is defined as the utricle with its three canals plus the saccule. It does not include the cochlea or the middle ear. Its structure and function are essentially the same in all vertebrates. It is a statocyst — or better, a "dynamocyst." The gradual evolution of the cochlea in the higher vertebrates, for reception of sound, will be described in the next chapter. We are here concerned only with the primitive vestibular part of the labyrinth. (See Figure 4.5.)

There are five distinct receptive structures in each of these paired

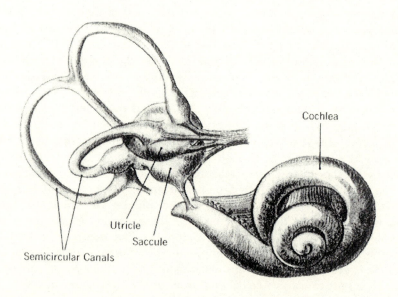

Figure 4.4. The labyrinth or inner ear. This is the membranous labyrinth, which lies within the bony labyrinth, floating in a fluid called perilymph. Its chambers and tubes are filled with a different fluid, called endolymph.

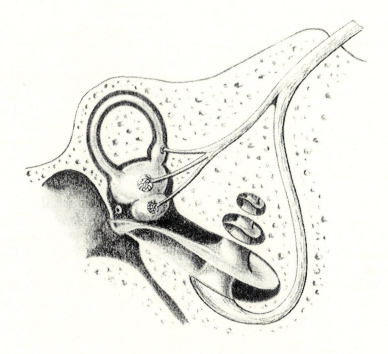

Figure 4.5   A schematic cross-section of the human labyrinth.
This shows the bony labyrinth sectioned to reveal one semicircular
canal, the utricle and saccule, and the cochlea at the lower right.
The point of view is not the same as in Figure 4.4. Converging
nerve bundles from the visible structures are indicated.

organs, two in the utricle and saccule and three in the semicircular
canals. All have a rich nerve supply. They are fluid-filled enclosures,
each having a heavily weighted gelatinous mass into which penetrate
the hairs of the receptors proper.

• THE MACULAE OF THE UTRICLE AND SACCULE. The statolith in the two
larger chambers is called a macula, and the two are set at an angle to
one another. Each weight drags continually on the hairs in accordance
with the posture of the head and also, by inertia, bends the hairs whenever there is a displacement of the head. The inertial lag signals the
beginning and the end of the motion. In walking, for example, these
masses presumably jog up and down with each step. They also jog up
and down with the irregularities of passive transportation in automobiles
and airplanes but then, it is significant to note, the stimuli are no longer
obtained but imposed. The jogging that occurs in passive airplane travel

has an entirely different effect on the individual from that which occurs in active walking. Being raised and lowered can make one seasick, raising and lowering oneself does not.

• THE CUPULAE OF THE SEMICIRCULAR CANALS. The masses in each of the three smaller chambers work in a somewhat different way. There is a swelling at the end of each tube (ampulla) nearly filled by a gate-like protuberance (cupula) from a base in which hair cells are imbedded (crista). The three ring-shaped tubes coming from the utricle and filled with its fluid are arranged in three planes at right angles to one another. (See Figure 4.6.) The six canals, three on each side, are thus suited to pick up a rotary movement of the head around any of the three axes of space.

The flexible cupula projects freely into the ampullar cavity like a camel-hair brush, and is capable of being bent like a swinging door within its chamber. Each tube, being open at both ends to the reservoir of the utricle, permits circulation of the fluid within it. When the head is turned on a given axis (actively or passively), the pair of canals perpendicular to that axis will circulate and the two little doors will swing, the deflection being proportional to the force of the turn. When the

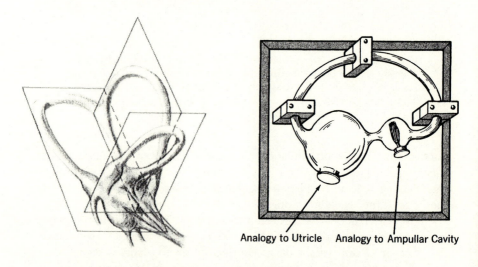

Analogy to Utricle   Analogy to Ampullar Cavity

Figure 4.6   The semicircular canals and Exner's model of a semicircular canal. The layout of the three canals in the three planes of space is shown on the left. On the right is a model to show the presumed action of a semicircular canal. It consists of fluid-filled glass tubing mounted on a base that can be rotated at the center. The flexible brush (cupula) in the smaller chamber bends and then recovers when the model is turned through any angle. (After an illustration in E. B. Titchener, *A Textbook of Psychology*, The Macmillan Company, 1928. By permission of the publisher.)

turn stops, the deflection is cancelled and the doors return to the null position, but meanwhile the firing of impulses from each sensitive crista has signalled the deflection.

The mechanical operation of this remarkable organ system was an evolutionary invention that has apparently not needed much improvement from fish to man. Note that a turn of the head on any given axis between the three principle axes (roughly the longitudinal, the lateral, and the dorsal-ventral) will yield three components of rotation, and three components of input, each proportional to the nearness of the given axis to the principle axes. The three fractions will always sum to unity and so, presumably, will the corresponding neural inputs.

The Use of Vestibular Information

We are now ready to consider locomotion as well as posture. The locomotion of any animal through its environment can be analyzed into *displacements* and *turns*. The vestibular apparatus provides information about both linear and rotary components of physical movement. We should keep in mind the fact that the movements of the body of an animal may be externally determined, i.e., imposed, or they may be spontaneous, i.e., voluntary. A passive movement elicits perception; an active movement is accompanied by proprioception.

The classical term for this information is simply *kinesthesis* (Boring, 1942, Ch. 14). The word means sensitivity to motion but, as we have noted, this is not simple. During active locomotion the animal *controls* the distance of his displacement and the amount of his turning. During passive locomotion he *perceives* the distance and the turn. Vestibular kinesthesis is useful for both behavior and perception. The animal can behave without necessarily perceiving, or it can perceive without behaving.

The contribution of the vestibular system to the proprioceptive and the perceptive systems can now be summarized.

1. The role of the chambers in bodily postural equilibrium is clear. It is a matter of reflex compensation. Along with equilibrium, however, goes an implicit awareness of the vertical and horizontal axes of the world, the gravitational frame of reference, and an awareness of the frame of the body, which has its own axes of reference, head-to-foot, right-to-left, and front-to-back. In experiential terms, we could say that the upright posture consists of keeping the bodily frame coincident with the gravitational frame, and that a reclining posture consists of permitting a discrepancy between the body frame and the gravitational frame, the discrepancy being itself perceived.

2. The role of the chambers in controlling spatial displacements (place-

to-place movements) is also fairly clear. The acceleration and deceleration of the animal's body are specified by the minute inertial displacements of the weighted masses in these chambers, and the duration of the movement is specified by the duration of the stimulus. Accordingly, at least crude information should be available about the distance of the movement, and therefore some perception of distance should occur. The *velocity* of the movement, to be sure, is not specified, but this physical abstraction varies from moment to moment with animate displacements and is irrelevant. The animal or human observer can register the amount of his linear locomotion, passive or active, for short distances even without vision.

3. The role of the semicircular canals in controlling turns is clear. The rotary acceleration and deceleration of a turn (or the turning component in locomotion over a curved path) are specified by the opposite deflections of the little swinging door in the ampulla of each canal. The angle or amount of turn is specified, within limits, by the temporal course of the stimulus. Information about the change of direction is available, and therefore some registration of the later direction relative to the earlier should be possible. The detection of the objective direction of the head after a turning movement is obviously a requirement if the individual is to remain oriented to the geographical environment. This does not wholly depend on the visual perception of "landmarks." When this perception fails, we say that the individual is disoriented, meaning that he is disoriented in the horizontal plane.

The orientation of the eyes in the head, the fact that they are stabilized relative to the optic array of ambient light, depends on compensatory movements of the eyes in the head and these depend in part on the action of the semicircular canals. As a result of stabilized eyes an individual can see the environment, and this level of orientation is the most elaborate of all, and the most trustworthy. The human observer can look in any number of directions, reach for or point to any number of things, and go to any number of places. This perceptual system will not be described until the end. The vestibular system is much older than the visual in terms of evolution. Crude though it may be, it is not negligible. Some animals can get about in darkness to a degree, and even a blind man has something of what we loosely call a "sense of direction."

The Limitations of the Vestibular Apparatus

Admirable as the mechanical functioning of these chambers and tubes may be, when it comes to the pickup of information the system has its limitations. In some circumstances it fails to specify different events as different and permits ambiguity.

• ILLUSIONS OF PASSIVE TRANSPOSITION. With respect to the chambers, the utricle and saccule, it is clear that an organ with a heavy statolith cannot by itself distinguish for its possessor between a *state of rest* and a *uniform motion in a straight line*, to use terms invented by Newton. It can specify starts and stops, pushes and pulls, or positive and negative accelerations in a horizontal direction. It can probably register short motions from place to place, but not motion as such. It is sensitive only to *transitions* between Newtonian steady states. This is why, so long as the jet airplane moves uniformly, the traveler cannot feel movement. The vestibular organ is suited to detect active locomotion or passive starts and stops but not constant-velocity transportation. For millions of years animals moved by rhythmic pushes, not as Newtonian bodies and not in railroad cars or airplanes. It is therefore reasonable that an individual should be susceptible to vestibular illusions when passively transported in a vehicle.

The statocyst was said to be an unfailing indicator of the direction "down." And so it is, except when subjected to a constant and sustained horizontal acceleration such as a speed-up, a slow-down, and a centrifugal force. The horizontal force then combines with the vertical force of gravity to yield a new vector resultant, and a shift in the apparent direction of "down." The statocyst cannot be expected to separate a gravitational from a sustained inertial force. The situation is diagrammed in Figure 4.7. The individual will feel himself tilted in the direction opposite the passive acceleration. In an airplane, for example, when speeding up one feels that he is in a climb, and when slowing down that he is in a dive, even though the line of flight may be perfectly horizontal. During an unbanked turn, one feels that he is tilted outward because the centrifugal force shifts the apparent direction of gravity. In such situations the pilot does well to control the airplane by his view of the horizon, or by his instruments. "Flying by the seat of his pants" is likely to get him in trouble. The research on illusions of the vertical during flight is well described in Geldard's book on the senses (1953, pp. 265ff.).

• ILLUSIONS OF PASSIVE HEAD ROTATION. With respect to the semicircular canals of the vestibular apparatus, it is clear that this organ by itself cannot specify the difference between a state of rest and a uniform rotary motion, or spin, once it is established. This fact is of no consequence to an individual who turns around, or changes direction while walking, since the rotary acceleration of the head passes over into deceleration without pause, and the flexible cupula of the horizontal canal first swings backward and then swings forward to its former neutral

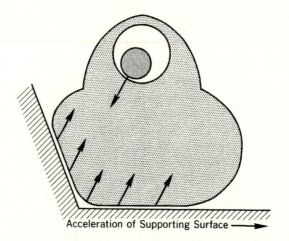

Acceleration of Supporting Surface ⟶

Figure 4.7   The simplified statocyst of an individual whose support is undergoing acceleration. The pull of gravity and the push of the surfaces of support both have been inclined from the normal direction by the fact of constant acceleration. Compare this diagram with Figures 4.1, 4.2, and 4.3.

position. The act is correctly specified. But it is of consequence to someone who observes his feeling of rotation while sitting in the rotating chair of the classical laboratory experiment.

The commonest way of demonstrating illusions of rotation is to seat the subject, start him, turn him around a number of times, and then stop him. During the period of constant spin, the flexible cupula in the stimulated canal probably tends to recover its null position spontaneously and thus ceases to specify a turn. During the negative acceleration, the gate swings *ahead of* the null position, thus falsely specifying a rotation in the opposite direction. Although the head is motionless, the organ continues to specify rotation until it returns again to neutral, yielding an illusory perception and also (as we shall observe in Chapter 9) forcing the eyes to compensate for a nonexistent turn of the head. The eyes show "after-nystagmus" and the observer experiences vertigo. This nystagmus should not be confused, however, with the compensatory eye-movements at the start of rotation, which are adaptive.

This experiment is instructive, although often misunderstood. The swinging gate has been deceived, as it were, into signalling a *start* with what is in reality a *stop*. But the deception results from the experimental intrusion of a coasting period between the real start and stop. The organ was evolved for the needs of active locomotion, not for swivelling chairs.

The illusion is hardly the fault of the organ, in view of its structure; the psychologist has simply *overstrained the capacity of the organ to register information*. Man has invented a great number of situations in which the natural information-gathering function of his perceptual systems is exceeded.

Postural Orientation: A Summary

From the statocyst of the simplest animal to the vestibular apparatus of man there has been a continuous development. At both extremes the structure is called a *sense organ*. But actually it is a tool of the nervous system for picking up information, part of a system for detecting facts. Even for the jellyfish it specifies the direction of *down*, but it probably does not yield a special mode of sensation. In human sensory psychology it has long been a puzzle why there are no introspectively clear impressions from this organ, and this is a "curious difficulty to psychology," as Titchener admitted (1909, p. 174). A man given a quarter-turn in a rotating chair, for example, perceives a quarter-turn but can report no qualitative impression that is specific to the cupula of the horizontal canal. How could a perception arise without sensation? If it can in this case, it might in other cases, and the implication is that sense perception need not be founded on sensation. This implication is accepted in the present book.

The vestibular apparatus interlocks with other organs and perceptual systems. By itself it is a force detector, providing orientation to the direction of gravity and making possible the upright posture, that is, equilibrium or balance. It does so by specifying any tilt of the body, forward or backward, to the right or the left, and initiating compensatory tonic reactions of the antigravity muscles. It also can specify the state of falling through the air, which is an alarming piece of information for terrestrial animals. In combination with the perceptual system of the skin, it provides orientation to the ground, the surface of support, which is usually but not always the same thing as orientation to gravity. The two perceptual systems together anchor another system, the awareness of the directions of the bones of the body relative to gravity and the ground, as will be explained in Chapter 6. The feeling of the position of the head, trunk, and limbs is thus a feeling in a body space of three dimensions, up-down, right-left, and front-back. Finally, the orientation of the head to gravity and the ground provides a stable platform, as it were, for the orientation of the organs of the head — that is, the ears, mouth, nose, and above all, the eyes.

The exploratory orientation of the ears to a source of sound, of the nose to a source of odor, and of the eyes to a source of light will be described in succeeding chapters. What is re-emphasized here is the fact that the pointing or directing of these perceptual organs depends on the upright posture of the head and body. The perception of external space, the dimensions of the vertical and horizontal and the third dimension, distance, is an accompaniment of the fact of body posture and equilibrium — that is, of orientation to the constants of the earth that have existed over millions of years of life.

Oriented Locomotion

Finally, we should consider the more elaborate kind of orientation mentioned at the beginning of the chapter, the kind that depends on both oriented posture and oriented organs of perception. Animals and men are mobile; they pursue prey, obtain mates, and find their way about. Rats get around in mazes and men get around in cities. In short, they are capable of oriented or directed locomotion.

The explanation of active locomotion, which is aimed or steered, as contrasted with passive locomotion, which drifts with the wind or current, has a long history in zoology. The lower organisms have various tropisms that move them toward or away from the bottom of the sea, toward or away from a source of light, into a current of water or away from it, upwind or downwind. These are conceived as "forced" movements and are supposed to be different from the "voluntary" movements of the higher organisms. The distinction is doubtful, however, since there is no dividing line between the behavior of the lower and the higher organisms and since all such directed locomotion can now be conceived as both automatic and purposive without contradiction. The swimming, crawling, flying, or walking is in all cases governed by a principle of symmetrical stimulation, and the individual directs the locomotion by balancing stimulation and then maximizing (or minimizing) certain features of it (Gibson, 1958).

. . . .

The Principle of Symmetrical Stimulation
in Orientation

Examples of the bilateral balancing of stimulation, of adjusting posture so as to make the input to the central nervous system *symmetrical*, are as follows:

For touch. In simple animals, there is the ventral earth reaction described above. In mammals, during infancy, there is a strong tendency when one side of the head is touched to turn so as to bring the mouth in contact with the touching object. A baby seems to find the mother's nipple in this way.

For odor. Animals as different as moths and hunting dogs, when they get the scent of mate or prey, will so move as to equalize the bilateral wind pressure on the front of the body. Orientation to the odor source is thus accomplished by orientation to the air stream.

For sound. Animals with two ears respond to a sound by turning the head so as to equalize the binaural intensity and synchronize the binaural transients. The head is then pointed toward the source, as we shall see in the next chapter.

For the ambient array of light. Animals with lateral eyes, when they register an interesting motion, form, texture, or color in the array, will turn the head so as to get the image symmetrically balanced in both eyes. They have then only to magnify this image in order to approach the object. Animals with frontal eyes that have concentrated foveas will also turn the eyes in the head so as to get the image centered symmetrically on each retina. We call the latter *fixation* (Chapter 9).

. . . .

In this book it is assumed that all the perceptual systems, chemical, cutaneous, auditory, and visual, can serve to govern directed locomotion. They are all orienting systems insofar as they can guide the individual to a goal. In various ways, as we shall see, the animals or man can approach a source of odor or withdraw from it, obtain comforting contact and reject painful contact, come close to a sound source or go away from it, and make a visible object loom large in his field of view or shrink. The determining cause of approach or withdrawal is the information in the odor, the contact, the sound, or the sight — the information that specifies the value of the source. Some sources are beneficial, some noxious. If the specification is real and if the information is detected and discriminated, the individual will be able to detect the values of things at a distance and move toward or away from them in accordance with what they afford.

The classification of tropisms, taxes, and kineses in lower animals has become increasingly complex under the biological assumption that what animals orient to is mere physical energy — radiant, thermal, chemical, and mechanical (Frankel and Gunn, 1940). The only alternative to an explanation in terms of forced movements has been one which grants animals a gift of mental powers. When it is assumed, however, that environmental energies convey information and that all animals get information, in their way, a higher-order control of locomotion is conceivable along with a lower-order control. The simplest animals detect only the simplest invariants; the complex ones detect the complex invariants; but all are moving adaptively.

Geographical orientation, as evidenced in the foraging, hunting, homing, and territorial behavior of animals and men, is a product of many perceptual systems in cooperation. The basic orienting system is at the root of it, but the haptic system, the olfactory system, the auditory system, and the visual system all contribute information, some of it unique but much of it redundant. The sensory control of maze-learning in the rat, the ability of a rat to run a maze when blinded, or deafened, or anosmic, or without vibrissae, or even partially paralyzed, shows that orientation does not depend on any one "sense." The orienting reactions of the sense organs, considered so important to behavior by Pavlov, are actually part of a hierarchical system for orientation. The moth and the flame exemplify one extreme; man's exploration of outer space exemplifies another; but both animals are, in their way, orienting to the world.

ヶ / The Auditory System

The sense organ for hearing is commonly said to be the ear. But the perception of sounds involves *listening*, not just hearing, and the listening system includes two ears together with the muscles for orienting them to a source of sound.

Anatomically, an ear is half of a listening system. Figure 5.1 shows this structure as it is found in man. It consists of (1) the outer ear (the auricle or pinna), (2) the ear passage (external auditory canal), (3) the eardrum (tympanic membrane), (4) the middle ear with its mechanical linkage, and (5) the inner ear with the cochlea containing the actual receptors. An "ear," then, is a subordinate organ which transmits vibrations from the air and converts them into nerve impulses. The complete organ is bilateral. The two half-organs are fixed on two sides of a mobile head; moreover, in the mammals below man each auricle is mobile. The system adjusts so as to turn first the ears and then the head toward the source of vibration. The individual is thus oriented to an event in the world. In perceptual terms, he can locate it.

The identity of a vibratory event, as contrasted with its location, is given by the temporal course and the frequency spectrum of the wave train, as suggested in Chapter 1. The pickup of this information, registering the meaning of the sound, can be accomplished by either half of the binaural system independently. But a single inner ear in the middle of the head could not locate a source.

The function of the auditory system, then, is not merely to permit hearing, if by that is meant the arousal of auditory sensations. Its exteroceptive function is to pick up the *direction* of an event, permitting orientation to it, and the *nature* of an event, permitting identification of it. Its proprioceptive function is to register the sounds made by the individual, especially in vocalizing. The hearing of one's own voice permits the control of sequential patterns of vocal sounds, as in bird songs, and the monitoring of vocal utterances, as in human speech. This loop, the

75

vocal-auditory act, is particularly well suited to be the basis of a social loop through another animals, and thus to facilitate social interaction.

Structure and Evolution of the Auditory System

The auditory and the vestibular systems of vertebrates are anatomically joined in the labyrinth but functionally separate. Both evolved from the statocyst of invertebrates like the jellyfish — an organ that might also be called a "dynamocyst." It is possible to imagine how this simple force detector could divide into two parts and become specialized in two directions. A weight of some sort attached to hair cells in a fluid-filled chamber could be elaborated in various ways. One part remained specialized for the slow pushes and pulls of locomotion; another part gradually became specialized for the rapid pushes and pulls of the medium. The stages of development of the cochlea in amphibia, birds, and mammals, are shown in Figure 5.2.

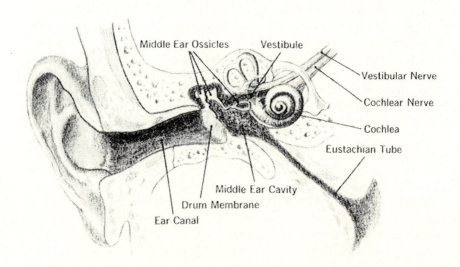

Figure 5.1 The anatomy of the human ear. The arrangement of the outer ear, the ear passage, the middle ear, and the cochlea is shown. The fact that these parts are adjacent makes them anatomically a single organ. Nevertheless the other ear is functionally united with this one, whereas the vestibular structure adjacent to this one is functionally separated from it. (After a drawing in N. L. Munn, *Psychology*, 5th ed., Houghton Mifflin, 1966.)

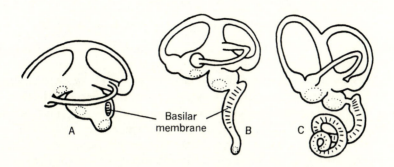

Figure 5.2 The membranous labyrinth at various stages of evolution. The vestibular part of the labyrinth does not show any evolutionary change from the turtle to the bird to the mammal, but the auditory part, the cochlea with its basilar membrane, does develop. The "otoliths" are shown by dotted ellipses; the basilar membrane is shown by parallel dashes. Presumably birds and mammals get increasingly more information from air vibration than amphibians, and are increasingly vocal. (From G. von Békésy and W. A. Rosenblith, Chapter 27 in S. S. Stevens, Ed., *Handbook of Experimental Psychology*, Wiley, 1951.)

The Development of the Cochlea

The utricle with its semicircular canals has remained essentially the same structure throughout vertebrate evolutions. The saccule, however, differs greatly from fish to man. In fish and frogs there is a small area of the saccule called the lagena, a primordial cochlea. In reptiles and birds, a real cochlea develops as an attachment to the saccule. In mammals, the cochlea elongates and spirals around, becoming a highly elaborate structure. As the cochlea developed, so did the active auditory system, and the ability of the animal to get information from the vibrations of the medium surrounding it.

As we noted in the last chapter, the vestibular organ registers linear starting and stopping with the utricle, and rotary starting and stopping with the semicircular canals. The cochlea, plus the middle and outer ears, seems to have developed so as to register *vibratory* starting and stopping, or *shaking*. Both structures show their evolutionary origin as a force detector. Both structures work on the principle of enclosing tissue being pushed or jarred relative to an inclosed weight of some sort, the heavy otolith or otoliths. Both the vestibule and the cochlea are sensitive to mechanical events. But the auditory system became sensitive to the special sort of micromechanical event we call sound.

The Development of the Middle Ear

When life emerged from the sea, animals had to develop air-hearing as well as air-breathing. In fish, since the fluid inside their bodies is similar to that outside, vibration of the medium is propagated directly to the receptors of the saccule. Underwater sound goes through the animal and the whole animal shakes relative to the otoliths. The auditory organ is rudimentary, and it is a question whether fish can be said to "hear," but the lagena is the precursor of the cochlea and it must respond to the simpler variables of wave trains. In amphibia and terrestrial animals, on the other hand, airborne vibration does not penetrate the body. These animals had to develop a way of admitting the sound pressures of the air and delivering energy to the receptors of the water-filled chamber that they inherited from their aquatic ancestors. Reptiles and birds did so by means of the middle ear. They possess an air channel for admitting sound, ending in the eardrum, a stretched membrane resonating with almost no latency or after-vibration, which has a mechanical linkage to the bony labyrinth of the inner ear. In this way, instead of the whole animal being shaken relative to the otoliths, only an inner membrane needs to be put into vibration relative to the otoliths. In short, the machinery of the middle ear converts air vibrations into fluid pulses in the cochlea.

In mammals the mobile outer ears developed, along with a more elaborate middle ear. With this went the elongation of the cochlea into the spiral shape of a snail shell. The localizing and discriminating of sound sources, accordingly, is very precise in mammals. Most of them can hear as well as we do, and some better.

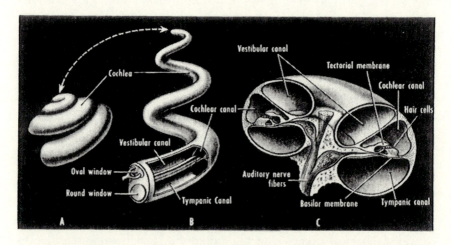

Figure 5.3 The structure of the human cochlea. In *A*, the cochlea is shown coiled in position; in *B*, it is shown as if extended and partially sectioned to reveal the internal canals; *C* shows a cross-section of one-half turn with the details of the receptive structure. (From N. L. Munn, *Psychology*, 5th ed., Houghton Mifflin, 1966.)

The Receptive Structure

The fully developed cochlea has as its essential feature a long and narrow flexible membrane, the basilar membrane, on which rests the *organ of Corti* containing the receptive hair cells. A cross-section of the cochlea is shown in Figure 5.3. Thousands of these hair cells are arranged in a column only four or five cells wide. They project into a gelatinous mass called the tectorial membrane, and it is assumed that these cilia, like the others in the labyrinth, are caused either to fire impulses by being bent or to modulate their spontaneous firing by being bent. As fluid pulses come up the cochlea the basilar membrane is probably affected by waves of displacement, or traveling bulges, which create a pattern of excitation in the column of hair cells, a pattern that is specific to the momentary frequency spectrum of the sound, and which changes as it changes.

The input of the cochlea to the fibers of the auditory nerve is not a matter of connections between single hair cells and single fibers. A single afferent fiber is activated by many hair cells, and there is much overlap among these groups. However the qualities of sound may prove to be specified in the neural input, the specificity is not a matter of fixed resonators in the cochlea, each attached to a specific neuron which signals that frequency to the brain.

. . . .

*The Action of the Cochlea and the Theory
of Auditory Sensations*

A great deal is now known about the mechanical and physiological action of the cochlea and its capacity to arouse sensations of pitch and loudness. An introduction to the subject is provided in the chapters on hearing in Stevens (1951) or in Geldard (1953). For the neurophysiology of the organ, see Wever (1949) and Davis (1959).

. . . .

The Potential Stimuli for the Auditory System

The propagation of compression waves outward from a mechanical disturbance was described in Chapter 1. Arguments over whether such a field should or should not be called "sound" can be avoided by realizing that the field is a potential stimulus. The ways in which it can become an effective stimulus will be described in the next two sections. But first let us examine the information physically existing in such fields — the information that *might* be picked up by an auditor.

Some examples of the kinds of mechanical disturbance that occur in the environment are (1) waterfalls, which broadcast continuously, (2) wind, or air friction, which is intermittent, and (3) the rolling, rubbing, colliding, or breaking of solids, which can be abrupt. In addition, there are (4) the behavioral and vocal acts of animals, (5) the speech and musical performances of man, and (6) the whole gamut of machine

Figure 5.4 A momentarily frozen field of vibration in air. Waves of compression are shown schematically as they would emanate from a buzzing mosquito. The equivalent sine wave is shown at the bottom. Actually this high-pitched hum is not a pure tone, and the waves are complex, not simple. A field of this sort, however, surrounds any vibratory event.

sounds of technological civilization. All of these events have a time course, and most have a beginning and end. The abstractly continuous pure tone with which the study of sound is often begun does not occur in nature, or not often enough to be typical.

A vibration field in air, disregarding reflections, consists of wave fronts that are concentric spheres (see Figure 5.4). The field passes around small obstacles with only small losses so that the "sound shadows" behind them are attenuated regions but not true shadows. At any station-point in air where an auditor might be, the wave fronts are essentially perpendicular to a line from the source. Along any radius of this field at any one time is a *train* of waves of mixed frequencies, the amplitude of the waves decreasing outward in theoretical proportion to the square of the distance. The wave front and the wave train are the important ecological facts for auditory perception.

The wave front is specific to the direction of the source. The train of waves is specific to the kind of mechanical disturbance at the source. The former affords orientation and localization. The latter affords discrimination and identification. The wave train, to elaborate, is specific to the vibratory event in two respects: first, the simultaneous mixture of frequencies is an exact copy of the mixture of frequencies of the vibratory event (e.g., whistling *vs* rumbling), and second, the sequence of transients in the wave train is an exact copy of the temporal course of the event. Note that the *amplitude* of the wave train at any station-point along a radius of the field is *not* specific to the event; it varies with distance and decreases to zero. It carries no perceptual information about the event. The *maximum* amplitude of the wave train at the source is proportional to the mechanical violence of the event, and determines the range of the vibratory field. But only the frequency spectrum and the transients of the wave train are invariant with distance; they are identical all over the field and specify the event anywhere within the field. The distinctive features of a sound, whether it be natural, animal, musical, or vocal, are all included within these two variables, and they mirror the physically distinguishing features of the source.

The pickup of wave-front information and of wave-train information will be described separately in the next two sections.

The Pickup of Wave Fronts: Orientation and Localization

Suppose that an individual with ears is somewhere within the range of a vibratory field and consider what happens when the first wave front, or any later one, reaches his head (see Figure 5.5). Most of the wave

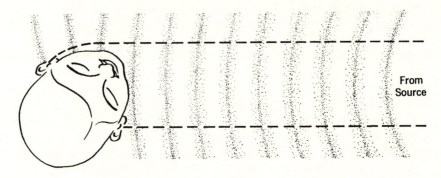

**Figure 5.5   The different paths of sound waves entering the
two ears.** Wave fronts from a sound source are shown approaching
the head. The first pulse enters the offside ear later than the onside
ear and with less intensity. Both the priority of onset and the disparity of intensity at the two ears are functions of the angle at which
the head is turned from the source.

will be reflected, but at the outer ears two small areas of the wave will
be funneled into each auditory canal. The critical fact is the angle between the frontal plane of the head and the wave front, that is, the
deviation by which the individual is not facing the source. It determines two kinds of covariant stimulus information. The wave front will
enter the offside ear a little *later* than the other (because it has farther
to go) and it will enter the offside ear a little *weaker* than the other
(because it is in the sound shadow of the head). In orthodox terminology, these are called the time difference and the intensity difference of
the sensations in the two ears. But it is very doubtful that there *are*
separate sensations in the two ears. If the bilateral ears are considered
a single perceptual system, the variables of prior onset and greater intensity in one or the other ear can be regarded together as a relational
stimulus for the system. They can vary between a left-right value, zero,
and a right-left value, and the two are normally correlated, i.e., covariant. Both specify the same fact. Priority of onset and disparity of intensity are therefore best conceived as a kind of stimulus asymmetry or
imbalance (Pieron, 1952, p. 235).

The two pulses from the first wave front reaching the head pass up the
auditory canals and push on the two eardrums. Each push is transmitted
through the middle ear, into each cochlea, and is then promptly converted to a burst of impulses in each auditory nerve. These proceed to
a common nerve center for the auditory system. The asymmetry of input
from the right and left could be represented by some kind of neural
action at this center.

The Adjustment Process: Orientation

The auditory system begins at once to adjust to any imbalance of stimulation. In the human auditor the head is turned automatically so as to nullify, for the pulses of sound following the first, the temporal priority and the intensitive difference. If this is not immediately achieved, the system "hunts" until the inputs to the two sides are symmetrical. The observer is then oriented to the source of sound, facing it with all the sensory equipment of the head. He is in a position to look at the rolling stone, at the maker of the cry of distress, or at the speaker.

In mammals below man, another auditory adjustment is superposed on this one. Each ear seems to orient by turning or twitching so as to funnel the maximum amplitude into its eardrum. And there seems to be a further auditory adjustment of certain muscles which can alter the tension of the eardrum. Both the orienting and adjusting responses of the auditory system, be it noted, are a circular feedback from the first input, modifying it in the direction of some optimum. Listening is what the system is for; hearing is incidental.

• ORIENTED LOCOMOTION. If the animal listens to a source of sound it it in a position to move toward or away from it. A lost duckling, for example, detecting the direction of the call of the mother, needs only to maintain the binaural balance of stimulation and waddle straight ahead in order to reach the family. The intensity of the sound increases as it progresses. The behavior is a sort of auditory tropism. Its formula is quite simple, and a neural mechanism to provide it can be conceived: keep the binaural input symmetrical and follow the head. The reassuring sound will become louder and the reassuring sight will appear and become bigger.

• SELECTIVE LISTENING. If there are several sources of sound in the environment at once, several different wave fronts will reach the head of an observer at the same time. Since the different wave trains will be physically blended at each eardrum, it might be supposed that the corresponding perceptions would also blend and be inseparable. Actually it is possible to listen selectively to different sounds, and the process of auditory orientation described probably helps to explain why this is so. The observer can, by turning his head around and tilting it if necessary, synchronize the binaural inputs for one sound while desynchronizing those for another, and can equalize the binaural intensities for that sound while unequalizing those for another. Presumably this makes it easier to listen to one voice while hearing but not paying attention to others. The problem of auditory "masking" will be considered again in Chapter 14.

The adjusting of the head and ears to a source in the world is a case of *overt* listening. There is another kind of listening, however, which is internal, and therefore *covert*. It must depend on some kind of selection at nerve centers rather than on the enhancing of stimulus information as described above. We shall find that these two kinds of attention are manifested in vision as well as audition, and will later need to be concerned with the central or secondary kind of attention, but the peripheral or primary kind is what we should first describe. Both kinds of attention are probably involved in what has been called the "cocktail party phenomenon" — the ability to select one stream of speech out of many concurrent streams in the sound flux produced by a roomful of speakers.

Priority of Onset and Disparity of Intensity as Cues for the Perception of Direction

The differences between artificially produced sounds at the two ears of an observer have been experimentally isolated and controlled in psychological laboratories for a long time. It was assumed that the difference in time of onset and the difference in intensity were *cues* or *clues* for a perception of the direction of the source relative to the head. In order to isolate them, experiments were performed with a blindfolded observer — with head held motionless at the center of a "sound cage" — whose task it was to point to or otherwise indicate the source of a sound. When localizing in this passive manner, the subject frequently made errors, confusing a direction in front of the head with a symmetrical direction in back of the head. The cues are indeed ambiguous in this respect, as an inspection of Figure 5.6 will show. When the head is kept motionless, a whole family of directions will yield the same degree of binaural time difference and intensity difference — all the directions lying on a cone-shaped "surface of confusion," the axis of which is a line joining the two ears.

These illusions of sound localization in the laboratory are the result of not permitting the ear-head system to explore and orient itself. When the head is allowed to move freely, the confusions disappear, as the experiments of Wallach have shown (1939, 1940). The static "cues" for sound localization in the dynamic situation are continually changing from moment to moment, being changed by the searching movement of the head, but the perception is accurate only when this seeming flux of information is present, not when the static cues are the only ones available.

It is significant that no observer in the static sound-localization experiment has ever been able to report having two separate sensations from the two ears which he can then compare. The binaural difference is never experienced as such; there is only an impression of the direction of the sound. This is why the present hypothesis of binaural asymmetry as stimulus information for the auditory system is preferable to the hypothesis of separate stimuli and sensations for the two ears.

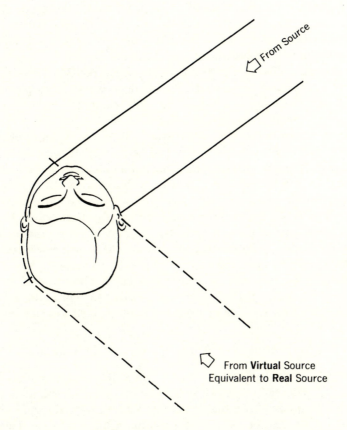

Figure 5.6 Two equivalent degrees of binaural asymmetry when the head is stationary. In this situation there is more than one direction from which the sound might come, since the priority of onset and the disparity of intensity are the same for the two sources shown. Actually there is a whole family of indistinguishable directions. However, when the head is allowed to turn and tilt, so as to nullify the binaural asymmetry, only one of the possible directions is specified for the source.

• THE PERCEPTION OF SOUNDS IN THE HEAD. If, for an external source, the binaural balance of auditory stimulation is linked to head movement, and covaries with it, then it is equally true that for a source inside the head, such as one's own voice, binaural balance is *not* linked to head movement and does *not* covary with it. In fact, a continuing balance of binaural input with head rotation should *specify* a sound within the head.

In this situation the sound ought to be heard inside the head. A person who wears a pair of earphones is in just this situation. He is strongly inclined to hear a mysterious invisible speaker inside his head, and it takes some practice to overcome the illusion.

Even a child who first listens to a telephone receiver hears the voice in or at his ear and is puzzled. The modern world of earphones, telephones, and loudspeakers does some violence to the natural orienting tendency of the auditory system toward sources.

The very great sensitivity of the system to the prior onset of a sound in one or the other ear was established by experiments with earphones. If a pair of identical clicks depart from simultaneity by as little as a few thousandths of a second, the click will be heard toward the right or the left ear according as the priority is in the right or the left earphone.

The illusion of perceiving a source within the head when it "really" comes from earphones is a necessary consequence of the perceptual ability to localize correctly the sounds of one's own voice, of eating, breathing, and the like, which are in fact within the head. The listening system normally provides not only information about the external loci of sounds but also about the locus of "here," to which the others are relative. It is thus capable of proprioception as well as exteroception.

The Pickup of Wave Trains: Identification

The train of pressure waves along any radius of a vibratory field in the air is a potential stimulus. It becomes an effective stimulus when it is funneled into an ear so that the front of the wave train starts cochlear activity and the rear of the wave train ends cochlear activity. The waves, no matter how complex, can be analyzed into an abstract combination of simple sinusoidal waves, each with a certain frequency and a certain amplitude. Physical acoustics makes just this analysis, invented by Fourier, and provides a neat theoretical basis for all the achievements of acoustical engineering. But the trouble with it is that the elementary sine waves have to be taken as eternal in time, without beginning or end (Licklider, 1951). It leaves out of account the transitions in time, the transients or "time language," of vibratory waves. It treats physical sound as a phenomenon *sui generis,* instead of as a phenomenon that specifies the course of an ecological event; sound as pure physics, instead of sound as potential stimulus information.

This mode of analysis has another defect. It assumes that a psychological sound, no matter how complex, can be analyzed into a combination of pure sensations of pitch. This is very dubious in fact. And the same objections about transitions and tempo apply to psychological as to physical sound.

Meaningful Sounds

A pure tone can be experienced only by neglecting transients and ordinarily only with an artificial stimulus. It can be produced with an audio-oscillator at a given frequency and a given amplitude, acting for a certain length of time at a fixed distance from an ear. The result is said to be a meaningless sensation having a pitch corresponding to the frequency, a loudness corresponding to the amplitude, and a certain duration. Meaningful sounds, however, vary in much more elaborate ways than merely in pitch, loudness, and duration. Instead of simple duration, they vary in abruptness of beginning and ending, in repetitiveness, in rate, in regularity of rate, or rhythm, and in other subtleties of sequence. Instead of simple pitch, they vary in timbre or tone quality, in combinations of tone quality, in vowel quality, in approximation to noise, in noise quality, and in changes of all these in time. Instead of simple loudness, they vary in the direction of change of loudness, the rate of change of loudness, and the rate of *change* of change of loudness. In meaningful sounds, these variables can be combined to yield higher-order variables of staggering complexity. But these mathematical complexities seem nevertheless to be the simplicities of auditory information, and it is just these variables that are distinguished naturally by an auditory system. Moreover, it is just these variables that are specific to the source of the sound — the variables that identify the wind in the trees or the rushing of water, the cry of the young or the call of the mother. The sounds of *rubbing, scraping, rolling,* and *brushing,* for example, are distinctive acoustically and are distinguished phenomenally.

For the study of perception, a better method of analysis than the classical one of reducing sounds to a combination of pure sine waves is the one provided by the sound spectrograph. This represents the relative amounts of energy at various frequencies — the sound spectrum at each moment of time from the beginning to the end of the event. A sound spectrogram shows the pattern of frequencies and the total intensity, together with the transitions of both and the tempo of these transitions (see Figure 5.7). It appears to map the distinguishing features of natural sounds fairly well, and it can be used for the analysis of animal cries, bird songs, and human speech. It is somewhat analogous to musical notation, but it indicates the continuity and irregularity of real sound instead of slicing it into the units of musical notes and confining it to the rules of musical composition.

Note that the vertical dimension on a spectrogram shows the sound spectrum at any moment of time. It is the pattern of the relative intensities of the different frequencies that are harmonics (i.e., whole multiples) of the fundamental frequency. The spectrum has to be sustained for some

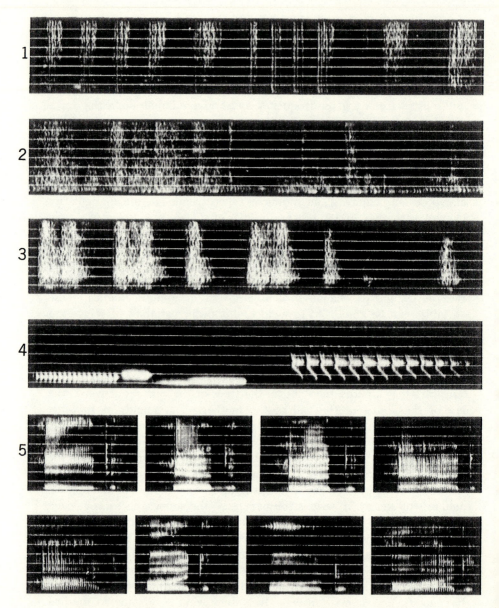

Figure 5.7 Spectrograms of several familiar sounds. From top to bottom: (1) Brushing with a whiskbroom. (2) Squeaky wheels (rolling a television set). (3) Barking by a dog (note that the first five barks are louder than the rest). (4) Some of the calls of the woodthrush. (5) The sounds of *heed, hid, head, had, hod, hood, who'd,* and *hewed*—eight different vowels uttered between the same initial and final consonants. (Spectrograms made at the General Electric Research and Development Center, Schenectady, New York. Courtesy of David E. Wood.)

time interval to be realized, of course, but it is not a tone. It should be thought of as a relational pattern, a configuration, not as a set of absolute frequencies, for the pattern is *transposable* with a shift of absolute frequencies. This fact is demonstrated in music by the equivalence of chords with a shift of key, and in speech by the equivalence of vowel qualities with a shift from male to female voice. The information in a sound spectrum seems to be given by the frequency ratios, not by the frequencies as such.

In general, a tone spectrum, not a tone, is the only kind of sustained sound that occurs in nature. Until the advent of tuning forks and oscillators it is very doubtful that an ear had ever been stimulated by a single frequency and that an organism had ever heard a pure tone. Presumably ears evolved to pick up relational patterns of frequencies and to distinguish different patterns.

Some Classes of Distinctive Sounds

The facts about the discrimination of auditory sensations are found in the handbooks and textbooks (Stevens, 1951; Geldard, 1953; Wever, 1949). What needs to be emphasized here is not the meaningless discriminations of pitch, loudness, and duration, but the useful discriminations that make it possible to perceive events.

For man there are classes, subclasses, and instances of identifiable sounds in countless variety, even if one limits consideration to those that can be named. In general they have not yet been studied under controlled laboratory conditions, with the exception of the fundamental speech sounds which are now being isolated and systematically presented to observers for discriminative judgment (e.g., Liberman *et al.*, 1961). But the classes and subclasses are open to ordinary observation, and deserve more study than they have had.

For example, the sounds of wind, of water, and of solids seem to be clearly distinguishable. Perhaps the vibratory events arising from gaseous flow, liquid turbulence, and mechanical action are characteristically different; it would be interesting to know why. With respect to the sounds of solids, rubbing, scraping, colliding, and rupturing seem to be clearly identifiable from their sounds, as noted above. If the physicist can specify the type of mechanical disturbance and the psychologist can obtain corresponding judgments, this type of psychophysics should prove to be more interesting than the psychophysics of abstract loudness and pitch.

The sounds made by various tools are specific to the mechanical action of the tool, as in sawing, pounding, filing, and chopping. The vibrations carry objective and external meaning insofar as they specify their sources. The question for the psychology of perception is how far the subjective meanings of a listener correspond to these objective meanings, and this is a question for experiment.

Consider animal sounds. The barking of dogs, the singing of birds, the buzzing of insects, and the croaking of frogs are never confused, either by us or by the animals themselves. The subtypes of these utterances are extremely diverse and quite specific — as to sex, parental status, or emotional state of the animal in question. The human auditor may be unable to perceive the emotional meaning of animal cries (unless he studies animal behavior), but the animal's own species does so readily.

Finally, consider the vocalizations of men. The sound of the infant, the child, the adult, and the aged person are all different. After childhood, the voice of the male and the female differentiate, the latter having a spectrum of higher mean frequency, and the sex of a person can usually be judged from the voice alone. The voice of every human speaker, in fact, is probably distinguishably different from that of all others in subtle ways, for we can all identify dozens or hundreds of persons by name from certain properties of the train of sound waves coming from a telephone receiver. A person's voice is like his face or his signature or his fingerprint in being specific to him only.

Even more interesting are the qualities of vocal sounds called *expressive*. They specify types and subtypes, differing in grosser or finer ways, of human emotions, moods, and feelings. The sound of laughter is unmistakable; so is the sound of weeping. There are growls of anger and grunts of effort, moans of pain and sighs of relief, shouts of triumph and croons of love. Vocalization of this sort existed long before speech, and it was from this repertory of spontaneous unlearned utterance in our hominid ancestors that conventional speech sounds developed. Exclamation still occurs along with speech, and expression occurs in the course of speech. However intellectual the words may be, the voice betrays the mood, feelings, intentions, and temperament of the speaker himself. This brings us to the sounds of speech considered as symbols, i.e., language.

The Pickup of Symbolic Speech

Vocal speech identifies the speaker, and specifies his emotion. It carries the *meaning* of the individual and his motives. But vocal speech does more than this. It contains symbols which carry the meanings of things in the common environment of *all* individuals. These enable men to *think* of the same things, to have concepts in common, and to verify their concepts jointly. Symbolic meaning is of a different order from perceptual meaning. The cry "wolf" has an entirely different function from either the cry of alarm at seeing a wolf or the howling of the wolf itself. This fact bears elaboration.

The relation of a perceptual stimulus to its causal source in the environment is of one sort; the relation of a symbol to its referent is of a different sort. The former depends on the laws of physics and biology, that is, on the ecology of stimulation. The latter depends on a *linguistic community*, which is a unique invention of the human species. The relation of perceptual stimuli to their sources is an intrinsic relation such as one of projection, but the relation of symbols to their referents is an extrinsic one of social agreement. The conventions of symbolic speech must be learned, but the child can just about as easily learn one language as another. The connections between stimuli and their sources may well have to be learned in part, but they make only one language, or better, they do not make a language at all. The language code is cultural, traditional, and arbitrary; the connection between stimuli and their sources is not.

In this book, a distinction will be made between perceptual cognition, or knowledge of the environment, and symbolic cognition, or knowledge *about* the environment. The former is a direct response to things based on stimulus information; the latter is an indirect response to things based on stimulus sources produced by another human individual. The information in the latter case is *coded;* in the former case it cannot properly be called that.

The pickup of sounds, including speech sounds, is a one-stage perceptual process. The apprehension of things referred to, however, is a two-stage process, since it involves both the discrimination of the vocal articulations and the learning of what they stand for. The acoustic sounds of speech specify the consonants, vowels, syllables, and words of speech; the parts of speech in turn specify something else. Both types of specification must be learned by the child, in some sense of the term, but the kinds of learning required are not the same.

If this position is correct, animals are not capable of symbolic speech and do not have a language. They communicate, of course, and the remarkable social signals of bees and porpoises which have recently been discovered deserve our admiration. But they do not deserve the name of language. Linguists have a fairly clear idea of what language is and is not. The study of the social organization of animals will only be confused by loosely comparing them to men. No animal has ever learned to generate a sentence or to interchange the parts of speech.

Articulation as the Source of Speech

The source of acoustical speech sounds is a human vocal apparatus backed up by a human nervous system. This apparatus is probably more versatile and elaborate than any other sound-maker in the world. The sounds arise from a series of exhalations produced by the breathing muscles of the chest and diaphragm. These may or may not be accompanied by vibrations of the larynx, but they are always accompanied by movements of the mouth, jaw, lips, tongue, and velum. The series of concurrent movements produces what is called the segmentation of speech — that is, the fact of segments in the flow of sound. This flow, voiced or unvoiced, is modified in spectral composition so as to make vowels. It is also cut up by pauses, stops, and transitions so as to make consonants. The vowels and consonants are the units of articulation. The muscular movements that create phonemes tend to be stereotyped. The fact is that, with a repertory of only a small number of letters of an alphabet — a phonetic alphabet — all combinations of speech sounds in all the hundreds of human languages can be represented.

Consonants and vowels usually alternate in speech to make syllables. Syllables combine to make words, which are said to have *lexical* meaning. Words in turn combine to make phrases, then sentences, and then discourse, at still higher levels of symbolic meaning sometimes called syntactical or grammatical meaning. The point to be noted is that the structure of speech can be analyzed at various levels, subordinate and superordinate, each having some sort of unit appropriate to it and each having a level of meaning appropriate to it. At each level, for the phoneme, the syllable, the word, the phrase, the sentence, and upward without limit, there is a stimulus unit for the perceptual system and a response unit for the vocal system. That is, there are lesser and greater units of stimulation and of response, the lesser units being nested within greater ones. This same structure of units within units will be found to apply to systems other than the auditory and to types of perception other than verbal.

The Stimulus Information for the Detection of Phonemes

The phonemes of human speech, vowels and consonants, can be specified in two equivalent ways, as responses and as stimuli. The first is articulatory specification, in terms ˙of the movements of the vocal apparatus. The second is acoustic specification, in terms of the spectrum and transitions of the sound waves. The classification of vowels by the shape of the mouth-space, and of consonants as plosives, fricatives, dentals, labials, and so on, is an old discipline. The classification of phonemes by the physically distinguishing features of the segments of a wave train depends on the use of instruments like the sound spectrograph and is a relatively young discipline. It was held back by the traditional belief that sounds could only be analyzed into physical variables of frequency, intensity, and time, and by the belief that perceptions had to be analyzed into corresponding component sensations of pitch, loudness, and duration.

The interesting fact about the sounds of speech is that they are to a striking degree invariant with changes of pitch, loudness, and duration. The effective stimuli are relational, not absolute; ratios, not quantities. As to pitch, a woman's voice may be a full octave above a man's but the vowels and consonants remain; either may speak in a high register or a low without loss of intelligibility; moreover a vowel can be sung on any note without destroying the pattern of "formants" that make it that particular vowel. As to loudness, a voice may be near or far, and the utterances may be shouted or spoken softly without change of the phonemes; most of them come through when they are merely whispered and not "voiced" at all. As to duration, speech may be emitted with extreme slowness or extreme rapidity, but if the *sequential pattern* is constant the phonemic units are constant. All these facts can be expressed by saying that phonemes are *transposable* over the dimensions of pitch, loudness, and duration, and that the stimulus information for detecting them is *invariant* under transformations of frequency, intensity, and time. The perception of a phoneme is therefore not reducible to sensations of pitch, loudness, and duration. Likewise, the relational stimulus for a phoneme is not analyzable as magnitudes of frequency, amplitude, and time.

One modern view of the phoneme in linguistic theory seems to be that it is a kind of relational entity, not an absolute. It is a cluster of contrasts between it and all the other phonemes. In the theory of Jakobson, a phoneme is reducible to a small concurrent bundle of "distinctive features," each acoustic feature corresponding to a contrast of articulation (Jakobson and Halle, 1956).

If the phonemes of human speech are thought of as at once the responses of a speaker and the stimuli for a listener (in the stimulus-response terms that a psychologist uses to think of them), it could be predicted that each speaker of a community would be compelled to make the same phonemes as others in order to be intelligible. Presumably this is part of what children do when they "learn to speak" — that is, they learn to pronounce in accordance with their language or their dialect, under pressure from playmates, parents, and schools. The sounds are then stereotyped for the community and can be said to have a valid objective reality, anchored in the habitual resonances, stops, frictions, and explosions of conventional articulation and specified by certain invariant properties of the wave trains of vibratory fields in the air. In this sense speech sounds specify their sources in the same way that natural sounds do. They are potential stimuli, as natural sounds are. But the fact that they are responses *at the same time* that they are stimuli makes them realities of a social group, not merely realities of a terrestrial environment.

The Physical Reality of Speech

There has been disagreement over the issue of whether speech is objective or only subjective, whether it has physical reality or only psychological reality. It depends on what the debaters mean by physics. An articulated utterance is a source of a vibratory field in the air. The source is biologically "physical" and the vibration is acoustically "physical." The vibration is a potential stimulus, becoming effective when a listener is within range of the vibratory field. The listener then *perceives* the articulation because the invariants of vibration correspond to those of articulation. In this theory of speech perception, the units and parts of speech are present both in the mouth of the speaker and in the air between the speaker and the listener. Phonemes are in the air. They can be considered physically real if the higher-order invariants of sound waves are admitted to the realm of physics. Speech is denied physical reality only when these invariants are excluded, when only the frequency and amplitude of sound waves are admitted to physics, and when the corresponding sensations of pitch and loudness are taken to be the sole basis for psychophysics.

Proprioceptive Hearing and its Implications

Audition is proprioceptive as well as exteroceptive. A speaker hears his own speech as well as that of others. Vocalizing is really vocal-auditory activity; all animals that have a vocal organ also have an auditory organ. In man, consonants, vowels, syllables, and words are no sooner created by the output of the nervous system than they are fed back into the nervous system. They begin with patterns and changes of muscular activity and end with patterns and changes of receptor activity. The loop from the mouth to the ears, largely by air conduction but also by a short-circuit of bone conduction, is inescapable and almost instantaneous.

There is an old theory to the effect that the human infant, in the babbling stage of speech development, learns associations between the sounds of speech and the acts of speech, or conditioned reflexes connecting a certain auditory stimulus to a certain vocal response. This is taken to be the basis of vocal imitation, and to explain why deaf children do not learn to speak. It is assumed by association theorists that children must *learn* the correspondence of hearing and speaking. Now it is perfectly true that any single elementary muscle contraction does not correspond to any single elementary sensory datum. But the *pattern* of contractions and the *change* of nervous output at the muscles *do* correspond to the pattern of excitation and the change of nervous input at the cochlea. There is no need for these to be associated, since they are identical. This being true, what probably happens during the babbling stage is the differentiating of pattern and change in the muscular output along with a parallel differentiating of pattern and change in the cochlear input. As the child learns to articulate the invariants of sound he learns to discriminate them. The practicing of vocal-auditory activity permits learning, but it is not associative learning.

Another old formula has it that when an individual hears his own speech he gets the same *stimuli* as when he hears the speech of another. If this were literally true it would lead to incredible confusion — the individual could not tell whether he or someone else had spoken! Actually the wave train invariants of stimulation are the same in the two cases, but the binaural balance of stimulation is not; the *symbols* are perceived as the same, but the *voices* are perceived as different. It will be recalled that the speaker's voice comes from his own head while the voice of another comes in a certain direction from outside. Consequently self-stimulation is binaurally balanced and unaltered by head-turning, whereas external stimulation is made to balance only by orienting the head. The stimulus information for location is not the stimulus information for symbolic speech, and each has its own level of perception. The individual perceives his own voice as "here" and the voice of another person as "there." He hears his own speech (the voice) as different from the speech of other men but nevertheless hears his own speech (the symbols) as *not* different from the speech of other men. Speech is at once vocal and symbolic, both personal and impersonal.

Associative learning enters into cognitive development as the child learns the referential meanings of the symbols—the speech code of his group. He has to learn what the words stand for or designate, and he begins to do so very early, but referential meaning is not the only kind and associative learning is not the only kind. The discussion of symbolic cognition, of knowledge *about* the environment, will be deferred to a later chapter.

The function of auditory self-stimulation is probably best understood if it is conceived not as a kind of audition but as a kind of proprioception. It monitors the flow of speech in the same way that other modes of proprioception keep track of the flow of other type of behavior. It thus enables articulation to be controlled. The next syllable depends on the previous ones; the feedback yields a running record of how far along the speech has got. The same thing applies to the words of a sentence and the sentences of discourse; what the speaker says next depends on what he has already said. Evidence for this control function comes from an experiment with apparatus that artificially delays the auditory feedback, using close-fitting earphones and delayed playback from a tape. When the sounds enter the ears a quarter of a second after they were pronounced, the articulation tends to disintegrate. Introspectively, speaking becomes a great effort. Evidently it is not sufficient that "voluntary" impulses begin in the brain; re-entrant impulses are necessary for volition to achieve its purpose (Cherry, 1957, Ch. 7).

The young child learns to guide the flow of speech sounds by auditory feedback. The adult can learn to guide a flow of instrumental sounds in much the same way. In either case the pattern and sequence of muscular action is controlled for a purpose. The blowing of flutes, the "lipping" of horns, the plucking, bowing or fingering of strings, and the flipping of drumsticks are not, in principle, unlike the articulation of the voice.

Summary

The intricate apparatus required for auditory perception evolved only because information about distant vibratory events could be picked up by animals from the vibrations of the medium. The sound waves corresponded to the event, and the wave fronts specified its direction; the act of listening developed to identify the event and to locate it. The information is carried not by the variables of sound heretofore emphasized in physics but by the invariants of the wave train and the geometry of the wave front.

A special case of auditory perception occurs with vocal-auditory behavior, when the vocalizer stimulates his own ears. In this case the source is the individual's own body, but the meaning of the wave train, expressive or symbolic, can be the same as that of the sound from another individual. Communication among members of the same species could thus develop. In man, this has led to the rise of linguistic communities having stereotyped speech sounds, and hence to the phenomenon of the accumulation of knowledge in libraries, and so to the complexities of the human condition.

VI / The Haptic System and its Components

What we mean by the *sense of touch* in ordinary parlance and what the psychologist means by it are two different things. When a person puts on his shoes in the dark or fits a nut to a hidden bolt, he says that he does it by "touch" or by "feel." The psychologist says that he does it with two separate senses, kinesthesis and skin pressure. In this chapter we will be chiefly concerned with what the ordinary person means by "touch."

The sensibility of the individual to the world adjacent to his body by the use of his body will here be called the *haptic system*. The word *haptic* comes from a Greek term meaning "able to lay hold of." It operates when a man or animal feels things with his body or its extremities. It is not just the sense of skin pressure. It is not even the sense of pressure plus the sense of kinesthesis. The analytical psychologist separates touch and kinesthesis by introspection and by laboratory control of stimulation. He then assumes that the set of these elementary impressions is all that the individual, animal or human, has available for perception. As we shall see, however, it is very possible that he is wrong in this assumption, since the inputs available for perception may not be the same as the inputs available for sensation. There are inputs for perception, and also for the control of performance, that have no discoverable sensations to correspond.

The haptic system, then, is an apparatus by which the individual gets information about both the environment and his body. He feels an object relative to the body and the body relative to an object. It is the perceptual system by which animals and men are *literally* in touch with the environment. When we say *figuratively* that a man is in touch with the environment by looking or listening, the metaphor is something to think about, but we can put this off until later.

The Sensations Taken to Underlie Haptic Perception

For a whole century, roughly from 1830 to 1930, investigators tried to make an exhaustive inventory of the sensations, as we noted in Chapters

2 and 3. Boring has written the history of this effort (1942) and his two chapters on "tactual sensibility" and "organic sensibility" describe the problems and frustrations of those who tried to classify the body senses and pin them down to corresponding receptors and stimuli. Aristotle's sense of touch, the fifth sense, did not seem to be unitary on careful examination. For one thing, it had no organ like the eye, ear, nose, or mouth, and the skin did not fit the idea of a sense organ. So it got subdivided. The first extra sense to be split off from touch was the *muscle sense*. It was then argued that *temperature* was a different quality from touch, and that *pain* also was different. Then *warm* was separated from *cold* when it was discovered that the skin of man contained different groups of spots yielding characteristic sensations of warmness and coldness. Spots for *pressure* and for *prickly pain* could also be mapped out, and they did not coincide. The sensitivity of the joints was then discovered, and this, with or without the muscle sense, was called *kinesthesis*. But what about feelings of *strain,* or of *deep pressure?* What about *cutaneous motion?* Some argued that the feelings of the body were so much allied as to be subsumed under one name — Boring has called it *somaesthesis*. Should hunger, thirst, nausea, and the other visceral experiences be classed as sensations? Is pleasure a sense if pain is? Is pain a single sense including both the sharp prick of a needle and the dull ache of indigestion? A vast realm of experience was discovered by these researches, but the aim of an *inventory* of all the basic sensations was never achieved. The whole effort, as Boring notes in his history, was inconclusive. Nevertheless, it was still accepted that there had to be so and so many senses because there were just so many sensory nerves, and sensations were taken to be specific to nerves. Sensations, moreover, were the sole basis of perception or knowledge. The inventory was necessary but could not be achieved.

The method of analytic introspection, aided by controlled artificial stimulation of the observer, is nowadays scarcely used except as an exercise in laboratory psychology. The climax of the research effort was reached under Titchener at Cornell in the early decades of this century. Little of it is now remembered but the general idea persists that the original sense of touch can be divided up into five senses of pressure, warm, cold, pain, and kinesthesis.

The investigators attempted to isolate sensory experiences from perceptual ones in several ways. First, the subject of an experiment was required to be passive and the stimulus was imposed by the experimenter, not obtained by the subject. Second, the stimuli were typically small, single, brief indentations of the skin made by a needle, a hair, or the point of a warmed or cooled metal cylinder. Third, the subject was told to report his awareness of the impression, not of the object making it. A report of the perception (what the object seemed like) instead of the sensation (what the skin felt like) was considered an error. Some component of perception must often have remained in these experiments, for observers found it difficult to avoid what Titchener called the "stimulus error." Left to himself, the observer tended to report the object of his experience instead of the mental content.

In contrast to the above, the investigator of haptic perception attempts to do the opposite. First, the subject of an experiment is not required to remain passive but may be allowed to obtain stimulation. The human observer can be encouraged to explore a surface, a substance, or a prepared layout, using his hands for active touching. Second, the indentations of the skin are not punctate, single, or momentary, but are of variable size and pattern, and move or change in pattern. Third, the subject is allowed to report what he perceives, including what it affords or might be used for, and he is not required to introspect upon it, or at least not in analytic terms. So far from being an error, this kind of report is considered right and proper. Experiments of this sort will be reported in the next chapter.

· ·

The Two Poles of Experience — Objective and Subjective

The fact seems to be that in touching a solid object one can attend either to the external resistant thing or to the impression on the skin. The reader should try it. Within limits, you can concentrate either on the edge of the table, say, or on the dent it makes in *you*. It is as if the same stimulating event had two possible poles of experience, one objective and the other subjective. There are many possible meanings of the term *sensation*, but this is one: the detection of the impression made on a perceiver while he is primarily engaged in detecting the world.

· ·

The Skin with its Appendages and
the Body with its Members

The haptic system, unlike the other perceptual systems, includes the whole body, most of its parts, and all of its surface. The extremities are exploratory sense organs, but they are also performatory motor organs; that is to say, the equipment for *feeling* is anatomically the same as the equipment for *doing*. This combination is not found in the ocular or the auditory system. We can explore things with the eyes but not alter the environment; however we can both explore and alter the environment with the hands. Similarly, the mouth is both perceptive and executive; it is used for perceiving and eating. The fact of overlap between the organs for perception and performance is not so strange if we remember that an organism is a system of organs, and that there are other instances in evolution of more than one use for a certain piece of anatomy.

In the evolution of the haptic system some animals have developed organs specialized for touching and exploring but not specialized for performing. The jointed antennae of arthropods and insects are both tactual and chemoreceptive; although popularly known as "feelers," they are chemotactile, combining what we call taste and smell and touch in a single piece of equipment. But they are not organs of performance as are the claws or mandibles.

For animals like ourselves, the two main parts of the haptic apparatus are the skin and the mobile body. But they are not simple, for the skin has various appendages and the body has a hierarchy of members based on a skeleton.

• CUTANEOUS APPENDAGES AS RECEPTIVE UNITS. The skin, even in man, is well supplied with hairs, and the digits have nails. Other mammals are covered with fur, and have specialized claws or hooves. Some have horns which may reach considerable dimensions. The skin of birds is primarily the base for the quills of the feathers. So the fact is that "touching" is very often an indirect mechanical disturbance of the skin mediated by an appendage, not a direct impression on the skin by an object, as we tend to assume. The follicles of hairs (see Figure 6.1) and the roots of nails, claws, hooves, and horns are wrapped about with nerve fibers so that the smallest leverage on the appendage is stimulating, but the actual contact between individual and environment is at the end of the appendage, not at its base. The tactual system is not, then, strictly a "proximity sense" as traditionally assumed, for the appendages of the skin protrude into the environment. The long-horned animal gets information at some distance from the skin; the man has only to scrape a surface with his fingernail to realize that he is aware of what happens at the end of the nail, not at the root, where the mechanoreceptive neurons are and where the sensations should theoretically be felt.

The capacity of vibrissae, hairs, claws, and horns to feel things at a distance is not different in principle from the ability of a man to use a cane or probe to detect the mechanical encounters at the end of the artificial appendage to his hand. The use of tools, from sticks, clubs, and rakes to more elaborate ones like screwdrivers and pliers or even fishing rods and tennis rackets, is probably based on a perceptual capacity of the body that is found in other animals.

The remarkable fact is that when a man touches something with a stick he *feels* it at the end of the stick, not in the hand. This is a difficulty for the theory of sensation-based perception; it requires some such postulate as the projecting of sensations outward from the body. But we entertain the hypothesis that information for the mechanical disturbance at the end of

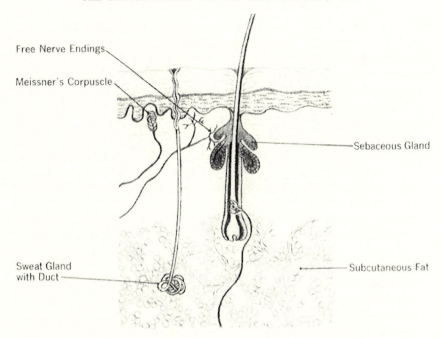

Free Nerve Endings

Meissner's Corpuscle

Sebaceous Gland

Sweat Gland
with Duct

Subcutaneous Fat

Figure 6.1   A hair follicle and its receptive mechanism.
The nerve fibrils wrapped around the base of a hair in human skin
are shown, together with the incoming (afferent) connection of
this tiny receptive unit. Also shown are two other types of nerve
endings found beneath the skin and two kinds of minute glands.

the stick is obtained by the hand as a perceptual organ, including information about the length and direction of the stick. The sensations in the hand
itself are irrelevant.

The surface of an organism, it should be remembered, is actually a
boundary between the organism and its environment, and the boundary
is not always or everywhere as clean-cut as the hairless human philosopher
tends to think.

• BODY MEMBERS. Vertebrates are built around a bony skeleton which is
jointed or articulated so that the animal's body has the advantages of both
mechanical rigidity and flexibility. Terrestrial vertebrates generally have
a head, a trunk with a vertebral column, and limbs with elongated bones.
The fact to be noted about these "members" of the body is that they form
an organized system — an aristocracy of membership, as it were, not a
democracy. The bones are linked by hinges to the spine and the head. The
trunk branches into four limbs and each limb branches into five digits.

The anatomist has Latin names for the corresponding bones in vertebrates generally. In order to understand touching, as well as locomotion and manipulation, we must keep in mind this relation of the body to its extremities. For the movement of any bone can only be a movement relative to the next bone inward. That is to say (considering the arm of a primate), the fingers can move only as the knuckles bend, the hand can move only at the wrist relative to the forearm, the forearm only at the elbow relative to the upper arm, and the upper arm at the shoulder relative to the trunk. The merest twitch of a fingertip, therefore, is linked to the spine by a series of some six joints. Movements fall into a hierarchy from large movements at the shoulder to small movements at the fingertip, the latter depending upon the former.

It has been observed in previous chapters that the upright body posture depends on a hierarchy of postures — of the head relative to the trunk, of the trunk relative to the legs, and thus of the whole system relative to the ground. It was noted that this system cofunctions with the vestibular orientation of the head relative to gravity, so that contact with the ground and orientation to gravity make a superordinate system. It should now be evident that the posture of each and every body member is an elaboration of this system (see Figure 6.2). For the angular position of every bone of the body out to the extremities is literally articulated with the body frame, and thus anchored to the direction of gravity and to the plane of the substratum. The sensitivity of the joints to their angles is evidently of crucial importance for this elaboration.

In this way an extremity can be oriented to both the frame of the body and the framework of space, even in the absence of vision. The disposition of all the bones, at any moment in time, can be thought of as a sort of branching vector space in the larger space of the environment, specified by the set of the angles at all joints relative to the main axes of the body. And now, be it noted, cutaneous touch re-enters the picture, for the *layout* of environmental surfaces in contact with the members of the body and the *disposition* of the members of the body go together. In this way a sitting man might feel the shape of the chair as well as the shape of his body in the chair. Thus a child who grasps a ball might feel the shape of the object as well as the shape of his grasping fingers. This fact, as we shall see, helps to explain why the haptic system can yield information about solid objects in three dimensions, whereas "touch," in the narrow sense of cutaneous impressions, has been supposed to be capable of yielding information only about patterns on the skin in two dimensions. The old idea that touch is strictly a proximity sense, as vision has been taken at the beginning of infancy, is based on a very narrow conception of the sense of touch.

• THE HAPTIC SYSTEM OF ARTHROPODS. Nothing will be asserted here

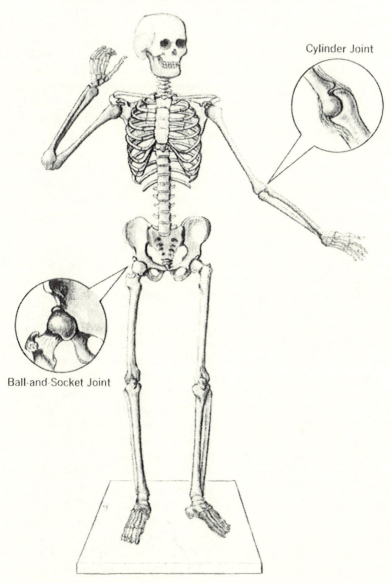

Cylinder Joint

Ball-and-Socket Joint

Figure 6.2 The human skeleton and its joints. The articulations or joints between bones are generally of two kinds — the cylinder-and-socket type, which can only bend like a hinge, and the ball-and-socket type, which can bend and also turn. The angles at which the bones are bent or turned seem to be continuously registered by the joints; the changes of these angles seem to be episodically registered by their input to the nervous system.

about the nature of the haptic system in those animals who have their skeletons outside the body instead of inside. A crab or an insect has a rigid surface, not a skin. But they are, no less than other animals, sensitive to touching and being touched. Their joints and appendages are known to be equipped with receptors. One might venture to guess, therefore, that an insect who grasps something with his mandibles or feels it with his antennae detects the object, that is, gets information about it, although by receptors quite different from those of a vertebrate animal.

• THE USE OF EXTREMITIES FOR TOUCHING. The higher terrestrial verte-brates not only are *in* contact with the environment, they also *make* con-tacts with parts of the environment. The animal can root or probe with its horns, explore with its mouth and gnaw with its teeth or paw with its front feet. The elephant can even do active touching with an elongated nose. The mobility of these organs can be exploited for information pickup as well as for fighting, eating, and getting about. The highest development of this exploratory touching is reached in the manipulation of primates. The use of the hands for groping, prodding, palpating, hefting, rubbing, and fingering is perhaps as important as their use in grasping branches, in wielding tools, and in the social grooming that is so characteristic of apes and monkeys. It is usually accompanied by looking, of course, and in the human case visual attention takes precedence over the haptic; but it will be shown that a surprising amount of information about objects is ob-tained by the haptic system alone. Many of the properties of substances are specified to both vision and active touch. Some, like color, can be registered only by vision and others, like specific gravity, can be registered only by the hand, but still others are doubly registered. The failure of the visual system by reason of darkness or blindness does not cut the indi-vidual off from the environment as much as is supposed.

The perception of the shape of an object by the exploring hand or hands is an especially interesting kind because of the puzzling relationship of haptic shape to visual shape and because, in the history of theories of perception, it has been the source of much argument. Could a blind man, given sight, tell a cube from a sphere on first seeing them, being already able to distinguish them by touch? We shall return to such questions in the chapter on pictorial vision; but first we should try to discover how a man *can* distinguish shapes by touch.

The Organization of the Haptic System

Mechanoreceptors and Mechanical Stimulation

The receptive cells and units of the haptic system are classed as mechanoreceptors, not as chemoreceptors or photoreceptors (Chapter 2).

This means that they are primarily affected by mechanical energy, not chemical or photic energy, having been specialized for this purpose during evolution. It is uncertain whether there is a fourth class, thermoreceptors, for heat energy, or whether temperature sensitivity is mediated indirectly by some kind of mechanical or chemical action at the skin. There seems to be no class of receptors specialized for electrical energy that is possessed by all animals. There are no receptors for magnetic fields or radio waves and no sensitivity to these. In short, a neat correspondence between the energy types of physics and the receptor types of physiology does not exist. There is no reason why it should, since the evolution of sensitivity was governed by the need for the information *in* energy, not for energy as such.

Mechanoreceptors are without question affected by some sort of mechanical action. But when the physiologist goes to the textbooks of mechanics to define and measure a mechanical stimulus, he gets little help. The units of mass, distance, and time; the assumptions of rigid bodies and particles; the variables of velocity and acceleration, force and pressure; the laws of motion—all these are much too abstract for his purposes. Consider pressure, as measured in units of force per unit of area. This is not a stimulus for the skin. As noted in Chapter 1, the pressure of the medium is not felt. What about a *gradient* of pressure along the skin? This is closer but still not adequate. The old experiment of immersing a finger in liquid and noting that the feeling of "pressure" occurs only at the boundary between liquid and air (see Figure 6.3) suggests that the continuous gradient of pressure from the surface downward is ineffective, and that

Figure 6.3   A finger immersed in mercury. The pressure deep in the liquid is much greater than that at the surface but only the discontinuity is experienced.

only the *discontinuity* at the boundary is a stimulus. A discontinuity in a stimulus array specifies a discontinuity of the environment, as will be evident again when we come to vision.

Boring has chronicled the search for some physical variable — *tension* for example — with which cutaneous stimuli could be measured (1942, pp. 487–495). The search has not yet succeeded. Evidently what is simple for mechanics is not simple for mechanoreception, and the biomechanics of stimulation is not now reducible to physical magnitudes.

All living tissue, from the single-celled protozoan up, seems to be sensitive to *deformation*. By that is meant a change of shape, a non-rigid motion. In large organisms the stimulation of tissue can scarcely be separated from the stimulation of receptors, for the latter are usually to be found throughout a whole mass of tissue. Such mechanical *disturbances*, although inelegant and arbitrary for theoretical mechanics and kinetics, seem to be the effective stimuli for mechanoreceptors in their surroundings. The receptors imbedded in the skin, muscles, joints, and other tissues are excited by stretching, squeezing, bending, pulling, rubbing, and the like, which can be specified by practical physics but not so easily by theoretical physics. The definition of stimuli in these terms, however, can be useful without its having to be a quantitative definition, a magnitude. The psychologist can therefore study the *meaningful psychophysics* of the haptic system, the relations between perception and stimulation, without first having to establish a *metric* psychophysics (Gibson, 1948). The ideal of a metric psychophysics linking the dimensions of sensory consciousness with the dimensions of theoretical physics has dominated the work of sensory psychologists for a century, but it is not the aim of this book.

The Location of Mechanoreceptors in the Body

The nerve supply of the body (see Figure 6.4), apart from the viscera, consists of an enormous number of nerve fibers, both afferent and efferent, the former terminating in receptors and the latter in muscles. From the periphery inward, they are gathered into bundles or cables of increasing size until they enter the spinal cord by way of the dorsal and ventral roots, where the afferent and efferent neurons are separated. The point to be noted is that there is scarcely a bit of tissue in the whole body that cannot deliver neural inputs from microscopic mechanoreceptive terminals in that tissue. The receptors are nearly everywhere. The only obvious exception is the brain itself, which is quite insensitive to mechanical stimulation or cutting.

The terminals are of many sorts, not easy to distinguish. First, there are free nerve endings, the bare branches of the afferent fibers that can spread out, spray, or cluster in basket-like or flower-like arrangements. These are extremely dense. To call them "receptors" may sound strange, but the fact

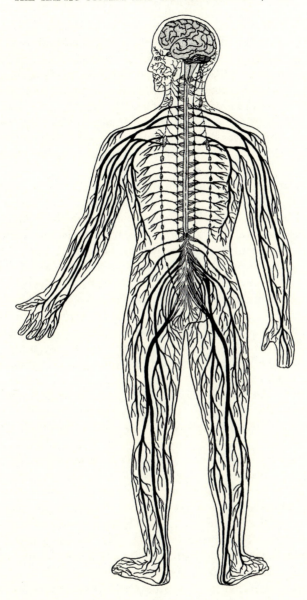

Figure 6.4 The nerve supply of the human body. The diagram represents the branching of the cables, bundles, and smaller nerves. Each is composed of nerve fibers, which are the axons of nerve cells. All of these lead into or out of the central nervous system, that is, the spinal cord and brain. The autonomic nervous system has been suggested but not fully represented here.

is that the naked peripheral nerve cell is excited by squeezing it, and it is therefore receptive. Second, there are encapsulated nerve endings, with tiny corpuscles, bulbs, spindles, and cylinders, that are found in many locations both in the skin and below it. And, third, there are the microscopic hair cells (not to be confused with hairs) with presumably the most delicate sensitivity to movement, that seem to be confined to special organs like the inner ear, at least in higher animals. It has long been a puzzle to the neuroanatomist why these types of structures do not correspond in any very clear way to the kinds of sensory qualities of introspective psychology.

These receptors are found all through the body, but in particular they are associated with the following parts and organs. *First,* they are thickly distributed in and below the skin. They cluster at the base of each hair or other appendage to the skin, they are present in hairless regions like paws or hands, and they penetrate the supportive and connective tissue below the surface. They are even found in the sheathing of bones. *Second,* they supply the joints and connecting ligaments between all the movable bones of the body — over one hundred in the human skeleton. *Third,* they interpenetrate all the muscles and the tendons attaching muscle to bone. *Fourth,* they are wrapped around the blood vessels, even the smallest, which dilate or constrict. *Fifth,* in the form of hair cells, they supply the flexible structures of the semicircular canals, the utricle and saccule, and the cochlea of the inner ear.

The notable thing which all these parts and organs have in common is that they are mobile. But they are mobile in different mechanical ways — that is, the families of possible motions are different for the elastic tissue, the socketed joints, the contractile muscles, the distensible blood vessels, and the variously weighted or damped structures of the inner ear. The skin moves in one set of ways and has one set of possible deformations. The joints move only by hinge action and have a fixed set of angular positions. The muscles can only contract or relax relative to their antagonists, with varying amounts of pull at varying lengths. The other tissues have their own motions and states. The information picked up by the receptors in any part of the body must be information about the particular motion or state of that part, not simply information about what part it is.

When the input of *information* from these receptive systems or subsystems is considered, as contrasted with their input of sensory qualities, Johannes Müller's problem of specific receptors and fibers for each quality becomes irrelevant. The information has to be specified, but this can only be carried by the input from combinations of receptors incorporated in a functional organ, not necessarily in an organ of anatomy, and firing in simultaneous patterns and successive transformations. Subjective qualities of sensation may well be anatomically specific to the nerve, when they arise, but perceptions must be functionally specific to invariant relations among nerves. In perception, nerves function vicariously.

Perceptual Subsystems

It is now possible to conceive how this fivefold distribution of receptors might be incorporated in different perceptual organs to yield different systems. The skin and deeper tissue can be stimulated without movement of joints or muscles. This would give perceptions of *cutaneous touch*. The skin and deeper tissue can be stimulated together with movement of the joints. This would yield perceptions of *haptic touch*. The skin and joints together can be stimulated in combination with muscular exertion. This would yield perceptions of what I will call *dynamic touching*. The combination of skin stimulation along with vasodilation or vasoconstriction might possibly give perceptions of *touch-temperature*. And the combination of inputs from the vestibular receptors and the joints and the skin together would yield perceptions of *oriented touch*, that is, of objects in relation to gravity and the ground.

The perception of *painful touch* is still a puzzle. Presumably some unknown pattern of excitation of some combination of nerve endings in the tissue specifies the onset of injury, and the mechanical event is then said to *hurt*. The free nerve endings in tissue cannot be exclusively concerned with the registration of pain, for they seem to participate in several other kinds of haptic experience.

The Difference between Muscle Sensitivity and Joint Sensitivity

Muscles and joints are quite different structures (see Figure 6.5). The muscle pulls; the joint rotates. The muscle varies in length; the joint varies in angle. The muscles are attached to the bones by tendons so as to form levers; the bones are fitted neatly together at bearings. These are either ball-and-socket bearings or cylinder-and-socket bearings, and they are held together with ligaments that encapsulate them. There are receptors in the muscles and tendons on the one hand, and in the ligaments and capsules of joints on the other hand, but their function is surely different. The mechanics of an elastic muscle is not the same as the mechanics of a bearing or a hinge. The evidence strongly suggests that muscle sensitivity is irrelevant for the perception of space and movement, whereas joint sensitivity is very important for it. In short, we detect the angles of our joints, not the lengths of our muscles. It is not often realized, even by anatomists, that it is the function of a joint not merely to permit mobility of the articulated bones but also to register the relative position and movement of the bones. In the old terminology, each joint is a "sense organ." Here it is called a receptive unit in a hierarchy of units.

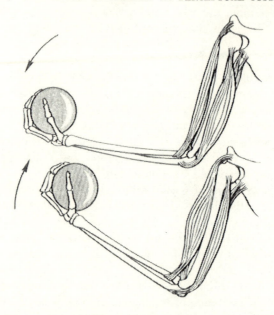

Figure 6.5 Bones, joints, and muscles. A pair of antagonistic muscles is represented, a flexor and an extensor of the upper arm. They are so innervated that when one is contracted the other is relaxed. The bending of the joint at the elbow through an angle of 30° is shown.

The leading authority on what is traditionally called the sense of kinesthesis has asserted that "the sense of position and movement of the joints depends solely on the appropriate receptors in the joints themselves. There is no need to invoke a mysterious 'muscle' sense to explain kinesthetic sensations, and to do so runs contrary to all the known facts concerning the muscle stretch receptors" (Rose and Mountcastle, 1959, p. 426). The evidence is that the spindle receptors clustering around the individual muscle fibers register the stretch of those fibers, and that the tendon receptors register the strain or pull of the whole muscle, but that neither could register the *length* of the muscle. The pull of a muscle, in fact, is not correlated with its length, since the same force can be exerted at different lengths. But it is the length of a muscle that would have to be registered if the position and movement of the limb were to be detected. Rose and Mountcastle have described the experimental discovery of the fact that joint receptors discharge at a given rate for a given angle of the joint, and that the rate changes when the angle changes (pp. 411–413). The pickup of bone angles is therefore a fact and the pickup of muscle lengths is a fiction.

There is a use, of course, for the muscle and tendon receptors. They probably register pull, or strain — that is to say, muscular effort as distinguished from movement. Their primary function seems to be the self-sensitivity of muscles. The reflex circle from each muscle back to the same muscle serves to maintain tonus and to resist gravity. But this is simply the primitive effort of life, a part of the state of being alive, awake, and active. An account of tonus, posture, equilibrium, and locomotion was given in Chapter 2. The so-called muscle sense should probably be ascribed no role in detecting the spatial postures and movements of the body, and therefore it had better not be called a sense. Muscular effort combined with the input of the skin and the joints yields information — for example, about the weight of an object handled — but this is not a unique quality of sensation.

The Use of the Term "Kinesthesis"

In this book *kinesthesis* will be used to mean what it literally denotes — the pickup of movement. But it refers exclusively to *body* movement, not movement of anything in the world. This is almost the same thing as proprioception, which was discussed in Chapter 2. Kinesthesis cuts across the functional perceptual systems. The discrimination of body movement from non-movement is too important for the organism for it to have been wholly entrusted to any single group of receptors. There are many kinds of movement that need to be registered. There is articular kinesthesis for the body framework, vestibular kinesthesis for the movements of the skull, cutaneous kinesthesis for movement of the skin relative to what it touches, and visual kinesthesis for perspective transformations of the field of view. In all these perceptions the sensory quality arising from the receptor type is difficult to detect, but the information is perfectly clear. Kinesthesis is a registering of such information without being sensory; it is one of the best examples of detection without a special modality of sensation.

The history of what can justly be called the muddle of kinesthesis is recounted by Boring (1942, pp. 524–535). The misunderstanding about a muscle sense only contributed to the confusion. The arguments of Charles Bell, who conceived it in 1826, should probably be interpreted in terms of what we now call re-entrant or reafferent input, or feedback, not in terms of a separate department of sense. To speak of the *sense* of kinesthesis, therefore, as the textbooks do, is merely to cover up ignorance and lump together facts that need to be kept distinct.

The Covariation of Skin Sensitivity and Joint Sensitivity

The cooperation of the supposedly separate senses of touch and kinesthesis is an old and controversial problem in psychology (Boring, 1942).

It has been reformulated here in terms of a perceptual subsystem, haptic touch, and the problem then becomes one of defining the information in a *combined* input from the skin and the joints. I have also postulated a system of *oriented* haptic touch with the further combination of input from the vestibular organ.

The question to be answered is this: How does a perceiver feel *what* he is touching instead of the cutaneous impressions and the bone postures as such? The animal registers the shape of the enclosure in which he is hidden; the man registers the shape of the chair in which he sits. The primate feels the branch that he grasps, and the proto-man must have felt the roundness of the stone he threw, the wedge shape of the hand-axe or the lip of the pot, even without looking at it. The sailor can feel the rope and tie the knot even in darkness. The violinist can feel the shapes and spaces of his instrument with extraordinary precision while keeping his eyes closed. The man with a walking stick can even feel stones, mud, or grass at the end of his stick. Yet all these perceptions come from the contacts between the adjacent surfaces and the skin and the contacts of bones upon one another (see Figure 6.6).

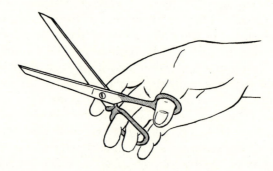

Figure 6.6 A hand feeling a pair of scissors. The pressures of the metal surfaces on the skin can be felt, but one is mainly aware of the separation and of the movements of the handle. In use, one actually feels the cutting action of the blades.

The question involves the perceiving of both the general layout of environmental surfaces and the particular layout of the surfaces of an object being manipulated. How is the arrangement or shape of these surfaces detected? The question is clearly related to that of so-called space perception. I have argued that the perception of the layout of surfaces *is* the perception of space (Gibson, 1950, Ch. 1). Completely empty space is unperceivable. There are dimensions or axes of empty space, to be sure, but they are embodied in a solid environment having a north-south, an east-west, and an up-down. This is the space to which an individual is oriented, with respect to which the posture and equilibrium of his body is maintained. The body itself, with its main axes of right-left, front-back, and head-foot, must never be confused with it. I called this a "vector space" on an earlier page, but it is not really a space. The body percept, or "body image," is a set of possible dispositions or poses — standing, or lying — relative to the substratum and to gravity. If it is a space at all, it is subjective rather than objective. And it is fluid instead of rigid, for it can adopt any of a vast family of poses by moving from one to another.

Now to answer the question. In brief, the suggestion is that the joints yield geometrical information, that the skin yields contact information, and that in certain invariant combinations they yield information specifying the layout of external surfaces. At any one moment the orchestrated input from the joints (the evidence for this will be given later) specifies a set of bone directions relative to the spine, to the head, and to the direction of gravity. The bones and the extremities are thus linked to the environment. At any one moment, the total input from the skin likewise specifies a pattern of contacts with touching surfaces, one of which is always the surface of support. The skin is thus also connected to the environment by this simultaneous pattern. Any change in the pattern of contacts with the skin is covariant and concomitant with a change in the branching of bones. The touch pattern and the vector pattern are altered together by the mechanical necessities of terrestrial movement. *The covariance of cutaneous and articular motion is information in its own right.* The neural input with covariation is different from either of the two inputs without covariation. A motor act normally yields both skin kinesthesis and joint kinesthesis. Together, they have a different meaning than would a simple movement of the skin or a simple movement of the bones. And a particular invariant unity between them specifies a particular external layout of surfaces.

One might ask, what about the detection of body disposition as such, unaccompanied by touch? A pose, as that of a dancer, can be perceived, but only as a pure case, for there has to be contact with at least a surface of support, and the vector pattern would have to be anchored to gravity by means of the statocyst. Conversely, one might ask, what about the detection of pure cutaneous location unaccompanied by joint kinesthesis? A man can say what part of his skin has been touched, or point to it, and any animal can scratch the spot where it has been stimulated, for example, by an insect. This capacity for locating on the skin has been the fact from which a great deal of theorizing has taken off in the history of psychology. A touch sensation was thought to include a *local sign*, a sort of signature of its locus on the skin, and there was a fruitless controversy over whether it was learned or innate (Boring, 1942, Ch. 1, 13). But the very notion of pure skin location is seen to be an abstraction when one realizes that skin and bones are parts of the same body, neither being primary. There is no such thing as location relative to the skin that is not also location relative to the body and the bones, and ultimately to gravity and the ground.

The skin is thus not a map, nor a picture. It is a closed surface in three dimensions, and the skin branches out in the three dimensions of terrestrial space just as the bones do. The "pattern" of contacts on the skin is accordingly not a pattern in the familiar sense of the term, for it surrounds the individual. Moreover the hands and the mouth can surround an object, so that the pattern of touches in grasping or eating is also a pattern in space. The classical misconception of local signs comes from the assumption that the skin is anatomically projected to the cortex of the brain by neurons and that each neuron has its own sensation. (The same assumption has been made for the retina.) But the fact is that the skin and the joints are *both* projected to the somesthetic area of the cortex, to the same area, and the joints cannot even be imagined to deliver a flat map to the brain. Bone space and skin space are all of a piece.

The layout of physical surfaces, according to this theory, is perceived by way of the disposition of body members when touch and posture are covariant. It is not that sensations from the skin and the joints are *blended* or *fused* when they occur together, as Titchener believed (1909, p. 161), but that the receptors then combine in one system to register one kind of invariant stimulus information.

The Differentiated Skin

On this theory, the sensitivity of the skin should not be conceived as that of a mosaic of receptors each with its own absolute local quality, but simply as being differentiated. A locus on the skin consists of the set of differences between it and other possible loci. The discriminations are crude in the embryo and the infant, but they get better. Right and left, head and foot, belly and back, are distinguished first; then the large divisions get subdivided into smaller divisions; finally the exploratory members of the body (fingers, toes, lips, tongue) develop the highest degree of cutaneous differentiation. It is not that the location of each spot on the skin has to be learned, but that parts of the skin have to be separated from one another by a joint process of maturation and learning.

The input of the joints and that of the eyes also differentiate at the same time. The cutaneous, articular, and visual systems are covariant during the exploratory activity of the developing individual. The "images" of the body — cutaneous, skeletal, and visual — thus come to coincide.

This conception of the skin as differentiated seems to contradict the fact that, using punctate stimulators the human skin can be mapped for the spots that are sensitive to pressure, pain, warmth, and cold. The laboratory demonstration that when a bristle attached to an "esthesio-meter" is made to indent the skin some of the square millimeters of a hairless region will yield sensations of touch and some will not has puzzled students for a long time, and has seemed to support the mosaic theory of sensitivity. But it may well be true that these sensory spots are mere artifacts of the method of stimulation. An indentation of the skin is not a point. Some indentations yield reportable sensations and some do not, but as Boring (1942) points out, this procedure "neglects all the vague sensory ghosts that can be aroused in the less effective regions between the spots" (p. 475).

VII / The Capabilities of the Haptic-Somatic System

The haptic system with its subordinate and superordinate systems constitutes a very elaborate perceptual apparatus. A great variety of perceptions can be achieved by it. But a systematic description of all these perceptions does not exist. Most experimenters on the sense of touch have concentrated on the sensations in controlled isolation, assuming that these were the components of perception.

There are scattered earlier studies or observations which can be drawn upon (e.g., Katz, 1925; Revesz, 1950) and one series of experiments has been performed by the writer on the range of information which an observer can pick up by touch (Gibson, 1962, 1963). But the following account must be considered exploratory and incomplete rather than definitive. The study of useful sensitivity, as distinguished from theoretically basic sensitivities, is only just beginning.

Perceptions Induced by Cutaneous Deformation: Passive Touch

If a blindfolded human observer is encouraged to report the nature of an object applied to his skin instead of the sensory impression, he finds the task quite natural. His reports are generally correct. For example, if the skin of his forearm is stroked by the experimenter in a standard manner with one of four instruments, having (1) a rounded wedge that "rubs" the skin, (2) a sharp wedge that "scrapes" the skin, (3) a small cylinder that "rolls" on the skin, and (4) a tuft of hair that "brushes" the skin, he distinguishes among them without error. This observation should be repeated by other experimenters, but I am fairly confident of it. These identifications must depend in part on differences in mechanical friction, for if the rounded wedge is polished and lubricated it may be indistinguishable from the rolling cylinder. One might guess that the same *dis-*

116

tinguishing features of rubbing, scraping, rolling, and brushing occur in the acoustic sequence when these events emit sound from a distance (Chapter 5, p. 87).

A depression of the skin, a so-called pressure, is by no means the only kind of effective stimulus, nor is it the elementary kind. For example, a *torsion* of the skin can be induced by twisting a rubber stimulator either clockwise or counterclockwise and the direction of this torsion is correctly perceived. One can try this with the rubber eraser of a pencil. A rubber-tipped forceps can be made either to stretch apart two skin regions or to pinch them together; these are not confused. If a lateral *traction* of the skin is induced with a rubber tip, the amount and direction of the traction are reported as "motion," but the stimulus involves no lateral displacement over the skin — that is, no successive stimulation of adjacent points as with the roller. In physics, a motion is a translocation in space, but in this case the stimulus is not a translocation over the skin.

In experiments of the above sort the observer reports the motion of the object in the environment rather than the complex motions of the skin and tissue. Seemingly quite different motions of tissue are equivalent as information for the perception of object motion. If a long rod is applied to a skin region and drawn lengthwise in the manner of a violin bow, the motion of an object is perceived, although the information can only exist in the directional friction at a single skin region (Gibson, 1962, p. 482).

The implication is that the passive skin, like the inner ear, detects the *source* of the stimulation whenever this external source is specified in the proximal mechanical event. It is the crawling insect, the scratching thorn, the brushing leaf, and the shaking branch that need to be distinguished. The prods, punches, pushes, and scrapes of the environment come from different objects that need to be dealt with in particular ways. So do the stroking, rubbing, and caressing from a partner, including sexual contact and infantile sucking; they come from objects that need to be dealt with in quite other ways. These are all mechanical encounters at the skin, but each is more or less specific to the object of the encounter and it is the information that normally gets attended to.

Perception of the Disposition of Touching Surfaces by the Disposition of Body Members

In 1898 Goldscheider experimented with the bending of a single joint, such as the shoulder, wrist, or knuckle, in an apparatus that held the other joints immobile. He showed that the observer could detect an angular movement as small as a fraction of one degree (Goldscheider, 1898; also described in Geldard, 1953, p. 235). Both the posture and the change of posture of the joint could be registered. These results have been confirmed, but no investigator has ever studied more than one joint at a time. The human skeleton contains over 100 mobile joints, on the authority of medical encyclopedias. They are arranged in a hierarchy of the body, its members, and its extremities, as we noted in the last chapter. Their total input is not a sum or a statistical collection. It follows geometrical laws, and the orchestration of this input to the central nervous system, simultaneous and successive, is not a collection of sensations but a structured perception. The angle of one joint is meaningless if it is not related to the angles of all the joints above it in the postural hierarchy. The branching vectors or directions of the bones constitute the "bone space" of the body and this is linked in turn with gravity and the ground. A certain *pose* of the body exists at any one moment, and the geometrical set of all body poses defines the set of all possible movements. Motor behavior consists of responses within this set.

What needs to be studied, clearly, is not the angular thresholds of posture and movement at each joint but the accuracy of the perception of poses. The directions of the bones of the limbs are especially important and the bone directions of the hand are the most interesting of all. When a blindfolded subject is asked to point his index finger straight forward in alignment with the direction of his head, the average error is only about two degrees, although seven or eight joints intervene between the finger and the skull. He can also point straight up or straight down with accuracy, although many joints intervene between the finger and the vestibular organ, and still more between the finger and the plane of the ground under his feet.

A subject can point with one of his bones. But he can also point with a rod or stick grasped in the hand, and about equally well by informal observation. The average error for aligning a rod held in the hand, or both hands, to the gravitational vertical or horizontal is only a few degrees (Gibson, 1937, p. 234). The average error for setting an invisible adjustable "palm-board" to a vertical or horizontal plane with the flat of the hand is two or three degrees (Gibson, 1962, p. 484). If, in this experiment, the hand is held behind the back, where it is not only invisible but also has never been visible in the course of experience, the error is still small.

A subject perceives not only the plane of the palm but also the plane-angle between his two palms. The average error in setting two adjustable palm-boards into parallel planes so that they feel neither divergent nor convergent is about 3 degrees, according to Gibson and Backlund (1963). There are some six joints between the two hands in this situation. Evidently the haptic perception of linear directions, of plane inclinations, and of geometrical parallels, is both possible and accurate withóut vision. *This perception occurs whether the body members are posed freely in the air or are touching a surface.* The haptic space of the hands can be either empty or solid, either "filled" or "unfilled."

What about dimensions and distances in haptic space as contrasted with directions? Some evidence exists. The space between the opposable thumb and the index finger (or any other finger) is clearly experienced. This use of the hand is like that of the mandible in an insect (Katz and MacLeod, 1949). With eyes closed one can measure off the diameters of familiar coins with some success (cf. Kelvin, 1954). The width of two blocks can be compared successively in this way, and small differences can be detected. Or the width and height of the *same* object can be compared by successive spanning with two fingers. In fact, the relative dimensions of an object can be simultaneously perceived by the relative spans between all five fingers, as we shall see. Note that when five fingers all touch an object, there are five distinct sensations of touch but there is a perception of only one object. This fact will be elaborated later. Multiple touching of this sort yields haptic perception in the literal meaning of "laying hold of."

If two invisible blocks are spanned between the opposed fingers of the two hands at the same time (see Figure 7.1), the widths can be readily

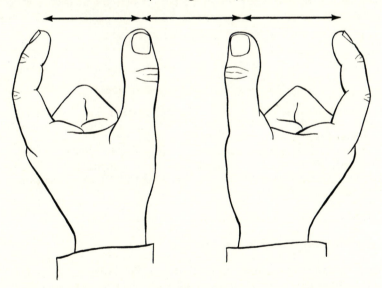

Figure 7.1 Two finger spans measuring off similar distances. One can feel the finger-thumb separation in both hands and compare them. One can also feel the separation between the two thumbs, although this depends on information from the shoulder joints.

compared, and a variable width can be matched to a standard. Köhler and Dinnerstein used this perception in theoretical studies (1949), although they called the experience *kinesthesis,* thereby perpetuating a confusion. I find that the finger spans of the right and the left hand are comparable whether the hands are posed close together or far apart, and that the arm span is itself perceived at the same time. This result is remarkable. It suggests that haptic distances are additive or constant over the whole universe of bone postures.

Conceivably the distance between each extremity of the body and every other, in any pose, is perceptible when the need arises. This pattern of distances goes along with the pattern of skeletal directions already described. If so, it is not surprising that the dimensions and proportions and slopes of surfaces or objects touching these extremities are also perceptible.

The sensitivity of a trained dancer to the geometrical pattern of the body, its members, and its extremities, is a demonstration of how exact the perception of pose or disposition can become. It is especially precise in ballet. Some choreographers have analyzed the movements and pauses of the human body in the effort to establish a dance notation (see Figure 7.2). One has only to study the elaborate set of symbols used (Hutchinson, 1954) to realize the richness of skeletal space perception. The input could better be termed osteoesthesis than kinesthesis.

. . . .

An Earlier Statement of Osteoesthesis

More than 30 years ago, L. T. Troland asserted that "posture is reducible primarily to patterns of relative angular disposition of the various portions of the skeleton," and went on to point out that "movement may be regarded as ordered successions of progressively different postures" (Troland, 1929, pp. 366–367). In the three volumes of his *Psychophysiology* (1929, 1930, 1932) he anticipated the spirit of the present book in many ways.

. . . . : . . . .

The Calibration of Subjective Skeletal Space

Some evidence is accumulating about the detection of skeletal space, the perception of the disposition of the limbs and branches of the body. It must be given as a hierarchy of bone directions, hinged together, relative to the vertebral long axis of the body (the cephalocaudal) and the two shorter axes (the dorso-ventral and the right-left). But clearly the three axes of this skeletal space must be anchored to environmental space if behavior is to be adaptive and perception correct. This can be

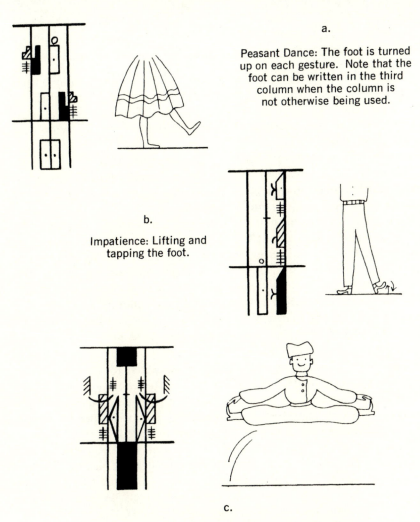

a.

Peasant Dance: The foot is turned up on each gesture. Note that the foot can be written in the third column when the column is not otherwise being used.

b.

Impatience: Lifting and tapping the foot.

c.

Cossack Jump: The feet point upward during the jump. Note the indication of contact between the foot and the hand.

Figure 7.2 Dance notation. Three examples are given of a method for recording successive postures of the human body and the movements between postures. The symbols refer to mobile members; they are read from the bottom up, in time. The center line represents the midline of the body and the columns represent legs and arms. The method, originating with Rudolf Laban, can become extremely complicated. The sketches and verbal notes accompanying each notation give the uninitiated some idea of the action. (From Ann Hutchinson, *Labanotation*, copyright 1954 by The Dance Notation Bureau, Inc. *Alphabet of Basic Symbols*, copyright 1954 by Rudolf Laban. Reprinted by permission of the publisher, New Directions Publishing Corporation, Phoenix House Limited, and Laurence Pollinger Limited.)

accomplished only if there is some sort of *calibrating* of the input from the articular system with other information. The haptic straight-ahead must be the same as the visual straight-ahead. The haptic vertical must coincide with the visual vertical. The body horizontal must coincide with the visual horizontal.

How such a calibration is accomplished in the brain is a problem. But there are experiments to suggest that a *recalibration* occurs when prolonged abnormal information is imposed on a perceptual system, and this may help us to understand the process.

There seem to be two logical possibilities. A perceptual system like that of the joints might normalize itself by some averaging process over time, taking the mean of its inputs as the criterion or straight-ahead, of vertical, and of horizontal. Or the brain might compare its inputs with those of another perceptual system, the vestibular or the visual or both, taking the other information as the criterion for recalibration. The former process would be one that occurs within the system; the latter would be one of reducing a discrepancy between systems, or what psychologists have called a "conflict of cues" between senses.

A process of spontaneous normalizing is suggested by experiments on the phenomenon of adaptation with negative after-effect (Gibson, 1937) or that of adaptation level (Helson, 1964). A process of comparison, on the other hand, is suggested by the history of experiments on an old issue — whether visual sensations must be validated by the sense of touch, as Bishop Berkeley believed, or whether, on the contrary, the feelings of limb location conform to the visual locations, as Stratton (1896) and others have found to be the case. The question of which sense to believe in, whether to trust what one feels or what one sees when the data conflict has never been answered, although it is still being debated (e.g., Harris, 1963). Perhaps both processes can occur — both spontaneous normalizing and cross-sensory reduction of discrepancy.

Normalizing of skeletal space perception certainly occurred in the experiments of Gibson and Backlund (1963), who found that the phenomenal slant of a palm-board from a normal plane decreased with time and that subsequently a normal plane felt slanted the opposite way. They also found that the apparent convergence (or divergence) of *two* palm-boards held between *two* hands tended toward parallel as such, and that subsequently planes that were parallel felt divergent (or convergent). There was no visual input in these experiments. On the other hand, Harris (1963) and others have shown that the felt position of the hand in pointing drifts toward the seen position of the hand when the latter has been artificially displaced by prisms in front of the eyes. It would appear that the haptic feeling of direction, of separation, and of position can be self-correcting in part and corrected by visual information in part. Presumably this perceptual system can work either in isolation or in cooperation.

Exploratory Perception with Haptic Touch

In discussing the capabilities of the haptic-somatic system we have so far been concerned with the *passive* registration of the environment by way of mechanical-geometrical information. We now turn to the *active* perception of the environment by touch. We are concerned with exploratory perception — active rather than passive, with obtained rather than imposed stimulation.

It is only half the truth to realize that animals feel the layout of the earth and its furniture. They also *seek* contact with things — at least some kinds of things and some kinds of contacts, for certain solids are beneficial and others are noxious. The infant clings to the mother and one adult clings to another in need. The earth itself has been compared to a mother in this respect. The metaphors of the search for contact hold true not only for the terrestrial, the sexual, and the social realm, but also for the cognitive and the intellectual. One can be "in touch" with other people, or with world affairs, or with reality.

Active exploratory touch permits both the grasping of an object and a grasp of its meaning. One may lay hold of the surroundings merely to obtain information. The hand can grope, palpate, prod, press, rub, or heft, and many of the properties of an object can thus be detected in the absence of vision. The properties we call "tangible" are (1) geometrical variables like shape, dimensions and proportions, slopes and edges, or curves and protuberances; (2) surface variables like texture, or roughness-smoothness; and (3) material variables like heaviness or mass and rigidity-plasticity. The material *color* (pigmentation) of a surface is not tangible but only visible. The relative temperature, however, is tangible but *not* visible. Haptics is not so inferior to optics as we suppose, since the blind depend upon it for a whole realm of useful perception (Revesz, 1950). I have referred to the double registration of some object properties in the last chapter.

We are not accustomed to think of the hand as a sense organ since most of our day-to-day manipulation is performatory, not exploratory. That is, we grasp, push, pull, lift, carry, insert, or assemble for practical purposes, and the manipulation is usually guided by visual as well as by haptic feedback. The perceptual capacity of the hand goes unrecognized because we usually attend to its motor capacity, and also because the visual input dominates the haptic in awareness. But the skin-joint sensitivity is inevitable. It always accompanies and underlies visual sensitivity when the eyes are open and the observer is looking, and it makes an even more fundamental contribution to the control of motor skill than vision. We become aware of haptic perception as such only when we must work in the dark, or without looking, or when, occasionally, it is actually more acute than visual perception. Examples of the latter would be when a butcher tests the sharpness of a knife with his finger, or a cabinetmaker tests the smoothness of his work by rubbing his finger over it.

• SHAPE. A method of investigating the perception of unfamiliar shapes by active touch is illustrated in Figure 7.3 (Gibson, 1962, 1963). Ten different sculptured objects were designed for the purpose of being felt with the hands. Familiar objects and utensils had proved to be so easy to identify when presented to a pair of hands behind a curtain that they did not test the limits of perception. Geometrical solids had proved unsatisfactory because familiar ones like the sphere, ellipsoid, and cube

Figure 7.3 Sculptured objects for studying the haptic perception of shape. One set of feelable objects is shown; a duplicate set is available for haptic comparison or for visual-haptic matching.

were too easy, and unfamiliar polygons made the subject resort to a semi-intellectual process of counting edges and corners by tracing them with a fingertip. Edges are important features of some objects but not all, and finger-tracing is one mode of haptic perception but not the only mode, or the fundamental one. The shapes designed were therefore compounded of convex, concave, and saddle-shaped surfaces on the front side, and a regular convex back side. All had six protuberances. They could conveniently be held in one hand and fingered with the other. The originals, and molds for the duplicates, were constructed by a sculptor interested in free-form work, using the above specifications and attempting to make each equally different from every other in shape.

When an observer is given one of these shapes to feel with his hands behind a curtain, he typically does the following things. (1) He curves his fingers around its face, using all fingers and fitting them into the cavities. (2) He moves his fingers in a way that can only be called exploratory, since the movements do not seem to become stereotyped, or to occur in any fixed sequence, or even to be clearly repeated. (3) He uses oppositions of thumb and finger, but with different fingers; he rubs with one or more fingers, and occasionally he seems to trace a curvature with a single finger. The activity seems to be aimed principally at obtaining a set of touch-postures, the movement as such being incidental to this aim. Introspection bears out the hypothesis that the phenomenal shape of the subject does emerge from such a series of covariant transformations. The tracing out of the surface with one finger, as if the observer were trying to draw a model of it or reproduce the shape, did not occur often enough to be typical. No subject ever tried to run his finger over the whole array of curves in a systematic manner such as that of the scanning beam of a television tube. The manual activity might be called scanning, but it is not the same as visual scanning, which will be considered in Chapter 12.

For testing discrimination of shape, the observer can be presented with a second object, either the same or different from the first, and asked to judge which it is. Errors are common with unpracticed subjects, but after an hour or more of training an adult is able to make an errorless run of such judgments. By this time, he is usually able to identify each of the ten objects when it is first put into his hand, and is often able to describe the distinguishing features, or feature, of each. It is possible for a subject to reach this level of proficiency without ever having seen the shapes.

The theory of the essential role of finger directions and finger spans, the "bone space," seems to be confirmed by these results. In tactual exploration of the above sort, the pattern that the various cutaneous pressures make to one another cannot be detected, but only the pattern which the parts of the object make to one another. The skin form is never perceived; the object form always is. The skin form changes from moment to moment as the hands move. With the possibility of ten different fingers touching the object in varying combinations, any number up to ten cutaneous pressure sensations can occur at any one time and the number can vary in time. The unity of the perception cannot come from the skin alone. It must come from the bones and the skin together in terms of the spatial invariants that relate them. This is not the traditional theory that skin sensations are the elements from which a perception of the object is constructed by past experience with kinesthesis. Instead, it would seem that the skin sensations, if they can be detected at all, are mere *symptoms* of cutaneous stimulation, incidental to the activity of the haptic system.

• SURFACE TEXTURE. David Katz (1925) was an experimenter who cared less about the theory of sensations than he did about the range of perceptual experience. In one of his experiments he obtained a dozen kinds of paper differing chiefly in the variable of rough to smooth, with blotting paper at one extreme and writing paper at the other. His observers, without vision, could distinguish among all of them "by touch." But they could not do so by mere contact or pressure, it was necessary to *rub* a finger over the surface, if only slightly, to obtain a perception of the texture of the surface. Presumably there had to be a mechanical friction with resulting lateral vibration of the skin. The stimulus information had to be *obtained*.

Several investigators have found that commercial grades of sandpaper can be distinguished in this way by untrained subjects (Stevens and Harris, 1962). This variable, it may be noted, is not rough-to-smooth but fine-to-coarse, since all the surfaces are rough. Still another variable is slipperiness. The analysis of the variables of surface texture is just beginning. Many variables of physical texture or microstructure are specified in the stimulation available by rubbing. A good many are also specified in the stimulation available by *looking* — that is, in the *optical* texture projected from the surface. The texture of a surface is probably even more important to animals than its pigment color in identifying it, but the discrimination of texture has scarcely been studied by sensory psychologists, whereas the discrimination of color has enlisted a disproportionate amount of research.

The capability of active touch to register information can be illustrated by another experiment. Binns (1937) studied the ability of wool graders to judge the *softness* of an untwisted rope of fibers from a fleece, a sample called a "wool-top." This quality seems to correspond to the physical variable of the fineness of the fibers, and determines the value of a fleece to the wool industry. The normal procedure was to pull a strand through one hand and look at it carefully, assigning a grade. Binns required his subjects to feel the wool-tops without being able to see them, and to look at them on a black background without being able to feel them. The tactual judgments of softness were in "remarkably good agreement" with the visual judgments. Furthermore he found to his surprise that non-professional, unpracticed observers using this method of active feeling without looking could give spontaneous judgments of softness about as well as the professionals.

Material Composition and Consistency: Dynamic Touching

The hand can discriminate the weight of an object as well as its surface layout and surface texture. The passive skin can be stimulated by an object resting on it, the amount of pressure (that is, skin deformation) being proportional to the weight of the object, but in this case discrimination is rather poor. It is much better when the object is lifted. Comparisons can be made either successively, or with one object in each hand. "Weights" of standard size and shape but varying in mass used to be standard equipment in every psychological laboratory, and hundreds and thousands of hours were spent by students in the discipline of comparing lifted weights. The lifting was performed in a stereotyped manner so that the sensations of strain or pull in the wrist could be isolated as the basis of judgment, all else being constant. But paradoxically the judgments were just as accurate if the objects were manipulated or passed from hand to hand. In this unorthodox procedure, a constant, external, objective perception of heaviness still occurs, although the flux of subjective sensations is so complex as to be unreportable.

The mass of an object can be judged, in fact, by wielding it in any of a variety of ways, such as tossing and catching, or shaking it from side to side. One can only conclude that the judgment is based on information, not on the sensations. The stimulus information from *wielding* can only be an invariant of the changing flux of stimulation in the muscles and tendons, an exterospecific invariant in this play of forces. Whatever specifies the mass of the object presumably can be isolated from the change, and the wielding of the object has the function of separating off the permanent component from the changes. The merely propriospecific information can thus be filtered out, as it were, leaving pure information about the object. This process takes time, for an invariant can only emerge from a series of transformations over time.

I suggested in the last chapter that this mode of haptic perception could be called *dynamic touching*. It involves synchronous inputs from the skin and joints, like the haptic touch that yields perception of the space and shape of objects, but it also involves a non-spatial input from the muscles and tendons that seems to yield a further perception of the *material substance* or *inertia* of the object. It is a perceptual subsystem in its own right. More than any of the others, its perception is blended with performance, for the information comes from muscular effort. One can perceive the inertial properties of something only by wielding it. Presumably this is the cognitive aspect of the ability to throw missiles and to use clubs — a formidable habit of the higher primates.

Besides weight, one can detect the rigidity, elasticity, viscosity, or softness of a thing by effortful touch. One might call this its *consistency* — what it consists of. The perception can be obtained by squeezing, or by pushing, prodding, or even stretching. Katz and Stephenson (1937) showed that the perception of elasticity obtained by lifting upward on a spiral spring is radically different from the perception of weight obtained by lifting up a mass. A handle was used in both cases. The mechanical force of the spring could not be equated to the gravitational force of the weight, and a large error was found when subjects attempted to match the two. Bearing this fact in mind, let us consider softness as perceived by squeezing.

The firmness or softness of a material substance is a property of the substance that is registered when forces are exerted on it by the hand. The firmness, however, is not the forces as such. Scott-Blair and Coppen (cf. Harper, 1952) investigated the perception of the firmness-softness of industrial substances (rubber, bitumen) by having the observer squeeze a cylindrical sample of the material to be graded. The "feel" of the material was quite clear at the end of this dynamic action. They concluded that the perception "had the nature of a Gestalt," but I would suggest instead that an invariant was isolated. They considered that firmness had to be conceived as subjective, or semi-subjective, since they did not think it was expressible as a physical magnitude; but I would argue that it is a fact of physics even if a complex one. Harper and Stevens (1964) assumed that the "hardness" of a substance, which must the the same as "firmness," is measured by a *ratio* — the ratio of the force exerted on it by a weighted steel ball to the amount of indentation produced by it. (A finger, of course, can also exert a force and make an indentation.) This ratio proved to be nearly invariant for different amounts of force. Their subjects pinched a sample of each substance from a varying collection by compressing it between thumb and forefinger. Judgments of hardness, or the reciprocal, softness, were in good correspondence with this ratio. Note that it could be detected only over time, and that pinching either strongly or weakly would reveal the invariant.

The ripeness of cheese, or fruit, can often best be detected by feeling it. Such "biochemicophysical" properties seem to be more easily apprehended by the hand than they are by physical formulae (Sheppard,

1955). The surgeon's techniques of percussion, palpation, and massage can often give him more information about the special states of the interior of the human body than any other medical test (Katz, 1936). Moreover, as we shall see, the consistency of a food substance in the mouth is detected with precision by the dynamic touching of the tongue and the jaws.

Summary of Perception by Haptic Exploration

By laying hold of something, a person can detect its size, its shape, its surface texture, and its material substance or consistency. Its relative temperature can also be perceived, as we shall note in the next section. All these qualities are picked up by exploratory manipulation, that is, by the hands considered as a perceptual subsystem. But the hands are not the exclusive possessors of these discriminative abilities. The feet are also quite capable, as scattered evidence indicates, although they are normally unused for perception by man. Other extremities can be substituted for the hands, as is demonstrated by the abilities of persons with amputations. And the mouth can make all the above discriminations with equal or better acuity. We think of the mouth as an entirely different organ belonging to a different modality but actually it overlaps with the haptic system. As part of its function in testing food substances the tongue in the oral cavity is sensitive to size, shape, texture, consistency, and temperature, as we shall observe in the next chapter.

The perceptual achievements of haptic touch and dynamic touching are only beginning to be investigated. Russian psychologists, having the concept of investigatory responses from Pavlov, understand the possibilities of discovery in this field. The evidence of the preceding pages is exploratory only.

Touch Temperature and Air Temperature

The perception of temperature, as distinguished from sensations of temperature, can be subdivided into two systems, one with cutaneous contact and one without. The first registers the relative temperature of a touching surface and the second registers the relative temperature of the medium, usually the air. The first is part of the haptic system; the second is part of the body's temperature-regulating system — it goes with shivering or sweating and partakes of motivation as well as perception. The first leads to an assertion like, "Your hand is cold," the second to an assertion like, "It is cold today."

The registering of the temperature of the medium partakes of motivation because warm-blooded animals (who regulate their own temperature) must be sensitive to the rate at which their bodies are gaining or losing heat, for they need to make adjustments to the rate of gain or loss. We feel "the heat" or "the cold" and act accordingly. When the outflow of heat is too great for physiological compensation, the individual must seek shelter, or increase the insulation at the skin, or put himself in the ways of external radiation, such as the sun by day or a fire by night. In the last case he will feel the inflow of heat from the source on one side of his body, and this will yield stimulus information as well as contentment. Even man has a tropism toward the fire on a winter night.

The stimulus for this perception is not heat as a level of physical energy, or temperature as measured in degrees above absolute zero. The effective stimulus is the *direction* of heat flow at the skin by radiation or conduction, this being the information needed for appropriate adaptation. The individual responds to the temperateness of the surroundings, as it were, not the temperature; to a relation, not a physical absolute, since his own temperature is constant and constitutes a *physiological zero* for temperateness. "Cold" is not recognized as a reality in energy physics, but it is a perfectly good reality for biophysics. Animals cannot live when the water in their cells is permanently frozen. Similarly, life generally stops when the water boils. In order to avoid these killing extremes animals have made various adaptations, one of which is perceptual sensitivity. Toward the extremes, the experience of pain merges with the experiences of cold and hot. In the intermediate range the experience is simply cool or warm.

In their commerce with the surroundings during evolution, animals have also achieved the perception of touch-temperature. This is the registering of the direction of heat flow of a substance in local contact with the skin — that is, a pickup of flow by conduction as contrasted with radiation. The object is perceived as cold, cool, neutral, warm, or hot, in addition to being rigid, elastic, or viscous. In this situation it is the object that seems to have the quality, not the skin, and the objectification seems to hold as much for the temperature as it does for the viscosity or the shape of the object. Information about a physical state is in fact detected. This state need not be conceived as subjective (a "secondary" quality or sensation) in contrast to its shape being objective (a "primary" quality or perception), despite John Locke's opinion to the contrary. The state of the object's being above or below the temperature of the skin is a fact of the animal's environment.

• ILLUSIONS OF TOUCH-TEMPERATURE. The perception of warmth and coolness is not exact, to be sure. It is subject to illusion because the stimulus information does not always correspond to the thermometer reading. An object of metal at the temperature of the surface of the skin will feel cool, whereas an object of cork at the same temperature will not, because the former conducts heat away from the skin faster than the latter, being a better conductor. The illusion does not extend to the extremes of temperature, however. Hot or cold objects will be perceived as such whatever the conductivity of the material.

Moreover, as is well known, the perception of the warmth or coolness of an object depends on the temperature of the skin touching it, which can vary. Hence a surface of neutral temperature will feel warm to a cool finger but cool to a warm finger, and hence the tissue in continuous contact with a cool surface, for example, will eventually be itself cooled, and thus cease to register the objective state. This fact is called temperature adaptation and the former fact is called contrast (or the negative after-effect of adaptation), but both are simply the consequence of the nature of the stimulus information, that is, the direction of heat flow. The perceptual system of the skin can be locally or temporarily out of calibration, as it were — the physiological zero of the tissue having been raised or lowered — and illusions are the result. The discalibration is somewhat analogous to that of the organs of the semicircular canals (Chapter 4), where it is known that the organ has a physiological zero in the form of a null position.

• RECEPTORS FOR TEMPERATURE. The receptive mechanism in the skin which initiates the nervous input is unknown, as we have already noted. According to one theory, the inflow or outflow of heat first induces vasodilation or vasoconstriction, respectively, of the tiny arterioles in the tissue which bring it the blood supply. Then, second, the wrapping of nerve fibers around these blood vessels specifies the thermal event by way of the mechanical size changes of these elastic tubes (Nafe, 1934). The complexities of fact and speculation about thermal reception are described by Geldard (1953, Ch. 11). It is possible that the information about heat flow at the surface of the body is multiple and complex. Sweating, for example, is an indicator of it, and even the erection of hairs, which serves a function in furry animals, may contribute to the perception.

Pain and Painful Touch

Pain has always had a doubtful status in psychology. It is sometimes considered as one of the senses because it yields a sensation like color or taste, but it is more often considered a motive or emotion like hunger or sex because it impels to action. It depends on nervous input, for it can be eliminated by blocking nerves, but no specific receptors have been identified. It is caused by certain kinds of physical radiation, certain chemicals, and certain mechanical events, but the only way to describe them simply is to say that they are toxic, noxious, or injurious.

Even then the correlation between pain and injury is imperfect. Undoubtedly pain has something to do with specifying damage to the cells of an organism. It is a symptom but a very puzzling one, as every physician knows. Internal pains do not carry much information about their causes or locations.

Cutaneous pain, however, when combined with haptic touch or locomotion or performance does carry useful information about the world. The subjective pain is not then experience so much as the painful object — that is, its noxious or dangerous character. Exploratory touching often includes cautious movements that cause a mild sort of pain as a feedback from the movement. In this sort of perception the onset of pricking or burning specifies an imminent injury, not an actual one, and serves to control further manipulation. Animals and children often need to touch or probe to find out whether something does or does not hurt. Sometimes the only way to discover whether a new contact with the world is or is not safe is to incur a certain degree of pain. Only thus can the dangerousness of the object be evaluated, and the margin of safety in handling it be determined.

Painful touch, then, is a kind of obtainable stimulus information about the environment. It combines with vision to yield perception of the negative values of certain things, i.e., their valences. Some afford injury, others afford benefit, and the developing individual must discriminate between them by attending to the stimuli that specify what is afforded.

Social Touch

Haptic touch, even without vision, makes an important contribution to the perception of the animate environment (Chapter 1). For the infant mammal, the mother is something soft, warm, roundly shaped, and mobile. It is also, of course, odorous, tasteable, audible, and visible, but basically it is tangible. It offers what Harlow has called "contact comfort" (1958). The stimulation provided to the infant by the mother is similarly provided to the mother by the infant, and this permits and controls their social interaction. The same can be said about each member of a sexual pair. Each partner is soft, warm, and suitably shaped to the other, and each touches when touched. Social touch, in fact, is a necessary basis of social life, and to be "in touch" with one's fellows, or to "make contact" with other individuals, is a requirement for the development of a mental life.

The perception of a concurrently soft, warm, round, and mobile thing is valuable to the young, and even to the old at certain times. They need it and seek it out, apparently, whether or not it yields satisfaction of hunger or sexual need. Matters are arranged so that it generally will, of course, but the perception itself is satisfying. We cling or clasp or embrace for its own sake. A demonstration of this fact has been provided by the use of artificial "mother substitutes" with infant monkeys (Harlow, 1958). A soft rounded object, as in Figure 7.4, is better than a rigid rounded object or no object, even if it is not fully responsive, and does not radiate warmth or provide food. In Harlow's experiments the infants clung to the best substitute available, and whether or not they perceived a mother, they obtained the closest approximation they could to the meaning of a mother.

Social touch is not, of course, always positively valued. Being touched

Figure 7.4 An infant monkey clinging to a soft mother-surrogate. (From H. F. Harlow, "The Nature of Love," *American Psychologist,* 1958, *13,* p. 679.)

by another individual may be painful, not pleasurable. The maternal contact may be a cuff instead of a caress, providing punishment, not comfort. Nurturing and sexual and affectionate touchings are not the only kind; there are the aggressive touchings of antagonists and competitors. These stimuli carry a different meaning and lead to quite different modes of social interaction, such as mutual attack, or flight and pursuit.

In social touch, the haptic system with all of its subsystems comes into full perceptual use. Simple cutaneous touch operates along with haptic touch, dynamic touch, and spatially-oriented touch, and touch-temperature, touch-pain, and touch-pleasure. There are perceptions of passive contact and of active touching. Exploratory perception merges with performatory activity. The haptic system provides an adequate means of social interaction and communication even without taking into account auditory-vocal perception, which has been described, or visual expressive perception, which remains to be described.

Summary of Chapters 6 and 7

More than any other perceptual system, the haptic apparatus incorporates receptors that are distributed all over the body and this diversity of anatomy makes it hard to understand the unity of function that nevertheless exists. Moreover, it is so obviously involved in the control of performance that we are introspectively not aware of its capability to yield perception; we allow the visual system to dominate our consciousness. Nevertheless the perceptions of the blind, and of blindfolded subjects, can sometimes rival those of seeing persons and this fact shows how much information is obtained by it. In many respects the system parallels vision. Animals with little vision depend on a sort of primitive haptics for their orientation to the adjacent environment, the muscles and skin cooperating with gravity detection to yield whatever they have in the way of space perception.

The inputs of reportable sensation, as these have been catalogued by introspection, are evidently quite inadequate to account for the richness of haptic perception. An example is the pattern and flow of geometrical information from the joints, which yield perceptions of body pose and the shapes of touching surfaces but not a collection of sensations from each joint.

A tentative classification of the subsystems of the haptic system of man has been offered, and they were named cutaneous touch, haptic touch, dynamic touching, touch-temperature, and touch-pain. They can operate in various combinations. The combination of haptic information with the unceasing input of vestibular information was called oriented touch.

The detection of heat flow relative to the surrounding medium was conceived as belonging to a different perceptual system from that of heat flow relative to an object.

The sense of touch in the everyday meaning of the term turns out to be an extremely elaborate and powerful perceptual system but not a sense in either the physiological or the introspective meaning of the term. Nor is it a clearly definable group of senses with just so many nerves and corresponding qualities of sensation. The common sense belief in touch as a way of getting information is justified.

VIII / Tasting and Smelling as a Perceptual System

We have all been taught that our ordinary use of the words *smell* and *taste* does not conform to scientific fact, and that most of what we call tasting when we eat is actually smelling. We accept this, but nevertheless we go on speaking of wine tasting, tea tasting, and food tasting without regard to what we have been taught. Why we do so is worth looking into.

Physiologists define a sense by the receptors that initiate impulses in a nerve, as was pointed out in Chapter 2. By this criterion the sense of smell depends on the stimulation of the cells in a small membrane in the uppermost nasal cavity. The tiny chemoreceptors there are connected to the olfactory nerve. The sense of taste depends on the stimulation of the taste buds in the tongue and mouth, and the chemoreceptors in these structures are connected to another nerve — a complex one. Odors are brought to the membrane by eddying currents of air, and solutions penetrate into the taste buds by diffusion in the saliva.

By these definitions the sense of smell is more than smelling external things, such as pigs on the breeze or flowers in the room, and the sense of taste is less than tasting what we eat. For smell is aroused not only by sniffing the air but also by food in the mouth. And taste is aroused only by the solutions coming from food and not by its aroma. Taste is reduced to the status of a minor sense, for distinguishing solutions. Smell is elevated to the status of a dual sense, for both sniffing the air and savoring food. As Titchener put it, we constantly make the mistake, when eating, of "attributing to taste what really belongs to smell" (1909, p. 115). A standard experiment, persisting from his day, was to show that when the nose is held closed, and air currents are thereby prevented from circulating into the nasal cavity, the tastes of apple, onion, and raw potato cannot be distinguished. Their solutions, in truth, do not differ.

Smelling and tasting however, need not be defined by receptors and nerves. They can be defined by their functions in use, smell being an accompaniment of breathing and taste of eating. The ordinary person

136

means by a sense what is here called a perceptual system — a perception sense, not a sensation sense. Sniffing the air has one function, chewing another. The different receptors for the volatile and the soluble components of food, located in the connected cavities of the head, can be incorporated in the same perceptual system. Conversely, the same olfactory membrane can be incorporated in a different perceptual system when sniffing occurs than it is when eating occurs.

In ordinary usage, to *taste* means first to sample a substance, as when the cook merely "tastes" the dish, and also to savor it, as when we eat. To *smell* means to detect a substance outside the mouth. And it can now be observed that these usages are not incorrect after all. When we stubbornly continue to mean by *taste* a mode of attention that cuts across the classification of receptors we are only recognizing the fact that receptors may be functionally united when anatomically separated. In fact, the word *palate*, although used in anatomy to mean the back of the mouth, is used in gastronomy to mean the whole complex of receptors contributing to palatability, that is, an organ of perception.

Taste has the status of a minor sense only as the channel of certain minor sensations. It is a major perceptual system, and a principal concern of life for many persons. No one can be wholly indifferent to it, and the cultivation of the palate is a mark of civilization. The discrimination of wines and culinary preparations can reach a high level. As to smell, I will only quote Piéron (1952, p. 187): "Thanks to a scent created by a perfume manufacturer, a woman will be able to express her own individuality which other persons will be able to recognize in this way. This will make it possible to distinguish from all others the traces of her passing, and it will guide the admirers following in her wake." Professor Piéron was a distinguished authority on the physiology of the senses, but he was also a Frenchman.

Titchener himself was struck by the "curiously unitary character" of the combined sensations of taste, smell, touch, and temperature when eating a peach or when drinking coffee. The "taste" seemed to be simple and unique. Nevertheless, he argued, the blend had to be analyzed, "and the foreign constituents referred to the sense departments to which they properly belong" (1909, p. 130). He assumed that special qualities of odor, feeling, and temperature combined with the sour-sweet quality of a peach and that the perception was a fusion of these associated qualities plus a context of associated memories of everything that had ever happened along with peach-eating. The hypothesis of peach specification by stimulus information was foreign to his way of thought. The chronic tendency of observers to detect objects instead of sensations, however, and to give even the sensory qualities objective names like salty, points in the latter direction.

The Tasting System

Tasting, as here conceived, is basically a system for the control of ingestion. It is part of the nutritive apparatus that all animals possess, but it has the special use of standing guard over eating, selecting certain things and rejecting others. Along with smelling, it is a component of the food-getting system. This last consists of a whole chain of activities — finding food, taking it, biting or chewing it, testing it for numerous qualities with numerous kinds of sensitivity, and only in the end swallowing it. As an alternative to swallowing, choking and coughing are possible in the later stages of eating.

Available Information in Tasting

There is a pickup of *all* the available information about a substance in the mouth. Here is a tentative list of such information.

The soluble fluid of the substance, the *sapid* component, stimulates the receptors in the tongue and nearby tissue lining the mouth.

The volatile part of the substance, the *odorous* component, stimulates the receptors in the olfactory cavity above the mouth.

The relative temperature of the substance stimulates the tongue and mouth in an unknown way.

The surface texture of the substance is registered by a sort of mouth palpation which detects such properties as slippery, smooth, and rough, as in butter, lettuce, and breadcrust.

The consistency of the substance is registered by chewing which detects such properties as viscosity, elasticity, and soft, hard, or brittle. Meat, raw vegetables, and peanuts differ in these respects.

In addition, the *shape, size, specific gravity,* and the condition of *wholeness* or *granularity* of the substance are probably registered by the haptic action of the mouth. These and the preceding three items all constitute haptic information, as described in the last chapter.

The mouth is an especially acute haptic organ, even more so perhaps than the hand. Both organs "lay hold of" the environment. The receptors for oral haptics are in the skin and tissue of the tongue, in the lips, in the lining of the mouth, in the muscles of the tongue, in the muscles of the jaw, and in the joints of the jaw (see Figure 8.1). The anatomical separation of these receptors does not prevent them from all being parts of one organ, in the present usage of that term.

The information obtained by tasting is evidently multiple. It is all specific to the same substance, however, and the inputs are all concomitant since the receptors are made to covary by the activity of the mouth. This activity is not only one that prepares the food for swallowing. It is also exploratory and stimulus-producing, since chewing releases

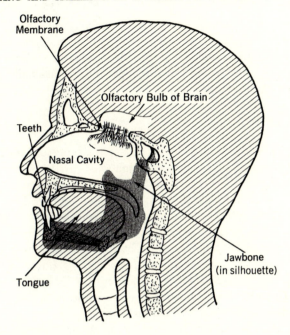

Olfactory
Membrane

Olfactory Bulb of Brain

Teeth

Nasal Cavity

Tongue

Jawbone
(in silhouette)

Figure 8.1   The Anatomy of the Human Nose and Mouth.

fluids and aromas, and the movements of the tongue bring them to the chemically receptive areas. Tasting is a kind of attention, and the mouth can be said to focus on its contents.

This perceptual system should no longer be called a chemical *sense*, inasmuch as only the first two types of information listed above depend on chemoreceptors. And in any case, as we shall see, the properties perceived are not those studied by straight chemistry. Rather, they are nutritive values or affordances. In man, they are gastronomic values. Such properties depend on facts of chemistry, physics, and biology, to be sure, but only as they relate to nutrition and cookery. Tasting is a detection of chemical values, not of chemical solutions.

The cavities of the mouth and nose register the effects of substances like pepper, horseradish, and mustard by receptors more like those found in the skin than like the chemoreceptors found in the taste buds and the olfactory membrane. The action of these substances, like that of the chemical menthol, is little understood. Mustard seems to affect the skin as heat does, and menthol as cold does, while pepper and horseradish yield something like tingling pain. Adults, but not children, often take pleasure in adding non-nutritive condiments to their food, presumably for the purpose of complicating the cutaneous sensations obtained in eating. For the same reason they like sparkling wines or carbonated drinks in which the breaking of bubbles yields sensations of tingle or tickle. Men are complicated creatures and they occasionally seek to have sensations for their own sake.

Sensations of Taste

The classical sensory qualities of taste are sweet, sour, salt, and bitter. They are the result of paying attention only to the solution receptors in the mouth. If these receptors are stimulated experimentally with drops of liquid, in isolation, clear sensations are evoked. Something approaching these pure sensations can be experienced by means of analytic introspection during eating but this kind of isolation is difficult to achieve and requires training. Only by experimental isolation with the punctuate stimulation of receptors, or by the method of fastening a device over the tongue which flows a solution over its surface, can the pure sensory qualities of taste be experienced by the ordinary person.

Most of the haptic sensations that ought to be present in ordinary tasting if Titchener's theory of perception is right cannot be analyzed out even with the most careful introspection. Since they also cannot be isolated by any known experimental procedure it is questionable whether they ever occur as sensations. Texture, consistency, shape, size, and granularity are qualities of objects, not qualities of sense.

The problem of the chemical correlates of sweet, sour, salt, and bitter will be discussed later. It can be noted, however, that the sweet quality is pleasant and that sweet substances often, but not always, have high food value. At the other extreme the bitter quality is unpleasant and bitter substances usually, but not always, have no food value. The evidence of animal behavior in eating often suggests that what is sweet or bitter for us is also sweet or bitter for them, but only within limits. There is some slight justification for speaking of intrinsically sweet and bitter substances, but on the whole the four classical qualities of taste seem to be the products of human physiology. When taste preferences are studied comparatively in a wide variety of animals, the theory of four basic sensations does not hold up. A leading investigator of taste in animals has asserted that "one cannot ascribe to animals the taste sensations experienced by man" and he believes that the results suggest "separate taste worlds for each species" (Kare and Ficken, 1963, p. 296).

The sensations of distaste other than bitter, are very complex and have not been fully studied by introspection. The negative selection of substances by spitting them out or later by vomiting has not usually been thought of as simply the complement of eating, but so it is.

The Limitations of Tasting as a Control for Eating

Taste in the full meaning of the term usually gives a correct detection of alimentary values, but not always. This is true for both animals and men. Noxious substances sometimes get eaten and nutritive substances fail to get eaten. There seem to be bad or nauseating tastes and good or delicious tastes, the values differing from one species to another, but the bad tastes are not always bad for nutrition and the good tastes are not always good for nutrition. There *are* toxic and nutritious substances in the environment for each species of animals, but the correlation with taste is not perfect.

In man, on occasion, a poison can be ingested without any warning of distaste or nausea. Then, reciprocally, a distasteful or nauseating substance which is perfectly harmless can be ingested so as to rid the stomach of both substances. The latter is called an emetic. The system is subject to misperception or illusion, like other systems. The food values of natural substances in the environment are extremely difficult to detect and what is surprising is that animals do as well as they do. The information obtained often has only *probable* instead of certain validity, to use the terminology of Egon Brunswik (1956). There have been attempts to study self-selection of diet in the human infant by "cafeteria presentation" of foods (Ausubel, 1958, pp. 243f.), but obviously the experiment did not include poisons, and the results suggest only that the infant tends to "balance" his diet over a period of days. In herbivorous animals, however, the self-selection of diet begins as soon as the young begin to graze, and there are great differences in the nutritive values of different plants, some being toxic. The evidence suggests that grazing animals select successfully by smell and taste, only rarely making such mistakes as eating the "loco weed" of the Western grasslands. There is good evidence to show that animals and children begin to manifest a preference for certain elements of diet, like salt, when their bodies are deficient in this element. Presumably the needed substance tastes better than it did before. But a "salt hunger" does not involve a lowered sensory threshold for the taste of salt, as was once supposed.

Civilized men have now so modified their environment that they seldom encounter natural food substances but only manufactured, processed, and packaged ones. Their diet is highly conventionalized. The capacity for rejection of noxious material by taste, such as it is, does not often get put to the test. It can be argued that it is fortunate for man that food technology should be substituted for the imperfect guardianship of taste perception. Bacterial infections and toxins that cause "food poisoning" often cannot be tasted but only eliminated from the diet by regulation. On the other hand, it has been argued that there are dangers in the chemical processing of food on large scale — that it is "unnatural," and that the natural choices of an omnivorous animal like man are more trustworthy. At the extreme this becomes food faddism, with overtones of mysticism. There is reason on both sides, but the former seems to have the best of it.

Hunger and Thirst

It has been taken for granted by physiologists and psychologists that all inputs to the central nervous system could be called "sensory" just as all outputs could be called "motor." This formula is an unfortunate choice. For one thing, it carries the implication that every input must be accompanied by a sensation corresponding to the stimulation of a receptor, difficult as it might be to discover. Hence, even the need states of the body like hunger and thirst which initiate behavior should be accompanied by sensations. This was the reasoning that led physiologists to search for the sensory basis of these drives. It was discovered that a sensation of hunger was reported by a human observer whenever the empty stomach contracted, and that a sensation of thirst was experienced whenever the throat was dry (Cannon, 1929; Boring, 1942, pp. 551–561).

But hunger and thirst do not consist of stomach contractions and throat dryness. They are states of the blood. Dehydration, for example, is more fundamentally the saltiness of the blood, that is, the salt to water ratio, then it is a dryness of the throat. It is now known that this ratio is registered directly by a nerve center in the hypothalamus of many animals. The activation of this center indicates a need for water whether or not the throat is dry. This kind of thirst is a sampling of the bloodstream by the nervous system without the mediation of receptors and sensory input. Animals drink compulsively when this center is aroused by electro-physiological means. A similar result is obtained with hunger. The conclusion can only be that sensory input and sensations are not necessary for a drive but that the pickup of information is. The information is what counts; the sensations are incidental.

The Uses of the Mouth

The organ referred to as the *mouth* is an active perceptual system. Anatomically, it includes a set of overlapping parts — the lips, jaw, teeth, tongue, palate, and throat — having a complex musculature. There are two chemoreceptive areas, in the oral cavity and the nasal cavity, and there are mechanoreceptors nearly everywhere. The mouth seems to be an apparatus for detecting the soluble and volatile components of a substance and its material qualities, like consistency, before swallowing it.

For the infant mammal it is an apparatus for sucking, as distinguished from eating. Hence, it is originally a means of feeling the mother's nipple and causing the mother to feel the infant's mouth — a means of mutual stimulation. This is perhaps the earliest kind of social interaction in animals of our sort. In man, the mouth remains an organ of sexual-social contact throughout life, as the act of kissing demonstrates.

The mouth is also an organ for haptic exploration in the infant, often with the cooperation of the hand. It explores objects brought to the mouth and the tactual acuity of the lips and mouth seems to arise earlier in development than that of the fingers. It is much used for autostimulation, in the sense of information-getting, and the baby appears to practice mouthing — to be interested in the regularities and possibilities of it. He drools and blows bubbles and sucks his thumb and learns how the mouth feels and what noises can be made with it. The adult often continues to suck a pipe or to use his mouth in other stereotyped ways. Freud called this "oral eroticism," but it is also surely the mere exercising of a perceptual system.

The mouth is also part of the complex organ system for vocalizing, the system that later develops the capacity for speaking. This complex feedback system, involving lungs, larynx, and ears as well as tongue, teeth, lips, and jaw, is of very high order indeed, as we saw in Chapter 5, and mediates the highest form of social contact.

In short, the mouth is a versatile apparatus. We use the mouth for all sorts of purposes, not just one. Its parts are used in various combinations and the same part can have different functions at different times. The organs of perception are often intermingled with organs of action and overlap with other organs of perception. This is typical of perceptual systems. They are not to be confused with the lesser organs of reception, the passive banks of chemoreceptors and mechanoreceptors which are identified with sensations.

• EXPERIMENTS ON THE HAPTICS OF THE MOUTH. The human adult does not use his mouth for exploratory haptic touching as the infant seems to do; or, more accurately, he does so only for food substances. "Putting things in the mouth" is tabooed after a certain age. Nevertheless this organ retains the ability to discriminate the shape, size, and solid geometry of objects without ever seeing them — an ability which the fingers also have. Experiments on this ability using sculptured nonsense shapes, with the hands behind a curtain, were described in the last chapter. The same kind of experiment can be performed with the mouth.

A set of geometrical shapes cut from plastic can be used, about a half inch in size, differing from one another considerably or only slightly. Copies of the set can be mounted on a panel in front of the subject's eyes. One of the shapes can then be put in his mouth and he is allowed to roll it about on his tongue and press it against the roof of the mouth or the teeth and lips. A remarkably clear perception of shape arises from this activity. The object displayed on the panel which matches the shape of the object in the mouth can be selected without error provided that they do not too closely resemble one another (Bosma, 1966).

My own observations suggest that the front part of the mouth, not the back, has the best acuity for this kind of discrimination and that some "manipulation" of the object by the tongue is necessary for it. There need be no tracing of the edges by the tongue, although this can occur. The tongue, teeth, and lips need only be fitted around the shape for it to be perceived. The equivalence of this spatial information to the spatial information picked up by the eyes — the matching of haptic to visual shape — is perhaps the most curious result of the experiment and it puts a considerable challenge to the traditional explanation of perception in terms of separate modes of sensation.

The Smelling System

If tasting is an accompaniment of eating, smelling is an accompaniment of breathing. Just as all animals must take in food, so all animals must take in oxygen. Tasting monitors and controls the intake of food. Smelling, however, cannot be said to control the intake of air, for the animal must breathe willy-nilly. Its main function is the detection of things at a distance by means of their odors or, more exactly, their effluvia.

Air as such, pure air, has no odor. A "foreign" substance in this normally constant mixture is a potential stimulus. The environment has many sources of such potential stimuli, each causing a field of diffusing volatile material. If it can be smelled it is an odor.

. . . .

The Constant Proportions of Gases in Air

Nitrogen	78.08%
Oxygen	20.94%
Carbon dioxide	.04%
Argon, helium, etc.	.94%
	100.00%

The additional water vapor depends on the relative humidity, but the proportion never exceeds 5 per cent by volume.

. . . .

Each animal is the source of an invisible cloud of diffusing vapor that seems to be specific not only to his type but also to him as an individual. The air is full of such overlapping clouds of emanation. It is likely that the diffusion field of a particular individual is not effectively stimulating to himself but only to other individuals. We do not know much about odors and odor fields. However, it is safe to say that they are streamed out by a wind, that they are dissipated by rain, that traces of a moving animal remain on the ground as a trail, and that the nest, burrow, or leavings of the animal as well as his own body are sources of specific odor. Only the animal himself is a continuing source; his traces and excrement are dissipated and diffused over time.

The specificity of an odor to its source holds for plants as well as animals. The flowers of plants are especially odorous because their pollination requires the cooperation of insects, often bees, and these can be attracted by particular odors. The fruits of plants are also characterized by "essences," to use a suggestive term from odor chemistry. So are plant products like resins and gums and spices. The state of a plant, like the state of an animal, is often characterized by a special emanation.

Finally, some natural events are advertised by the fields of their volatile products. Burning yields smoke, and the oxidation of different things yields different smokes. Mineral springs and fumaroles, swamps and seashores, all have specific odors that are detectable from a distance when the wind is right. So also, as modern man knows, does the glue factory.

Dogs can identify other animals, other dogs, and man, including individual men, by smell. They can also follow a trail made by any of these. Cats smell mice and mice smell cats. Skunks repel enemies by odor; females attract males by odor. Certain flowers attract certain insects; carrion flowers attract carrion flies. Female moths at the right stage of the reproductive cycle emit a scent so powerful that males of the appropriate species, but no other, find them by flying upwind to the source from a distance of several miles (Kalmus, 1958). Even men are capable of fine odor discriminations when they choose. No one mistakes frying pork chops. Perfume blenders and tea tasters become very expert at perceiving by smell within the range of objects that interest them. And a blind woman "is said to have been employed in the Hartford Asylum to sort the linen of its multitudinous inmates, after it came from the wash, by her wonderfully educated sense of smell" (James, 1890, p. 509).

The Uses of Smelling

The act of sniffing brings the foreign component of the inspired air into contact with the olfactory membrane, whereupon it is presumably absorbed into the mucous coating and caused to stimulate the microscopic receptors. Repeated sniffing probably maximizes the absorption of this vapor when its concentration is low. Sneezing presumably clears the air in the nasal cavity of the foreign substance and stops the absorption, or the irritation. Some odors are "good" and the individual acts to maximize their intensity. Some odors are "bad" and the individual acts so as to minimize their intensity.

The function of this perceptual system is, first, to evaluate and identify the source of the odor in the environment and, second, to orient and control behavior, including locomotion, with respect to the source. We shall take these up in order.

• THE IDENTIFICATION OF SOURCES BY ODOR. In a natural environment the sources of odor are other animals and their products, plants and their products, and a few types of inorganic things. By and large, the minerals of the earth, the air, and the water — the lithosphere, atmosphere, and hydrosphere — are odorless.

Organic odors contribute potential stimulus information about their sources but the whole range of this information is not perceived and responded to by any one species. The pickup of an odor depends on its relevance to the animal. The evolution of perception by smell did not take the same course in all species, since what constitutes food for one does not always constitute food for another. Carnivores might be expected to detect the odor of meat better than the odor of clover while herbivores would do the reverse. The total spectrum of detectable odors for insects is quite different from that for mammals. It is reasonable to suppose that the odors of whatever objects constitute food for a species will also constitute effective stimulus information for the smelling system of that species. The pickup of this information will be unlearned in the young of some animals and partly or wholly learned in the young of other animals, depending on how soon they must forage for themselves. The responses of animals to food scents, insofar as these have been observed, are consistent with this hypothesis (Matthews and Knight, 1964).

Likewise the potential mates of a species should be identifiable by odor, and the readiness of the female for mating should be uniquely perceivable by the male, as the bitch dog in heat seems to be. The young of certain species should theoretically be discriminable by the adults, and the mother should be particularly sensitive to her own young in the case of herd animals. The evidence suggests that the odor of a lamb is "imprinted" on the perceptual system of the ewe soon after birth by the activities of licking it and allowing it to suck. After a certain interval an infant that does not smell right is butted away by the mother.

Predatory animals should come to be sensitive to the odor that specifies their prey, whether by maturation of perception or by learning. The cat smells the mouse. Reciprocally, the preyed-upon animal needs to be sensitive to the odor that specifies a predator, and this should develop early, since an error of discrimination is fatal and cannot be corrected. The mouse smells the cat. Note that the affordance of prey odor is different from that of predator odor, the one being positive the other negative. The information registered depends on the animal registering it. For a scavenging species, the odor of carrion is attractive; for others repulsive.

Plants, foliage, flowers, and fruit are objectively specified by odors but are differentially attractive to different animals depending on the biochemical constitution of the animal in question, that is, on his diet.

What the individual picks up in smelling is primarily what the source affords — the "invitation quality" or "demand quality" of the stimulus (Lewin, 1935). The quality cannot be explained as a cluster of associations to a bare sensation. It must be conceived as a kind of information — the quality of being edible or inedible, ripe or unripe, mate or stranger, own species or foreign species, young or adult, prey or predator, alive or dead, safe or dangerous. The individual distinguishes the important differences. He does not, of course, identify everything in the environment by odor — first, because not everything is potentially specified by odor, and second, because he does not need to distinguish everything from everything else. The same is true of man. He smells what interests him. The perceptual system, however, is capable of more discriminations than are usually demanded of it. A man can learn to discriminate wine if he chooses to do so, and a police dog can easily be trained to discriminate among men.

Not very much is known about the process of learning to recognize places, things, animals, and people by their odor, but there is some evidence to suggest that it is a simpler, less conscious kind of recognition than that by sight or sound. The power of smells experienced in childhood to reinvoke old memories in the adult has often been commented on. On another level, the salmon "remembers" the smell of the stream in which it was hatched (Hasler and Wisby, 1951) and can detect it in all the tributaries of the river up which it has to migrate when it returns to lay its own eggs in later years. It is as if the chemoreceptive system, once attuned to a particular identifying substance in the medium, retains this special sensitivity during the whole life of the animal. In the salmon, to be sure, smell and taste have not been separated into two perceptual systems, so the words we use to describe them are inappropriate. The theory that the nervous system *resonates to information* as an explanation of recognizing and remembering will be elaborated in Chapter 13.

• THE ORIENTATION OF BEHAVIOR BY ODOR. The identification of more or less specific things in the environment and the orientation of behavior to such things develop together in the individual, although logically identification is necessary for orientation. The question "what is it?" must receive some answer before the question "what to do about it?" can arise. Admittedly, the priority of one or the other of these questions is a theoretical issue in psychology, but the position adopted in this book is that identification comes first. We must now consider what an organism *does* when its perceptual system has detected an odor.

For the moths referred to above, the scent emitted by the female when her eggs are ready for fertilization lures only males of the same species, and not males of other species. How does the appropriate male orient when his antennae pick up a trace, even the faintest trace, of this specific substance? What does he do? His compound eyes are inadequate to specify the female except at very close range and, in any case, he may be miles away. The gradient of concentration of the odor is likewise insufficient to specify the direction of the female until he is almost upon her. One kind of directional information does exist, however, if there is a wind. He can equalize the bilateral pressure on the front of his body caused by airflow, and fly upwind. The streaming out of an odor field, in short, creates a sort of air track. Orientation to a breeze is the same as orientation to an odor source if the odor is carried by the breeze. Flying animals can in fact orient their bodies relative to an airflow by detecting the symmetry or asymmetry of stimulation of sensory hairs or feathers on the surface of the body. Even a man can move with the wind in his face, and the touch of the wind is not confused with the touch of an object. The feeling of airflow is one of the factors that enables animals to fly better than airplanes — at least in some respects.

Dogs and carnivores also seem able to use this information; they can follow the air scent carried by airflow, as well as the ground scent from a track (Kalmus, 1955). Predatory animals locate prey by combining these methods. The rule for oriented locomotion is quite simple: move in such a way as to keep and maximize the smell of food. Later in the hunt a similar rule may operate: move in such a way as to maximize the *sight* of food. At a maximum intensity of smell and the maximum of optical size, the rule is simply *bite*. The prey is captured. Taste then takes over.

This is the rule of the chase. The rule of flight is precisely the opposite: move so as to minimize the scent of the predator, or the sight or the sound of it. Orientation to the wind may also be involved in flight; when a herd of deer catch the scent of a mountain lion they generally take off downwind. In short, what seems to us highly complex motivated behavior may be only an automatic orientation to stimulus information — a servomechanism, requiring the balancing of neural inputs and the maximizing or minimizing of an identified stimulus value. The behavior is nonetheless purposive for being automatic. But some perception of the value, of what is afforded, of the information in the stimulus, is implied in all such oriented action prior to the action itself. "What is it?" comes before "what to do about it?"

The Sensations of Smell

A man can attend to the subjective experience while smelling, instead of attending to the source, and then he has what can be justly called a sensation. An effort to find out by introspection what the elementary irreducible qualities of these sensations are has been made by a number of investigators (Boring, 1942, Ch. 12), but they do not agree with one another. The qualities of smell are not like sweet, sour, salt, and bitter, or like red, yellow, green, and blue. There seem to be no outstanding primary qualities from which the others can be derived as blends or compounds. Henning's list, embodied in the "smell prism" (see Figure 8.2), consists of *fruity, flowery, spicy, resinous, burning,* and *putrid,* but other experts consider this scheme too simple. Note, in any case, that these words are names for classes of objects or events (fruits, flowers, spices, resins, fires, or decaying bodies), not classes of chemical substances. The supposed qualities seem to be perceptual, not sensory. What could be the *stimuli* for these qualities, as distinct from the *sources* of stimulation? The whole question is very puzzling.

The puzzle has been well stated by Boring (1942, p. 446): "Although smell is always said to be one of the two chemical senses, there is no clear evidence that *chemistry* will eventually provide the knowledge of the essential nature of the olfactory stimulus. The mere fact that different substances have different smells and also different chemical constitutions does not make smell a chemical sense. Different substances have likewise different colors and different chemical constitutions, and yet color vision is not for this reason a chemical sense. The nature of the olfactory stimulus still escapes the psychologist." The implications of this quotation will be followed up in the next section.

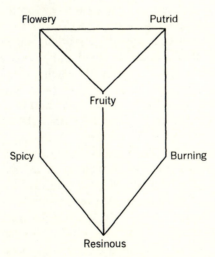

Figure 8.2 Henning's classification of odor qualities. The intermediates between these six supposedly pure qualities are conceived to lie on the surface of the prism but not in the interior.

The Search for Chemicals as Stimuli
for Smell and Taste

For more than a century, physiologists have been trying to discover the chemical causes of sweet, sour, salt, and bitter tastes, and of the bewildering array of smell qualities. Suggestions of correspondence between the chemical and the psychological realm have been obtained, and they are enough to keep the investigators working at the task, but exceptions have turned up for every tentative rule. Sugars are sweet, more or less, but so is saccharine. Acids (hydrogen ions) are sour, but so are other chemicals. Salts are often but not always salty. Alkaloids are bitter but no one knows what the necessary and sufficient cause of bitterness is. The same situation holds for smells. Pfaffman (1959) and Adey (1959) have recently summarized the evidence for taste and smell respectively. The chemist cannot predict what the smell or taste of a chemical will be until he tries it, for no theory is available. Conversely the psychologist cannot explain a smell or taste in chemical terms for, as Boring has said, he does not know what the stimulus is.

• THE BEGINNING OF A THEORY. A *substance*, of course, is not the same as a chemical *compound*. Most natural substances are mixtures of chemical compounds. The latter are "pure" chemicals; they can usually be synthesized and reproduced and each is composed of molecules of the same type. Natural substances cannot ordinarily be reproduced by a chemist and, not being standardized, are not satisfactory for experiments. In medicine, the study of the effect of drugs on the organism has proceeded successfully on the principle that a drug is essentially a molecule. This permits controlled experiment. The study of smell and taste has proceeded on the same principle, but with little success. We cannot correlate the configuration of a molecule with the odor or taste of a compound as we can correlate the wavelength of light with its color, and the frequency of sound with its pitch. It is conceivable, however, that the effective stimuli for smell and taste, what the systems discriminate between, are *not* pure chemicals but are what the chemist calls mixtures or complexes. The foods and odors of the environment are mixtures; so are the culinary preparations of the cook and the odor blends of the perfume manufacturer.

At the beginning of the chapter, it was suggested that the smell-taste system reacts to chemical *values*. It was emphasized that stimulus information is not the same as stimulus energy. The odor of a source specifies it but is not chemically identical with it, and the sapid juices of food identify it without being the same thing as the food. Smoke corresponds to fire without being fire; the body odor of an individual corresponds to his body but does not have the same chemical composition; an extract is not the thing it was extracted from. This relation of correspondence is different from the relation of identity between a laboratory chemical and its vapor or its solution in water. But the latter relation is presupposed when we assert that smell and taste are chemical senses, meaning that they distinguish chemicals, that is, compounds defined by their formulae.

The puzzle described by Boring in the quotation above may be resolved only when a new sort of chemistry has been developed, a chemistry that recognizes values and considers the problem of stimulus information instead of merely that of the chemical excitation of receptors. It would be a sort of ecological chemistry, based on the assumption that some vapors and some solutions carry information about their sources without necessarily being chemically identical with them. The so-called essences of flowers and fruit are characteristic of them without being expressions of their inner nature or of their true substance.

Of course it is true that pure chemical molecules often will excite the chemoreceptors. Similarly, as we shall see in the next chapter, single wavelengths of light will excite the photoreceptors. But these stimuli do not excite them in the particular invariant combinations that the perceptual system has been evolved to register, the combinations that constitute information. The *organs* of smell and taste probably respond to mixtures or spectra of molecules, by analogy with the retina as a whole, which responds to spectral mixtures of light. The specific reactions to molecules and wavelengths may prove to be merely incidental.

The chemistry of nutritive value is like the chemistry of pigment color: neither is now understood. But it is conceivable, strange to say, that the nose and the eye understand them, when the chemist does not. Consider ripe and unripe fruit, which primates needed to distinguish when their perceptual systems were developing. Ripeness is characterized by a type of odor tending to be "fruity" and a type of color tending to be red rather than green. The chemical causes of ripening and redness are enormously complex. But the nose and eyes of the arboreal animal may have evolved to pick up just this complex information by way of the class of essential oils we call "fruity" and the class of absorption spectra we call "reddish." What is complex for chemistry and physics may prove to be simple for the nose and eyes.

The Perception of Chemical Values in the Sea

It is now possible to make electrical recordings of the activity of the chemoreceptors of some animals. If a horseshoe crab, a very primitive creature, is hooked up to an apparatus, and his chemoreceptors are stimulated with chemical solutions of the sort we call sweet, sour, salt, or bitter, they do not respond strongly. But an extract of clams causes a violent burst of activity (Autrum, 1959, p. 376). The essence of clams is not known to the chemist but it is to the crab. There are also men who find clam broth uniquely delicious.

Fish and aquatic animals can detect such essences diffusing from a source in the medium. The ability is like smell in this respect, but it is also like taste, of course, in respect of being a sensitivity to solutions. Does the fish smell or taste? The impossibility of any answer betrays our anthropocentric prejudice when we think of the senses and their sensations as being those that we possess, and it betrays the fallacy of assuming that a fixed set of "sensory" data are the causes of behavior in all animals. The fish has a taste-smell perceptual system, primitive but nevertheless informing to the fish. When the amphibians emerged from the sea the sensitivity to essences had to differentiate into two systems, one for odors in the air and one for solutions in the saliva. Smelling and tasting, then, are senses only as any sense is an apparatus for perceiving. There are not just so many modes of perception as there were thought to be just so many modes of sense. Perception is flexible, opportunistic, multiple, and redundant.

Summary

The senses of taste and smell have previously been defined by the banks of receptors connected to the nerves that are called respectively gustatory and olfactory. But the perceptual systems of tasting and smelling, corresponding to the ordinary meanings of these terms, cut across the receptors and nerves and register information with invariant combinations of nervous input.

The mouth, among its other functions, focuses on its contents so as to select what will be swallowed. It is primarily an ingestive control system, getting all the available stimulus information about a substance besides processing it by chewing and mixing it with saliva. The system tests for solubility, volatility, temperature, texture, consistency, and shape. These tests are not like those of the chemist in his laboratory, analytic and reductive, but for the purpose of testing palatability and edibility they surpass any the chemist now can employ.

The sensory qualities of solution taste must surely reflect the activity of the receptors in the taste buds in some way, but the causes of sweet, sour, salt, and bitter are still a mystery. Their stimuli cannot be chemically specified.

The nose, in the popular meaning of the term, is a perceptual system which is an adjunct to breathing. By virtue of odor fields in the medium, and the laws of diffusion, streaming, and the leaving behind of traces on the ground, it permits the perception of distant sources in the present environment and even of the places where animals have been in the past. This information depends on the specificity of odors to their sources, a remarkable but little understood fact of biochemistry. The pickup of this information, that is, the identifying of the source, seems to be partly unlearned and partly learned, depending on the species of the animal, its evolutionary history, its individual history, and its diet.

Orientation to a source of odor, positive or negative, becomes possible when the animal has some degree of perceptive discrimination. But the stimulus for orientation is the information or value in the volatile substance, not the chemical energy as such.

The detection of chemical values as distinguished from chemicals, the problem of the stimulus for perception as distinguished from the stimulus for the mere firing of chemoreceptors, is a great puzzle. The suggestion has been made that the information lies in the profile, the relative proportions, of true chemicals in a mixture, not in chemical molecules as such.

IX / *The Visual System: Evolution*

The usual exposition of the sense of sight begins with the anatomy of the eye and an explanation of how the light from an object makes an inverted image on the retina. Then there follows an account of the visual sensations, with emphasis on color, brightness, and form as they are related to the photosensitive cells of the retina, the rods and cones. Binocular vision is then introduced, which leads to the problem of depth perception and the question of how it could be accounted for by learning. The whole treatment is in terms of human vision.

We shall begin, however, with the question of what eyes are good for, and with an examination of the eyes of animals other than men. Many of these do not have camera-like eyes as we do, yet they behave as if they could see. Along with the retinal image we will consider the ambient light from the environment and the ways in which animals have come to respond to it. The peculiarities of human vision will be reserved until the end. This chapter will deal with the evolution of vision. Chapter 10 will deal with the problem of stimulus information for vision, and how it is registered.

Visual perception is so important to all of us, and so curious a process when studied, that we cannot help having preconceptions about it. Some of these come from the theories handed down to us from centuries of investigation and some come from our own private observations of how we seem to see. We have long been told, for example, that perception is a matter of the interpretation of visual sensations by the brain. The reader will be asked to question this preconception. We are told that an eye works like a camera and that the retinal image can be compared to a picture. The reader will be urged to consider the possibility that this analogy is misleading. We take it for granted from our own observation that the only way to see something accurately is to look at it. But this, although true for human vision, is not true for the vision of many other animals who can see all around at the same time, and who do not have a center

154

of greatest acuity in each eye. We have prejudices about how it feels to see from our own behavior as human lookers. We also have preconceptions about visual perception from a long history of theorizing about it. The best way to avoid these biases is to begin with the vision of animals.

Only in the last few decades has the evolution of vision become clear, with some understanding of function as well as of anatomy. The long treatise by Walls on *The Vertebrate Eye* (1942) is a monument to this progress, and it provides much of the groundwork for this chapter. The comparative study of visual perception is now possible, and evidence is accumulating. This approach is quite different from the traditional one. The classics of vision were unaffected by evolutionary considerations or by knowledge of animal behavior but nevertheless they dominate the theories of perception. The two greatest were probably Berkeley's *New Theory of Vision* in 1709, and Helmholtz' *Physiological Optics* in 1865. Both were preoccupied with the puzzle of how men could see depth and distance in the face of the fact that retinal images were flat and visual sensations were depthless. Another landmark in the history of the subject, Koffka's *Principles of Gestalt Psychology* (1935), was mainly concerned with how we see an object in relation to its framework, a figure on a background, and it kept to the question of why things look as they do to *us*.

In my book, *The Perception of the Visual World* (1950), I took the retinal image to be the stimulus for an eye. In this book I will assume that it is only the stimulus for a *retina* and that ambient light is the stimulus for the visual system. This circumstance, the fact of information in the light falling upon an organism, is the situation to which animals have adapted in the evolution of ocular systems. The visual organs of the spider, the bee, the octopus, the rabbit, and man are so different from one another that it is a question whether they should all be called *eyes*, but they share in common the ability to perceive certain features of the surrounding world when it is illuminated. The realization that eyes have evolved to permit perception, not to induce sensations, is the clue to a new understanding of human vision itself.

The Uses of Eyes

If vision was gradually evolved, as we know it was, the question is, why? What benefits are conferred by seeing? What purposes does it serve? If one asks people what vision is good for, the answers reflect only what they are most aware of as human beings. They say "for reading," or "for looking at pictures," or "for recognizing my friends." A woman may note that vision is necessary for threading a needle, and a man may observe that it is necessary for operating a steamshovel. A few people will realize that eyes are necessary for the basic act of getting about. Scholars are apt to reply with something like the answer given by Bishop Berkeley. "For this end" he said, "the visive sense seems to have been bestowed upon animals, that they may be able to foresee the damage or benefit which is likely to ensue upon the application of their own bodies to this or that body which is at a distance." Berkely was the philosopher who made us think of vision as a space sense, and he conceived of spatial vision as a "foreseeing" of what it will be like to touch an object before one touches it.

It is clear that all these answers are anthropomorphic. The objective study of animal behavior is a better guide than introspection to the utility of vision. When one surveys the whole realm of behavior that is controlled by light, from the phototropisms of the simplest creatures to the hunting behavior of the octopus, the dragonfly, and the hawk, a classification of the following sort emerges. Vision is useful for (1) detecting the layout of the surrounding, (2) detecting changes, and (3) detecting and controlling locomotion. In each of these ways, vision may pick up (a) only gross differences, (b) intermediate differences, or (c) all these plus small and subtle differences.

Detecting the Layout of the Surroundings

• SKY-EARTH DISCRIMINATION. One of the simple invariants of nature is the law of strong light from above and weak light from below. As we noted in Chapter 1 and again in Chapter 4, this difference is ordinarily coincident with the pull of gravity and the push of the substratum. The animal with mere photoreceptive spots on its outer skin can orient to the sky-earth differential by keeping its upper eyespots more strongly stimulated than its lower ones. Note that, in our terms, this is already a response to a difference of light in different directions, to an array, not simply a response to "light." It is detection of an invariant, not a response to energy; a *sky*tropism, not a *photo*tropism; and it is registered by the *relation* between stimulated eyespots, not by the stimulation of an eyespot.

Under the sea, as well as on land, the strongest light comes from above (see Figure 9.1). In a medium of water it is true that the "sky" is not a hemisphere, as it is in a medium of air, but instead is a cone of about 98° angle (Walls, 1942, p. 378). This is because light from the sky outside this cone is reflected instead of being refracted into the water. Nevertheless this cone of greater intensity, this "window," as Wall terms it, is the underwater equivalent of the overarching sky, at any depth, and serves the same purpose for orientation. The sky is smaller for the fish than for the lizard but it is always above.

• DETECTING THE GROSS FEATURES OF THE ENVIRONMENT. The sky-earth difference is the primitive one but there are also smaller differences in

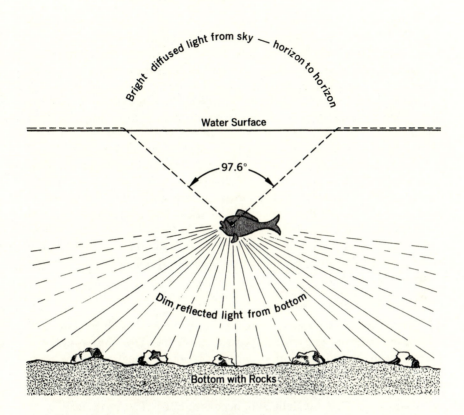

Figure 9.1 The ambient light in the underwater environment. The invariant features of this kind of an optic array must have governed the evolution of ocular systems in aquatic animals. The bottom would not be visible in deep water but the cone of light coming from the sky would be constant. Information about the flat or rippled character of the surface would be specified by the presence or absence of motion in this cone. (Adapted from G. L. Walls, *The Vertebrate Eye,* Cranbrook Institute of Science, Bulletin No. 19, 1942.)

ambient light. For example, the sky may be occluded by an obstacle in a certain direction. This will be specified by a darker patch in the array, and such a dark patch will mean a "thing." On level terrain the surface of the earth is structured by rocks and vegetation and this will be specified by some sort of patchwork in the lower hemisphere of the total array (see Figure 9.2). On a sloping terrain the patchwork will have a different arrangement than it will on a level terrain. Vision will permit the animal to distinguish the geographical layout, at least grossly, if it can register the geometrical arrangement. Vision may also permit the animal to distinguish the character of these surfaces — for example, earth *versus* water — and which of them therefore provides footing. It will even enable the animal to detect a falling-off place or cliff in the substratum if his ocular system can pick up the information that specifies it.

• IDENTIFYING OBJECTS AND OTHER ANIMALS IN THE ENVIRONMENT. The detachable, separated, movable parts of the environment that Berkeley called "bodies" are only parts of it, not the whole. The ground or air from which objects are detached cannot be neglected, although we tend to do so. The detachment of objects from their background has to be specified somehow in the ambient light. If the objects are either small or far away, they are hard to identify. If they move spontaneously, they are apt to be other animals. If not, they are apt to be sticks and stones and things of that sort. Obviously it is very useful to be able to distinguish among them and to locate them, and the farther off the better. But this requires a highly developed visual system, for the distant ones are specified only by the fine structure of ambient light.

Detecting Change or Sequence

• DISTINGUISHING DAY FROM NIGHT. The environment has always had lawful changes in time as well as a lawful geometry. The diurnal cycle of alternating light and dark, of strong and weak illumination, is the most obvious of these changes. It correlates with higher and lower temperature, and many other ecological and biological rhythms. Many animals wake up when stimulated by light and become active. The gross change of illumination with sunrise and sunset is analogous to the crude difference of intensity at the horizon of earth and sky, although one is a difference of sequential order and the other is a difference of adjacent order. Both kinds of differentiation are information about the world, even if the contrast is only between day-night and up-down. It is merely two-alternative information instead of many-alternative information. Eyes with high acuity are not needed to pick up this information — only the simplest eyespots connected to a simple nervous system.

• DETECTING GROSS MOTIONS IN THE WORLD. A single photoreceptive organ serves to pick up a change of illumination such as is caused by the covering of the sun by a cloud or the hiding of the sky by something approaching from above. Abrupt darkening as such, merely as a flicker, is useful information. But this is not the information given by motion. A looming silhouette in the optic array is more useful; it is specific information for something approaching. Is it approaching from the right or from the left? For obtaining this perception a group or mosaic of photoreceptors is needed, and the transformation of their individual flickers has to be sent into the nervous system. With directional photoreceptors and a more

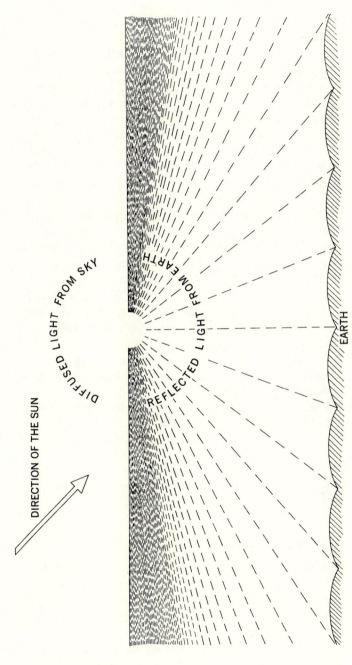

Figure 9.2 The ambient light in a terrestrial environment. The structure of the array represented is general, or abstract — that is, it would be the same at any other station-point on the earth's surface. The principal invariants to be noted are (1) the *greater intensity* of light in the upper hemisphere of the array than in the lower, (2) the *texture* of the light in the lower hemisphere as against the upper, and (3) the increase in density of texture in the lower hemisphere outward from its center. The material texture of the earth is represented simply by regular adjacent humps whose size is not specified. The fact that the actual substratum is structured at various levels of size from grains to hills is not represented, nor is the fact that it is differentially colored. This diagram will be discussed again in Chapter 10.

complex nervous system the distinguishing of simple transformations in the optic array becomes possible, and thereby some perception of the direction in which a thing moves in space. Note that an optical transformation is a correlation of arrangement and sequence, a pattern that changes in a regular order, not a disorderly array of flickering regions such as can be observed in the scintillation or "snow" of a mistuned television screen.

• DISTINGUISHING AMONG MOTIONS AND EVENTS IN THE WORLD. When the environment is illuminated, nothing can move without the fact being broadcast in the network of intersecting rays that fills the medium (Chapter 1, p. 12). The flutter of a leaf, the fall of an acorn, the twitching of a tail, and the lifting of a man's eyebrow, not to mention larger movements, are specified in the flux wherever the lines of sight are not intercepted. Only the motion of the wind is invisible. The motion of an object is by no means copied in the motion of the light rays, it is true, but it is specified by exact and elaborate laws of perspective. The ambient light coming to the position of an animal, therefore, carries a vast amount of information about what is going on around him. A certain scurrying motion specifies prey; another special motion specifies the courtship display of a mate; a peculiar rippling of light specifies a surface of water. The ambient array with transformation carries more information than the same array without transformation. The *form of motion* often specifies more than the *form as such*, as will be shown in the next chapter.

There is evidence to suggest that a visual system can have good acuity for distinguishing among the forms of motion in ambient light without necessarily having high acuity for distinguishing among the static forms. The compound systems of certain insects like the spider seem to be examples of this type. Man has fairly acute vision for both, but we are so preoccupied with form as such that we take for granted the subtleties of transformation in our field of view.

In varying degrees, then, vision makes possible the perception of objective motion. But it also is used for the detection and control of subjective movement, that is, the movement of the animal himself in the environment.

Detecting and Controlling Locomotion

• REGISTERING LOCOMOTION. Animals that swim or fly have the problem of how to avoid being carried away from their accustomed habitat by a flow of the medium — water or air. A fish in a stream or a bird in a wind must, like the Red Queen in *Alice in Wonderland,* run in order to stay in the same place. Turning upstream or upwind is an automatic response in this situation, and it is governed by the balance of mechanoreceptive stimulation, but this rheotropism, as it is called, is not enough. The only way the animal can stay in the same place is to anchor himself visually to the bed of the stream or the terrain of the earth. He must be able to register *optical* flow as well as airflow. The flow of the whole array of ambient light away from the pole that coincides with the direction of locomotion is less familiar than the flow of a current, but more predictable (Gibson, Olum, and Rosenblatt, 1955). This panoramic streaming is an unfailing index of locomotion with respect to the earth (see Figure 9.3). and the absence of streaming is an absolute index of non-locomotion. The way to keep from drifting with the tide of water or air is to cancel the optical flow. If it expands ahead and contracts behind, one is "gaining

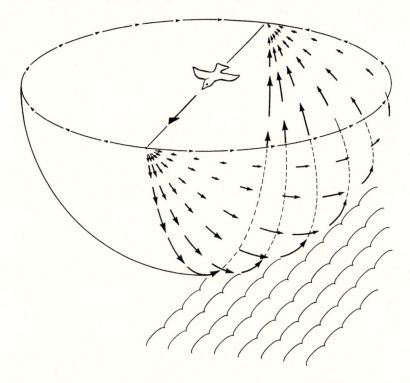

Figure 9.3   The flow of the optic array during locomotion in a terrestrial environment. When a bird moves parallel to the earth, the texture of the lower hemisphere of the optic array flows under its eyes in the manner shown. The flow is centrifugal ahead and centripetal behind — i.e., there are focuses of expansion and contraction at the two poles of the line of locomotion. The greatest velocity of backward flow corresponds to the nearest bit of the earth and the other velocities decrease outward from this perpendicular in all directions, vanishing at the horizon. The vectors in this diagram represent angular velocities. The flow pattern contains a great deal of information.

ground"; if it contracts ahead and expands behind, one is "losing ground."

A visual system does not have to be sensitive to fine detail in order to register this flow pattern, especially if the system is highly panoramic. The seeing of small landmarks is not required; only the overall streaming of gross structure need be detected. A relatively small number of directional photoreceptors each accepting a different cone of the total array might serve. Some insects and crustaceans possess no more.

The flow pattern of ambient light should be distinguished from the rotation of ambient light around the animal. The former specifies translocation of the animal from one place to another; the latter specifies turning of the animal in the same place. Actually a rotation of the array relative to the animal is always caused by a rotation of the animal relative to the array, except in a certain experimental circumstance never found in life. The animal takes rotation as information for being turned, as when, for example, he is whirled around by an eddy in the medium. This was illustrated in Figure 2.1.

Consequently, if an animal is put on a small platform at the center of a textured cylindrical environment which is then artificially rotated, he shows what are called optokinetic reflexes, (or compulsory optokinetic nystagmus). Their function again, is to keep the animal anchored to the optical environment for as much of the time as possible. In this experiment there is no stimulus information from the statocyst organs, only information from the eyes. We shall return to this experiment when describing compensatory reactions.

• GUIDING LOCOMOTION. It is useful to be able to see whether or not one is moving; it is better to be able to see vaguely where one is going; it is best to be able to see exactly where one is going. Visually guided locomotion is a matter of going to a specific goal in the environment, and this requires that the goal be identified in the array of ambient light. The form in the array on which the focus of expansion is centered corresponds to the place toward which the animal is proceeding. If it is the right form — if it specifies prey, or a mate, or home — all he has to do is magnify it in order to reach the object. He governs the muscles of locomotion so as to enlarge the form, to make it loom up. The same rule of visual approach holds true for swimming, flying, or running: keep the focus of centrifugal flow centered on the part of the pattern of the optic array that specifies the attractive thing or the inviting place. The controlling rules for steering among obstacles, for avoiding collision, and for stopping without collision are all related to this rule for aiming locomotion. The cybernetics of pursuit, evasive flight, and landing depends on the pickup of certain invariants in the optical flow pattern (Gibson, 1958). The human aircraft pilot must learn to detect them, but the bird and the bee, with their panoramic eyes, seem to find it easy to do so.

• COMPLEX FEEDBACK. When the forms of an optic array at one station-point are supplemented with all possible transformations to other station-points, and when sequence over time is added to order in space and all motions are considered, it is obvious that the specifying capacity of this super-stimulus is unlimited (Gibson, 1961). It is an inexhaustible reservoir of potential information about the world and about the individual's behavior in it. Vision can develop into the dominant system in our species, the "queen of the senses," because the opportunities for perception are so vast. When *sequence* is combined with *scene*, vision makes possible the achieving of geographical orientation, the feats of navigation over time, and the cognitive mapping of the environment. It also makes possible the control of skilled movements and the coordination of hand with eye in primates. In man, the ability to control the movements of the hand by vision has led to picture-making and even to ideographic or phonetic writing, from which a new level of cognition emerges. There is visual feedback at all levels of activity: upright posture, locomotion, homing, and the control of vehicles; manipulation, tool-using, mechanical problem-solving, and graphic representation. As the informative feedback becomes differentiated the skill can become learned.

The foregoing ninefold classification of the uses of vision is not exhaustive. It is offered to illustrate the opportunities for development of visual organs and their neuromuscular systems, and the possibilities for exploiting the information in light. The classification should also loosen our human and historical fixation on the retinal *image* as the stimulus for seeing. We now turn to the evolution of visual organs.

The Evolution of Visual Systems

The distinction between receptors and organs has been emphasized in the preceding chapters. For vision it is the distinction between photo-receptors and eyes. A photoreceptor responds to light, usually to a beam of light coming from a certain direction if it is pointed in a certain direction. An eye responds to a sheaf of light beams each coming from a different direction. An optic array, the stimulus for an eye, consists of differences of light in different directions. How *many* differences in direction an eye can resolve depends on the anatomy and physiology of the organ.

There are two ways in which an eye could accept an array of converging beams of light coming from an environment, either with a convex mosaic of photoreceptors or with a concave mosaic of photoreceptors. The two ways are diagrammed in Figures 9.4 and 9.5. In the first case the receptors embrace a converging sheaf directly, whereas in the second case

Figure 9.4 **The acceptance of light rays by a convex or compound eye.** The receptors embrace a converging sheaf of "pencils" of light and register the differences in different directions.

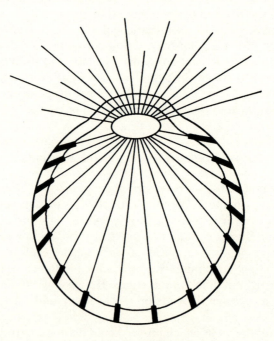

Figure 9.5 **The acceptance of light rays by a concave or camera eye.** Here also the eye embraces a converging sheaf of light rays, but the receptors register differences in different directions by means of an inverted image formed by a lens.

they encompass the diverging sheaf of rays after it has converged. The first case is unfamiliar except as it is partly exemplified in the recent study of fiber optics. The second case is a familiar one in optics, involving the formation of an inverted image on a surface. The image is often compared to the picture formed on the plate of a photographic camera. In the first case, however, no image is formed — at least nothing that could possibly be *seen* in the way that a retinal image can be seen by peeling off the back of an eye taken from a butchered ox and looking at the translucent retina. Nevertheless, in both cases, in the convex eye as much as in the concave eye, *the adjacent order in the external array is preserved in the order of stimulation at the receptor mosaic.* What-is-next-to-what remains constant; there is no shuffling or permutation of order. It is true that the order is inverted by the concave eye and not by the convex eye but this is a matter of no consequence.

The eye as we know it best — the concave, chambered, or camera eye — is a possession of vertebrates, the animals with internal skeletons (Walls, 1942). The convex eye, known as a compound eye, is a characteristic of arthropods, the animals with external skeletons. These two phyla diverged a long time ago and have provided perhaps the two mainstreams of animal evolution. The higher vertebrates like the birds and mammals have efficient vision by means of a concave retina; the higher arthropods like the bees have efficient vision by means of a convex mosaic. Another phylum, the molluscs, includes certain forms that abandoned their protective shells and became free-swimming, the squids and octopuses. These also have efficient eyes of the concave type. They were evolved independently of vertebrate eyes and show fundamental differences, but the characteristics of the camera (the pupil, lens, and chamber) are common to both and are cited as an example of convergent evolution. It is a fair guess, however, that the convergence of eye development in the vertebrate fish and the invertebrate squids was governed by the necessity of choosing either one or the other of two optical systems.

The three kinds of eye are shown schematically in Figures 9.6, 9.7, and 9.8. They are the culmination of a long history, and they had to be constructed or compounded out of simpler organs. The lower animals do not have eyes at all, as the term is here used, but only eyespots, ocelli, or directional photoreceptors (see Figure 9.9).

The Simplest Visual Systems

A minimum photoreceptor must consist of cells containing photochemicals at the branching terminals of an ingoing neuron. Actually a number of photosensitive pigment cells are gathered together in a cup or vesicle and several nerve fibers are usually grouped in a bundle. Moreover, even in the simplest eyespots of animals like the jellyfish, the photosensitive

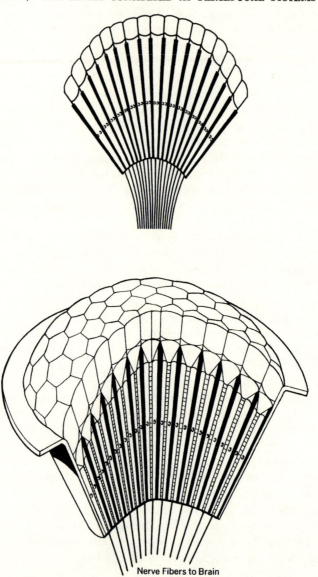

Figure 9.6 The compound eye of an arthropod. Essentially, this organ is a set of narrow tubes called ommatidia, each one insulated from every other. Hundreds or thousands of them may be packed together. The three-dimensional cutaway drawing shows how each tube points to a different direction in space. (After Hesse. From R. Buchsbaum, *Animals Without Backbones*, University of Chicago Press, 1948. Reprinted by permission.)

material is screened so as to prevent light from falling on it from all directions. Often the vesicle is a tiny shaded chamber with a relatively small opening so that the receptor is highly selective in direction. And usually the opening is filled with a bulge or thickening of transparent cuticle which is called a lens and can be seen under a microscope. But the function of this lens is certainly not to form an image; it is only to gather more luminous energy than could otherwise be obtained through a small opening and concentrate it on the little cluster of photosensitive cells. This is analogous to the use of a lens as a burning-glass, not to its use as an information projector in an optical instrument. The eyespot or ocellus of lower animals has the *form* of a subminiature camera but not the *function* of one. It is this crude similarity of form, I believe, that has misled zoologists into calling the organ an eye when it should have been thought of as merely a directional photoconcentrator.

A number of these primitive organs on the surface of an organism will enable it to get some information in ambient light, at least the information in the difference between earth and sky. There is an advantage in having many of them instead of only a few, since the number of different ambient patterns that can be registered as nervous patterns increases enormously; the number of possible changes of pattern that can be registered, the form of motion, likewise goes up. The more photoreceptors an animal has, the closer it can come to seeing, the more motions it can distinguish, and the more it can govern its locomotion. The pressure in the course of evolution, then, was to increase the number and density of these simple organs. On the other hand, there was also pressure to increase the efficiency of the

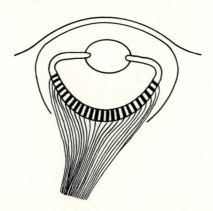

Figure 9.7 The chambered eye of a mollusc. This organ has a lens which forms an image on a retina of photosensitive elements and receptive units, connected by a tract of nerve fibers to the animal's brain.

organs as such, and to improve their capacity to gather light in dim illumination by enlarging the lens and multiplying the sensitive elements.

These two pressures were contradictory, for the following reason. If
the little chambers were to be multiplied and packed together they had
to remain small, but if each chamber was to be packed with photosensitive
elements they had to become large. This can explain, I think, why the
convex or compound eye was an alternative to the concave or camera eye,
and why the two lines of evolution diverged. The arthropod developed
eyes by *multiplying* ocelli; the early vertebrates and the later molluscs
developed eyes by *enlarging* ocelli. The compounding of directional receptors required that they become elongated and thin, each in the form of
an ommatidium (Figure 9.6). The elaborating of a directional receptor
required a large lens, pupil, and a many-celled retina for registering
details of the image, but at the cost of having only one organ on each side.
The lower animals have experimented with all possible shapes and structures of these pre-ocular organs (Milne and Milne, 1959) but true eyes
seem to have evolved only in the above two ways.

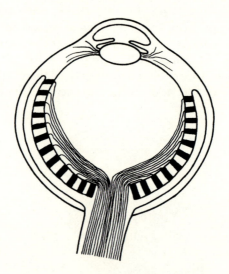

Figure 9.8   The chambered eye of a vertebrate. This organ
also has an image-forming lens but the retina is *inside out* as compared to the mollusc eye. That is, the nerve fibers from the receptive units are gathered together in front of the retina, not behind it,
and emerge through a hole in the retina. The vertebrate optic nerve
thus constitutes a flexible cable, an arrangement that permits the
eyeball to be freely mobile within its bony orbit.

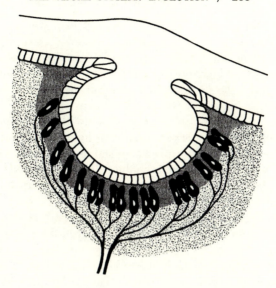

Figure 9.9   An ocellus or eyespot. The light-gathering vesicle illustrated is one of many kinds found in lower organisms. This one is found in the horseshoe crab. It is tiny and the drawing has been much enlarged. (Limulus after De Moll. Redrawn by Lorus and Margery Milne, in Chapter 14 of *Handbook of Physiology*, Vol. I, *Neurophysiology*, The American Physiological Society, 1959. By permission.)

The Evolution of Ocular Systems in Vertebrates

The chambered eyes of our own relatives, from fish to mammals, have been studied in great detail. They are all built to a standard plan, as we shall observe, but even so they are astonishingly various in different orders of vertebrate animals. Some of these ocular systems, and the corresponding ways of seeing or looking, are radically unlike our own. They are all adaptations to an environment and a way of life, and these differ. Each system is said to be "a cluster of harmonious parts and the changes which have converted one type of eye into another through evolution have necessarily involved most of its parts [with] the whole complex remaining harmonious and workable at all times. It is now possible to tell a well-connected story of the evolution of almost any particular vertebrate eye" (Walls, 1942, p. iv).

It will be worthwhile to consider at length some of the factors that have governed the development of these visual systems and some of the expedients adopted by different animals for seeing what they needed to see.

In this context the peculiarities of the eyes of man will be more understandable.

• POSTURAL STABILIZATION OF THE EYES. Vertebrate eyes are set in sockets of the skull called orbits, and the posture of the eyes therefore does not have to be the same as the posture of the head. It is very useful to be able to turn the head without having to turn the eyes, for when they are turned they lose their orientation to the surroundings. Eyes need to be anchored to the array of ambient light as much of the time as possible if they are to work. In order to stabilize the eyes without being forced to stabilize the head, or immobilize the whole body, the animal must make a compensatory rotation of the eyes for every rotation of the head. Eye movement and head movement need to be reciprocal. Vertebrates meet this need more efficiently than arthropods or molluscs do, for the eyes of the latter are more closely attached to the neighboring tissue of the body or, as in bees, are rigid parts of the head. Some arthropod crustaceans have had to develop eyestalks to make the eyes mobile.

The posture of the vertebrate eye is governed by three balanced pairs of muscles and these are controlled by the three pairs of semicircular canals that register turns of the head. As a result of this, and other supplementary neural hookups, the eyes compensate for a turn on any axis — a yaw, pitch, or roll, or any combination of these. The result is compensatory nystagmus, the adaptive kind of nystagmus that keeps the eyes oriented to the fixed features of the world (Chapter 4). If the turning of the head continues beyond an angle for which the eyes can compensate, they jerk to a new stable posture and once again maintain it.

Figure 9.10 shows the placement of the eyes in a typical fish, with the field of view of each eye indicated. Note that the binocular system can pick up nearly the whole array of ambient light. When the fish turns right or left, up or down, or rolls on one side, the eyes counter-rotate. Midway during a turning maneuver the eyes will jump ahead to a new posture and then continue to counter-rotate until the body has caught up to their new posture. For only a brief moment are they out of touch with the array. Fundamentally, this is the way the eyes work in any vertebrate whatever.

For the great majority of fishes and many other animals, this is the *only* way the eyes can move relative to the head. There is no need for exploratory eye movements — that is, for scanning the array by successive fixations — since these animals have no especially acute foveal areas in the retinas and no centers of clear vision to correspond. They see equally well in all directions, and they do not have to "look" in order to see. This is a kind of visual perception which we, as human lookers with frontal eyes, may find it very hard to conceive, but it is a kind that is much more common than our own.

The orienting of the eyes to the array explains the experimental arousal of optokinetic reflexes in animals when the environment is rotated around

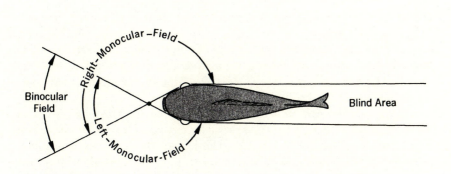

Figure 9.10   The total field of view of a typical fish. Each eye embraces more than a hemisphere of the ambient array, so that there is a double registration of the field in front and nearly panoramic vision. (After G. L. Walls, *The Vertebrate Eye*, Cranbrook Institute of Science, Bulletin No. 19, 1942.)

them, as noted above. Vertebrates adjust by nystagmus of the eyes, whereas crustaceans and insects must do so by movements of the head or of the whole body, but all, in one way or another, try to keep in contact with the structure of light.

• THE FOCUSING OF A DEFINITE IMAGE. During the millions of years when the prevertebrates were converting a light-gathering vesicle into an image-forming chamber (if this is what they did), the development of the lens mechanism and of the retinal mosaic must have gone hand in hand. A retinal image need be no better than the neural equipment behind it, and the differential capacities of the retina cannot be more exact than the image formed on it. The primitive lens had only to gather a cone of light and concentrate it on a sensitive area, but the advanced lens had to preserve the differences of light in different directions within this cone by reducing to a minimum what we call *blur*. The primitive retina with its small bundle of neurons had only to *summate* the input of its photosensitive elements, but the advanced retina had to *differentiate* the input by groups and subgroups of elements, and also by the sequence-groupings of elements that specified motions. The retina developed not only by multiplying the elements of the anatomical mosaic but also by grouping them in overlapping functional units for detecting information. These are the *receptive units* described in Chapter 2.

As eyes got larger and the retinas included more and more elements and groupings the shape of the lens became more critical than before. Moreover, when the width and focal length of the lens increased sufficiently, there arose a need for accommodating it differently for the near and the far environment, since the "depth of focus" of a large lens is reduced. As more light was admitted to the chamber and the elements became more sensitive, the need also arose for a contractile pupil of some sort to moderate the intensity in high illumination. The variable-focus lens and the variable pupil are interrelated, and both are connected with the development of retinal elements for dim illumination (rods) and retinal elements for bright illumination (cones).

Accommodation can be achieved either by moving the lens toward or away from the retina, as it is in fish, or by changing its curvature, as it is in mammals (Walls, 1942, Ch. 10). The lens of the fish's eye is not lens-shaped but spherical, and it has to be so strongly curved because the supplementary focusing power of the cornea, which works well in a medium of air, will not work at all in a medium of water. For either kind of accommodation (see Figure 9.11), it should be noted, the muscular reaction is an adjustment to the "blur" of the retinal image, and it is significant that even the simple retina of a fish registers blur and minimizes it, or to put it the other way, causes the lens mechanism to hunt for the maximal "sharpness" of the image, which presumably yields the best pickup of the potential structural information in the external array. The neural system of feedback that brings about this optimal state of sharpness is a fascinating puzzle for neurophysiology. Note that it is not a "reflex," if by this is meant a response to a simple punctate stimulus.

As Walls (1942) points out, "the small eye needs no accommodation at all" (p. 254) and not all vertebrate eyes accommodate for distance. The comparison of eyes with cameras or projectors is misleading, and the investigators of human vision, where the eye is not very large, have overstated the importance of focusing the lens, as if it were like the focusing of a picture on a screen. The human eye loses most of its power of accommodation at the age of 50 or 60, but if it was normal to begin with it remains a fairly efficient organ. There are some vertebrate eyes, Walls suggests, that escape the need for accommodation entirely by means of a sloping retina which keeps the ground in focus at different distances, like the "ramp retina" of the horse (p. 225).

The retinal image, thus, is simply a method of getting some of the information in light, and only one method at that, although a good one potentially. The retinal image is a stimulus for a retina but not the stimulus for an eye and certainly not for an ocular system. It is a long way from being analogous to a picture. The *structural* properties of a retinal image are what count, not its *visible* properties. Structurally, it should not be called an *image* at all, for that term suggests something to be seen. *The structure of a retinal image is a sample of the structure of ambient light, obtained indirectly from an inverse ray-sheaf,* as was shown in Figure 9.5.

The use of an image (in the pictorial sense) for producing an array will be discussed in Chapter 11. It is usually a matter of reproducing a

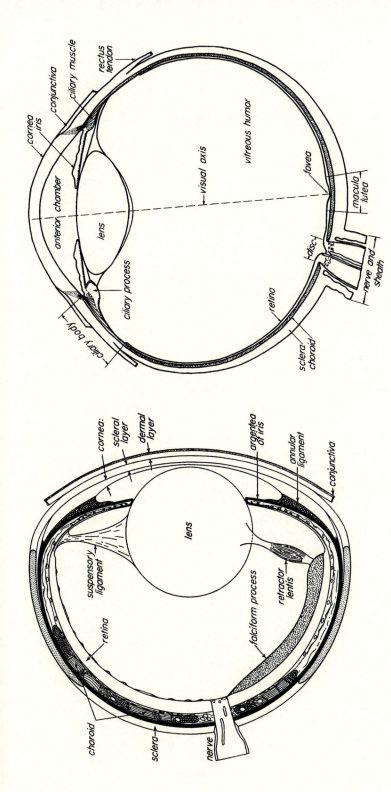

Figure 9.11 The eye of a fish and that of a mammal. The eye of a teleost (left; a vertical section) can be compared here to the right eye of a man (right; a horizontal section). The shape of the lens is quite different, the focusing mechanism is different, and the human eye has a fovea. (From G. L. Walls, *The Vertebrate Eye*, Cranbrook Institute of Science, Bulletin No. 19, 1942.)

particular array that an artist wishes to preserve for the benefit of other observers.

• THE USES OF FRONTAL EYES AND LATERAL EYES. The fish shown diagrammatically in Figure 9.10 has lateral eyes with some overlap of the binocular fields in front. This is typical of many animals, including terrestrial ones. Other animals, such as the carnivorous cats, have eyes placed in more nearly frontal orbits of the skull and thus obtain much greater overlap of the binocular fields. The advantage of lateral eyes is that they afford a more nearly panoramic field of view. The advantage of frontal eyes is that they afford a double assurance of information pickup in a wider angle of the field ahead. Preyed-upon animals generally have lateral eyes while predatory animals generally have frontal eyes. It would be useful to have both advantages, of course, but they conflict. The various adaptations or anatomical expedients that have developed are described by Walls (1942, Ch. 10).

One compromise is to widen the scope of each eye. The horse, for example, has nearly complete panoramic vision but also a considerable binocular overlap because each single eye can see through an angle of 215°. The rabbit, defenseless and watchful, is said actually to have binocular overlap in the region behind the head as well as that in front of it. For him light is a truly global stimulus. No one can sneak up on a rabbit from behind.

Note that a tendency toward frontal eyes does not imply that the eyes necessarily point to the front, nor does binocular overlap in the frontal array necessarily imply "binocular vision" in the human sense of the term. Eye-pointing is a separate and distinct capacity. Frontal eyes do not always have concentrated foveas. The literature of vision is muddled and confusing about binocular pickup. But it seems clear that a horse, for example, can turn both eyes more or less to the front without fixating both eyes on the same detail of the array. Frontal vision with two eyes can be useful merely as two hands are useful in touching things; they yield an extra input of the same information, a redundancy of input which helps perception. Eyes can be turned forward without being fixated forward.

The compulsory convergence of the centers of both eyes on the same bit of the world is a characteristic of the primates and man, and it probably goes with the effort to use a separate and distinct kind of information about the layout of things, that given by the *disparity* of the overlapping arrays which coexists along with their identity.

• THE ADVANTAGE OF CONCENTRATING THE RECEPTORS IN SPECIAL REGIONS. As eyes became more efficient in the course of evolution, providing better adaptation to the special environment in which they operated, the nervous equipment behind the eyes had to become more elaborate too. The system as a whole became more acute. But there were alternative ways of using this discriminative capacity, (1) by dispersing the resources of the system evenly over the whole array encompassed by the eye, or (2) by concentrating these resources in a smaller region and sacrificing it in the remainder. This principle held for the compound eye as well as for the chambered eye. A retinal area where the receptors are somewhat concentrated is called a macula, and a small one where the receptors are densely concentrated is called a fovea. The human retina has a fovea that corresponds to the subjective *center of clear vision,* or the external *point of fixation.* That beam of light which falls on the fovea determines the *gaze-line* or what is sometimes vaguely called the *line of sight.*

Certain directions-from-here, in which things need to be seen, are more important than other directions, depending on the animal's way of life. The general direction *ahead* is often more significant than the direction *behind,* as already noted. The direction *above* may be more significant for some species than the direction *below,* but this significance can be reversed for other species. The directions *to the right* and *to the left* would seem to be equally significant for all species. Evenly dispersed panoramic vision in all directions is therefore wasteful, and some animals adapted to this fact by concentrating the resources of each eye, that is, by a tendency toward foveation.

But note that the full development of frontal eyes with foveas must be accompanied by the development of the ability to *look* — that is, to explore the optic array by scanning it. If panoramic vision is restricted, the ability to look around must be substituted. The parts of the array must be fixated in succession; there must be exploration and selection of certain items of interest to the neglect of other items. This is nothing less than visual attention; it demands what physiologists have called "voluntary" eye movements, although the term is unfortunate. The exploratory fixations can be carried out by the eyes alone in vertebrates with freely mobile eyes; otherwise they must be performed with the head, as happens in many birds, or with the whole body, as happens in many arthropods. Exploration makes possible a better overall registration of the ambient light, but only over time, since the simultaneous registration of the whole array has been partially sacrificed. This temporal integration has been considered a puzzle. If it is conceived as a process of remembering retinal images, the process is made to seem an advanced intellectual achievement. It is surely not that, for it began in the fish. This problem of scanning will be considered more fully in Chapter 12.

The evolution of visual attention began early, but it did not take the same course in all species and it did not end up with the same kind of visual attention that we primates have developed. Some fish have centers of acute vision in each eye pointing outward to each side and thus can "look" with either eye or, probably, with both eyes at the same time. Some birds (see Figure 9.12, for example) have two foveas in each eye, one for fixation to the side and another for fixation forward. Other birds have a strip fovea, a band of concentration in each retina such that a horizon of clear vision results (Prince, 1956, p. 798). Still other expedients are possible, such as that of the "four-eyed fish" who can see both above and below the surface of water. The varieties of foveation are described by Walls (1942, Ch. 10). Indivisible concentration or fixation of visual attention is surely not the only kind; attention can be divided or distributed simultaneously in several ways.

The need for developing an eye that could fixate, even though it had to jump about in order to explore, carried with it a special advantage — it made possible the fixation of a moving object in the environment. The ability to follow a moving object, to "track" it with the gaze-line, was

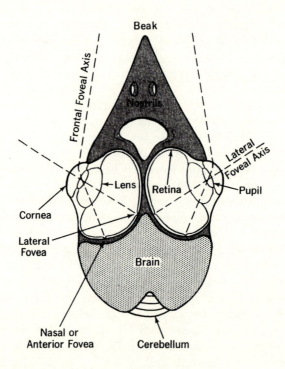

Figure 9.12   The eyes of a barn swallow showing three directions of especially acute vision. A horizontal section is shown. The bird can fixate straight ahead, to the left, and to the right, simultaneously. It also can see nearly all the way around at once. The eyes can rotate in the head, but only through a small angle. (After S. L. Polyak, *The Vertebrate Visual System,* University of Chicago Press, 1957. By permission.)

useful, since it thus became easier to distinguish detail in the moving patch of the array and to classify the source as inanimate or animate, as friend or enemy, and as predator or prey. The eyes did not have to be at the front of the head, of course, for this ability to develop. This *pursuit movement* of the eye, as it is called, could be developed from the slow phase of the compensatory nystagmus. The quick exploratory movement of the eye from one stationary fixation to another, the *saccadic movement*, could be developed from the fast phase of the nystagmus.

• THE ADVANTAGE OF COMPULSORY CONVERGENCE OF BOTH EYES. With eyes having central foveas and also a frontal position in the head, the stage was set for our particular style of visual attention, the coordinated pointing of both eyes. Primates need to look at their hands, or whatever the hands grasp. The gaze-lines converge so that both foveas register the same detail. As the eyes move upward toward the horizon, the convergence lessens until the gaze-lines are parallel, but they can never diverge from parallel. There is double assurance of seeing with a fovea, but the eyes have lost their independence. The anatomical arrangement that goes with this style of vision is shown in Figure 9.13.

Each eye can no longer explore the array on its own, for the saccadic movements have what is called compulsory conjugation. Rotations are equal in angle and synchronized. This is necessary, of course, if the fixations are to coincide at the end of a movement. The same is true of pursuit movements. The human ocular system has been compared to the front wheels of an automobile — the eyes move as if connected by an invisible tie-rod, and the analogy is heightened by the fact that both have a certain degree of toe-in, or convergence.

The nervous equipment necessary for the delicate balancing of the eye muscles in this automatic converging and conjugating must obviously be exact and subtle. If convergence is to be maintained at all times, the system has to register even the slightest mismatch of detail at the two foveas so as to correct it. The center of the pattern of the optic array entering one eye has to coincide with the center of the pattern of the array entering the other eye. The forms at the two foveas have to be congruent forms, and the system has to detect incongruence of form in order to maintain convergence. As the eyes move upward from the hands, to the ground nearby, to the distant horizon, the convergence of the gaze-lines must always be relaxed just enough to eliminate disparity of pattern at the foveas.

The neurophysiology of this adjustment is another fascinating puzzle. It is called a "fusion-reflex" — wrongly, I think, because that implies an operation of putting one pictorial sensation on top of another.

The optic array from the terrain to one eye cannot, however, be made wholly congruent with the optic array from the same terrain to the other

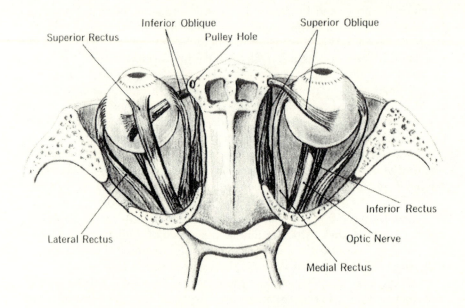

Figure 9.13   The human binocular equipment. This is the oculomotor system of man as seen from above in a dissected head. The flexible cables of the optic nerves are shown, together with the partial crossing-over of their fibers at the optic chiasma. The pairs of opposing eye muscles are labeled. On the left, a portion of the *superior oblique* has been cut away to reveal the *inferior oblique.* On the right, the *superior rectus* has been removed to reveal the *inferior rectus* under the optic nerve, Note how each oblique muscle operates by means of a tendon running through a hole or pulley in the side of the bony orbit. (After G. L. Walls, *The Vertebrate Eye,* Cranbrook Institute of Science, Bulletin No. 19, 1942.)

eye. As Figure 9.14 shows, there will always be disparity of pattern outward from the center if the world slants away. One array is skewed relative to the other by a slight perspective transformation. And by inexorable laws of perspective the distribution of disparity in the two overlapping arrays specifies the layout of the surfaces from which the light is reflected. If a binocular system can register the disparity, it can register information about the environmental layout.

In human observers binocular disparity can be studied experimentally with a stereoscope, and the resulting perception of pictorial depth is taken to demonstrate stereoscopic vision or, more properly, *binocular* stereoscopic vision. Primates other than man have not yet been tested with

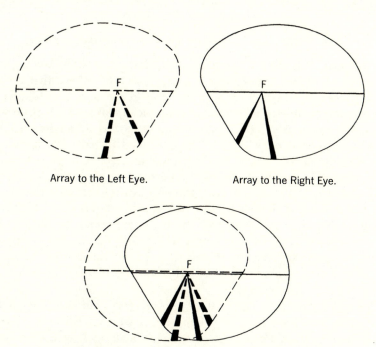

Array to the Left Eye.   Array to the Right Eye.

Disparity of the Two Arrays when Fixating the Horizon.

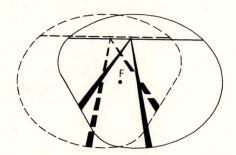

Disparity of the Two Arrays when Fixating a Near Point.

Figure 9.14   The disparity between the optic array admitted to one eye and that admitted to the other. The observer is look-ing down a road to the horizon. The left eye is closer to the left-hand side of the road; the right eye to the right-hand side of the road. The array in one eye is skewed relative to that in the other, and the disparity increases from the horizon down to the locus of the observer's own body, as shown. When the observer's eyes con-verge and fixate on the road 30° downward from the horizon, the disparity above this point changes in sign but the skew relations are not altered. Note that these diagrams are cross-sections of the light sampled by each eye, not retinal images. (After Gibson, 1950.)

stereoscopes (it is hard to get an ape to look into one, or to know what he would see if he did!), but there is every reason to believe that they can use disparity information for getting about in the trees and for the control of manipulation. The *simultaneous* pickup of two perspectives on the environment is a valuable supplement to the *successive* pickup of different perspectives, which will be described in the next chapter (see also, Gibson, 1950, Ch. 7). If the foregoing account is correct, animals other than primates must rely on the perspective of motion for unequivocal spatial information, whereas primates can rely on both the perspective of motion and the perspective of disparity. Squirrels and birds and flying insects seem to have excellent depth perception by means of the information resulting from motion parallax, but the depth perception of monkeys, apes, and man is doubly insured by the use of information resulting from binocular parallax. Historically, these have been called "cues" for depth perception.

Compulsory convergence of the eyes with conjugation of their shifting fixations is *necessary* for the pickup of disparity information. It is also *dependent* on the pickup of binocular mismatch, as I have tried to suggest. The adjustments depend on the detection and the detection depends on the adjustments. But the calibration of the system is fragile and frequently imperfect. The whole thing is a sort of perceptual luxury. A good many persons have some degree of imbalance of the eye muscles and accordingly do not perceive the extra depth in a stereoscopic picture that is geometrically afforded. In these persons the visual system fails to register the extra information. They do not really need it for perceiving depth in the environment, since they have motion parallax.

Compulsory convergence of the eyes, as contrasted with the merely optional convergence found in other animals, seems to entail a complete loss of the ability to perceive two different objects at the same time with two eyes, or two scenes at the same time. When each eye is given a different pattern, by optical trickery such as that of a haploscope, or by putting quite different pictures on the two sides of a stereoscope, the result is binocular rivalry in perception, one pattern supplanting or inhibiting the other. Non-primates, certainly animals with lateral eyes, should have no difficulty in seeing one pattern with the center of one eye and another pattern with the center of the other eye. Surely the rabbit who sees half the world with one eye and the other half with the other does not go blind in one eye when the other is in use.

• THE ADVANTAGES OF A NIGHT RETINA, A DAY RETINA, AND A DUPLEX RETINA. Little has been said so far about the photosensitive cells in a retina, the microscopic pigmented rods and cones that are packed into it at one of its many layers. They are the energy receivers as distinguished from the information receivers. More is known about the transduction of energy than about the translation of information, and we are mainly concerned with the latter. But we must not forget that there can be no information without some energy to carry it, even if only a minute quantity. There is no seeing in utter darkness.

The energy level of ambient light at night, an average night, is said to be on the order of a millionth of what it is in the day, an average day. The differences of intensity in different directions, accordingly, are very slight. Nevertheless the evolutionary pressure to be able to see at night was compelling, if only to detect patches or shadowy motions and loomings. The same held for seeing at dusk, or in the deep sea, or in caves. Hence, the developing of highly sensitive photoreceptors with very low energy thresholds had value for survival. In fact they were evolved, in the form of the rod-like cells found in vertebrate retinas (see Figure 9.15).

This trend in evolution, however, was contrary to another trend, since a maximum sensitivity to light is not compatible with a maximum acuity for information. Sensitivity is promoted at the expense of acuity. One reason for this is that an increased number of cells all connected to one fiber improves the chances of firing the fiber, by summation, but decreases the opportunity for multiplying the number of cell groups and subgroups in the retina. The greater the ratio of elements to the number of ingoing neurons, the less light is needed; but the greater the number of ingoing neurons, the more an image can be differentiated in various ways. The amount of this convergence of cells upon fibers in the human retina is estimated as about 100 to 1, since there are over 100 million rods and cones but only about one million fibers in an optic nerve. The known facts are given by Polyak (1957).

In the face of this alternative, some animals developed a rod-retina and adopted a nocturnal way of life. Others developed a cone retina and adopted a diurnal way of life. The former had to avoid the dazzling sunlight and confine their activity to the night because of day-blindness; the latter had to shelter at night and forage during the day because of night-blindness. These were only the extremes, however. A good many animals, like the primates, were able to compromise with a *duplex* retina containing both rods and cones, and to get along well enough in either a brightly or a dimly illuminated environment. The cones operate in the high-intensity range but they stop functioning and the rods take over in the low-intensity range.

The explanation of visual phenomena by the duplicity theory, the concept of two photochemical systems in one, is a great achievement of visual physiology. The facts of dark adaptation, with the associated loss of color discrimination, with the blindness in the foveal center of the field, and with the substitution of shadowy patches and motions for sharp textures and details, all fit neatly together with other facts. The

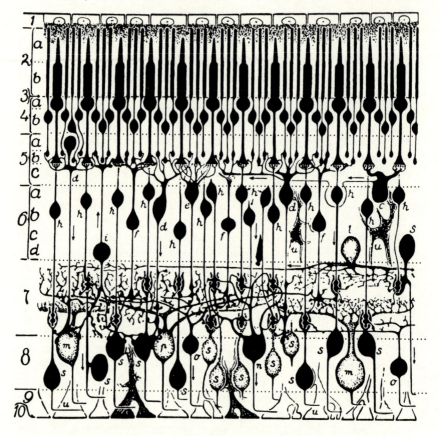

Figure 9.15 **The complexity of the microscopic layers of the human retina.** The rods and cones, the cells containing photochemicals, are at the top of the diagram. All the other layers of the retina consist of nerve cells that are probably grouped into complex overlapping receptive. units. The layer of long nerve fibers running from these units to the hole in the retina where the optic nerve emerges is below the bottom of the diagram. What is shown is the innermost layer, lying toward the interior of the eye. Nerve cells, being transparent, do not interfere with the focusing of an image on the outermost layer. (From S. L. Polyak, *The Retina*, University of Chicago Press, 1941. Reprinted by permission.)

theory is described in many textbooks, with applications to our own perceptions at night.

Other expedients besides the dual retina are possible in the attempt to register the surroundings despite the million-to-one variation in the intensity of light (Walls, 1942, Ch. 8, 9). The adjustment of the pupil is only one of these. There can be photomechanical changes in the retina as well as photochemical changes. Nocturnal animals often have a mirror behind the retina, the tapetum, to enhance the photon pickup; this explains the "eyeshine" of cats at night. All such adaptations, it seems to me, are intelligible as efforts to extract the information from the energy in light, and to keep the organ functioning without being either swamped by too much energy or stalled by too little.

• THE ADVANTAGES OF COLOR VISION. Finally, we come to the utility of being able to distinguish the colors of surfaces — to detect the color as well as the slant, the layout, and the shape. The meaning of the term *color* is one of the worst muddles in the history of science; the controversy will not be discussed here, but a definition must be given. I will use the term to mean the pigmentation of substances in the environment. This includes both the selective pigments that yield hues and the unselective pigments that yield black, gray, and white. In this sense of the term, the color of a thing helps to specify the material substance of it — that is, what the object is composed of. Hence the ability to discriminate colors is part of the more general ability to discriminate substances, as described in Chapters 6 and 7. It can arise merely as the ability to distinguish the black-white character of a surface — the proportion of light reflected from it (and this is probably possessed by all animals with good eyes) — and also as a more specialized ability to discriminate some of the chromatic qualities of a surface — the *differential* proportions of the *spectrum* of light reflected from it (and this has developed in different degrees in different animals).

As for the spectral "colors" which have been the concern of optics since Newton's discovery of the different components in sunlight, let us only note that there is no advantage whatever for any animal to be able to see rainbows, or sunsets, or spectral fringes at the edges of objects. He needs to detect the composition of substances at a distance, the pigment qualities of flowers and fruit, of feathers and fur, of rock and earth and vegetation. The "colors" of light as such, of mere illumination, are nothing to him. It is true that the colors of surfaces must be somehow specified in the "colors" of light. One can only see surfaces by means of light. It would follow that an observer cannot distinguish the colors of objects without having the incidental ability to distinguish the "colors" of the spectrum. But it does not follow that sensations of "pure color" are entailed in the seeing of surface color. The sensations are what I call useless dimensions of sensitivity. The problem is full of complexities and we will return to it in the next chapter.

Among vertebrate animals, the ability to see the texture and pigmentation of a surface is probably connected with the development of the cone system in their retinas — that is, the high-acuity daytime retina that functions only with strong illumination. Some species, notably the birds and the primates, seem to have developed a specialized cone system enabling them to see varieties and dimensions of chromatic pigmentation. (If it were not so, the colorful display of the peacock's plumage and the baboon's behind would be wasted on the eye of the beholder!) The retinal cones must have differentiated into three types, or perhaps four or even more, and arguments about this have a long history. We still do not fully understand the photochemistry of the cones, although it may soon be clarified (Graham, 1959).

Among the arthropods with compound eyes, the differences among surface pigments, especially those of flowers, are known to be perceived since they make a difference for behavior. But the flower colors seen by insects like the bee are surely different from those that we see, or those that any other vertebrate sees, inasmuch as the spectral sensitivity of the ommatidia extends into the ultraviolet wavelengths and falls short of the red wavelengths. The compound eye, in fact, registers not only a somewhat different spectrum of light but also a rather different sample of other information than does the camera eye. It can pick up the pattern of polarization of light from the sky, which is something our eyes cannot do at all (see Figure 10.16).

Summary

Visual systems presumably developed in order to take advantage of the information in ambient light. Eyes, including the nervous equipment to back them up, are of two general sorts: the convex or compound eye, and the concave or chambered eye. Both seem to have evolved from the simple ocellus of the lower organisms. In the arthropods, these photoceptors were multiplied so that each would register one direction. In the vertebrates and higher molluscs, the organs were reduced to a pair, each registering many directions by image-formation. But an eye does not have to focus a camera-like image in order to be a useful perceptual organ, as had been assumed. It need only register differences of light in different directions, as the compound eye does.

Lower animals pick up less of the available information than higher animals. The sky-earth difference is at one extreme and the millions of directional differences that we see are at another. As the distinguishing of spatial differences developed, so did the distinguishing of motions and the detecting of locomotion relative to the solid environment.

Different species of animals get somewhat different types of ambient information and sample it in different ways. Our way is not the only one.

Some have panoramic vision, some frontal. Some have dispersed sensitivity, some concentrated. Some do not fixate the eyes, some do. The primate visual system with compulsory convergence of both eyes on the same detail is a special type. It has its virtues, but the popular notion that our supplementary capacity for binocular depth perception is the only genuine kind of depth perception is a misconception.

The evolution of the retina accompanied the evolution of the eye and the nervous system, each depending on the other. Some retinas are efficient at low illumination, some at high, and some are dual. The reciprocity of acuity and sensitivity, however, sets limits on the efficiency of any receptive mosaic, including that of the compound eye. In general, eyes developed in accordance with the uses to which they might be put.

X / *The Visual System: Environmental Information*

The difference between *energy* and *information* has been emphasized in all of these chapters but the difference has not yet been made explicit. I have suggested that while energy is relevant to receptor-cells, information is relevant to organs, and that the stimulus for an organ or a perceptual system is of higher order than the stimulus for a cell. The heart of the question, however, is to explain how stimulus energy may carry or contain information. It is not how information might be picked up that needs to be decided first, but simply whether it exists.

The question is especially puzzling where light is concerned, for it has been asserted with some plausibility both that light carries information about the world and that it does not. This is an old puzzle. Is it true that objects get into the eye in the form of images, as certain Greek thinkers believed? Or is it true that nothing gets into the eye but light energy? We now reject the idea that objects constantly send off little copies or replicas of themselves in all directions. Must we then assume that *no* information can be projected to a distance by mere rays of light? If so, we are forced to the conclusion that the mind, or the brain, somehow builds or creates an image of the world from the light rays.

How can we accept the physical theory of light and believe at the same time that information about an external object must be conveyed by light? The latter is implied whenever we say that the object stimulates the eye. The outline of an answer was suggested in Chapter 1 (pp. 12–13, 14–15). We can escape the paradox by distinguishing between radiant light and ambient light — that is, between light emitted from an energy source and light reflected by the environment as a source. The conveying of information about surfaces by light of the latter kind is conceivable. To justify such a theory, however, the known laws of physical optics need to be supplemented with quite unfamiliar laws of ecological optics.

. . . .

Proximal and Distal Stimuli

A thoughtful discussion of the relation between objects and the light rays reflected from them to the retina was offered many years ago by Heider (1926). Many of the problems considered in this chapter were treated by him. But he believed that light could only *mediate*, not *convey* information, and that an optic array contained only "spurious" units, not genuine ones. In the end, he concluded that some postulate of a creative process in the organism was necessary to explain perception, as Köhler and Koffka did. He anticipated a good part of the modern theory of information, however, and saw very early that the concept of stimulation was inseparable from the concept of environment.

. . . .

An effort will be made in this chapter to combine optics with ecology. There is not much precedent for doing so. Brunswik (1947, 1956) conceived of what he called an ecology of visual cues, but with wholly different assumptions than those here, and with opposite conclusions. There have been tentative formulations of ecological optics (Gibson, 1958, 1961; also Purdy, 1960) but the present one will be more elaborate. This protodiscipline cannot be expected to have the mathematical elegance of classical optics, but it is closer to life.

Let us begin by noting that *information about* something means only *specificity to* something. Hence, when we say that information is conveyed by light, or by sound, odor, or mechanical energy, we do not mean that the source is literally conveyed as a copy or replica. The sound of a bell is not the bell and the odor of cheese is not cheese. Similarly the perspective projection of the faces of an object (by the reverberating flux of reflected light in a medium) is not the object itself. Nevertheless, in all these cases a property of the stimulus is univocally related to a property of the object by virtue of physical laws. This is what I mean by the conveying of environmental information.

In this chapter it is assumed that *information* means *information about*, or *specification of*. In the next chapter another and quite different meaning of the term will be recognized — information as *structure*. Ambient light must have structure if it is to carry information about the environment, but not all structure carries this sort of information.

The Principles of Ecological Optics

The light by which the terrestrial environment is seen is far more complex than the light by which the sun and stars are seen. In order to make the complications intelligible, let us consider them in stages. I will describe stages (1) radiation from a luminous source, (2) reflection of light from surfaces, (3) the network of projections in a medium, (4) the ambient light at a single convergence point, (5) the optic array at such a point, (6) the ambient light at a *moving* convergence point, (7) the figural motions in an ambient array, and (8) the principle of moving optical occlusion.

Introduction

The description of ambient light begins at Stage 4. A diagram of the light at a single stationary convergence point for a terrestrial animal was given in Figure 9.2. It was supposed to represent the basic features of the motionless optical environment in daylight during all the ages of terrestrial evolution. It consisted of two hemispheres, the upper caused by the cloudless sky and the lower caused by the earth. Radiant light was not represented in this diagram except as a narrow beam, since it must come from the sun, which is millions of miles distant.

The upper hemisphere consists of diffused light, the rays having been scattered in all directions when the sunlight entered the atmosphere. It has no margins anywhere except at the disk of the sun. The intensity of this light decreases gradually over the sky as a function of angular separation from the sun, but in the absence of margins it is textureless, i.e., without intensive structure. Its polarization, however, varies continuously over the sky as a function of the position of the sun. The marginless quality specifies endless air — that is, something a bird could fly into without meeting obstacles.

The lower hemisphere consists of reflected light. Although of lesser mean intensity than the upper, it is strongly textured since it has been differentially reflected from different parts of the terrain (faces and facets having various inclinations and various pigmentations). It has an arrangement and may properly be called an optic *array*. This light specifies the solid state of matter, not the gaseous state — that is, rigidity and resistance, instead of the non-resistance of a medium. It is said to have *surface* color as distinguished from *film* color.

In Figure 9.2, the earth was represented as consisting of evenly spaced faces or "humps." This layout, of course, is a simplification. The actual structure of a terrain consists of parts within parts, both larger and smaller in size, and the spacing is only stochastically regular. But the simplified diagram served to show how the density of the optical texture increases without limit (or how the angular interval between margins *decreases* without limit) as it approaches the horizon of the optic array. This method of illustrating the gradient of texture-density is more revealing than the method of representing it on a picture-plane, which I have previously used (Gibson, 1950, Ch. 6; see also Purdy, 1960). However it is represented, the gradient is simply a consequence of the geometrical laws of perspective.

Ambient light as thus represented is typical, but it fails to include a very important fact of ecological optics. The diagram does not indicate any of the peculiarities of pattern that make each optic array on the earth unique to its station-point. There are no "landmarks." I assume that no two places in the world are wholly identical. We need to describe the light at some more particular place in the world, a man-made enclosure, for example. For the detailed consideration of ecological optics in the eight stages listed above, I will use the example of a room having a rectangular layout of surfaces, with artificial illumination. At Stage 5 a human observer will be introduced to the room.

Radiation from a Luminous Source (Stage 1)

Figure 10.1 illustrates radiation. A hot body emits energy in rays, each beam containing a spectrum of frequencies. A lamp is represented, but the sun, or a fire, or a candle flame would do the same. The rays

Figure 10.1   Radiation from a Luminous Source (Stage 1).

diverge from the source, and if they were in empty space they would continue indefinitely. Only a few are represented but they should be thought of as infinitely dense. The shadow behind an opaque barrier in space would be absolutely dark. Unless the rays were reflected, there would be nothing for an observer in a radiant field to see but a luminous spot — that is, there would be no ambient light.

Is there any kind of information in radiant light? The answer must be yes, for the spectrum of any radiant beam specifies vibrations in the atoms that emitted the energy. The astronomer with a spectroscope can identify the substance of a star. One could aim the instrument at a luminous object and determine whether it is incandescent, fluorescent, bioluminescent, etc. But note that an eye cannot do this; it cannot register the distribution of wavelengths and cannot measure their absolute intensities. This is not the *kind* of information an eye can pick up.

Figure 10.2 Scatter-reflection of light from surfaces (Stage 2).
A dense space-filling network of reverberating rays results from the scattering shown, consisting of convergent and divergent pencils of light rays.

A single spot of light in darkness conveys only a minimum of information to an eye.

Scatter-Reflection of Light from Surfaces (Stage 2)

Figure 10.2 represents reflection. It is not the abstract reflection of a single ray at an ideal mirror, for the surfaces indicated are imperfectly smooth, and a beam is therefore scattered in various directions depending on the microstructure of the surface — that is, on the arrangement of a large number of "micromirrors," each being a tiny facet of the surface. This scattered or diffuse reflection is characteristic of environmental surfaces. Degrees of scattering are indicated in Figure 10.3. The incident light on any part of a surface is scattered, but the amount reflected at the symmetrical angle is always greater than the amount reflected at any other angle. This is important to remember.

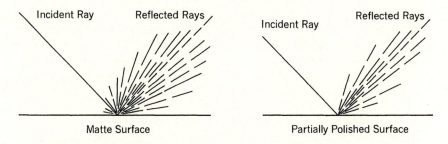

Figure 10.3 Two degrees of scattering of light by a matte surface. A single incident ray is shown, with two hypothetical distributions of reflected rays. A surface is assumed to gain in gloss, shine, or luster as the degree of scattering is reduced. When the scattering is eliminated the surface constitutes a mirror.

The result of scattering when there is a layout of *facing* surfaces is multiple reflection or reverberation. The light bounces from surface to surface endlessly. At this stage the environment is said to be illuminated. An infinitely dense network of rays is formed, consisting of pencils of rays intersecting at every point in the medium. This network of convergence and divergence cannot be represented and must be imagined by the reader. It ceases to exist the instant the source is extinguished.

The Set of All Convergence Points in a Medium (Stage 3)

The complete set of all convergence points in the room shown has remarkable properties. It constitutes the permanent possibilities of vision — that is, the set of all places where a mobile individual might be. Its properties are like those of a mathematical group in being ordered on any number of parameters. It can be shown (1) that each pencil of rays is unique, that is, different from every other, (2) that the set of all pencils is unique to the room, and (3) that every series of adjacent pencils is unique to a possible path of locomotion in the room. Hence the specifying power of the set is unlimited.

The manifold of convergence points can be considered in continuous sequence, as if a potential observer moved from one place to another, or simultaneously, as if a crowd of potential observers stood in the room. The set of all convergent pencils from the table, for example, could be sampled either by a single observer who changed his point of view or by a multiplicity of observers each with a different point of view. This is the basis for asserting both that the single moving observer could continue to see the same table and that the group of stationary observers could all simultaneously see the same table.

The room, of course, is only one part of the terrestrial environment. There exists a still larger set of convergence points for the house, the street, the town, and in fact for the whole world. There is an infinite number of vantage points from which an observer could look at his surroundings. The most indefatigable tourist could only sample them. But they all exist as permanent possibilities for vision.

The Ambient Light at a Stationary Convergence Point (Stage 4)

Next consider a single station-point in the room, as shown in Figure 10.4. The radiant light has been omitted in this diagram. The ambient light consists wholly of light that has been modified by reflection. (There is no diffused light from the sky because the room is windowless and has a ceiling.) This global stimulus also contains an unlimited amount of information but not as much as the complete set does.

Only the rays from the *faces* of the surfaces and objects in the room are shown, not those from the *facets* of things. The latter, the "micromirrors," cannot be represented, but the structure of the surfaces and the pencil of converging rays should both be thought of as having unlimited density. It can be observed that each face, as defined by the edges or corners of the surface, corresponds to a perspective projection in the ambient array, depending on its slant to the line of sight. The same is true of each subordinate face or facet of a surface. The structure of the environment at all levels of linear size is mapped into the structure of the array at all levels of angular size. But note that the structure of the world is analyzed by faces and facets, not by particles, and that the structure of the array is analyzed by forms, not by points. More will be said about perspective mapping later on.

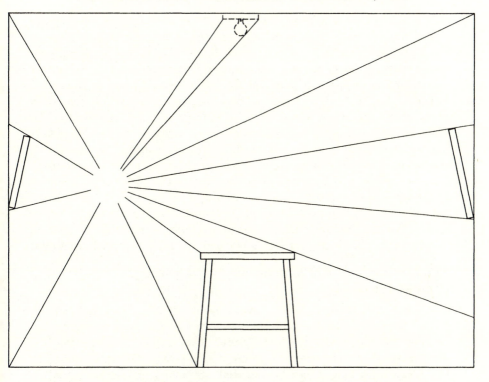

Figure 10.4 Ambient light and the main boundaries of the stationary array (Stage 4). The lines in this diagram are different from those in all the preceding diagrams: they represent *borders* instead of rays. Only the main borders in the optic array are shown.

It should be especially noted that the lines in this diagram have a different character from those in previous diagrams, corresponding as they do to the edges and corners of surfaces facing in different directions. They are no longer beams of light shrunken to lines; they are the boundaries between pencils of rays. They are no longer the paths of photons; they are relations. Hence they no longer represent energy but information. The angular pyramids of the ambient light carry energy of course, but the *borders* of the adjacent pyramids are merely relations of contrast. A relation, I think, cannot be said to carry energy. A boundary, margin, border, contour, or transition is nevertheless justly considered a stimulus for an eye, or more exactly, stimulus information for an eye, and this is the central problem of the present chapter.

The reason for boundaries in the array is that the faces of the room reflect different amounts and colors of light to a convergence point. No two adjacent faces (or facets) will project the same intensity if they are at different angles of inclination to the source. Moreover, no two adjacent faces (or facets) will project the same intensity if they have a different composition or pigmentation, that is, a different reflectance. Either of these differences alone or both together will yield a border in the array; either a slant difference between two surfaces of identical gray or a black-white difference between two surfaces of identical slant. The differences in reflectance, furthermore, are usually reinforced by differences in spectral reflectance, that is, differences in color in the usual sense, so that borders are doubly guaranteed. In short, an array is structured, i.e., caused to have borders within it, by (1) the physical inclinations of the faces and facets of surfaces, (2) the reflectance of the substances, and (3) the *spectral* reflectance of the substances, or chromatic reflectance. We shall consider the causes of structure in more detail later in this chapter, adding another factor not here considered, namely shadows.

The Effective Array at a Stationary Convergence Point (Stage 5)

We can now bring in an observer. Figure 10.5 shows a man in the room. His eye admits a solid angular sector of the ambient light, embracing something under a hemisphere. This is the effective array for a given eye-head posture at a given station-point. The information in this array is no longer merely potential; it can be picked up, since for every border in the array there is a corresponding border on the retina of the eye.

The textures and details of the room are specified by the textures and details of the array, although neither can be represented in the figure. A man, it will be remembered, has to explore the ambient array with successive fixations in order to register the finer details. He can turn his eyes without moving his head, he can turn his head and eyes without moving his body, or he can turn his body and head and eyes without moving from the same general location. As the exploratory movements ascend in this hierarchy, the successive overlapping arrays admitted to the eye extend to the total array of ambient light. The observer can thus perceive the whole room, although the momentary array for a single fixation is less than a hemisphere, and the cone admitted to the center of the eye is only a few degrees wide.

Only one eye is shown in the illustration. The two simultaneous overlapping arrays admitted to the two eyes are quite another factor in the perceptual situation. Since they converge to station-points that are separated by about two and a half inches, they are not the same array. They are slightly different perspective mappings of the room; therefore, when they are treated as overlapping fields the pattern of one is not congruent with the pattern of the other, as noted in the last chapter.

Figure 10.5   The effective array at a stationary convergence point (Stage 5). The solid lines represent the sample of the total optic array that is admitted to a human eye in a given posture. The dashed lines represent the remainder of the array, which is available for stimulation but not effective at this moment.

The Ambient Array at a Moving Convergence Point (Stage 6)

Figure 10.6 suggests a principle of ecological optics that is even less familiar than the ones already given and more radically different from the principles of physical optics. It is not easy to diagram or to phrase, but it is crucial for the hypothesis of information in light.

It is evident from the illustration that whenever an observer moves, the array changes. Every solid angle of ambient light — each one of the adjacent pyramids in the diagram — is altered. Every form that would be projected on a sphere centered at the eye is altered by a perspective transformation, and every form projected on the retina, of course, undergoes a corresponding transformation. For convenience, I will refer to the transformations in the ambient optical field instead of the inverted retinal field.

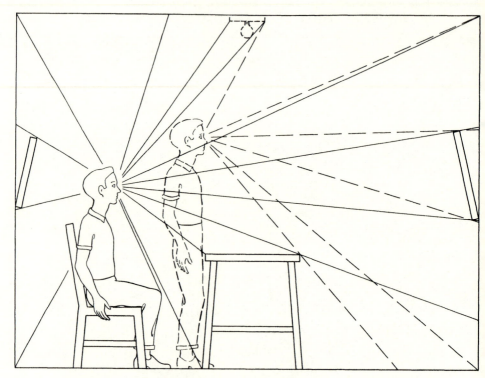

Figure 10.6   The transformation of the optic array obtained by a locomotor movement (Stage 6). The solid lines represent the optic array before the observer stands up, the dashed lines after he has moved. The path of locomotion of the head is forward and upward. The whole array is transformed, including the invisible portion behind the head, but the latter is not represented in the drawing.

. . . .

On the Use of the Term "Transformation"

The simplest meaning of transformation is the change of form of a surface, as when a cloud billows or a baby's face smiles. But we must refer to optical, not environmental forms, and to a change in the array, not in the surface. Hence the use of the term here is similar to that in projective and perspective geometry. It is not quite the same, however, since abstract mathematics has not yet been applied to the problems of ecological optics. There is a vast variety of optical "motions," and to all these I will apply the term *transformation* (Gibson, 1957).

. . . .

Analytically, this total transformation of the array appears to mean that the elements of its texture are displaced, the elements being considered as *spots*. Introspectively, the field is everywhere alive with motion when the observer moves. If we had the angular coordinates of the field we could describe the displacements of all the elements by a formula. This would express the global motion parallax for a given environmental layout. The formula was obtained for a movement of the observer relative to the earth's surface some years ago (Gibson, Olum, and Rosenblatt, 1955). All spots in the field of view are displaced, with the sole exception of the two spots at opposite ends of the axis of locomotion, i.e., the focus of expansion and of contraction, and all the spots on the line of the horizon of the earth. The optical velocities of these spots can be plotted as vectors on a graph. Figure 10.7 is a graph of the spot velocities in

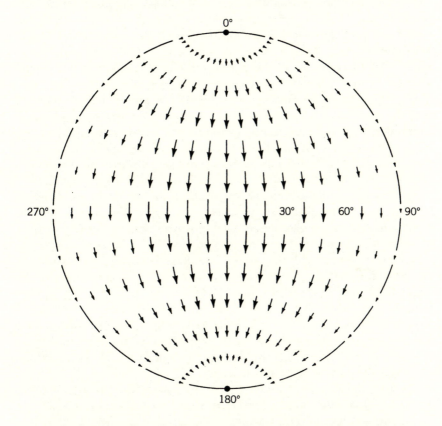

Figure 10.7 The flow velocities in the optic array reflected from the surface of the earth. This is the flow pattern obtained with locomotion parallel to the earth in the direction of the pole at the top of the graph. The vectors are plotted in angular coordinates. This is a view from above, whereas Figure 9.3 was a view from the side. (From J. J. Gibson, P. Olum, and F. Rosenblatt, "Parallax and Perspective during Aircraft Landing," *American Journal of Psychology,* 1955, *68,* p. 376. Courtesy of the publisher.)

the hemisphere of light projected from the surface of the earth during locomotion by an observer parallel to the surface. It should be viewed as the inner aspect of a hemishere, looking down, and it may be compared with Figure 9.3 in the last chapter, the flowing optic array of a bird in flight.

There is something wrong with this graph, however. It is analytical, not topological. The vectors, of course, represent the velocities of points. Accordingly there is a temptation to think of the graph as a collection of stimulus motions analogous to the physical motions of particles in space, but this thought would be very misleading. The insubstantial motions of margins in an optic array are not analogous to the substantial motions of particles. Optical motions have no inertia and do not collide with one another; they are a set of relations, not of independent elements. The optical flow in the graph is not to be thought of, therefore, as a collection of separately moving parts, each perceptible by itself. The analysis of spot velocities is useful, but it should be remembered that the optic array does not consist of spots. If a terrestrial layout is analyzable by *faces* and *facets*, then its optic array is analyzable into *forms* within *forms*. Every form, even the smallest, undergoes a transformation, but this fact is not shown by the graph. Nor does this graph take into account edge information, which will be discussed later.

The streaming of the ambient array with a movement of the observer is a corollary of the change of perspective, that is, of the altered point of view. Flow perspective is closely related to size perspective in that both decrease with distance. Perspective geometry has so far been concerned only with the latter kind, because its laws have been applied to painting, and were first stated by men who were painters. It is customary to formulate the laws of perspective for a picture-plane, instead of for a panorama as we do here. But they hold for both and they can be extended to angular motions as well as to angular sizes. As a stimulus for an eye, however, motion perspective is vastly more informative than static perspective, in that it specifies more about the geometrical layout of the environment. Let us make this assertion explicit.

Consider the stationary array shown in Figures 10.4 and 10.5 (Stages 4 and 5). Inasmuch as the lines correspond to the edges and corners of flat surfaces, not to their textures — that is, so long as the angles indicate the faces of the room, not the facets — a distorted room could be substituted for the normal room without the observer being any the wiser. The faces might consist of slanting trapezoids, for example, instead of horizontal and vertical rectangles, without its making any difference in the array, except for its fine texture. The perspective mapping would be identical for a family of rooms with different edge-and-corner layouts.

Distorted rooms with unpatterned walls and floors have actually been constructed in several psychological laboratories in recent years. They demonstrate the fact that the stationary perspective of light does not specify the gross physical layout of its source. The information in the static array diagrammed is ambiguous in this respect. The observer of such an abnormal room gets an illusory perception of a normal room, and this result is highly suggestive for the classical theory of how we construct perceptions out of sensations. But the demonstration works only so long as the observer sees the distorted room with a motionless head and with only one eye. If he moves, or looks with two eyes, the actual layout is perceived. This correct perception is just as interesting as the illusion, and even more important. Motion perspective or binocular perspective eliminates the ambiguity in static perspective and provides information for perceiving the objective slants of the surfaces and the abnormal proportions of their edges.

A careful examination of the two arrays in Figure 10.6 (Stage 6) will confirm the hypothesis that the optical flow from one to the other, the transformation, is specific to that layout of surfaces and to no other. There could be a family of optically equivalent rooms for the seated man; there could be another family of optically equivalent rooms for the standing man; but there could only be that particular rectangular room for the particular motion perspective obtained when he stands up.

The *slant* of a surface in the room is specified by the continuous gradient of flow velocities of its optical texture, if it has a physical texture to project (Flock, 1964). The *edge* of a surface in the room is specified by a discontinuity in the flow of optical texture, as at the tabletop. The *corner* of a surface in the room, the angle of two planes, is specified by another kind of discontinuity in the flow. (For the static optical geometry of edges and corners, see Fig. 10.8.) There are several possible kinds of *topological breakage* in the distribution of optical flow. They can more easily be displayed by a motion picture (e.g., Gibson, 1955) than described in words (Gibson, 1957). As I will phrase it, texture can undergo "wiping" or "shearing" at a margin. That is, one texture can be "wiped out" by another or "cut across" by another. This kind of optical discontinuity corresponds to a separation of surfaces in the world. It will be described in more detail later. The motion perspective for an environment is theoretically loaded with information about its layout, and the experimental tests that have been made so far agree in showing that this information is effective for human perception. There is increasing experimental evidence to suggest that it is just as effective for animal perception (Walk and E. Gibson, 1961; Schiff, Caviness, and Gibson, 1962). When a kitten avoids a cliff it presumably sees the edge; when a rat turns a corner it must see the corner; when a monkey shrinks from collision it must see the oncoming obstacle.

Figure 10.8 The stationary optical information for detecting an edge and a corner. An *edge* consists of one surface in front of another (left), and a *corner* consists of one plane surface joining another (right), as these terms are used here. Two kinds of mathematical discontinuity in an array are illustrated, corresponding to these two features of an environment. For a fuller discussion, see Gibson (1950, pp. 92 ff.).

• VISUAL KINESTHESIS. The flow of the ambient array from the centrifugal to the centripetal pole contains information with subjective reference as well as information with objective reference. It specifies locomotion of the individual with respect to the world at the same time that it specifies the layout of the world. As we noted in the last chapter (pp. 160–162), a movement from place to place can be either a case of passive transportation without muscular effort, or a case of active behavior with effort. The feedback of vestibular kinesthesis, articular kinesthesis, and cutaneous kinesthesis from voluntary movement (Chapter 6) does not always correctly specify a movement from place to place. The only trustworthy information for locomotion in the world is *visual* kinesthesis. Thus, it is only by observing on what part of the world the focus of optical expansion falls that one can see where he is going.

It is only a *total* motion of the structured ambient array that specifies movement of the self, not a part motion of the array. The latter specifies motion of an object in the world. Accordingly, the total motion induces a perception of being moved, not a collection of sensations of motion. What is picked up is the information, not the vectors of velocity. Neither the bee nor the human flier sees the world expand in front of him when he comes down for a landing; instead he sees himself approaching a rigid surface. The human observer, if he introspects, can notice a sort of elastic expansion of the visual field ahead during approach, but these sensations have nothing to do with his perception. They are sensations accompanying visual kinesthesis, that is, visual impressions incidental to the pickup of locomotor information.

A transformation of the whole optic array specifies a movement of the observer. It is propriospecific. Invariants under transformation of the whole optic array specify invariants of the layout of the environment. They are exterospecific. The separation of the information about the world from the information about the observer's *movement* in the world, the isolation of the invariants from the motions, is something that a visual system does in its dual role of being both exteroceptive and proprioceptive.

Figural Motion within the Ambient Array (Stage 7)

If one imagines, considering our hypothetical room, that the picture frame on the wall falls to the floor, or that the table is overturned, or that a second person enters the room, another phase of ecological optics can be illustrated. A part motion will occur in the ambient light without motion in the remainder of the array. Such a figural motion, as distinguished from the global motion of Stage 6, specifies something happening to an object of the environment, that is, an external event.

A *physical* motion, either rigid or elastic, must not be confused with the *optical* motion produced by it. We are tempted to get them mixed because both can be called *motion,* but they belong to entirely different orders. The former is an event while the latter is a stimulus; the former involves mass and inertia while the latter does not; the former applies to physical bodies while the latter applies to insubstantial margins between pencils of light. An optical motion can specify a physical motion without itself being one. The proximal stimulus event at the eye is not the same as the distant event in the world.

A physical motion can be described fully by six components, three of translation and three of rotation, on the axes of a coordinate system. This assumes a rigid body like the falling picture or the overturning table. An elastic motion, including that of a walking man with his gestures and facial expressions, could be analyzed into a set of rigid motions of elementary particles if one wished to do so, but it is better thought of in terms of components like bending, flexing, stretching, skewing, expanding, and bulging. The movements of animals in all their variety, the animate motions, are of this non-rigid sort. Animals are non-rigid bodies.

The figural motion corresponding to a body motion, rigid or non-rigid, is a transformation of the figure. For every translation of a body in space there is a corresponding transformation of its figure in the field of view, and the same is true for every rotation of a body in space. All these can be called *perspective* transformations. All of them are usually observable on the screen during an ordinary movie. The reader should have no trouble in visualizing them, although some of them are more "like" their solid physical counterparts than the others. They have been described and illustrated abstractly by the author (Gibson, 1955, 1957).

The *non-rigid* motions of a body in space are much more difficult to order or classify, and physics has scarcely attempted to do so. The corresponding transformation of figures will be called *non-perspective* transformations. Many of these, too, can be noticed on the ordinary motion picture screen and, in fact, most of the meaning of a film, the "live action" as contrasted with the "scene," is carried by non-perspective transformations. Some of the types are hinted at in topology — "rubbersheet" geometry — but they are enormously various, as much so as the events they project. The forms of the possible changes of form have never been exhaustively classified by geometry. Nevertheless the rubbery motions of a smiling face and a snarling face are specified by different transformations, and these are easily distinguished by the human eye.

The difference between a perspective transformation and a non-perspective transformation can be expressed by saying that more properties of the figure remain invariant in the former than in the latter. Rectilinearity, for example, is preserved under perspective transformation but not under topological transformation. Presumably these invariants specify the rigidity of the object during its motion in the first case, and the absence of these invariants specifies the elasticity of the object in the second case. The kind of non-change that persists during change is obviously important information for perception. Can it be picked up by an eye? There is evidence to suggest that it can, for Gibson and Gibson (1957) found that the perspective transformation of a patterned silhouette on a translucent screen was perceived as the motion of a rigid object, and Fieandt and Gibson (1959) showed that when the transformation of a patterned shadow caused by foreshortening was compared with the transformation of the same shadow caused by elastic contraction the perceptions were quite different, the latter not having the immediate phenomenal quality of a rigid surface. The invariants that specified rigidity were not noticed by the naive observers; they simply perceived it.

The detection of non-change during change when an object moves in the world is not as difficult as it might appear. It is only made to seem difficult when we assume that the perception of constant dimensions of the object must depend on the correcting of sensations of inconstant form and size. The information for the constant dimensions of an object is normally carried by invariant relations in the optic array. Rigidity is specified.

Kinetic Optical Occlusion and Edge Information (Stage 8)

Let us return to the room where an object hanging on the wall falls to the floor, and consider what happens in the optic array. Since a translatory motion of the object occurs in space, one might assume that a corresponding translatory motion of its pyramid of light rays will occur or a corresponding motion of its image over the retina. One might conceive that the stimulus for motion is simply motion. But this would be a serious misconception. Many students of vision have been guilty of it, including the writer (Gibson, 1954). The displacement of a body in space is mapped *not* as a displacement of a figure in an empty visual field, but as a figural transformation. Moreover, such a transformation involves the "wiping" and "shearing" of optical texture referred to above — the stimuli that specify edges in the world.

As the object moves through the air it progressively covers and uncovers the physical texture of the wall behind it. In terms of optical texture, there occurs a *wiping-out* at the leading border, an *unwiping* at the trailing border, and a *shearing* of texture at the lateral borders of the figure in the array. These aspects of transformation involve a rupture of the continuity of texture, a sort of topological breakage, as it was called in the last section.

Now the fact of one surface behind another, the ordinary everyday optics of hiding, interception, or occlusion, is so familiar to us that we do not realize the need for explanation or analysis. Static occlusion or "superposition" is recognized in the textbooks as a cue for depth in pictures, but *kinetic* occlusion is what occurs in life. The wiping-out and shearing-across of texture in the array specify depth at an edge in the world. This stimulus occurs without fail whenever one surface moves relative to another and whenever the observer himself moves.

Edge-depth in the environment is often, but not always, specified by an intensive border in a stationary array (Figure 10.5). There is ambiguity, because an intensive border may also come from a corner or from the margin between two flat pigments. But in a *kinetic* array (Figure 10.6), which is the prevalent stimulus for men and animals, edge-depth is specified without ambiguity by wiping and shearing. In a stationary array, to be sure, edge-depth is usually also specified by an abrupt increase in the density of texture at a border (Figure 10.8), as well as by an intensity difference; but the best specification, with the best ecological validity, is provided by the phenomena of kinetic occlusion.

The information provided by kinetic occlusion and its variants is extremely rich. It specifies the existence of an edge in the world, and the depth at the edge, but it does even more. *It also specifies the existence of one surface behind another, that is, the continued existence of a hidden surface.* When, in Figure 10.6, the figure of the falling object is occluded by the figure of the tabletop, the fact of *going behind* can be detected. We say loosely that the object "disappears," but we do not mean that it disappears by vanishing or fading, for which the stimulus information would be quite different; we mean that it disappears *behind* something else. The wiping out of border and texture is one stimulus; the fading of border and texture (as when a puff of smoke dissipates in the air) is quite another stimulus. Hence the seeing of one thing behind another in this situation is not a paradox, for there is information to specify it. The same reasoning can be applied to *emerging from behind* as to *going behind;* it specifies appearance, but not the materialization of a ghost.

Koffka asserted, in the *Principles of Gestalt Psychology* (1935, p. 180), that he could "see" the top of his table extending behind the book that lay on it. He considered this an example of the figure-ground phenomenon and explained it by spontaneous neural organization of the visual inputs to the brain. But insofar as his head moved and the texture of the table was wiped and unwiped by the edges of the book, he had information for perceiving the table behind the book.

• THE EXPERIMENTAL ANALYSIS OF KINETIC OCCLUSION. The experimental isolation of this information in light does not seem to have been accomplished except in some degree by Michotte. Figure 10.9 shows one of the elegant experiments from his laboratory (Michotte, Thines, and Crabbé, 1964, p. 26). Described in terms of the pictorial source, a black

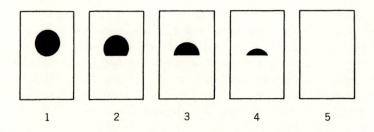

1   2   3   4   5

Figure 10.9   Five Successive Forms in the Continuous Transformation that Specifies the Occlusion of a Disk (Stage 8).

disk moves over an empty screen. (This can be accomplished by such means as shadow projection.) Abruptly the leading contour stops while the trailing contour continues to move. The circular contour is transformed in this manner until it finally flickers out. The perception is very striking. All observers see a slit in the background behind which the disk goes. The disk seems to keep its circular identity throughout and does not vanish; it is simply hidden. The perception of the slit is especially interesting, for there is no phenomenal slit at Stage 1 and it fades away after Stage 5. The appearance of the slit is produced by nothing but the transformation of the contour. This transformation is mathematically unique; Michotte calls the phenomenon *covering* or *screening*, and this is indeed what is perceived. But a term is needed for the transformation as such — that is, the stimulus that *specifies* something being occluded.

Essentially, this is what happens to every form and subform and texture-element in light when one thing goes behind another. The transformation is not easily classified mathematically. It is reversible, for if the stages diagrammed in the illustration are reversed, a slit opens up as before but then the disk *emerges* from behind it. The perception of the edge is what Michotte calls *amodal:* there are no visual sense data on which to base it. Here, then, is a paradox — a sensationless perception. It simply cannot be seen as a mere change of shape. The paradox is resolved by the present theory that stimulus information exists for the perception and that sense data would be irrelevant in any case.

Michotte's "tunnel effect" is a demonstration of the perception of an object during an interval between the stimulus for *occlusion* displayed on one side of a screen and the stimulus for *emergence* displayed on the other side. An object is almost literally *seen* while it is in the "tunnel." As I would put it, an object is seen in the visual *world* although not in the visual *field* (Gibson, 1950, Ch. 3), and I would maintain that stimulus information exists for perceiving this part of the visual world, although no sense data exist for perceiving it. These and other phenomena of temporal perception have been thoroughly established in the Louvain laboratory. The phenomena are described and the relevant references are given in the recent monograph by Michotte, Thines, and Crabbé (1964). It should be added that Koffka also understood the implications of seeing one thing behind another, as noted above, but he investigated it only with static pictorial stimuli and conceived it only as a special kind of sensory organization (1935, pp. 153ff.).

The detecting of occlusions caused by moving objects and by movements of the observer himself is something that every animal and every child must become capable of, either by learning or by development of the nervous system or by innate endowment. Detecting the *permanence* of the objective environment behind barriers or outside the momentary field of view or behind one's back is entailed in the fact of intelligent behavior. In the human child, as Piaget (1954) has shown, it develops slowly. But this development need not be conceived as an intellectual construction of reality from data that do not contain the reality; it can be conceived as a process of learning to extract the information from light that does convey reality. We shall return to this problem later.

The Connected Set of Convergence Points for a Geographical Environment

The principles of ecological optics outlined above suggest a new basis for explaining certain kinds of behavior. Our hypothetical man has so far been boxed into a room. Let us go back to Stage 3 and consider the space-filling network of rays outside the room as well as the network inside. We must now assume a door in the room and allow the man to walk out of it. The room presumably is in a house, on a street, in a town, in a valley, and so on. The man gets about in this geographical maze, as a rat does, and as any exploratory animal does in its habitat. What are the stimuli that enable him to do so?

The network of rays with its set of convergence points is not perfectly continuous over the face of the earth. For the man it is partially broken up by walls, houses, and hills; for the animal, by barriers of a similar sort. Any given ambient array is usually occluded by obstacles to loco-motion. When the individual goes from one place to another, as in Figure 10.10, he has a different *vista*. What is the connection between one vista and another? The answer is interesting; the transition is another edge phenomenon, an "emergence-from-behind."

When the man in the room walks up to and through the door, the edge of the doorframe expands to uncover the new array of the next room. The same unwiping of the new array (or wiping out of the old one) occurs in reaching the corner of a street or the brow of a hill. If the man had panoramic vision, he could see the old array gradually being wiped out behind his back. The specification for a hole in the world, an aperture, window, or space between obstacles, is that it "opens up" on an optically denser array. This is information for controlling locomotion without collision, and it helps to explain why vision to the front is more important than vision to the rear.

The permanent possibilities of optical stimulation in a geographical environment can be said to consist of the set of all moving convergence points in it, and these correspond to the set of all paths of locomotion. One vista leads to another in a set of continuous connected sequences. Over time, as the individual moves about the house, the street, the town, and the country, the sequences come to be perceived as a scene, and the fact that the transformations all make a group becomes evident to him.

Figure 10.10   The Optical Transition from One Vista to Another.

The individual is then able to find his way from place to place, but more than that, he is able to *see one place behind another* on a larger and larger scale. He is then geographically oriented. Even when he is shut into the room he is able to apprehend the house, the street, the town, and the countryside in relation to the room. He can point to the kitchen, the post office, or the Old Mill Stream. He can move directly to get a cup of tea, or post a letter, or go to a rendezvous with a girl; he has a sort of cognitive map of his environment. He can not only perceive things in the room that are for the moment hidden; he can also perceive places outside the room that are hidden by its walls. We call the latter kind of perception "knowledge" and assume that it depends on "memory," but I venture to suggest that it is only an extension over a longer period of time of the principle of seeing one thing behind another. This unorthodox suggestion will be elaborated in Chapters 12 and 13.

The Structuring of Ambient Light

The answer to the question put at the beginning of the chapter — how energy may convey information — should now be clearer, at least for light. Radiation carries information about a terrestrial environment after and only after it has been modified by the environment. In the terminology of communications engineering, radiation can be "modulated." By the time it reaches a convergence point, after many vicissitudes, it is specific to what has happened to it.

The leaves of a tree face in all directions so as to pick up the *energy* in ambient light and use it for photosynthesis. But the tree cannot pick up the *information* in ambient light and use it for behavior. The animal can. His receptors use energy, of course, for photochemical reactions and nervous excitation, but his eyes use differences of energy in different directions. The information lies in the *structure* of ambient light, that is, in its having an *arrangement* or being an *array*. The structure may change in regular ways, as we have noted, but it has to be present for the information to exist, and even for the change to occur.

It will be useful to examine with some care the ways in which light can be structured by the environment, the ordinary causes of an optic array. After that, in the next chapter, we can consider critically the study of structure as such, the difficult and never-solved problem of what it is.

The Causes of Structure in Reflected Ambient Light

• DIFFERENTIAL FACING. The main reason for the existence of borders in an ambient array is the faces of reflecting surfaces — that is, the differing inclinations of their planes to the prevailing illumination. The result is differing amounts of light reflected to the convergence point. This was illustrated at Stage 4. The same principle of differing inclinations applies to the smaller facets of the layout as well as to the larger faces. On this account, borders will exist in the array in a hierarchy of structure. At a fine level the array may be said to have *texture*; at a coarse level it has *form*; but there is no clear separation between them.

A facet of the world that faces the sun will be strongly illuminated and will reflect a considerable amount of energy. A facet that is inclined to the sun's rays, or parallel to them, will not be strongly illuminated and will not reflect much energy. It is said to have less "brightness." A facet that faces *away* from the sun's rays is weakly illuminated, reflects little energy, and is said to have an "attached shadow" (see below).

For example, a *concavity* causes a difference in the light intensity reflected by its two faces. A *convexity* causes the same difference except that the direction of difference is reversed. An *extended* concavity, a "valley," causes a difference between the light reflected from its two slopes. An *extended* convexity, a "ridge," does the same, except that the light-dark border is in this case a dark-light border — the transition as such, however, being invariant. Note that concavity and convexity are reciprocals, and that these principles work at all levels of size. They are illustrated in Figure 10.11.

• SURFACE COMPOSITION. A second reason for borders in the array is

Figure 10.11 Convexities and concavities in the surface of the earth as specified by transitions of intensity. This is an aerial photograph of hills and valleys, but the same principle applies to any layout of convexities and concavities — namely, that the different inclinations of their faces to the direction of illumination determine different relative brightnesses in the array. Presumably the bare earth of these desert hills has everywhere the same reflectance.

the differing reflectances of adjoining substances in the world caused by their differing chemical compositions. *Reflectance* is defined as the proportion of the incident light that is reflected (or transmitted) back into the air instead of being absorbed. It is sometimes called the *albedo* of a surface. In commonsense terminology, it is the *whiteness* of a substance, the variable from white to black. A surface composed of substances of different reflectance is shown in Figure 10.12.

Reflectance is of two sorts, unselective for wavelength or selective for wavelength. In the first sort, the spectrum of the reflected light from the

Figure 10.12   A conglomerate of different substances in a flat surface. Each different kind of wood has a characteristic grain when cut. This one is ash. (U. S. Forest Products Laboratory, Forest Service, U. S. Department of Agriculture.)

face is the same as that of the incident light; in the second sort, the spectrum of the reflected light from the face is altered from that of the incident light. A difference in unselective reflectance between two surfaces is a difference in whiteness; a difference in selective reflectance is a difference in color (chromatic color). A border in the array will be caused by either of these differences or by both in combination. Some difference of chromatic pigmentation usually goes with a difference of achromatic pigmentation for different adjoining substances, and a physical color contrast usually reinforces a physical whiteness contrast, but not always.

• THE COMBINATION OF INCLINATION AND REFLECTANCE. The principle of differing inclinations of the faces and facets of surfaces and the principle of differing reflectances of surfaces may combine to cause borders in the ambient array. That is, they may cooperate, providing a double assurance of a border; or either may cause a border independently of the other (see Figure 10.13). For example, one kind of wallpaper may structure light only by being embossed, having no differences of color or printed pattern. Another kind may structure light only by differences in pigment or ink, having no appreciable roughness of texture. But a common sort of wallpaper has both embossing and printing in coincidence. The same thing happens in nature with surfaces of rock and vegetation. One or the other kind of optical structuring, if not both, is practically guaranteed in nature. For this reason the information for the existence of a surface as against empty air is usually trustworthy.

Conceivably these two principles could work in exact opposition to one another. It is theoretically possible to construct a room which would be invisible at a fixed monocular station-point. It could be done with very smooth unpatterned surfaces by a precise counterbalancing of inclination and reflectance so that all borders in the array corresponding to the junctions of planes in the room disappeared. The room would simply

Figure 10.13 Embossing without printing and printing without embossing. Letters can be made by altering only the inclination of a paper surface or by altering only the reflectance. (Photo by Benjamin Morse)

blank out. This would be troublesome to set up experimentally, and as far as I know has never been done. The author once made, with a great deal of effort and the help of many colleagues, an arrangement of apertures in the form of a tunnel which looked like a void beyond the first aperture because the real edges were not specified by borders of intensity in the optic array (Gibson, Purdy, and Lawrence, 1955, p. 8). The inside of an optical integrating sphere is an example of an invisible room (e.g., Cohen, 1957). Another example of this possibility is the temporary occurrence of "whiteout" in the arctic environment of a level snow plain, especially when the overcast sky and the terrain happen to reach the same intensity so that the horizon therefore vanishes. For all that one can see anything, one might as well have translucent diffusing plastic hemispheres covering both eyes (Gibson and Waddell, 1952).

All these cases demonstrate that borders of intensity must exist in the ambient light at an eye for a layout of surfaces to be visible. Likewise a structure of differential intensities, an optical "texture," must exist for a *surface* to be visible, on the principle that a surface is composed of *facets* just as a layout is composed of *faces*. But the information in light for the existence of both the large-scale layout of faces and the small-scale layout of facets in the world is not *always* present, and when it is not the observer does not perceive either layout or surfaces. He usually then reports that he sees "nothing," that is, no *thing*, although he may also use words like "fog," "film," or 'sky" (Gibson and Waddell, 1952).

• ATTACHED SHADOWS. The relative inclinations of terrestrial surfaces facing the main source of illumination cause differences in the structure of light, as noted above, and so do the relative inclinations of surfaces facing *away* from the illumination, but the latter get much less light to reflect and are said to have *attached shadows*. The plane angle, or dihedral angle, between a surface facing toward and a surface facing away from the illumination therefore yields an especially strong border. These contrasts are weakened as the illumination becomes more diffused but they almost never disappear completely. A curvature between two such surfaces, as distinguished from a plane angle, yields a gradual transition of intensity instead of an abrupt one, as was illustrated in Figure 10.11. In short, the structuring of light by attached shadows is a special case of the structuring of light by the inclination or layout of surfaces.

Diffused illumination is described by artists and photographers as "flat." But the term only means, I think, that edges and curvatures are less insistent in experience on a cloudy day than on a sunny day, not necessarily less evident. When all edges and corners vanish, the world vanishes, but it does not do so by becoming literally *flat*. It was suggested above that contrasts are "weakened" by diffused illumination. This probably means that when the ratios of intensities (luminances) at borders in the array become small, the borders themselves become less effective stimuli. Nevertheless it is known that very low ratios across very abrupt borders are effective, even when they are as low as 1 per cent.

• CAST SHADOWS. A cast shadow is produced on a surface facing the illumination by anything that stands between it and the radiant source. It is produced to the degree that the directional illumination exceeds the diffuse illumination; hence, this kind of terrestrial shadow is also weakened on overcast days. The form of a cast shadow is a geometrical projection of the form of the object. The shadow produces margins in the optic array just as the object does (see Figure 10.14). Where is the

Figure 10.14 Cast shadows on a surface. The penumbras of these shadows and their transparent or filmy quality are evident. Hence they are perceived as shadows, not as objects or colors on the surface. (George Daniell from Photo Researchers, Inc.)

information to specify shadow instead of object? It is found in the fact that the border for the shadow, unlike the border for the object, has a *penumbra*. If a cast shadow had no penumbra it would yield the same stimulus as a *stain* on the surface — that is, an area of dark pigment — and this, in fact, is what a sharply outlined shadow looks like (e.g., MacLeod, 1947). A shadow, moreover, does not occlude the texture of the background as the object does, nor wipe it out when it moves. Hence a shadow is usually distinguishable from an object and also from a stain on the background.

• THE COMBINATION OF INCLINATION, REFLECTANCE, AND SHADOWING. In summary, there seem to be three main ecological causes of the structure of ambient light from an illuminated environment; first, the different *facing* of different surfaces, either large or small; second, the different *whiteness* of reflecting surfaces, either large or small; and third, the different *illuminatedness* of different parts of a surface, that is, differential shadowing. A transition in the optic array may be caused by any one of three kinds of change in the world in isolation from the other two — a change of slant, a change of pigmentation, or a change from illuminated to shadowed. The first has to do with the space of surfaces, the second with the color of surfaces, and the third with their quality of being lighted or darkened.

Let us consider three examples. A pure case of *layout-structuring* would be one in which the material substance has a uniform chemical composition and is uniformly illuminated without cast shadows, but which is modeled or faceted. This has been illustrated in Figures 10.4 and 10.11. The structure of the optic array depends solely on differential facing. A pure case of *pigment-structuring* would be one in which the material substance is a uniform plane, without modeling or faceting, and uniformly illuminated without shadows, but which is composed of different chemical substances. The structure of the optic array then depends solely on differential reflectance. This case is met approximately by the surface of any painting or photograph; another example is the conglomerate of Figure 10.12. A pure case of *illuminatedness-structuring* would be one in which the material substance is a uniform diffusing plane, of uniform chemical composition, but which is unevenly lighted because of cast shadows. The structure of the optic array then depends solely on differential illumination. One example is the shadowing of the ground by a tree in sunlight; another is a projection screen on which is cast the more elaborate shadow we call an image.

If these are indeed the causes of structure in reflected light, the question arises, how can the light specify separately the three different causes of its structure? How could a perceiver distinguish slant from whiteness from illumination? Why is change of slant not confused with a change of color on a flat surface? Why is a change of slant not confused with a cast shadow on a flat surface? Why is a change in color not regularly confused with a change in illumination? The last is a puzzle of long standing, the problem of whiteness constancy, or color constancy.

I would argue that there has to be special information in the array to specify a slant as against a color, or either as against a shadow. When the distinguishing information is lacking the distinctive perceptions should become impossible. The fact is that stimulus conditions can be arranged in a psychological laboratory so that the slant, the intrinsic color, and the illuminatedness of a surface all become indeterminate and the only remaining experience is that of "film" or "fog" (Katz, 1935). The conditions favoring such reduction of information are monocular vision, elimination of head movement, restriction of the optic array to a narrow angle (as with an aperture or tube), low illumination, and a fine-grained, uniformly pigmented surface.

On this theory the perception of the layout, the shadowing, and the reflectance of surfaces are mutually dependent. One cannot get information about space without at the same time getting information about illumination and color, nor about illumination without also getting it about layout and color, nor about color without the specifying of layout and illumination. The last assertion is consistent with a good deal of the experimental evidence concerning whiteness constancy and the conditions for achieving it; only when layout and illumination are specified is the reflectance of a surface fully detectable.

The seeing of things as black, gray, or white is not at all a simple matter. We have long known that these qualities were not simply sensations. It now seems likely that they are features of the world on the same level as geometrical space and the fact of sunlight. Whereas previous theories began with sensations of color or light and went to perceptions of space, we begin with the interrelated problems of detecting color, lighting, and space, all having the same footing.

The present theory predicts that the face of an object, a surface in a differentially slanted layout of surfaces, will look blacker than it really is if exactly this face but none of the others around it is artificially shadowed. An invisible shadow is equivalent to a decreased reflectance. Likewise, the theory predicts that one surface in a layout will look blacker than it is if its inclination to the illumination is increased without there being any other depth information for the increase. An invisible slant is equivalent to a decreased reflectance. Although experiments to test these predictions have not been published, I believe they hold true. Illumination on and reflectance of an isolated face of the environment may counterbalance one another, and so may the inclination and reflectance of such a surface. The latter is demonstrated by an experiment of Hochberg and Beck (1954), which leads into the whole question of reciprocal determination.

The Structuring of Light by Means Other Than Reflection

The last section was entirely concerned with the differential reflection of light from opaque surfaces, not with the light coming from water or glass, from a mirror, from the sky, or from a radiant source like the sun or the stars or fires or fireflies. The latter sources also make a contribution to the structuring of ambient light, but they do so by transmitting light, by reflecting it ideally, by polarizing it, or by refracting it, or by straight-line radiation. The latter sources of optical stimulation are not as important for terrestrial perception as the former, inasmuch as the environment consists mainly of opaque surfaces, and since the surface of the earth is the main background for all of them. But we need to consider these other sources, since they too pattern light, and they too are visible.

• TRANSMITTED LIGHT AND TRANSPARENT SURFACES. A pool of clear water or a pane of glass, if perfectly smooth and plane, and if conditions are such that no "highlights" are reflected from it, will quite simply be invisible. Under such conditions a man may try to walk through a glass door, to his great discomfiture. The optical texture from whatever is behind the water or the glass is transmitted as if through the air, and this is the only surface perceived.

But if the water is rippled or speckled with floating material, as in Figure 10.15, or if the glass is imperfectly smooth or even filmed with dust, it will texture the reflected portion of the light falling on it and will be visible, but with the special quality of *transparency*. One surface is seen in front of another, as in Stage 8, but this is a special case of it. The perception of transparency has also received some study. In one experiment, the optical information for transparency was shown to be kinetic — a type not easily named but describable as one texture "flowing across" another (Gibson, Gibson, Smith, and Flock, 1959) as a result of the parallax of the two surfaces. However, there can also be *static* optical information for transparency, as Koffka has shown (1935, pp. 260–264). This is also illustrated in Figure 10.15.

• MIRROR REFLECTION. A textureless plane *opaque* surface acts as a mirror — that is, it reflects light ideally by the laws of the equal angles of incidence and reflection. (Scatter-reflection, however, is characteristic of textured terrestrial surfaces; mirrors are usually human artifacts.) The extraordinary characteristic of a mirror is that it yields the same stimulus (the same optic array except for reversal) a hypothetical observer would get if he were *behind* the mirror, and that consequently one

Figure 10.15 The stationary information for seeing one
thing through another. The quality of transparency illustrated
here in two quite different situations is described in more detail in
the accompanying text. A. "Study of Transparency" by Clifford
Eitel, from G. Kepes, *Language of Vision*, Paul Theobald and
Company, 1944. Reprinted by permission of the publisher. B. H.
Armstrong Roberts.

can perceive a *virtual* layout (see Figure 10.16) of surfaces in an illusory space behind the plane as well as the actual layout of surfaces in the genuine space in front of the plane. The information carried by the reflected array is detailed, and it is correct with respect to all features of the source except its direction and orientation. This contrast between "appearance" and "reality" has interested men for centuries, but further consideration of the problem, and its relation to the slippery concept of an *image*, will be deferred until the next chapter.

• IRREGULAR REFRACTION. The regular refraction of light transmitted through a wedge, i.e., prism refraction, is described in the textbooks. But light may also be transmitted through an irregular surface like "pebbled" glass, in which case a special structure is imposed on the optic array by the irregularities. The substance can be perceived with varying degrees of *semi-transparency*. If it is moved, the optical texture undergoes complex changes that may approach a sort of random scintillation. Such changes are more radical than transformations, for they involve the breaking of continuity in *both* adjacent and successive order. But these effects have scarcely been studied at all.

• DIFFERENTIAL POLARIZATION OF SKY LIGHT. Ambient light from the cloudless blue sky does not have an intensive structure and carries no surface information. In fact, it carries trustworthy information for *no*

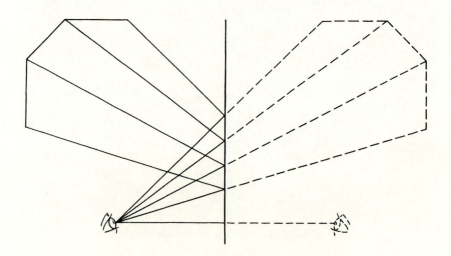

Figure 10.16 A reflected optic array providing information for a virtual layout behind a mirror. A cross-section from the side. The ceiling and wall of the mirror room may be indistinguishable from those of the real room. The observer can look back and register this array directly, although it is not shown in the diagram.

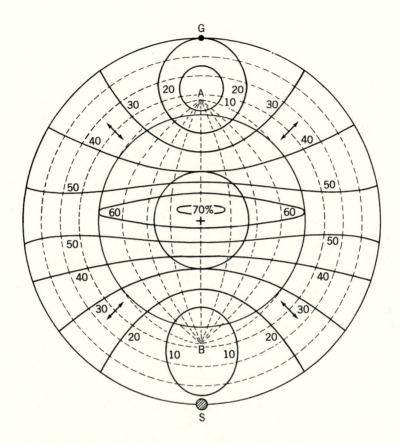

Figure 10.17   The pattern of polarization of the sky by day.
The sun is at the bottom and the observer at the center of the graph.
The direction of polarization is at right angles to the dashed lines
(see double arrows). The amount of polarization is given by the
percentage figures on lines of equal polarization. *A* and *B* are neutral
points where polarization reaches zero. (After von Frisch, 1950.
From Thorpe, *Learning and Instinct in Animals,* Methuen and Company, Ltd., 1963.)

surface, that is, nothing to collide with. However, it does have a pattern
of another kind, surprising to us because we cannot detect it — the pattern of polarization (see Figure 10.17). It is utilized by insects with
compound eyes. It specifies the position of the sun in the hemisphere,
and a sufficient patch of blue sky specifies its position even when the
sun itself is obscured by clouds. Hence it is potential information for
geographical orientation, and the demonstration by von Frisch (1960)
of the use of this information by bees for navigation to and from the
hive is very striking. It provides an example of a kind of pattern vision
wholly foreign to us but nevertheless an example of perception.

• STRUCTURING OF AN ARRAY BY RADIANT SOURCES. We now come to a vexing question. The central thesis of ecological optics is that illumination instead of radiation is the typical stimulus for an eye, and the one which it is adapted to register. A single point of light in ambient darkness, corresponding to a single ray in the divergent pencil of rays emanating from a point source, carries the minimum of information because a single point has no structure. A *patch* of light in ambient darkness, however, corresponding to a radiating object that is large enough or near enough, can have structure. It begins to be an array, and the greater the angular scope of this array the more information it will carry. At some visual angle an eye will be able to register it and the observer will be able to identify a luminous object. As one gets closer to a bonfire on the hills at night, it becomes distinguishable as a fire instead of a star.

The assertion that radiant light does not convey information to an eye (Stage 1) has to be qualified. A point does not, but a structure begins to do so. Flames and fire and lamps and even fireflies can broadcast information about themselves directly; they do not depend on the broadcasting of their perspectives in the reverberating flux of illumination. The latter has been emphasized in this chapter because it has been neglected by physical optics.

Students of vision have long assumed that the forms and patterns of light are constituted by points of luminous energy, since this is implied by optics. They have taken the night sky with its star-points as a prototype of the visual stimulus. A constellation like the Big Dipper was assumed to be a primitive kind of form even by the Gestalt theorists, that is, a configuration of points with various relations of separation. An optic array, however, to use our terminology, is assumed not to be built up from points but instead to consist of transitions. The night sky, then, is not the case with which to begin the analysis of stimulus information; a textured surface is better. I believe that no matter how many relations of proximity one conceives between theoretical points of light, one cannot arrive at the optical structure that specifies a surface visible to an eye. Points of light can structure the darkness at night, to be sure, but it is not the kind of structure that evokes a perception of space.

Summary

This chapter is concerned with the structuring of ambient light by the environment. We are concerned primarily with the environment that is illuminated, not with the parts of the environment that are luminous. Moreover, we have excluded a whole realm of things that structure light in a civilized environment — the images, pictures, models, tracings, and writings of men — since they pattern light in a special way, and this deserves a chapter to itself.

Ambient light is structured as an array at a point of view in accordance with laws of ecological optics. The array at a stationary point consists of the perspective projections of things in the world — the surfaces, corners, curvatures, and edges of the permanent layout — and the changing perspectives of moving or changing things.

Only if ambient light is structured can that structure be transformed. Change of structure can occur in either of two general ways, by a movement of something in the world or by a shift of the point of view.

The most obvious cause of the structuring of light is the geometrical structure, the layout, of the environment. Layout can be analyzed either on a large scale (faces) or on a small scale (facets). The faces and facets of things, the edges, corners and curvatures, are mapped into the array by virtue of a law relating the inclination of a surface to the amount of light it reflects in a given direction. But there are two other causes of structure that combine with this one — the chemical composition of a substance that determines its reflectance (surface color), and the existence of cast shadows. Layout, pigmentation, and illumination can interact in producing optical structure. There is information in the ordinary daylight array to specify all three kinds of physical fact — spatial, chemical, and optical — but the isolation of these kinds of information remains a task for ecological optics and psychology.

Other causes of optical structure exist, but the facts they specify are not so vital for the behavior of animals, at least not for the behavior of all animals. Some of these are transparent substances, mirrors, irregular refracting surfaces, rainbows, and stars. The pattern of skylight polarization is a kind of optical structure, although it is effective stimulation only for insects.

The parts of the environment that are luminous, as against those that must be illuminated, constitute a special case. If they are large enough, they radiate both energy and information directly. But the field of visual information surrounding a campfire, for example, is quite different from the field of visual information surrounding an illuminated object, and it is the latter we principally seek to understand.

Supplementary Note for Students of Optics

Anyone who has studied modern optics as this mixed body of knowledge exists today will be puzzled, and perhaps offended, by what is here called ecological optics. Such a discipline does not, in truth, exist. But it purports to be a new basis for a science of vision, put together from parts of physical optics, illumination engineering, ecology, and perspective geometry. It is part of the author's attempt to reformulate more precisely the concept of the stimulus in psychology (Gibson, 1960).

Vasco Ronchi (1957) has argued eloquently that optics cannot be defined merely as the science of light, its origin, propagation, and detection by instruments; it must have some ultimate reference to an eye. Optics is the science of *vision*, not of *light*. Otherwise, he asserts, there are contradictions at the very heart of the discipline. I agree. But Ronchi, a physicist, assumes that an eye transmits nervous impulses that are "turned over to a mind which studies their characteristics and compares them with the mass of information in its files. In conclusion it creates a luminous and colored figure which it places where it believes the initial group of atoms to be" (p. 288). This is precisely what I, a psychologist, do not assume. Instead of making the nervous system carry the whole burden of explaining perception, I wish to assign part of this burden to light itself. Ecological optics is my way of doing so. This concerns light that is *relevant* to an eye, leaving aside radiation that is *irrelevant*. But I do not assume that light is *dependent* on an eye, as Ronchi seems to do.

The physicalist view of optics is so strongly entrenched in this country that, as Fry suggested (1957), "the only way the eye can get included in the field of optics is by virtue of the fact that the eye itself is accepted as an optical instrument" (p. 977). This is a prejudice in the opposite direction. What we need is a branch of optics which is neither mentalistic nor physicalistic, but which simply treats light as a stimulus.

Supplementary Note for Students of Visual Sensation

The reader who knows the facts of visual psychophysiology and psychophysics may wonder why no reference has been made to them in this chapter. Nothing has been said about the measuring of light intensity in patches by methods of photometry, or about the sensation of brightness that theoretically ought to correspond to the luminance of each patch in the optic array, or about the nature of this correspondence. The reason is that these elegant quantitative studies become irrelevant to perception, if the assumptions made in this chapter are correct. An excellent introduction to the complexities of measuring brightness sensations is provided by Hurvich and Jameson (1966).

An optic array has been defined in terms of the margins between its patches of luminance, not in terms of the luminances. The former are invariant with changes of illumination, but the latter are variable; the former are relations (that is, information), while the latter are the quantities measured by a light meter.

The sensation corresponding to a given luminance depends so much upon the other luminances in the array, and upon other conditions in the world, that it can never provide an explanation of the perception of the world. It is a laboratory curiosity of great interest. If we did not know so much about it, the present theory could never have been formulated. But nobody ever really sees a color sensation of this sort in the ordinary environment. Instead, one detects the pigmentation, facing, and illuminatedness of surfaces, all three together; and these invariants of the world can only be specified by invariants among the variable luminances of the optic array. Space perception is not based on sensations of brightness and color. For this reason, we do not need to review all the efforts of psychologists to measure and scale these sensations, and all the controversies to which they have led. Interesting as they may be, they are not in the line of inquiry that ends with perception.

Supplementary Note for Students of Philosophy

The reader who is familiar with John Stuart Mill's *An Examination of Sir William Hamilton's Philosophy* (1865) will notice a similarity between his hypothesis of the "permanent possibilities of sensation" and the notion of permanent optical possibilities of vision in an illuminated space. Mill even assumed *groups* of possibilities of sensation, as I have assumed connected sets of possible perspectives of a room, available to the observer who moves about. But the difference is that Mill could not conceive of invariance under transformation. His sensations were mere fugitive pictures in consciousness. He believed that their grouping constituted the basis for our *belief* in an external world, but this is far from asserting that the possibility of detecting stimulus invariance is the basis for *contact* with the external world.

XI / The Structuring of Light by Artifice

The groundwork for an understanding of how light is structured by the environment was laid in the last chapter. We may now consider a special case: how light is structured by artifice or art, that is, by man. For uncounted thousands of years, men have been altering the terrestrial environment in one manner or another. One of the ways in which they have done so is by making *displays*. They have made scratches or grooves on surfaces, have traced or painted upon surfaces, and have molded or manufactured substances into new surface-shapes. But something new happened about twenty or thirty thousand years ago. Evidence suggests that men of a group called Cro-Magnon made a startling discovery, the discovery of representation. Scratching, daubing and shaping began to be used for a new purpose — to make reliefs, pictures, and sculptures, that is, *images*.

The earliest methods of artificially structuring an optic array correspond to two of the three principal ways which the natural environment can itself structure an array — that is, by variations of, first, surface layout and, second, surface reflectance. Reliefs and sculptures are alterations of surface layout. Paintings are alterations of surface reflectance. The third main way in which the environment structures ambient light — by the casting of shadows on flat surfaces, thereby varying the surface illumination — was not used by man until much later, with the invention of shadow pictures. Examples are the oriental shadow plays and the screen pictures projected by a "magic lantern."

Displays, either non-representative handiwork or representative images, are thus substantial surfaces. Like any other surfaces of the world, they must be illuminated (or transilluminated or self-luminous) in order to convey information to an eye. They cannot be seen in the dark. They are sources of optical stimulation. But the peculiar fact about displays and images is that they are modifications of pre-existing surfaces, made for the special purpose of being looked at.

224

A representative display, an image, provides stimulus information about something other than what it is. More exactly, as I have suggested elsewhere, its optic array yields some of the same structural information as would the optic array from another part of the environment at a distant place or a different time. It is a substitute or surrogate, and thus provides for a kind of perception that is mediated instead of direct, a perception at second hand. An image is a means by which the artist can enable others to see what he has seen (Gibson, 1954). But a non-representative display, one that is not an image, is not any of these things. Its optic array does not copy that of another object. The graphic or plastic display that is not "iconic" has long puzzled artists, philosophers, and students of vision. Does it or does it not provide any information? Can it have meaning or is it nonsense? What is the use of finger painting, scribbling, forming, designing, and non-representative painting? The answer suggested is that such activities are useful to the human individual, whether artist or observer, as exercises in the production of optical structure and in the distinguishing of its limitless variations. They are exercises in perception if not of representation.

The structure of a natural optic array, including its invariants under transformation, specifies its source in the world by the laws of ecological optics. The structure of an artificial optic array may but need not specify such a source. A wholly invented structure need not specify anything. This last is a case of structure as such. It contains information, but not information *about*, and it affords perception but not perception *of*. The distinction will be elaborated later. For the present, we should note only that the human practice of making and seeing forms for their own sake permitted the assigning of arbitrary meanings to them. A few thousand years ago conventional alphabets were invented, that is, writing. Only because of this previous practice, I think, could our ancestors create graphic symbols and thus become literate.

The main themes of this chapter have been outlined above. Now, the outline needs to be filled out. The first thing to be clear about is the problem of representation. What is meant by an *image*?

The Original and Derived Meanings of the Term "Image"

The meaning of *image* is a slippery one and no end of confusion has resulted. In this chapter the word always means an environmental source of optical stimulation, the cause of an optic array but not the array itself. An image can be a solid model, sculpture, or statue, on the one hand; or a flat relief, picture, painting, drawing, or photograph, on the other.

The plastic image broadcasts its perspectives in all directions, while the graphic image yields a perspective only from in front. But both are delimited material objects producing an optic array of limited scope within the total array of ambient light. Even a so-called panoramic picture cannot present a view in all directions, a complete panorama of the environment including the hemispherical arrays from earth and sky.

Sculptures, paintings, and the intermediate case of reliefs were the only kinds of images known during prehistory and a good part of recorded history. But men eventually became curious about mirrors and lenses, and the developing science of optics inevitably borrowed the term *image* and used it to describe the results of operations on light rays. Most of the so-called images of instrumental optics, however, are fictions, not things. An optical instrument such as a microscope or telescope is an adjunct to an eye, and all it can do is deliver a magnified optic array to an eye. We should not confuse the "images" seen through eyepieces or in mirrors with paintings or sculptures, although we tend to do so.

The so-called retinal image is another fiction. It is not a picture. When Isaac Newton asserted that a visible object was "painted on the back of the eye" by rays of light, he misled us, and the error has persisted for two centuries. A dark chamber with a lens in one wall will indeed yield a visible inverted image on the opposite wall for a man in the chamber, a screen image. The camera with a sheet of ground glass in back will make the screen image visible from outside. The photographic camera will preserve such an image and make it visible later. But the eye is not a camera in the sense of a device producing a visible image. If it were such a device there would have to be a man to look at the retinal image, or a little man in the brain to look at the image "projected" on the brain. This man would have to have an eye to see the image with, so we are back where we started. Worse off, in fact, for we are faced with the insoluble paradox of an infinite series of nested individuals, each little man looking at the brain of the next bigger man.

The fallacy of supposing that the eye is a picture-taking instrument employed by the brain, or by a homunculus in the brain, is almost unquestioned by physicists and physiologists, and it equally confuses psychologists. They are accustomed to talking about visual after-images, memory images, and mental images — still another extension of the original meaning. This metaphorical usage leads to the theory that memory is the "storing" of images so as to permit later "retrieval" and that thinking consists of the little photographer in the brain looking at his collection of snapshots. The cerebral image in the brain, the physiological image in the nerve, and the retinal image in the eye are all fictions.

If we could think of an image in the derived sense as a complex of relations, as the invariant structure of an arrangement, in short as information, there would be no great harm in extending the original meaning of the term. But this is hard to do, for it carries too much weight of history. It is better not to try. It would surely be false to say that there is a phonograph record in the ear, and the same error tempts us when we say that there is an image in the eye.

The Distinction between Real and Apparent
Sources of an Optic Array

Physical optics makes a distinction between "real" and "virtual" images. In optics, what I have called a screen image (the picture made by projecting shadows on a surface, the structuring of an array by artificial variations of illumination) is called a "real" image, and so it is. What I call an optic array (the structured stimulus for an eye, chambered or compound) when it comes from a mirror or a lens is said to produce a "virtual" image. It is virtual, a virtual object, but not an image in my terminology. The apparent face in the mirror and the apparently near thing in the field of a telescope are objects in effect, nor in fact, but they are not pictures or sculptures or screen images. *The "virtual" image of optics is nothing more than a consequence of the fact that perception is caused by stimulation and depends on stimulus information.* One sees what the optic array entering the eye determines. A natural optic array specifies an object. If an optic array has been reflected by a mirror or magnified by a lens before entering the eye, the information specifies an object in the mirror or an object close to the eye. Such an object may properly be called illusory or apparent or phenomenal or virtual, but the stimulus has been produced by optics, not art.

There are two ways of artificially producing an optic array to an eye, causing the perception of an object, event, place, or person that is apparent but not real. All the various methods fall into two types, depending on whether they come from optics or art. The optical illusionist starts with the array from an environmental source and operates on it with mirrors, prisms, and lenses before it reaches the eye. The artist-illusionist fabricates a new source, a model, sculpture, relief, drawing, painting, photograph, or screen picture — in short, an image — and allows the array to reach the eye directly. There is an "illusion" in both cases, but they are of different sorts. The object in the mirror is not there at all. The object represented by an image is not there either, but *something* is — the image itself and this is interesting in its own right.

The riddle that classical optics, for its own convenience, has created for perception is illustrated by a celebrated dictum of Helmholtz, written at the beginning of his treatise on physiological optics. "Whenever an impression is made on the eye, with or without the aid of optical instruments, such objects are always imagined as being present in the field of view as would have to be there in order to produce the same impression on the nervous mechanism" (Helmholtz, 1925, p. 2). Insofar as this says that *the same stimulus coming to the eye, however produced, will always afford the same experience,* it is surely true (see below). But insofar as it says that visual perception consists of the imagining of external objects and the projecting of them into the field of view, it is mischievous. This doctrine is completely contrary to all I have been suggesting. The difference lies in stimulus *information.* Helmholtz assumes mere sense impressions made on the eye, while I assume information about objects entering the eye. The information may be partially falsified by instruments, but the objects are surely not products of imagination. To suppose that perception depends upon imagination is to put the cart before the horse.

The Origin of Images in Prehistory

Our ancestors of the Ice Age were successful cooperative hunters, with a variety of stone tools and tools made of bone or wood. They could work flint with great skill, and used needles, scrapers, borers, knives, axes, and the like to perform a great variety of tasks connected with fire-making, food-getting, and sheltering. In short, they were good with their hands, that is, with the visual control of manipulation and manufacture. They could mold clay, and decorate it. The watching of the hands, and the observed alterations of a substance that the hands could produce, had become very highly developed.

They often lived in rock shelters that, in certain protected valleys, had deep recesses behind them. They sometimes ventured into these caves and made finger tracing on walls glistening with dampness or made handprints on surfaces filmed with clay. There are examples of such doodling, designing, and finger painting still preserved after tens of thousands of years. Men had presumably been making and looking at such playful displays for ages previous, as children do today, tracing, scratching, and shaping available surfaces. But in certain deep caves, notably those of the Dordogne Valley in France, there are found unmistakable images, both pictures and sculptures (Daniel, 1955). The best of the paintings, made with pigments and charcoal, can be dated as more than twenty thousand years old. There are excellent portrayals of mammoths, for example, that have been extinct for nearly that long. Something very important for the psychological development of man had been discovered, perhaps suddenly, namely the image.

Let us consider what the first artist did, or more exactly, what the first limner did and what the first beholder perceived. The artist contrived a display that made the beholder and the artist alike see something that was not there, or more exactly, that was there and yet not there. A mammoth appeared on the wall of a cave! To perceive this for the first time, in the light of a flickering torch, must have been astonishing. The paradox would surely have puzzled this ancestral observer. The apparent mammoth would give him to think and it would tend to make a philosopher of him. The artist knew that he had made the mammoth appear with his own hands. Hunting magic and religion would come into the puzzle, no doubt — a dim awareness of *apparent* and *real, form* and *substance, spirit* and *body* — but the artist who paid attention to the technique of the image would also learn a new way of communicating, without speech, and a new way of looking at the world around him.

Before considering the psychological consequences of representation for man, however, let us consider the antecedents of it, the skills of eye and hand that made it possible.

The Fundamental Graphic Act

Manipulation of all sorts is guided by visual motions as well as by motions of bone hinges. To thread a needle, for example, demands close attention to the relative motions of hole and thread. In such acts the visual feedback disappears when the act is over. The act of trace-making, however, is a special case, in which there results not only a transient visual motion but also a persistent visual source. The motion, as we say, "leaves a trace," which outlasts the act. Making a trace on mud or clay with a finger or a stick *displays* the movement of the hand in a stationary form. There is a persisting record of the manipulation, and a newly created source of stimulation. Proprioception leads to perception. The making of traces on a surface is a fascinating act, as every human child discovers for himself at an early age, by finger painting or scribbling. Our human or semihuman ancestors too must surely have discovered it — long before the men of the Ice Age discovered representation or how to make images.

Linear trace-making might be called the *fundamental graphic act*. It is easy. One can leave a line on almost any surface except water. It can be done in two ways, by making a groove on the surface or by leaving a deposit on it. A finger will often serve for either, although a tool of some sort may be better — a sharp point, a charred stick, a chalky stone, or a chewed twig dipped in pigment. All these were used by the cave artists.

The *fundamental plastic act* can be distinguished from the fundamental graphic act, but there is no sharp division between them. Indenting and hand-printing pass over into molding and modeling; grooving and digging pass over into flaking and carving. The making of pots and tools preceded the contriving of sculptures or solid representations just as the making of traces preceded the contriving of pictures or surface representations. The graphic art is of more concern to us because eventually it permitted the invention of alphabetic writing.

The essence of the graphic act is *to change progressively the capacity of a surface to structure light by layout or pigment, the progress of the change being coincident with the movement of the hand*. This will serve as a definition. Examples are to scratch, chisel, mark, daub, paint, draw, trace, or write. The controlling of the displayed trace is necessary, I suggest, before a man can learn to depict or to write.

Experiments on the Graphic Act

The studies that have been made of the development of scribbling in young children are not very revealing, except to show that children seem to enjoy it. But scribbling is not simply play, or an opportunity for the child to "express himself"; it is an opportunity for the educating of visual attention and for learning to perceive in new ways. It would be interesting to know whether children continue to scribble when they are given a crayon that leaves no visible trace. (An experiment in progress as this book goes to press seems to prove that they refuse to do so.)

The importance of the progressive visual trace as distinguished from the motor act is suggested by an experiment of Michotte (1963, p. 289). A red square appears on a screen; it moves and, as it does, a black rectangle appears to elongate immediately behind it. This peculiar optical transformation yields a compelling perception of a *trace being made* and of its *being made by the red square* (see Figure 11.1). There are no sensory data for a tracing tool or a guiding hand, but observers report that the red square *writes*, or *draws*, or *paints*. Slight changes in the transformation destroy the effect. Michotte seems to have abstracted the visual stimulus information that goes with tracing.

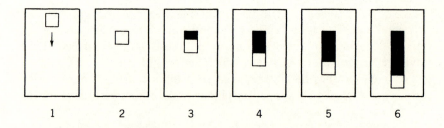

1   2   3   4   5   6

Figure 11.1   An optical sequence that yields the perception of trace-making. These pictures represent six moments of a continuous event, reading from left to right. The event perceived is a moving thing leaving a trace behind it.

The Consequences of Pictorial Representation

Since the cave paintings, men have been making and observing images at an accelerated rate. Every culture has its art. Sculpture was perfected by the ancient Greeks. With the discovery of the technique of pictorial perspective in the Renaissance came the flowering of representative painting. With the nineteenth-century photography arose to cheat the painters of their role in society; then came photo-engraving, and recently cinematography, and now the moving vacuum-tube image. A complete history of representation has not yet been written. The methods are extremely various, and it is hard to separate technology from art, and art from psychology (Gombrich, 1960; Arnheim, 1954). In the welter of confusion, it will not be easy to establish a science of pictures comparable to the science of linguistics. But if we can agree, first, that what an artist or technician does is to structure light by the same methods that structure light in the environment, and second, that the structure of light carries information, we might be able to make a start.

The Illusion of Reality in Pictorial Perception

The painters of the Renaissance, especially Leonardo da Vinci, began to apply the emerging concept of light rays to the making of faithful pictures. They thought of a picture not as a mammoth appearing on a wall, or a king on a stone cliff, or a warrior on a vase, or an angel on a gilt panel, but as a *window*. A whole scene could thus be represented, a sector of the ambient light surrounding a person. This kind of picture required a frame. The principle is shown in Figure 11.2.

After two centuries of progress with this wondrous method, an English mathematician could say, in a book entitled *Linear Perspective*, "We must consider that a Picture painted in its utmost degree of Perfection ought to affect the Eye of the Beholder so that he should not be able to judge whether what he sees is only a few Colours laid artificially on a cloth or the very Objects there represented, seen through the frame of the Picture as through a Window. To produce this effect, it is plain the Light ought to come from the Picture to the spectator's eye in the very same manner as it would do from the Objects themselves" (Taylor, 1715).

Such pictures could indeed deceive the eye of the beholder, and he might well take an image for a reality if a real window were substituted for the frame of the painting — that is, if he looked at the canvas through an aperture. He would have to keep his head still, however, and position one eye at the station-point of the picture-plane for the deception to be complete. The least amount of transformation, either from successive positions of one eye or different positions of two eyes, would specify the flat image (Gibson, 1954, 1960). No man has ever been permanently deceived

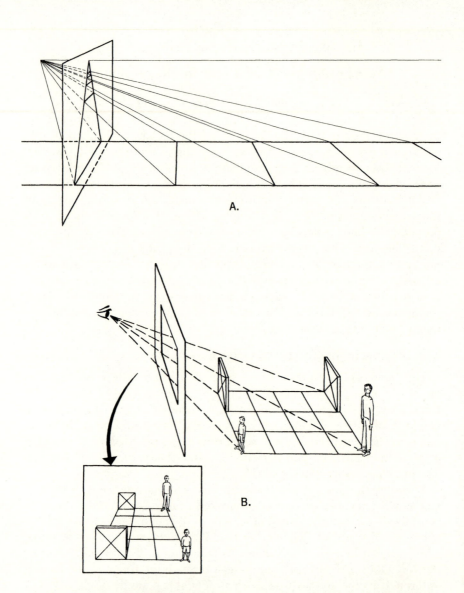

Figure 11.2 The principles of pictorial representation. The projection on a picture-plane of a regular pavement extending into the distance is shown in A. The main laws of linear perspective can be observed, especially the vanishing point at the horizon. The projection of a scene on a window of the picture-plane is shown in B. Note the angular size relations and the transformations of square-into-trapezoid. Straight edges are projected as straight lines in the picture (straightness is invariant). The perspective of surface texture is not shown, only what are called *outlines*. In both cases, note that it is the optic array that is the stimulus, not the image. (A. From J. J. Gibson, *The Perception of the Visual World,* Houghton Mifflin, 1950. B. After Julian E. Hochberg, *Perception,* © 1964. Adapted by permission of Prentice-Hall, Inc., Englewood Cliffs, N. J.)

by such an arrangement. Nevertheless, the illusion of reality, given a "suspension of disbelief," is present. The search for realism in painting has been discussed by Gombrich in *Art and Illusion* (1960).

In our terms, the more closely the stationary structure of an optic array from a picture approximates the stationary structure of the optic array from a window opening on a hypothetical environment, the more nearly a beholder will get a perception of that environment. The information for the perception is contained in the structure of the array. Its intensity does not matter much, and therefore a painting (or a transparency) can be strongly or weakly illuminated (or transilluminated) without affecting the perception. The surfaces and their colors, textures, slants, edges, corners, curvatures, and shadows can be specified by optical structure. There are not merely "cues for depth" in the array; there is information for the whole layout of surface and space in reciprocal relationships to color and illumination. This formula of the *interdependence* of space, color, and illumination was stated in the last chapter.

The geometrical laws of linear perspective on the picture-plane, as illustrated in Figure 11.2, hold only for the edges and corners of represented surfaces, their junctions, not for their colors and degrees of illumination. The junction of two surfaces in the world becomes a line in the picture. Linear perspective was therefore appropriate for representing and conceiving buildings, and it was architects who developed linear perspective to its fullest extent (Ware, 1900). But the perspective of reflectance and illuminatedness must be included in order to represent the curvatures and tones of flesh, or the textures and shadows of a sunlit landscape. It seems to have been the French painters of the nineteenth century who strongly rebelled against the painting of edges and corners and began, as they said, to paint *light*. They called themselves impressionists largely, I think, because sensations of light and color, sense impressions, had by that time been advertised as the basis of all vision by physiologists, psychologists, and philosophers. Artists are often right for the wrong reasons.

The striving for an approximation to immediate first-hand experience explains also the efforts of the past century to overcome certain limitations of the framed picture. Some of them may be listed. (1) Panoramas of battles scenes were constructed with the painting almost surrounding the observers, who stood on a platform in the center. There is a popular one in Gettysburg still, and there are others in Europe. (2) The parlor stereoscope with two pictures was devised to "add depth" to a picture, binocular depth, although much of the improvement was no more than would have been obtained by looking at it with one eye at the proper station-point through an aperture that hid the frame (see Schlosberg, 1941, on stereoscopic depth from single pictures). (3) The devising of ridged surfaces that permit the head to move while still delivering two disparate arrays to the two eyes has been achieved and this does indeed yield a stereoscopic picture. (4) The motion picture (including the television screen) is another matter. It dramatically freed the observer from having to perceive only a single unique view of the apparent environment, the observer being forever fixed to one spot and the environment frozen in time. (5) The binocular-stereo motion picture ("3-D movies") was tried out on the public at one time, but the added information is anomalous, of necessity; objects sometimes protrude into the air from the screen and the perception is unnatural. (6) The semipanoramic motion picture in the existing commercial form called "Cinerama" yields an extremely vivid illusion of reality, including that of vicarious passive locomotion in all sorts of vehicles from roller coasters to airplanes. This is the widest window so far contrived on distant parts of the world, and it is a far cry indeed from the painted mammoth on the cave wall. It is a good show—that is, it *shows* the beholder events he would never see if he stayed at home. But it is not the success its promoters hoped it would be. Just why is an interesting question.

Note that the information in a still picture consists of the variables of structure in its optic array. The information in a motion picture contains the additional variables of transformation in the array with all the invariant variables under transformation remaining to take the place of the formerly frozen structure. A motion picture is therefore much richer in information than a still picture.

The Consequences of Perception at Second Hand

The process by which an individual becomes aware of what exists and what goes on around him is perception. The process by which a human individual is *made* aware of things outside his immediate environment is one stage higher. It is mediated perception. It involves the action of another person besides the perceiver. A man or a child can, as we say, *be told* about things, or *be taught*, or *be given to understand*, or *be informed*, or *be shown*. Speech, that triumph of the human species, is the earliest and perhaps the principal vehicle for this indirect apprehension. But speech symbols have their limitations, and a powerful supplement to speech was acquired in the discovery of image-making.

The human learner, from childhood on, often needs to be given an acquaintance with objects, places, events, animals, persons, and facts that he has not yet encountered. Pictures, models, diagrams, and maps will do this in a way that words cannot. The information in a train of sound waves broadcast from a vocal apparatus can specify many properties of things but the information in the optic array from a representation can specify other properties of things that the former cannot — subleties of shape, for example, for which words do not yet exist. Both symbols and images are surrogates for other things, but the former must specify by the relation of *convention*, while the latter can specify by the relation of *projection*. So, at least, I have argued (Gibson, 1954). My examples of these two kinds of relations are the correspondence between an automobile and its license plate, and the correspondence between the automobile and its shadow.

The correspondences between surrogates and what they stand for have to be learned. One might guess that the more nearly a surrogate specifies an object by convention, the more associative learning has to occur; while the more nearly it specifies by projection, the less associative learning has to occur. The perceiver must learn in any case to distinguish among the objects of the world and must learn to distinguish among the surrogates of his culture; but the added burden of arbitrary associative learning is less for images than it is for symbols.

The consequences of mediated apprehension by surrogates, that is, by words and images, were momentous. Animals and men alike can have what William James called "knowledge of acquaintance," but only men can have what he called "knowledge about." The latter is a case of second-hand acquaintance. This is a great advantage of socialized knowledge over individual knowledge. But the virtue of images over words seems to be that they permit socialized knowledge to be closer to immediate apprehension, i.e., closer to knowledge by direct acquaintance. The cultural heredity of man fortunately includes the arts of representation as well as the arts of language.

The Consequences of the Pictorial Attitude for Psychology

There is a curious paradox about a picture — it is neither a pure display on the one hand nor a pure deception on the other. The stimulus conveys information for both what it is physically and what it stands for. The painted mammoth (Figure 11.3) could therefore be seen as either paint or mammoth, or both.

The first pictorial artists and all of them since have had to pay attention to the paint as well as the mammoth. They had to watch the traces being made, and the progressive alteration of the surface. They could not fail to perceive outline and form and they surely became puzzled by the difference between the line on the surface and the edge-depth of the object, between the flat form and the solid form. This puzzle is as old as art, and formed one of the roots of philosophy.

There is a difference between *perceiving* and *seeing in perspective*. When the artist attends to the thing pictured he is perceiving, but when he attends to the picture he is seing in perspective. The latter is having sensations. It was, I suggest, a new kind of seeing when it first occurred. It required a special attitude of perception — the pictorial attitude. It had

Figure 11.3   The cave painting of a mammoth. This picture
was made on a cave wall, probably with charcoal pigment. The
texture of the rock surface has been omitted from the reproduction.
The distinctive features of a young mammoth have been carefully
observed and rendered. (Bettman Archive)

to be learned, as presumably it has to be learned by every human child.
To see an animal in perspective requires doing so from the front, side,
back, or above. (The cave artists chose the profile exclusively.) I am suggesting that men had not paid attention to the perspectives of things until
they learned to draw and to perceive by means of drawings. Before that
time they needed only to detect the specifying invariants of things that
differentiated them — their distinctive features, not their momentary aspects or frozen projections. Young children are also, I think, not aware of
aspects or forms as such until they begin to notice pictures as surfaces.
The *invariants* in a pictorial array, the information *about* the dog, cat,
man, house, or car, are picked up very early, but the embodiment of the
ghostly shape of an object is not noticed, and children do not take a
pictorial attitude toward ordinary objects until they learn to do so.

    As a consequence of the pictorial attitude toward the environment,
men began to be self-conscious about perception. They began to notice

the patchwork of the visual field, the forms and colors of light as distinguished from the shapes and pigments of the world. They began to have sensations. They noticed that a form seemed to appear smaller as the distance of the object increased, that one form took a piece out of another when one object was in front of another, and that the world, with this attitude, could look flat. They noticed that the patchwork changed when they moved their eyes. They noticed double images. Eventually they noticed spots before the eyes, and after-images from glancing at the sun, and the blind spot. I have described the differences between the experience of the visual field and the experience of the visual world in a previous book (Gibson, 1950, Ch. 3). A man, if he tries, can *almost* see the world as it would project on a glass plate in front of his face — the inverse of his retinal projection, or a so-called retinal "image." He can never quite do so, for there is always some compromise with natural perception. If it were easy to detect pure sensations, we could all be representational painters without training.

. . . .

The Visual Field and the Visual World

A halfway stage between the present theory of information-based perception and the accepted notion of sensation-based perception is represented in a debate between the author and Professor Boring some years ago (Boring, 1952a; Gibson, 1952a; Boring, 1952b). The question was how to define the experience of the visual field, sensation, as contrasted with that of the visual world, perception. Boring argued that the field was a *reduced* experience, that is, perception reduced to its fundamental data. I maintained that they were *alternative* experiences, but my argument was weak since I was not then bold enough to assert that the data for perception, the invariants of available stimulus information, were quite independent of the data for sensation, the retinal images considered as pictures. I would now maintain that the optical (not retinal) gradients and the other invariants that carry the information for perception are often not open to analytic introspection, and that perception is therefore, in principle, not reducible to sensations.

. . . .

The theory of sensations as the basis of perception presumes that the infant at birth must see the world in this way, as a flat picture. Only the infant has the completely "innocent eye" that the painter must try to recover if he is to paint truly (Ruskin, quoted in Gombrich, 1960, p. 296). For more than two centuries investigators have been trying to test this assumption. One method has been to question persons blind from birth who had later been given sight by the operation of removing a cataract (von Senden, 1960). They did not report seeing things on a plane in front of the eye, or *in* the eye, unless this was suggested to them.

The supposedly pictorial vision of the infant has thus not been verified, but in the absence of any alternative to sensation as the basis of perception, psychology and philosophy have assumed it, and have thus been faced with the puzzle of explaining depth perception.

The problem of depth perception considered as the conversion of two-dimensional experience into three-dimensional experience seems to me quite insoluble. In this book, and implicitly in my earlier book (Gibson, 1950), the problem disappears. If sensations are not entailed in perception at all, why speculate about how they might be changed into perceptions?

The Consequences of the Pictorial Attitude for Art

Consider again the primitive artist who had to pay attention to both the paint on the wall and the mammoth in the world. An image, paradoxically, is both an object in its own right and a surrogate for some other object. This division of attention and this paradox may explain why artists have wavered between the aim of trying to show us something about the world and the aim of trying to interest us in form as such.

The non-representative display is much older than the image. The fundamental graphic and plastic acts, the manipulations that leave records on the environment, had to precede the contriving of pictures and sculptures. And so the artist, even when most meticulously specifying a real piece of the environment, must have been aware of the "medium," as he calls it, or the technique — in short the operation he is using to structure light. The Dutch still-life painters of the seventeenth century, who could render a drop of water (Figure 11.4) on a flower so that it seemed to stand out from the canvas, were attending very carefully indeed to the rules of display. The artist takes pleasure in the image for its own sake and so does the observer. Such motivation can be called esthetic, but that is a very elegant term for it.

The trouble was that the various rationalizations for this interest got mixed up with philosophical and psychological puzzles. Forms were taken to be something ghostly instead of substantial. Images were appropriated by optics and were said to be unreal. The eye was said to contain a picture. After photography, non-representative patterns were claimed to have a meaning of their own, and it was said to be the mission of artists to discover and show us this meaning. Perspective was rejected and was said to be a mere convention, but artists were supposed to be able to paint "space" (whatever that is). The legitimate endeavor of working artists to practice the art of structuring light, as here defined, was obscured by intellectual confusion. It is no wonder that so many artists refuse to talk about their work.

Figure 11.4 Drops of water with insect. In this detail of a still life, the actual microstructure of an optic array has been produced by the painter with tiny applications of pigment to canvas, working under a magnifying glass. (Detail from the painting, "Vase of Flowers" by Jan Van Huysum. Courtesy, Museum of Fine Arts, Boston. Bequest of Stanton Blake.)

The Concern with Optical Structure as Such

No one, artist or psychologist, has ever been quite sure what a *line* was, or a *boundary, margin, contour, texture, pattern,* or *form.* The status of these things was in doubt. They might be real or unreal, concrete or abstract, in the world or in the light, or only in the mind. I attempt to resolve this uncertainty by asserting that the structure of an optic array must be distinguished from the causes of structure in the array. The main causes of optical structure seem to be of three sorts: illuminated surfaces of the environment that face in different directions (geometrical or layout structure), illuminated surface colors of the environment (pigment structure), and variable illumination of the environment (shadow structure). Ambient light from the terrestrial environment has structure from all three causes in combination. The structure of an array from a sculptured or engraved display depends on geometrical structure. The structure of an array from a painted display depends on pigment structure. The structure of an array from a screen depends on shadow structure.

What the artist and the perceptionist are ultimately concerned with, therefore, are the boundaries, textures, patterns, and forms of light, the optical stimulus; but what they have to work with are the boundaries, textures, patterns and forms of surfaces, pigments, and shadows, the sources of the optical stimulus. These are not the same, but we tend to confuse them because the words are the same. The optical texture of painted velvet, for example (Figure 11.5), is not the texture of the pigments on the canvas, although there is a relation of correspondence between them. And neither is at all the same as the woven pile of the textile itself, the physical texture, although they can specify it.

The kinds of information conveyed by optical structure are a problem for the artist and the psychologist alike. Artists have been working on the problem for centuries, although they have not put it into these words. Psychologists are now beginning to work on it. Each can learn from the other. The artist Kepes, in *The Language of Vision* (1944), has shown many of the variables of optical structure that yield variables of visual experience, and so has Metzger, a psychologist, in *Gesetze des Sehens* (1953). Formal experiments on this kind of psychophysical correspondence are hard to set up, but they will surely be increasingly successful in the future.

The variables of optical structure that carry information, it is now clear, include much more than the variables of "form." There are textures, and densities of texture, and gradients of density of texture. There are forms within forms, subforms down to the limits of acuity and superforms up to the earth-sky separation. There are abrupt transitions and

Figure 11.5 The textures of velvet and fur. Presumably the optic array given by the photograph is nearly the same as that given the naked eye at the appropriate station-point. The painter achieves an array like the photograph by skillful application of pigments. Compare Figure 11.4. (Painting "Sir Thomas More" by Hans Holbein the Younger. Copyright, The Frick Collection, New York. Photo by Susan McCartney.)

gradual transitions. There are symmetries and asymmetries, regular patterns and irregular patterns. The notion of "formless" or "unstructured" stimulation is based on the fallacy that simple regularity is the only kind. Inkblots, clouds, and the spattering of paint have structure, even if it is not simple. Proportions and ratios of higher order may specify facts of higher order, and the "golden" proportions of Greek architecture were conventions, not laws of nature. Above all, it should be remembered that the informative variables of optical structure are *invariant under changes in the intensity of illumination and changes in the station-point of the observer.*

The Structuring of Light by Alphabetic Writing

Several thousand years ago a new use was found for the graphic act of tracing. Display marks, it was gradually discovered, could specify the sounds of speech besides being able to specify objects. The sounds of speech could already specify objects by their names, and a great deal more (propositions, commands, questions), but they were impermanent, since the voice left no record of its action as the hand could record its movement. Pictures, as they had developed into the forms called pictographs, ideographs, or hieroglyphs, could specify objects somewhat better than names could (although they were incapable of stating, commanding, and questioning); but they were also themselves objects and could be carried about, observed by anyone, and used by one generation after another. When the virtues of the spoken language were combined with the advantage of permanence, a great step forward was taken. Men could talk, as it were, across distance and time. Social interaction became possible without a face-to-face meeting. Messages could be sent over great distances. Knowledge could accumulate in storehouses. The young could be taught by the wisest teachers, living or dead. History and civilization began.

A string of syllabic or phonetic graphs (see Figure 11.6), to be sure, had to be converted into speech by the observer before it could mediate apprehension, whereas a series of pictorial graphs did not. The connection between grapheme and phoneme and thence to the referent is conventional and arbitrary, whereas the connection between picture and referent is more like that between stimulus and source. One has to discriminate the graphemes in order to learn to read, and in old-fashioned schools one had to "learn the alphabet." Some children find it difficult to learn to read. Literacy is more demanding than second-hand knowledge by way of pictures. But literacy makes available the abstract insights and considered admonitions of philosophers and prophets. Art,

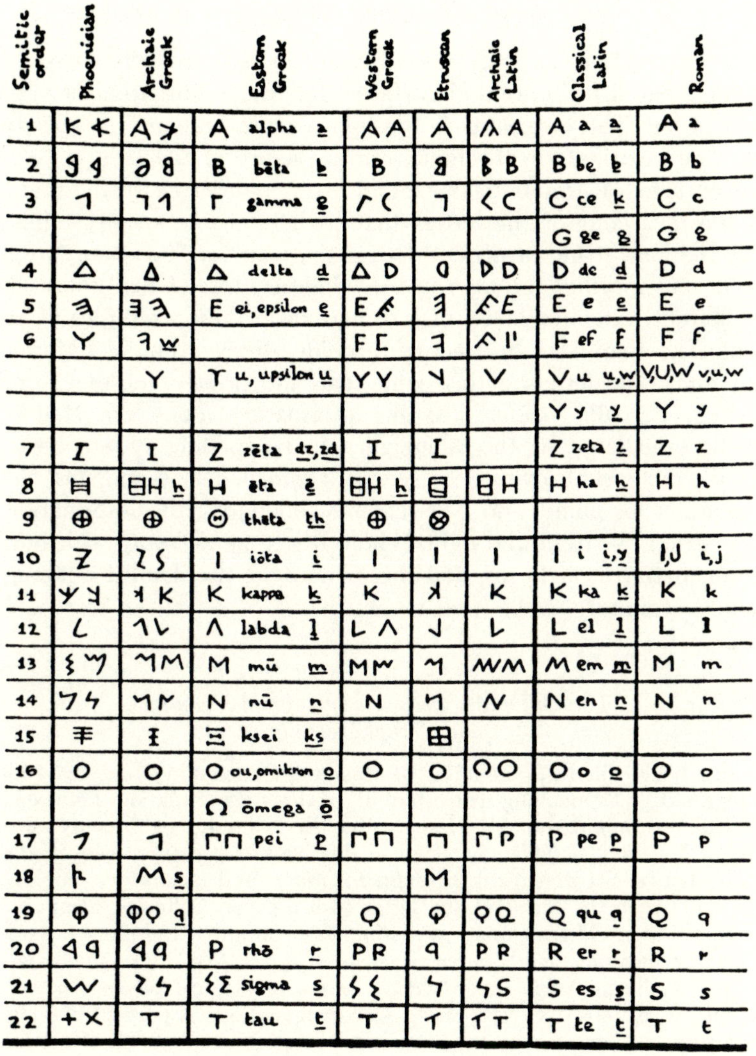

Semitic order	Phoenician	Archaic Greek	Eastern Greek	Western Greek	Etruscan	Archaic Latin	Classical Latin	Roman
1	K ⟨	A ⟩	A alpha a	A A	A	∧ A	A a a	A a
2	9 ⟨	∂ 8	B bēta b	B	8	⟨ B	B be b	B b
3	⟨	⟨⟨	Γ gamma g	Γ ⟨	⟨	⟨ C	C ce k	C c
							G ge g	G g
4	△	△	△ delta d	△ D	◁	▷ D	D de d	D d
5	⟨	⟨	E ei, epsilon e	E ⟨	⟨	⟨ E	E e e	E e
6	Y	⟨ w		F ⟨	⟨	∧ Iʹ	F ef f	F f
		Y	Υ u, upsilon u	Y Y	⟨	V	V u u,w	V,U,W v,u,w
							Y y y	Y y
7	I	I	Z zēta dz,zd	I	I		Z zeta z	Z z
8	⊟	⊟H h	H ēta ē	⊟H h	⊟	⊟H	H ha h	H h
9	⊕	⊕	⊙ thēta th	⊕	⊗			
10	Z	⟨⟨	I iōta i	I	I	I	I i i,y	I,J i,j
11	⟨ ⟨	⟨ K	K kappa k	K	⟨	K	K ka k	K k
12	⟨	⟨⟨	∧ labda l	L ∧	⟨	L	L el l	L l
13	⟨ ⟨	⟨M	⟨ mū m	M⟨	⟨	∧∧M	M em m	M m
14	⟨ ⟨	⟨⟨	N nū n	N	⟨	N	N en n	N n
15	⟨	I	Ξ ksei ks		⊞			
16	O	O	O ou, omikron o	O	O	⟨⟩	O o o	O o
			Ω ōmega ō					
17	⟨	⟨	ΓΠ pei p	ΓΠ	Π	Γ P	P pe p	P p
18	⟨	M s			M			
19	φ	φφ q		Q	φ	φ Q	Q qu q	Q q
20	⟨⟨	⟨⟨	P rhō r	P R	⟨	P R	R er r	R r
21	W	⟨⟨	⟨Σ sigma s	⟨⟨	⟨	⟨S	S es s	S s
22	+ X	T	T tau t	T	⟨	⟨T	T te t	T t

Figure 11.6 Early alphabets. This table represents the descent of the western alphabet, the Roman, from the Semitic. (Reprinted from *The Triumph of the Alphabet: A History of Writing*, by A. C. Moorhouse. By permission of Abelard-Schuman, Ltd. All rights reserved. Copyright 1953 by Henry Schuman, Inc.)

at its best, cannot generalize as literature can — not in the same ways.

Consider the structure of light reflected from a series of adjacent letters. They can be written on stone, clay, papyrus, vellum, or paper, and can be made by stylus, brush, charcoal, pen, or typeface. This structure carries information, as does the structure of light reflected from naturally pigmented or contoured surfaces, but the information is of much higher order. The invariants in the light from a human face specify the man. The invariants in the light from a picture of the face can specify the man. The invariants in the sound of his name specify the man, and thus the invariants of the letters that spell his name specify him. And finally the long string of printed letters that can say "this man is wanted for murder" specifies the man in the whole context of his group. There are different orders or levels of information in these examples of stimulation. The man and his picture provide direct stimulus information about him. The letters of his name, and the printed message, provide what may be called *coded* stimulus information about him, that is, information mediated by the language and the spelling system.

At all four visual levels, (1) seeing the man, (2) seeing his picture, (3) reading his name, and (4) reading about him, the information has to be carried by structured light. There has to be an array with borders, textures, patterns, or forms, and this is why the problem of defining the structure of an array is so fundamental.

. . . .

The Difference between Perceptual Meaning and Verbal Meaning

In a book called *The Meaning of Meaning*, Ogden and Richards (1930) suggested that meaning consisted of a three-way relation between a *thought*, a *symbol*, and its *referent*. But this is surely not the only meaning of meaning. I have suggested in this book that a three-way relation exists between a *percept*, a *stimulus invariant*, and its *source*. The relations between the terms in the latter case are very different from those in the former. The meaning of a stimulus invariant is therefore different from the meaning of a symbol, such as a word. A stimulus invariant is related to its source in the world by laws of ecological physics, whereas a word is related to its referent by social convention. A percept is related to a stimulus invariant by the resonance of a perceptual system (as I shall argue), where a thought is related to a word by the learning of an association. The differences are diagrammed below:

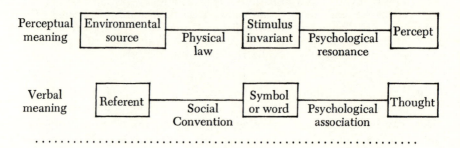

. . . .

Two Conceptions of the Information in Stimulation

Perhaps it is now possible to understand more clearly two different conceptions of stimulus information, both of which are valid but only one of which has been emphasized so far in this book. One is information *about*. The other is information considered as *structure*. The former permits perception *of*. The latter allows perception considered as *discrimination*.

In the last ten or fifteen years there has arisen a mathematical tool, called "information theory," which has many applications in psychology (Attneave, 1959) and other disciplines. It suggests methods of describing the stimuli for psychological experiments in quantitative terms. A stimulus may be treated simply as "what it is not but might have been," and information is defined as the reduction of uncertainty. This can be measured. A letter of the alphabet, for example, is differentiated by not being any of the other 25, and that, you might say, is all there is to a letter. Note that the meaning of a stimulus (what it stands for, or the source of a stimulus) is excluded from consideration. With this approach, the psychologist can provide stimuli for perception or learning in pure form, without having to worry about the puzzle of epistemology.

Garner has recently written about *Uncertainty and Structure as Psychological Concepts* (1962), suggesting that the structure of visual or auditory stimulation is the basis of what others have called information. One has to agree that spatial and temporal structure are requisites for perception since otherwise there is nothing to be discriminated. But this is information only as it provides the opportunity to *distinguish*, not the opportunity to *perceive*.

The psychologist's concern with optical structure as such is comparable in some ways to the artist's. The mere distinguishing of its limitless variations is interesting. The psychologist wants to test the limits of the capacity to distinguish; the artist wants to know the distinguishable variables of display. The case is similar for the musician concerned with the structure of instrumental sounds. Whether or not pure art and pure music have "meaning" is another question; at least they have structure. The structure of light and sound, the higher-order variables of simultaneous and successive order, constitute information in a special sense of the term, and a legitimate one. But this modern sense of the term is not the original one. According to the dictionary, information is "that which is got by word or picture," and nothing is said about structure.

Let us review the proposals made so far. Stimulus energy, unless it has structure, conveys no information. The natural structure of stimulation from the near environment conveys information directly. The structure of stimulation from representations conveys similar information, but indirectly. The structure of stimulation from socially coded or conventional signals conveys information still more indirectly. All these are *information about the environment*, although an increasingly remote environment. Finally the structure of stimulation from the displays of artists and experimenters on perception, from "abstract" art and the various devices for stimulating human eyes by artifice, conveys information in a pure mathematical sense. I have called it information *as such*.

Equivocal Information from a Picture

There is a class of pictorial displays that has long interested both psychologists and artists, in which alternative perceptions may be evoked by the same display. It is as if there were two things represented in the same place. The examples from experimental psychology are called the reversible figure-ground illusion and the reversible perspective illusion (Figure 11.7). In the former, a border or margin representing the edge of one surface superposed on another is arranged so that the apparent depth at the edge can reverse direction, the object becoming background and the background object. A goblet becomes a pair of faces, or vice versa. In the latter, a line representing the dihedral angle of two or more surfaces, the junction or "corner," is arranged so that the apparent convexity or concavity can reverse, and what formerly protruded is now hollow or vice versa. The back of a book becomes the front of a book, as shown, or a whole staircase from above becomes a staircase from below.

The reversibility of ridges and valleys was illustrated in Figure 10.11, and this is also a case of ambiguous convexity-concavity. There can be ambiguity in a frozen representation of a layout of surfaces. The absence of perspective transformations to specify the directions of slant is characteristic of such a picture. The ambiguity may even appear in different parts of the same apparent object as illustrated in Figure 11.8. The phenomenal object or surface layout is then "impossible."

The fact that alternative perceptions can arise from the same optic array is very puzzling. The stimulus has two different effects. This would seem to refute the assumption stated above (p. 228), that *the same stimulus coming to the eye will always afford the same experience*. The structure of the light has not changed when a pair of faces is seen instead of a vase, but the percept has changed. Doesn't this fact disprove the supposed dependence of perception on stimulation and prove instead that it also depends on the observer? The reversibility of perception with a constant stimulus has been so interpreted. It has even been taken to mean that there is no hope of discovering a lawful correspondence

Figure 11.7 Reversible surface-or-air and reversible con-vexity-or-concavity. On the left are two examples of ambiguous figure and ground (the goblet-faces display and the alternative Maltese crosses). On the right are two examples of reversible "perspective" (the ambiguous book and the ambiguous staircase). Stare at the center of each drawing for a time; observe what happens.

between stimulation and perception (Gibson, 1959). But let us examine the facts more closely.

In the goblet-faces display, the stimulus is the same for the two percepts but the stimulus *information* is not. In the absence of texture and parallax, the information for edge-depth or superposition has been arranged to specify two opposite directions of depth. There are two counterbalanced values of stimulus information in the same "stimulus." The perception is equivocal because what comes to the eye is equivocal. In such displays, the information for one-thing-in-front-of-another must

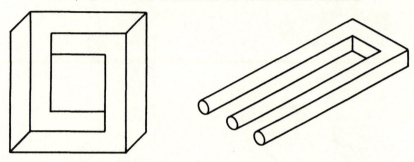

Figure 11.8   Impossible surface layouts in outline drawings.
When lines are used in a drawing, as distinguished from pigments
in a painting, they can be ambiguous in their representation of surfaces. Contradictory values of the information for layout may be
counterbalanced, as in these two examples.

come from variables of the mutual contour at the optical junction of the
two things. The complexity of such variables is illustrated in Figure 11.9,
where superposition may go one way, or the other way, or neither.

In the displays of reversible convexity-concavity and of paradoxical
transitions between substance and space, the same suggestion can be
offered, that contradictory counterbalanced information about surface
layout may coexist in the same picture. We are accustomed to the idea
of "conflicting cues" from different senses, but the idea of conflicting information from the same sense is unfamiliar. There is nothing implausible
about it, however, once we grant that sensations of light and dark are
irrelevant to the problem.

The hypothesis of stimulus information can now be restated more
generally. *The same stimulus array coming to the eye will always afford
the same perceptual experience insofar as it carries the same variables
of structural information.* If it also carries different or contradictory variables of information it will afford different or contradictory perceptual
experiences.

The puzzle of two or more reactions seemingly caused by the same

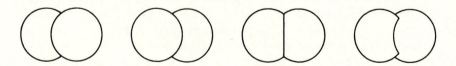

Figure 11.9   What makes one disk appear in front of the other?

"stimulus" arises, of course, for overt behavior as well as for perceptual activity. It has long been a difficulty for the stimulus-response hypothesis. Long ago it was found that the display of $\frac{6}{4}$ to a human subject would sometimes evoke the response "10" and sometimes the response "2". The puzzle was resolved by assuming that the response was a function of the subject's "set," the *aufgabe* or "determining tendency," as well as a function of the stimulus (Gibson, 1941). The response to the display depended on a task set to *add* or to *subtract*. But note that the display is ambiguous, unlike that of $6 + 4$ or $6 - 4$. The apprehension of the task itself depends on stimulus information; in the absence of information it is got by "context," or by whatever information there may be in the "total situation." The paradox of different responses to the same "stimulus," then, can be resolved by analyzing the stimulus for the information it contains as well as by appealing to subjective determining tendencies. And these latter will generally turn out to be forms of attention. A discussion of abstractive attention, and of the education of attention, will be offered in Chapter 13.

XII / The Pickup of Ambient Information: Scanning

The perceptual systems are capable of *obtaining* external stimulation, not merely of having it imposed on their receptors. This was the theme of Chapter 2. The principle has been exemplified in succeeding chapters. The auditory system can obtain equal stimulation at the two ears. Smelling and tasting obtain chemical stimulation at the receptors. The haptic system obtains tactile stimulation by exploratory movements of the hands. Above all, the human visual system obtains new samples of the array of ambient light by the activity called *scanning*. Scanning is defined as looking at parts of an array in succession. The obtaining of successive incoming cones of light, be it noted, is analogous to the obtaining of successive touches from a surface layout.

Samples of external stimulation are obtained for the sake of the information they carry about the environment, not for the sensations that may (or may not) accompany them. As a general rule, the individual explores, samples, or scans the sea of energy around him for what this proximal stimulation will specify about its ultimate sources. There are special cases, of course; the human individual can visually scan a picture for its design, but what he is generally in search of is meaning. The esthete may practice discrimination and enjoy the structure of a painting or the composition of music, but this is a sort of perceptual luxury.

In order to *search*, an active perceptual system has to be propriosensitive as well as exterosensitive, that is, it has to be self-guided in order to home in on the external information. This is true of looking, touching, smelling, tasting, and even listening. How the input of information is separated from the feedback of the system itself, or how it differs from the feedback, is not yet clear. An examination of the temporal course of perception in scanning may help to explain how this isolation or extraction occurs.

The last two chapters have been concerned with the available information for vision. Here we consider the actual pickup process. In man, visual attention is a matter of looking. Exploratory looking is somewhat like exploratory feeling as the process was described in Chapter 7. Each perceptual system has its own peculiar mode of attention, but these two are especially capable of sampling in discrete acts. Active smelling and tasting are less clearly episodic, and listening is the least capable of selective sampling.

The Problem of Perceiving by Scanning

The man in the dark who gropes with his fingers, like the insect who gropes with his antennae, seems to get a succession of contact stimuli, not a simultaneous pattern of them. Nevertheless, it is surely the simultaneous layout of the surfaces that he detects, whether or not he experiences a succession of sensory impressions. Similarly, a man who looks around the world, like any animal whose eyes are in the front of his head, seems to get a succession of optical stimuli, not a simultaneous panorama. What he ordinarily perceives, however, is the visual world, not a succession of visual fields.

The perception of a constant object that is explored by touching and the awareness of a constant environment that is explored by looking present a difficulty. It is especially a difficulty for the theory of sensation-based perception. How can a series of touch sensations be converted into the impression of a single thing? How can the sequence of retinal sensations be converted into the apprehension of a scene? The only solution to this difficulty seemed to be an appeal to memory. More exactly, the brain must be supposed to construct a simultaneous composite from the sequence of sensory data. This requires that each sensory datum be held over, or temporarily stored, in the form of a trace, so that the series can be put together at one time. Problems then arise as to how all the traces can be stored, at what place in the brain, and once stored, how they can later be retrieved. These problems are as yet unsolved. The theory of information-based perception can avoid these difficulties by denying that sensations combine with their traces to be converted into perception. It need not assume that perception requires a simultaneous composite in the brain — either a process of integrating successive data or one of organizing simultaneous data. The perception of a unitary constant object over time, or of a unitary visual world over time, might be explained by the assumption that unchanging information underlies the changing sequence of obtained stimulation, and that it gets attended to. This new assumption, of course, may seem to present equally serious difficulties, but perhaps they can be overcome.

Apprehension by scanning, or more generally, by sequential sampling, is a problem for vision and touch, but it ramifies into other fields of psychology. Awareness of things in time, and awareness of time, as Boring notes (1942, Ch. 15), has a long and obscure history. The relation of memory to learning puzzled Lashley (1951) — he called it the "problem of serial order in behavior." We will consider the problem only in relation to vision and touch but we will recognize its generality. In order to comprehend the problem, let us take it up piecemeal.

The Equivalence of Successive Sampling to Simultaneous Grasping

The detection of an adjacent arrangement has been taken to be simpler than the detection of a successive arrangement, on the grounds that the former requires only perceiving whereas the latter requires both perceiving and remembering. But this usage of the two terms is not consistent with the fact that a successive order may be equivalent to an adjacent order. An observer can apprehend a five-place number, say, when it is presented to vision in adjacent order (in the window of a tachistoscope) or when it is presented to audition in successive order (by speech). The same thing is true of a printed word and a spoken word; both are within the span of *apprehension*. It violates the facts to suppose that adjacent letters are governed exclusively by a span of *perception* while successive sounds are governed exclusively by a span of *memory*. Within limits, perception spans both kinds of order, spatial and temporal. This consideration seems to imply that the brain does *not* have to construct a simultaneous composite in order to register a sequence of items. The impossibility of sharply dividing perception from memory has led to the notion of "immediate" memory, or "primary" memory, or "short-term" memory, but these compromises do not solve the difficulty.

Now the remarkable fact about visual scanning is that awareness of the succession of temporary retinal impressions is completely absent from the perceptual experience. There is awareness of the simultaneous existence of all the objects in the world, or all the parts of a picture, despite the fact that the objects, or parts, are fixated one after another — at least with our kind of vision. The whole physical array seems to coexist phenomenally although it has been looked at sequentially. No one has ever been able to count his eye fixations while inspecting the world, or a picture, although it is easy to count the number of objects in the array. The retinal-impression theory of perception has an elaborate explanation of this puzzling fact in terms of a presumed *internal cancelling* of the retinal motions and an unconscious combining of retinal impressions (Helmholtz, 1925, p. 570). But it might be accounted for as a case of the equivalence of successive sampling and simultaneous grasping.

In the evolution of vertebrate vision, it should be remembered, the fish began with panoramic eyes that could encompass most of the ambient array at once. Later, as Walls (1942) suggests, some animals sacrificed the simultaneous grasp of ambient light for the advantages of frontal eyes. But this requires turning the head in order to get a full view of the surroundings. Overlapping, successive part views had to be substituted for the full view, and the nervous system of the animal had to be adapted to this substitution. The brain had to trade space for time, as it were.

The equivalence of successive to simultaneous pickup is also demonstrable in tactile scanning with the human observer. The experiment on the identifying of unfamiliar objects by haptic perception, reported in Chapter 7, showed that the shape of a sculptured solid could be detected by simply holding it motionless with the five fingers of one hand (or the ten fingers of two hands). In this method the shape is *grasped*, figuratively as well as literally, by means of the simultaneous compound input of the skin and joints. But the shape could also be detected as well or better by another method, in which the fingers were allowed to move over the layout of the solid, exploring its convexities and concavities, one by one or in various combinations. The simultaneous input, the momentary pattern from the skin and joints, was then not noticed. Neither was the sequence of the transformed patterns of input. Instead, the invariants of the object's shape emerged clearly from the successive transformations. Evidently, exploratory movement of the fingers can be substituted for a grasping posture of the fingers, and the information about convexities and concavities can still be picked up. Again, the brain seems to be able to trade space for time.

The Stable and Unbounded Character of the Phenomenal Visual World

The visual world as I once described it (Gibson, 1950, Ch. 8) has the property of being stable and unbounded. By stability is meant the fact that it does not seem to move when one turns his eyes or turns himself around (Figure 12.1) and that it does not seem to tilt when one inclines his head. By unboundedness is meant the fact that it does not seem to have anything like a circular or oval window frame. The phenomenal world seems to stay put, to remain upright, and to surround one completely. This experience is what a theory of perception must explain. The visual *field*, which seems to be experienced when one concentrates on what it feels like to see, does seem to be displaced when one turns the eye or head, it does rotate when one lies on his side, and it does have a sort of window-like boundary between inner content and outer nothingness, or indeterminacy. The mosaic of retinal receptors is displaced

Figure 12.1 A sequence of visual fields from left to right in the act of looking around a room. The man is sitting in an easy chair with his feet up. He is looking around the room. The drawings represent the visual field of the left eye in four stationary postures of the eye. His gaze is horizontal and the center of each field represents his point of fixation. Each is a wide-angle field; the

reader's eye would have to be very close to the picture for it to project the same angular array that was admitted to the man's eye. His nose appears at the right of each field. His body appears at the bottom of the field when he is looking forward. What does the man see? The answer is that he has four successive pictorial sensations but *he perceives the room.*

correspondingly relative to the retinal image and is rotated relative to the retinal image, and the mosaic has an anatomical boundary. Note that it is the retina that moves relative to the image projected on it, not the other way around, as we have been taught. The retina moves relative to its image *and relative to the pattern occupied by excited receptors.* The doctrine of the "transposability" of the retinal image is therefore stated backwards; usually it is the retina that is transposable over its relational pattern of excitation — a pattern that is projected from the outer world (Cf. Gibson, 1950, pp. 55ff.).

The sensation of the unstable and bounded visual field, I now suggest, comes from a vague kind of detection of the retinal mosaic. It is a matter of sensing the retina as such, not the image and not the relational pattern occupied by excited cells. Only insofar as one detects the qualities of the neurons, as required by the doctrine of Johannes Müller, does one have a sensation of a moving window. Insofar as the brain detects the relational pattern of places occupied by excited cells instead of the anatomical pattern of cells that are excited, one gets a perception of something stationary. The perceptual experience of the stable, unbounded visual world comes from the information in the ambient array that is sampled by a mobile retina.

The reason the world does not seem to move when the eye moves, therefore, is not as complicated as it has seemed to be. Why should it move? The movement of the eye and its retina is registered instead; the retina is propriosensitive. Even if a conscious visual sensation should arise from this retinal stimulation, and it seldom or never does, it would not affect the perception of the world.

The reason the world seems to surround the observer instead of having a window-like boundary is primarily that the ambient optic array surrounds the individual and has no boundary. Note again that, since the retina moves relative to the image projected from the array, it is the *retina* that has a boundary, not the *image.* The eye successively samples the available array, and its retina successively samples a corresponding potential image. This latter concept is a very strange one inded, and it will be considered later.

Ecological Optics and the Visual
Scanning Process

We can now treat successive sampling by the visual system in greater detail. The experimental study of human eye movements has been pursued since the beginning of the century (e.g., Woodworth, 1938, Ch. 23). It is an important problem for education, for example in reading (Carmichael and Dearborn, 1947). A great deal is known about how the eyes behave. The evidence has been interpreted in terms of retinal-image optics, but it can be understood just as well or better in terms of ecological optics. The physiology considered has been that of the retina, the eye, the optic nerve, and the eye muscles; but I shall try to consider the higher-order physiology of the whole visual system consisting of two eyes in a head on a body in an environment. The movements and postures of the eyes can only be understood in relation to the movements and postures of the head, and in turn to those of the body. The compensatory movements in this hierarchy that enable the eyes to maintain a stable orientation to the world have been described in Chapter 2.

Consider first the definitions of ambient light, of its parts, and of its temporary cones or samples. Then the various postures and movements of the head and eyes can be coordinated to these definitions.

Ambient Light and the Ambient Array

Ambient light was defined in Chapter 9 as the set of differences between light in different directions at a point of view, either stationary or moving. It is the available stimulus for the visual system, and it must be structured if it is to afford perception. The optic array was defined as the projection to a point of view of the faces and facets of the material environment, in consideration of their layout, shading, reflectance, luminosity, and the like.

The ambient array has parts of various solid-angular sizes. It contains forms within forms. Objects and interspaces (holes) project forms or figures in the array; the fine structure of a surface projects a texture in the array. A contour form may correspond to such varied things as a human face, the face of a clock, a picture, or the page of a book; or it may correspond to a window in a wall. These angular sectors of the ambient array are not to be confused with temporary *samples* of the array.

The transformation of an isolated part of the array results from a motion or an event in the world. The concurrent transformation of *all* parts of the array results from locomotion of the observer.

The Temporary Sample of an Ambient Array

There are two levels of sampling, one for a head with its two eyes, and one for a single eye.

• THE FIELD OF VIEW OF A HEAD. This can be defined as the light intercepted by the ocular system of any animal without a complete panoramic field. For man it is roughly a hemisphere, since the orbits have migrated to the front of the head and the entering light is limited by the eyebrows above and the nose and cheeks below. It spans about 180° horizontally and 150° vertically. When the head it turned on any axis, the oval field sweeps across the available ambient array, uncovering its structure at the leading boundary and covering it at the trailing boundary.

• THE FIELD OF VIEW OF AN EYE. This can be defined as the array that enters an eye. Depending on its anatomy, the eye may accept a cone of varying solid angle; in man it is considerably less than 180°. It was diagrammed in Figure 10.5, as Stage 5 in the discussion of ecological optics. As the eye turns on any axis (its swivelling movement on the sagittal axis being very limited), the cone sweeps across the field of view of the head. The temporary field of view of an eye corresponds in some respects to the temporary retinal image.

• THE FOVEAL FIELD OF VIEW OF AN EYE. This can be defined as a central cone within the entering cone of rays that projects on the fovea, when such exists. Vertebrate eyes have different kinds and degrees of foveation (Chapter 10; also Walls, 1942). In man, foveation is concentrated, and the central cone is therefore a narrow pencil. The sampling of the head's field of view by an eye of this sort can be confined to a small part of the field, such as that corresponding to a book page.

What, then, is the retinal image?

• A TEMPORARY RETINAL IMAGE. This is something not at all easy to define; its complexities are described in ponderous textbooks of ophthalmology and it is widely misunderstood, as we have noted in the last chapter. Roughly, it is an inverted projection on the interior of a sphere of the light intercepted by an eye. The intensity of the light, however, has been moderated by pupillary adjustment, some wavelengths have been filtered out, and the fine structure of the array in the center of the field is made registerable by the focusing of the image, eliminating blur, where it falls on the fovea. This is automatically accomplished by the accommodation of the lens, which "hunts" for an optimum state.

This complicated event is highly selective; it is selective with respect to the physical properties of light and it is also a temporary selected sample. It is surely a sample of something. But a sample of what? It is very hard to say. The question reveals the difficulties of retinal-image optics when it must face the problem of vision by scanning. Could it be that the retinal image is a sample of a *permanent* image?

• THE POTENTIAL RETINAL IMAGE OVER TIME. The retina sweeps over the retinal image, let us recall, just as the field of view of an eye sweeps over the field of view of the head. This means that the boundary of the retina uncovers a new portion of the image and covers an old one when the eye moves. There must exist, therefore, a sort of potential image that is only sampled by any single instance — something that can only be realized over time. It is inside the eye globe, and inverted. What an astonishing conception! It is nevertheless required by the facts of eye-movement if the retinal image is taken to be the basis of visual perception (Gibson, 1950, pp. 155–162). When extended, the potential image becomes an inverted microcosm inside the eye, like a panoramic painting of the world shrunken to the interior of a 1-inch sphere. It now seems to me an unnecessary fiction, since the optic array can be considered instead.

Exploratory Visual Attention

Now to describe the behavior of the eyes relative to the head and body in a way that connects it with the environment. First, the eyes are stabilized relative to the ambient array, being compensated for movements of the head or the head-and-body. Second, they are fixated on parts or details of the ambient array. Third, they selectively sample this array by jumping from one fixation to another. The body can be stationary or moving with reference to the environment, the head can be stationary or moving with reference to the body, and the eyes can be stationary or moving with reference to the head.

At the largest level of behavior, the body explores the environment by means of locomotion. There is a set of possible transformations of the ambient array for the paths of travel in a room, in a house, along a street, and so on. It is presumably by exploring this set that the individual gets a cognitive map of his environment. At the next level down, the ambient array at a station-point is explored by head-turning, the hemisphere intercepted at each head posture being a temporary sample of it. The set of overlapping samples exhausts the possibilities of vision at that station-point. When a man comes into a strange room, for example, two 90° turns of the head to left and right will encompass the whole room. The eyes, of course, will have been making compensatory and exploratory movements during these turns. At the smallest level of the visual system, that of the eye, the hemispherical field of the stationary head is explored by saccadic movements. This process is scanning in the narrow meaning of the term.

If a part of the ambient array projected from a colorful book, say, specifies an item of interest for the man who has entered the room, he may fixate on it, magnify it by locomotion and manipulation to an angular size of 10 or 15 degrees, and then begin to scan the print with the narrow central cones of his eyes. In this case, he scans in a special way, moving from left to right and top to bottom. The twitches will be very frequent, up to 10 per second, but they are so rapid relative to the pauses that during 90 per cent of the time the eyes will be fixated. The remarkable type of scanning required for reading has to be learned, in contrast with the natural zigzag scanning that occurs when the man looks around the room, or at a picture on the wall. In the latter case the items of interest in the array have not been conventionally laid out in an arbitrary adjacent order that corresponds to the sequential order of speech sounds.

Another type of fixation is possible for the human eyes, pursuit fixation. The man who enters a room may find another person there who is, let us assume, pacing up and down. The face of this person reflects a pinkish patch in the array, a patch that wipes across the background texture and undergoes complex deformations. Our observer will almost certainly apply his foveas to this small patch and track it with his eyes, for this part of the array probably carries more interesting information than any other. He will even scan its fine details, with minute fixations superposed on the pursuit fixation, identifying a smile, and observing whether the other person does or does not look directly at *him*. The optical information for this environmental fact — being or not being looked at — is extremely subtle, consisting of form relations in the light reflected from the dark pupils and white scleras of the eyes in proportion to the form of the face (Gibson and Pick, 1963). Nevertheless, as experiment shows, the information is registered with very high acuity. Men learn to watch the eyes of other men so as to detect their motivations. We can and do perceive the direction in which other people are looking, as Figure 12.2 illustrates.

How are the exploratory shifts of fixation guided or controlled? What causes the eyes to move in one direction rather than another, and to stop at one part of the array instead of another? The answer can only be that interesting structures in the array, and interesting bits of structure, particularly motions, *draw* the foveas toward them. Once it is admitted that the variables of optical structure contain information or meaning, that they specify what their sources afford, this hypothesis becomes reasonable. Certain loci in the array contain more information than others. The peripheral retina registers such a locus, the brain resonates vaguely, and the eye is turned. Subjectively we say that something "catches" our attention. Then the orienting reactions begin and continue until the retino-neuro-muscular system achieves a state of "clearness," and the brain resonates precisely. The focusing of the lens is just such a process and it, of course, accompanies fixation.

Experiments have shown that the periphery of the field of view of an eye does in fact register crude information. If an observer is required to fixate an uninteresting spot on a screen, and if a motion, pattern, form, or color is then displayed at some angular distance outward from the spot, he can identify certain features of the display but not others. If this experiment were pursued in an attempt to determine what variables of information can be reported instead of what qualities of sensation the peripheral receptors possess, it might be very revealing.

Figure 12.2 The perception of the gaze line. The pattern of each child's face shows the direction in which he is looking. (Syd Greenberg from Design Photographers International, Inc.)

The Persistence of Invariant Structure in Successive Samples

We now have a resolution of the difficulty described at the outset. The sampling of the world by locomotion, the sampling of the ambient array by head-turning, the sampling of the head's field by eye-turning, and the detailed sampling of parts of this field by foveal exploration, are all similar in one respect. The set of sequential samples is a unit in the sense that it comprises a mathematical group. The same structure persists throughout the series.

Take the samples of an ambient array obtained by combined head-turning and eye-turning. As noted above, the set constitutes the possibilities of vision at that station-point (Ch. 10, p. 194). Any two successive samples have a large overlap, since the maximum excursion of an eye movement cannot approach the angular field of the eye, and the same is true of a head movement. The amount of overlap is the amount of structure common to the two samples. It is the permanence in change or, in mathematical terms, the invariance under transformation.

The "problem of perceiving by scanning," the puzzle of how a sequence can be converted into a scene, only arises if each sample is assumed to be discrete from its neighbors in the series. This is what the traditional theory of sensations assumes. The retinal mosaic is taken to be sensed (in accordance with Müller's law), and its own stationary pattern of excited places, relative to which it moves, is overlooked. Each sensation, the "oval window" described, would then indeed be discrete and the sequence would have to be converted into a scene by an elaborate central operation, including memory. But if the sequence *contains* the scene, as just explained, it does not have to be converted into one.

The oval window of colored spots, corresponding to single receptors and their connected neurons, scintillates when the retina moves or twitches, and does so even when there is the slightest tremor of the eye muscles. The structure of these spots is wholly altered from one moment to the next. But this is structure relative to the *anatomy* of the system, not to the function or physiology of the system. The anatomical units of the system function vicariously. The structure of the bits of the *array* is unaltered from one moment to the next. The nervous system detects this structure without necessarily having to project a sample of it, spot for spot, on the surface of the brain by neural connections. The anatomical fact of an approximate "wiring system" from retina to brain has nothing to do with perception. It is evidenced on occasion, as when an after-sensation burned into the retina persists at the photochemical level. This illusion then seems to sweep across the structure of the optic array when the eye is turned; it "moves with the eye," as we say. But the nervous system surely did not evolve to pick up these subjective sensations. They are incidental.

The Superfluous Appeal to Memory

It should now be clear that the brain does not have to integrate successive visual sensations in immediate memory. There is no necessary reason to suppose that the fixations have to be retained. The invariance of perception with varying samples of overlapping stimulation may be accounted for by invariant information and by an attunement of the whole retino-neuro-muscular system to invariant information. The development of this attunement, or the education of attention, depends on past experience but not on the *storage* of past experiences.

The very idea of a retinal pattern-sensation that can be impressed on the neural tissue of the brain is a misconception, for the neural pattern never even existed in the retinal mosaic. There can be no anatomical engram in the brain if there was no anatomical image in the retina. The retina jerks about. It has a rapid tremor. It even has a gap in it (the blind spot). It is a scintillation, not an image. An engram impressed on the brain would have to be divided into two changing parts in the two halves of the brain, which is impossible. The whole idea stems from the persistent myth that there has to be something in the brain that is visible, and from Johannes Müller's assumption that the nerves telegraph messages to the brain.

. . . .

Why is the blind spot of the retina "filled in" even when the eye is fixated?

One of the standard experiments of the psychological laboratory is to have an observer close his left eye and fixate a black spot on a white cardboard screen with the right eye. Off to the right of his fixation point is an area of the screen corresponding to the blind spot of the retina — the place where receptors are missing because their fibers exit through this anatomical gap. The whole screen looks white. The margins of the "blind" area can be mapped, however, by finding where a moveable spot on the screen disappears or reappears. It is usually about a two-inch irregular circle at a screen distance of three feet.

The fact can now be established that any property of color or texture possessed by the surface *surrounding* the blind area (if the surroundings go out far enough) is also perceived *inside* the area. It is said to be "filled in" so that the color, or the newsprint, or the cloth, or fur, or striped wallpaper, or checkerboard pattern is continuous across the gap. My observations suggest that the slant of a surface, or the curvature, or an edge or a corner is also continued within the area. The only thing that disappears is an *exceptional* feature of the surface, or an *object* whose edges fall wholly within the area. If a form, a line drawing or a picture, is presented in this region of the field, what is perceived depends on how much of the drawing falls outside the area and whether these lines are diagnostic of something.

Is it necessary to conclude from this experiment that the anatomical gap in the retina is "filled in" by the brain, or that a process of organization in the cortex completes the image by a tendency toward "closure?" An alternative, surely, is to conclude that the receptive units of the retina surrounding the unreceptive disk of the optic nerve register whatever structural information they can, although their acuity is hampered by the scarcity of receptors.

The reason the surface area corresponding to the blind spot can look black or white or colored or striped or checkered or slanted is that it *cannot* appear to be a hole or gap in the surface. To see a hole or gap requires stimulus information, and that is just what the blind spot cannot pick up. "Filling in" is a misnomer, therefore, since there never was a phenomenal hole in the world to be filled in.

. . . .

It has been shown in previous chapters that the anatomical equipment of the body is not divided up neatly between the so-called senses, and that perceptual systems do not have exclusive possession of certain organs. The same organ may be employed for different uses at different times; the nose can either sniff the air or smell the contents of the mouth; the hand can be a sense organ or a motor organ. The study of evolution repeatedly exemplifies more than one use by an animal for a certain piece of anatomy. This equivalence of function in different settings must also hold true for the neurons of the nervous system. A nerve cell is not the same thing in different combinations of nerve cells, Müller notwithstanding. Lashley (1929) demonstrated this fact for parts of the brain, concluding that a given area of the cortex functioned vicariously, that it was equipotential to some degree for various kinds of performance. The principle should apply equally to the smallest units of the brain, the single cells. Especially it should apply to the receptors and the receptive units of the retina, for they have quite different uses at different times.

The Tuning of the System to Invariant Information

An individual who explores a strange place by locomotion produces transformations of the optic array for the very purpose of isolating what remains invariant during these transformations. It is not that he has to remember a series of forms but that the space emerges from these optical motions. What went out of sight as he moved one way comes into view as he returns; it does not vanish like smoke, but disappears by being hidden. Hence he does not have to *remember* it when it is occluded, but only to apprehend its place behind what covers it. The sensation of its form has vanished like smoke, to be sure; and if that were the basis of his perception, he would have to remember it, as one can remember an object consumed by fire. But perception, i.e., sensationless perception, detects the permanent layout, and the man walks back and forth so as to isolate the information for permanence.

Similarly, the individual who scans a strange room actively produces new samples of the array so as to establish its permanent features. The field of view behind his head does not have to be remembered, for it overlaps the other samples he has obtained. The sequence of impressions is irrelevant.

The trouble with the classical theory of memory as applied to apprehension over time is that it begins with passive sensations in a supposedly discrete series. It presupposes that the oberver gets only a series of *stimuli*. But in active perception for the sake of information a series of transformations and transitions has been produced. The series is a product of the activity and, since the perceptual system is propriosensitive, the changes merely specify exploratory responses. Memory in the traditional sense of stored engrams is not required. But a kind of memory in a new sense of the term is definitely required if we are to explain not apprehension over time but *repeated* apprehension over time. For the fact is that an observer learns with practice to isolate more subtle invariants during transformation and to establish more exactly the permanent features of an array. This theory will be treated more fully in the next chapter. An effort will be made to show that the old ideas about memory will have to be reformulated if the old ideas about perception are.

XIII / The Theory of Information Pickup

Up to the present time, theories of sense perception have taken for granted that perception depends wholly on sensations that are specific to receptors. I have called these theories of sensation-based perception. The present theory asserts the possibility of perceptual experience without underlying sensory qualities that are specific to receptors, and I have called this a theory of information-based perception. It is a new departure.

The various theories of perception constitute a main branch of the history of psychology, and they have been described by Boring (1942). They need not be reviewed here, but it is worth noting the main issues over which they divided, since we should ask how the new proposal deals with them. The liveliest issue, now centuries old, was that between nativisim, and empiricism. More recently, another issue has been raised by Gestalt theory in opposition to elementarism.

Consider first the debates between the nativists and the empiricists. One aspect of the controversy was a purely theoretical issue; whether the human being can be said to have a mind at birth — any sort of innate rational capacities or any basis for knowledge before the fact of actual perceiving — or whether, on the other hand, the infant starts life with nothing but a capacity for meaningless sensations and only learns to perceive the world by means of memory and association after an accumulation of past experience.

Another aspect of the controversy is a difference of emphasis, not of theory: whether to stress the influence of heredity on the development of perception or the influence of learning. Since both kinds of influence are known to have some effect, the decision is not one between supposedly logical alternatives.

If the theory of information-based perception is accepted, the first controversy becomes meaningless and the logical issue can be thrown out of court. The second controversy is still meaningful, but it takes a new form. The perceptual capacities of the newborn, animal or human, for getting information become a matter for investigation. The relative proportions of the unlearned and the learned in perception might be expected to depend on the degree of maturity of the infant at birth, which in turn depends on his species and on the kind of environment the young of his species have been confronted with during evolution.

Consider next the question of whether perception was compounded of elements or organized into structures. The empiricists argued for learning or association as the only organizing principle in perception; the Gestalt theorists argued for autonomous field-forces in the brain as the organizing principle. The issue has not been resolved. According to the theory here proposed, this issue also disappears, for the neural inputs of a perceptual system are *already* organized and therefore do not have to have an organization imposed upon them — either by the formation of connections in the brain or by the spontaneous self-distribution of brain processes.

The evidence of these chapters shows that the available stimulation surrounding an organism has structure, both simultaneous and successive, and that this structure depends on sources in the outer environment. If the invariants of this structure can be registered by a perceptual system, the constants of neural input will correspond to the constants of stimulus energy, although the one will not copy the other. But then meaningful information can be said to exist inside the nervous system as well as outside. The brain is relieved of the necessity of constructing such information by *any* process — innate rational powers (theoretical nativism), the storehouse of memory (empiricism), or form-fields (Gestalt theory). The brain can be treated as the highest of several centers of the nervous system governing the perceptual systems. Instead of postulating that the brain constructs information from the input of a sensory nerve, we can suppose that the centers of the nervous system, including the brain, resonate to information.

With this formula, an old set of problems for the psychology of perception evaporates, and a new set of problems emerges. We must now ask what kinds of information pickup are innate and what are acquired? What *is* the process of information pickup? How are the facts of association to be reconciled with the formula? The facts of so-called *insight*? What is the relation of perceiving to remembering in the new approach? The relation of perceiving to recognizing? To expecting? How is the detecting of information that has been coded into language related to the detecting of information that has not? These questions will be taken up in order.

What is innate and what acquired in perception?

The theoretical issue that divided nativism and empiricism was whether the interpretation of sensory signals did or did not presuppose inborn categories of understanding, or "innate ideas." The empiricists wanted to show that perceiving could be learned — all of it, including the perception of depth. Neither camp ever doubted the assumption that sensations were innate, i.e., that the repertory appeared full blown at birth, when the sense organs began to function. This abstract issue can now be disregarded, but a concrete question remains: Considering the infants of a given species, what mechanisms of detection appear at birth and what others depend on learning?

The theoretical assumption that sensations are innate, incidentally, can now be examined. It seems very dubious. Perhaps men *learn* to experience visual sensations, for example, to become aware of the field of view, or even sometimes to notice the excitation of receptors.

The concrete question of innate and acquired mechanisms in perception is not a two-way issue, for we now know there are intermediates between what is inherited and what is acquired. Pure genetics is one thing; pure learning is another thing; but in between there are types of development that we call growth or maturation. The anatomy and basic physiology of the organs of perception depend mainly on genetic factors as determined by evolution. The maturation of the perceptual systems depends on genetic and environmental determiners in concert. The education of the perceptual systems depends mainly on the individual's history of exposure to the environment. So there are really three questions: How much does perceiving depend on organs? How much does it depend on growth? How much does it depend on experience?

The answer to the first question has already been suggested in Chapters 4 through 8. The working anatomy of the vestibular organs, the ears, the ingestive equipment, the appendages, and the eyes has been described for man, and the evolution of these structures has been outlined so far as this is known. The organs with their receptors set limits on the kinds of stimulus information that can be registered. The five modes of attention, listening, smelling, tasting, touching, and looking, are specialized in one respect and unspecialized in another. They are specialized for vibration, odor, chemical contact, mechanical contact, and ambient light, respectively, but they are redundant for the information in these energies whenever it overlaps. Their ways of orienting, adjusting, and exploring are partly constrained by anatomy, but partly free. The basic neural circuitry for making such adjustments is built into the nervous system by the time of birth, but it continues to develop in man for a long time after birth.

The answer to the second question has been suggested, but a fuller knowledge of how the perceptual systems develop in the child over time depends on evidence that has been accumulating only recently. We need to know more about overt attention, as in looking, listening, touching, and so on, and more about the inner, central nervous resonance to selected inputs that also occurs. In this country, experiments are beginning to appear on the growing ability of infants to fix their eyes on certain kinds of visual structure (Fantz, 1961). Studies are being made on those features of an optic array that demand notice, such as the information for a human face (Ambrose, 1961) or the information for a "visual cliff" (Walk and Gibson, 1961) or the information for "imminent collision" (Schiff, 1965). In Europe, Jean Piaget has for many years pursued the study of perceptual development (e.g., Piaget and Inhelder, 1956), but his emphasis is on the inner intellectual aspect of perception. He inclines to the belief that the child *constructs reality* instead of detecting information. His experiments show, however, that the ability to attend to the higher-order features of objects and events develops in graded stages. At least the results can be interpreted in terms of information. In any case it seems to be true that the child cannot be expected to perceive certain facts about the world until he is ready to perceive them. He is not simply an adult without experience, or a sentient soul without memory. The ability to select and abstract information about the world grows as he does.

The answer to the third question, the extent to which perception depends on experience or learning in the theory of information pickup, is this: it does so to an unlimited extent when the information available to the perceiver is unlimited. The individual is ordinarily surrounded by it; he is immersed in it. The environment provides an inexhaustible reservoir of information. Some men spend most of their lives looking, others listening, and a few connoisseurs spend their time in smelling, tasting, or touching. They never come to an end. The eyes and ears are not fixed-capacity instruments, like cameras and microphones, with which the brain can see and hear. Looking and listening continue to improve with experience. Higher-order variables can still be discovered, even in old age. Getting information to the receptors becomes troublesome when the lens of the eye and the bones of the ear lose their youthful flexibility, but higher-order variables in light and sound can still be discovered by the artist and musician.

However, this is not the kind of learning that the theory of association, or of conditioning, or of memorization, has been concerned with. It is not an accrual of associations, an attaching of responses, or an accumulation of memories. Perceptual learning has been conceived as a process of "enrichment," whereas it might better be conceived as one of "differentiation" (Gibson and Gibson, 1955). What can this differentiation consist of?

The Probable Mechanism of Learning to Perceive

Despite the ancient doctrine that sensations left behind ideas in the mind, or the modern version that they could become reconnected with responses in the brain, there has always been plenty of experimental evidence to suggest a different sort of learning. This neglected evidence was surveyed and reinterpreted some years ago by Eleanor J. Gibson (1953). Even the supposedly sensory correspondence between physical intensities and phenomenal brightnesses and loudnesses has been shown to improve with practice in making comparisons. Similarly, the psychophysical correspondence between physical frequencies and phenomenal qualities of pure color and pitch improves with practice. Even the detection of physical separations of points on the retina and the skin, supposedly basic sensory acuities, can get better. When *patterns* of intensity, frequency, or separation are presented to an observer, learning is the rule, for patterns may carry information. A great number of psychophysical experiments have shown decreasing errors in discriminating, estimating, detecting, and recognizing, even when the observer is kept in ignorance of his errors. The rule holds for every department of "sense." The author of this survey concluded that the observer learns to look for the critical features, to listen for the distinctive variations, to smell or taste the characteristics of substances (perfumes or wine) and to finger the textures of things (wool or silk). Both she and I now consider this an education of attention to the information in available stimulation.

This increase of discernment is not confined to the detection of finer and finer details. The *span* of attention is increased with practice. It can (within limits) be enlarged in scope. It can also be extended in time. A pilot, for example, can be trained to keep track of a whole array of aircraft instruments, and a production engineer can be trained to watch over a long sequence of mechanical operations if each episode is part of a whole. This increase of the span of apprehension over both space and time is very suggestive. It is probably a matter of detecting progressively larger forms composed of smaller ones, and progressively longer episodes composed of shorter ones. The spatial relations in an array, and the temporal relations in a sequence, permit the information to be taken in progressively larger and longer units or "chunks." One can finally grasp the simultaneous composition of a whole panel of instruments or a panorama, and apprehend the successive composition of a whole production line or a whole symphony. Note that this extension and protension of grasp is not inconsistent with the concentration of attention on smaller details of an array, or on briefer details of an episodic sequence.

The "differentiation theory" of perceptual learning proposed by Gibson and Gibson (1955) was programmatic at the outset, but the mechanisms for this learning are becoming clearer. The process is one of learning what to attend to, both overtly and covertly. For the perception of objects, it is the detection of distinctive features and the abstraction of general properties. This almost always involves the detection of invariants under changing stimulation. The dimensions of transformation are separated off, and those that are obtained by action get distinguished from those that are imposed by events (Chapter 2). The exploratory perceptual systems typically produce transformations so that the invariants can be isolated (Chapter 12). And the action of the nervous system is conceived as a resonating to the stimulus information, not a storing of images or a connecting up of nerve cells.

The "resonating" or "tuning" of a system suggests the analogy of a radio receiver. This model is inadequate because there would have to be a little man to twiddle the knobs. A perceiver is a *self-tuning* system. What makes it resonate to the interesting broadcasts that are available instead of to all the trash that fills the air? The answer might be that the pickup of information is *reinforcing*. This is essentially the answer that Woodworth suggested twenty years ago, in a paper on the "reinforcement of perception" (1947). Clarity in itself, he asserted, is good, is valued. A system "hunts" until it achieves clarity. The process can occur at more than one level. First, the pickup of information reinforces the exploratory adjustments of the organs that make it possible. And second, the registering of information reinforces whatever neural activity in the brain brings it about. We know something about the adjustments — for example, the accommodating of the eye where the clarity of detail is somehow "satisfying" to the ocular system. We do not know much yet about the neural action of resonance at higher centers, but it too may prove to be the reaching of some optimal state of equilibrium. If the neurophysiologists stopped looking for the storehouse of memory perhaps they would find it.

A perceptual system, to repeat, is not composed of an organ and a nerve. The nervous system is part and parcel of any perceptual system, and the centers of the nervous system, from lower to higher, participate in its activity. Organ adjustments are probably controlled by lower centers, selective attention by intermediate centers, and conceptual attention by the highest centers.

. . . .

The elaboration of this theory and the marshalling of the evidence for it is too much for this chapter, or for this book. Another book is needed. It will be published under the title, *Perceptual Learning and Development*, by Eleanor J. Gibson.

. . . .

How are associations between events detected?

Psychologists have become accustomed to thinking of an association as something that is formed between two sensory impressions or between a sensory impression and a response. They realized, of course, that there had to be a physical conjunction of events — fire and smoke, for example — before the psychological association could be formed, but this was not what they were interested in. Let us consider, however, the *fact* of ecological associations, as distinguished from the *formation* of associations. The result of this fact is an invariance of stimulus combinations. Brunswik considered the ecology of stimulus combinations (1956), but he treated them only as probabilities of sense data. To the extent that a fire *always* conjoins an optical flame with an acoustic sound, a cutaneous warmth, and a volatile odor, the combination is invariant and constitutes a stimulus of higher order; more exactly, each component contains the same stimulus information (Chapter 3, p. 54). If a peach *always* yields a certain color, form, odor, texture, and sour-sweet quality, the discriminated features are all characteristic of the same thing and constitute a single combination (Chapter 8, p. 137). The act of perceiving a fire or a peach, then, might just as well be considered the pickup of the associated variables of information as the associating of sensory data. Two things are necessary: the dimensions of quality must have been differentiated, and the invariant combinations of quality must be detected. The formation of associations is not necessary.

Can the classical conditioning of responses be explained without resorting to the theory of association? Sign learning, at least, can be subsumed under the theory of information pickup. Consider Pavlov's dog isolated in a cubicle containing a food tray and a bell. The rule of this special environment was that whenever the bell sounded, food appeared. The dog in the cubicle soon began to salivate to the sound. The latter stimulus is then said to be *conditioned* (the sight and smell of food being associated with it) and the response of salivation is said to be conditioned *to* it. We say that a new stimulus-response connection has been formed — that the dog has a new stimulus for his old response of salivating, or a new response for his old sensation of a bell. But we might as well say that the dog has learned to detect the bell-food invariant in the cubicle situation. As long as Pavlov chose to make this improbable sequence a law of the cubicle (and only so long as he did), the dog might be expected to detect it.

What about the instrumental conditioning of responses? We must now consider Skinner's rat isolated in a box containing a lever and a food cup (1938). Skinner had created this little world (perhaps in six days, resting on the seventh) so that depression of the lever caused delivery of a food pellet. In order to detect this strange invariant, the rat had to behave before he could perceive, but in the course of exploration the utility of the lever became evident: it afforded food. When Skinner made the law merely probable instead of certain, or willfully abolished it, the rat's attention to the food affordance of the lever still persisted. The rat would continue to press the lever long after it had been disconnected from the food magazine, and a single success would send him off again.

What about the learning of nonsense syllables? Surely, you may say, this is a process of forming associations. Even here, it can be argued, Ebbinghaus required the learner (usually himself) to perceive the pairing or sequence of YOK and LIF in an arbitrarily created list. This was not even an invariant that held for the laws of discourse, much less one holding·for the world outside his laboratory, but it was an invariant of the task nevertheless.

Learning by association is defined in stimulus-response theory as an increase in the capacity of a certain stimulus to evoke a certain response, the increase having been produced by associating the stimulus with another one that regularly evokes the response. This formula takes no account of stimulus *information*. In perception theory, at least in the kind being advocated, the response of interest is that to the *association*, not to either one of the stimuli alone. In short, learning *by* association becomes the learning *of* associations.

What is learning by insight?

Ebbinghaus, Pavlov, and Skinner have all given us experimental methods for studying learning by association. Köhler's (1925) observations on the learning of lifelike tasks by apes, however, did not fit into the theory of association. A famous example is the chimpanzee in a barred cage with food set outside his reach and a stick behind him. After many vain attempts, the animal suddenly turns, seizes the stick, and rakes in the banana. The animal is said to have perceived the relations between the elements of the situation and to have learned by *insight*.

The explanation offered for the chimp's perception was that a spontaneous reorganization of his phenomenal field had occurred which included the banana, the stick, the bars, and his body in one configuration. But again, a different interpretation is possible if the hypothesis of stimulus information is accepted, and this is fore-shadowed in Köhler's description of the ape's behavior. Conceivably what he did was to perceive or notice the *rake-character* of the stick. This object, by virtue of a certain thickness and length, was graspable and reach-with-able. The information for its useability was available in the ambient light. There is no need to postulate reorganization in the brain — only perception of a fact.

This assertion about the useability of the stick does not imply that the chimp had any innate idea that a certain thickness was graspable or that a certain length was reach-with-able. The detection of these meanings emerges, no doubt, from grasping (or having grasped) and from reaching (or having reached). The perceiving of rake-character may have developed slowly, after much primate manipulation. The suddenness of insight has been justly questioned (Thorpe, 1956, Ch. 6). The point is that these meanings do not *consist of* the memories of past manipulation, or of the acquired motor tendencies to manipulate. The acts of picking up and reaching with *reveal* certain facts about objects; they do not *create* them.

The hypothesis of the "invitation qualities" of objects, their valences, or what they afford, was central to Gestalt theory, especially as developed by Lewin (1936), but the phenomenal field in which they appeared had an uncertain status, neither wholly internal nor wholly external. If these valences are taken to be invariants of stimulus information, the uncertainty disappears. The stick's invitation to be used as a rake does not emerge in the perception of a primate until he has differentiated the physical properties of a stick, but they exist independently of his perceiving them.

The invitations or demands of one animal to another, the affording of sexual partnership, for example, are usually specified by color and shape. But often, as if this were not enough information, the availability of a mate will be advertised by special movements called *expressive*. The optical transformations specify the fact, and seem to be registered with little previous experience. Displays of this sort are called "releasers" for instinctive behavior (Tinbergen, 1951), but it should be noted that they constitute stimulus information.

. . . .

Insight vs. Association

The controversy over learning by insight as against learning by association is full of complications and is too big a subject for discussion here. We might, however, consider the physiology of the two processes. Insofar as the Gestalt theorists thought of insight as a neurological process of organization (e.g., Köhler, 1929), their theory was similar to that of the stimulus-response psychologists who thought of association as a neurological process of reinforcement (e.g., Hull, 1943). That is, both theories started from sense data, although they differed as to the kind of neural interaction ensuing. But insofar as the Gestalt theorists recognized the *prior* organization of stimuli, insofar as they acknowledged the "seeing" of structure (e.g., Wertheimer, 1945), their theory was similar to the present one. They did sometimes think of insight as detection. But they could never quite bring themselves to assume that environmental stimulation always *has* structure. The Gestalt theorists failed to realize that even dot patterns or inkblots cannot be wholly "unstructured." Hence their emphasis had to be on a hypothetical process that *imposed* structure on stimulus inputs.

. . . .

What is the relation of perceiving to remembering?

All theories of learning by association presuppose some kind of central enrichment of an impoverished input to the nervous system. The supplementation, no matter how conceived, is supposed to depend on memory, that is, on some cumulative carryover of the past into the present. It may be conceived either as an accumulation of nervous bonds or connections, or of images or engrams, but at any rate an accumulation of traces in some sense of the term.

Lashley sought to discover the physiological basis of memory during a long career of investigation. But he had to conclude in the end that "it is not possible to demonstrate the localization of a memory trace anywhere within the nervous system" (1950, p. 477). Neither connections between neurons nor between images impressed on the tissue were consistent with the results of his experiments. The "search for the engram," as he put it, had failed. He could only suggest that "the learning process must consist of the attunement of the elements of a complex system in such a way that a particular combination or pattern of cells responds more readily than before the experience" (p. 479). This hypothesis of tuning or resonance implies something quite different from the accumulation of traces. When it is combined with the hypothesis of information pickup, it suggests a surprising possibility — that learning does not depend on memory at all, at least not on the re-arousal of traces or the remembering of the past. Let us follow up this possibility.

. . . .

Hebb's Theory of Reverberation

Hebb, a student of Lashley, conceived of a way in which the brain might resonate or reverberate, described in a book called *The Organization of Behavior* (1949). But the reverberation was supposed to occur in the cortex, and the aim was to explain the awareness of a visual form, say a triangle, together with the engram of such an experience. Hebb was influenced by the theory of an *isomorphism* between visual form and cortical form, the notion that the firing of nerve cells must somehow be *like* consciousness. The resonance of a retino-neuro-muscular system at various levels to the information available in optical structure, to the variables of form but not to the forms as such, is quite different from Hebb's reverberating circuits. Only the concept of a circuit is the same. But both theories stem from Lashley.

. . . .

The essence of memory as traditionally conceived is that it applies to the past, in contradistinction to sense perception, which applies to the present. But this distinction is wholly introspective. It depends on the feelings of "now" and "then," not on the facts of life. The experience of "now" is the result of attention to the observer's own body and to the impressions made on it — to sensation, not perception. *Information* does not exist exclusively in the present as distinguished from either the past or the future. What is exclusively confined to the present is the momentary sensation. The stream of consciousness as described by William James (1890, Ch. 9, 15) exhibits the travelling moment of present time, with a past extending backward and a future extending forward, but this is the stream of self-consciousness, not the process of perception. Physical events conform to the relation of before and after, not to the contrast of past and future. Resonance to information, that is, contact with the environment, has nothing to do with the present.

The ordinary assumption that memory applies to the past, perception to the present, and expectation to the future is therefore based on analytic introspection. Actually, the three-way distinction could not even be confirmed, for the travelling moment of present time is certainly not a razor's edge, as James observed, and no one can say when perception leaves off and memory begins. The difficulty is an old one in psychology, and Boring (1942) has described the efforts to get around it in his chapter on the perception of time. The simple fact is that perceiving is not focused down to the present item in a temporal series. Animals and men perceive motions, events, episodes, and whole sequences. The doctrine of sensation-based perception requires the assumption that a succession of items can be grasped only if the earlier ones are held over so as to be combined with later ones in a single composite. From this comes the theory of traces, requiring that every percept lay down a trace, that they accumulate, and that every trace be theoretically able to reinstate its proper percept. This can be pushed into absurdity. It is better to assume that a succession of items can be grasped *without* having to convert all of them into a simultaneous composite.

The idea that "space" is perceived whereas "time" is remembered lurks at the back of our thinking. But these abstractions borrowed from physics are not appropriate for psychology. Adjacent order and successive order are better abstractions, and these are not found separate.

Even at its simplest, a stimulus has some successive order as well as adjacent order (Chapter 2, p. 40). This means that natural stimulation consists of *successions* as truly as it consists of *adjacencies*. The former are on the same footing as the latter. A visual transient between light and dark is no more complex than a visual margin between light and dark. The information in either case is in the direction of difference: *on* or *off, skyward* or *earthward*. The visual system in fact contains receptive units for detecting both kinds of information. It is absurd to suppose that these sequence detectors have to make a comparison of intensity *now* with the memory of intensity *then*.

The improvement of information pickup with experience is thus not necessarily the dependence of perception on memory in the commonsense, introspective meaning of that term. The "attunement of a complex system," in Lashley's words, need not entail the reinstatement of earlier experiences, that is, recalling or recollecting. This proposal does not in the least deny that remembering can occur. It denies only that remembering is the basis of learning. Perhaps conscious remembering is an occasional and incidental symptom of learning in the same way that sensations are occasional and incidental symptoms of perceiving.

The ability of the human individual to contemplate parts of his past history is no mean achievement; the experimental psychologist as well as the psychotherapist and the novelist has reason to be fascinated by it; but there is some question whether it has to intervene in the simpler ability to perceive and learn.

The question of whether or not thinking always involves images was a controversy in psychology many years ago (Humphrey, 1951). The weight of the evidence indicated that problem-solving and reasoning could sometimes proceed with no awareness whatever of any copies of previous experience. If it is agreed that one can think without remembering, there is no great step to the conclusion that one can learn without remembering.

The "image" of memory and thought is derived by analogy to the image of art. The "trace" of a percept is analogous to the graphic act. The "storehouse" of memory is analogous to the museums and libraries of civilization. As we observed in Chapter 11, these inventions do make possible the preservation of human knowledge for subsequent generations. But to assume that experiences leave images or traces in the brain, that experience writes a record, and that the storage of memories explains learning, that, in short, the child accumulates knowledge as the race has accumulated it, is stultifying.

What is the relation of perceiving to recognizing?

It has often been pointed out that memory has quite different manifestations. To recognize is not the same as to recall. One can identify the same place, object, or person on another occasion without recalling it. "I recognize you," one says, "but I cannot recall your name, nor where we met." Often there is a mere "feeling of familiarity" or a bare judgment of "same as before." Nevertheless, both are considered forms of memory and the theory of traces requires that, even for recognition, the present input must somehow retrieve the stored image of the earlier experience. If the input matches, recognition occurs; if not, recognition fails. This act of comparison is implied by the commonly accepted theory of recognition. There is, however, an alternative theory. It is to suppose that the judgment of "same" reflects the tuning of a perceptual system to the invariants of stimulus information that specify the same real place, the same real object, or the same real person. The judgment of "different" reflects the absence of invariants, or sometimes the failure of the system to pick up those that exist.

The "successions" of stimulation include both non-changes and changes, and therefore the detection of *same* is no less primary than the detection of *different*. One is the reciprocal of the other and neither requires an act of mental comparison. This is quite evident in the simplest possible case of recognition, in which one encounter with an object is followed immediately by another, as when one sees an object in two perspectives, or feels it on both sides. The invariants provide for the detection of *same thing* along with the detection of *different aspect*. In recognition over a long interval, when encounters with other objects, other places, or other persons have intervened, the attunement of the brain to the distinguishing features of the entity must be deeper and stronger than in recognition over a short interval, but the principle need only be extended to cover it.

The same object is usually not encountered in wholly separate places; it is usually met with in the same place, to which one returns after having passed through other places. As we observed in Chapter 10 (Figure 10.10), places are linked by the transformations of *vistas* and the transitions between them. A vista, it will be remembered, is an array that "opens up" in front and "closes in" behind. Locomotion thus eventuates in a sort of cognitive map, consisting of the invariants common to all the perspectives. This helps to establish the recognition of the objects contained in the perspectives.

The problem of why phenomenal identity usually goes with the same physical thing and why phenomenal distinctiveness usually goes with different physical things are actually two sides of the same problem. Identification and discrimination develop together in the child as reciprocals, and the experimental evidence shows it. Identifying reactions improve at the same time as discriminative reactions (Gibson and Gibson, 1955). Recognition does not have to be the successful matching of a new percept with the trace of an old one. If it did, novelty would have to be the failure to match a new percept with any trace of an old one after an exhaustive search of the memory store, and this is absurd.

What is the relation of perceiving to expecting?

No one has ever been able to say exactly where perceiving ceases and remembering begins, either by introspection or by observation of behavior. Similarly, it is not possible to separate perceiving from expecting by any line of demarcation. Introspectively, the "conscious present," as James observed, merges with both the past and the future. Behaviorally, the evidence we accept as showing that the subject of an experiment *expects* something, food or electric shock, is the same evidence we accept as showing that the animal *remembers* something or has *learned* something.

The theory of learning advocated by Tolman (1932) was characterized as a cognitive or perceptual theory. He argued that all kinds of learning consisted of expectations, the actual movements of behavior being secondary, and that the explanation of learning was to be found in the confirming or disconfirming of expectations, not in the reinforcing of responses by reward or punishment. The animal learned what led to what, not reactions. A conditioned stimulus, for example, came to arouse an expectancy of food or shock. The lever in a Skinner box came to induce an expectancy of food in the cup below. The successive alleys of a maze after running through them led to the anticipation of the goal box, which might or might not contain food. The marking on a door in a discrimination box or a jumping stand came to arouse an expectancy of food behind it. This emphasis on the animal's orientation to the future made it plausible to think of behavior in terms of "means-end readiness," and to conceive behavior as purposive.

It has already been suggested how these kinds of learning might be explained without any necessary reference to the future, namely as cases of perceiving or detecting an invariant. The causal connection in these experiments, the contingency, is one created by the experimenter. It was he that designed the conditioning experiment, the box with a lever, the alleys of the maze, or the discrimination apparatus, and he that decided what the law of the experimental environment would be. The causal structure of this environment, its machinery, might not be very similar to that of the natural environment of a rat but it was predictable and controllable. The causal law of "what led to what" was present in the situation on repeated trials. If the animal could identify it over the series, he could be said to have learned, inasmuch as his behavior came to be determined by it. Whether or not the animal could fairly be said to expect, anticipate, or imagine the future, he could surely be said to have detected something.

Tolman's *confirming of an expectation*, it may be noted, is similar in principal to what has here been called the discovering and clarifying of information as a consequence of exploratory search. To call the process one of predicting an event and then verifying its occurrence makes it seem an intellectual accomplishment and dignifies the rat undeservedly. The rat's perception is more primitive than this.

The apprehension over time of the motion of an object, one might suppose, has nothing in common with the learning that may occur in the event sequences described above. The motion, we say, is simply perceived; remembering and expecting do not come into it. A kitten perceives the course of a rolling ball, an outfielder perceives the trajectory of a batted ball, and that is all there is to it. Nevertheless, in a sense, the kitten and the ballplayer *expect* the ball to continue on a predictable path, and that is why they can both start out on a dead run to intercept it. This foreseeing is much like ordinary seeing, and not much like Tolman's expectancies, for it depends on a continuous flow of stimulation. But the two kinds of situation do have something in common. The unbroken continuation of the optical motion is a consequence of the invariant laws of inertia and gravity in physics. The ball continues in a straight line, or a trajectory, because of Newton's Laws. The invariant is implicit in the motion. Both the kitten and the ballplayer may have to practice and learn in order to detect it accurately, but in a certain sense what they are learning is to perceive the laws of motion.

The experiments of Schiff, Caviness, and Gibson (1962) and Schiff (1965) on optical magnification of a silhouette in the field of view demonstrate that "looming," the visual information for imminent collision, is often detected by young animals who have never had painful encounters with an approaching object. They shrink away or blink their eyes, or otherwise make protective responses without having any reason to "expect" collision by reason of past experience. In this case the visual nervous system is presumably attuned to the information at birth. The behavior of human automobile drivers suggests that there are various degrees of attunement to the foreseeing of a collision when something starts to expand in the field of view.

What is the effect of language on perception?

Both men and animals perceive the environment, but the human perceiver has language while the animal does not. When the child begins to communicate by speech, and to practice speaking, he starts on a line of development that makes his knowledge of the world forever different from what it would have been if he had remained a speechless animal. What are these consequences? We might suppose that the effect of language would be to make perceiving easier and better. But it has been argued that there is an unfortunate and unavoidable effect which tends to make it distorted and stereotyped instead.

The argument seems to be based on a fact about language, but only one, and not necessarily the most important — the fact that it is a *code*. Language substitutes words for things. It depends on the lexicon, that is, on a sort of social agreement as to the signals that will stand for certain percepts. Every child must learn the code of his social group, and it is supposed that he learns it by forming associations between things and words, or by acquiring conditioned verbal responses to things. There are of course, many more things in the world than there are words in a language. Not everything can be coded. The verbal responses, it is argued, must therefore categorize or cut up the real world in conventional ways that are necessarily inadequate to its full complexity (Whorf, 1956). If, now, it is further assumed that perceptual identifying is not theoretically separable from verbal naming, then perceiving is perforce limited, as verbalizing is limited, and perception is to that extent distorted.

This line of reasoning presupposes an association theory of perception, assuming that words are utterances (or tendencies to utter, or auditory memories of utterances, or visual memories of writing) and that they have been attached to the stimuli from the world by association. The theory of information pickup, however, starts with a different assumption about words and ends with a different conclusion as to the effect of language on perception. Let us try to pursue the new line of reasoning.

For the child who is learning to use language and at the same time learning to perceive the world, words are *not* simply auditory stimuli or vocal responses. They embody stimulus information, especially invariant information about the regularities of the environment. They consolidate the growing ability of the child to detect and abstract the invariants. They cut across the perceptual systems or "sense modalities." The words are like the invariants in that they are capable of being auditory or visual or even tactual (as Braille writing is). They even cut across the stimulus-response dichotomy, for they can be vocal-motor or manual-motor. Hence, the learning of language by the child is not simply the associative naming or labeling of impressions from the world. It is also, and more importantly, an expression of the distinctions, abstractions, and recognitions that the child is coming to achieve in perceiving. Insofar as a code is a set of associations, the terms of the code have to be learned by association. But a language is more than a set of associations and the learning of language is therefore more than learning by association.

A language is more than a code because it permits *predications* as well as labelings. It has a grammar as well as a vocabulary. So the child's discovery of facts about the world can be predicated in sentences, not simply stereotyped in words. Predication can go to higher and higher levels, so the limitations of vocabulary do not set the same limits on the codifying of facts.

The learning of the language code as a vocabulary should be distinguished from the child's learning to consolidate his knowledge by predication. He gets information first by focusing, enhancing, detecting, and extracting it from nonverbal stimulation. Later, the extracting and consolidating go on together. Perceiving helps talking, and talking fixes the gains of perceiving. It is true that the adult who talks to a child can educate his attention to certain differences instead of others. It is true that when a child talks to himself he may enhance the tuning of his perception to certain differences rather than others. The range of possible discriminations is unlimited. Selection is inevitable. But this does not imply that the verbal fixing of information distorts the perception of the world.

In the theory of information pickup, the spontaneous activities of looking, listening, and touching, together with the satisfactions of noticing, can proceed with or without language. The curious observer can always observe more properties of the world than he can describe. Observing is thus not necessarily coerced by linguistic labeling, and there is experimental evidence to support this conclusion.

Behavioral theories of perception get their force from the conviction that behavior is practically useful. In a behavioral theory of perception, however, exploratory activities are treated simply as responses. Perception must then be learned by the reinforcing of stimulus-response connections. The conclusion is unavoidable that perception is biased by the needs that motivate practical action, for discrimination serves only the interests of practical action. One should fail to see anything that leads to unpleasant consequences and should see anything that leads to satisfaction. Both psychic blindness and hallucination ought to be common occurences. But in the theory being advocated, discrimination is *itself* a kind of useful action — an activity reinforced by clarity, not by punishments or rewards — and autism, or wishful perceiving, ought to be an uncommon occurrence.

The issue between the two kinds of theory can be illustrated by the following question. Does a child distinguish between two physically different things only after he has learned to make different responses to each, names, for example; or does he first learn to distinguish them and then (sometimes) attach names? On the former alternative he must learn to respond to the things; on the latter he must learn to respond to the difference.

From the first alternative it would be predicted that a child should be able to say names correctly before he can say "bigger" correctly; on the latter alternative the reverse would be predicted. This issue is deep and far-reaching. It cannot be compromised or avoided.

The Probable Kinds of Development in Learning to Perceive

Associating, organizing, remembering, recognizing, expecting, and naming — all these are familiar psychological processes, and all of them have been appealed to in the effort to explain the growth of knowledge. But all these processes were first conceived as operations of the mind upon the deliverances of sense, and they still carry some of this implication. They have now been examined, one by one, and I have suggested that, as commonly understood, they are incidental, not essential, to the developing process of information pickup. They need to be reinterpreted. The deeper, underlying kinds of perceptual development seem to involve exploration and attention. What can be said by way of summary about the more fundamental types of development?

Differentiating the Range of Possible Inputs

Consider a very simple perceptual system — for example, that for detecting the direction of gravity (Chapter 4). The input of a statocyst is presumably different for every different position of the weight resting on its hair-cells, altering as the animal is tilted leftward, is upright, or is tilted rightward. But a given input of excited hairs constitutes information about the direction "down" *only in relation to the other possible inputs of excited hairs.* The range of inputs, from a horizontal posture through vertical to horizontal again, defines the meaning of any given input. Consequently the animal's nervous system must have differentiated this range if it is to detect "down" and make compensatory righting reactions. For this, the animal must have been subjected to the range of postures, or perhaps have explored the range of postures. The development might be prenatal, or innate, or even learned, but it must be a development.

The same differentiating of the range of inputs must occur for other perceptual systems as well as the vestibular. The dimensions of variation in the haptic and the visual system, for example, are much more elaborate than are the inputs of a statocyst. Discriminative learning may be required instead of neural growth or maturation. Active testing of the limits of the range may occur. *Any perceptual system, however, has to have each of its inputs related to the other available inputs of the system.*

Establishing the Covariation of Inputs between Different Systems

The "orienting system," it will be recalled, is actually a redundant combination of vestibular, tactual, articular, and visual information. The input of a statocyst is covariant with the input of the skin, the joints, and the eyes whenever a young individual rolls, crawls, walks, or gets about. Consequently there must be another simple type of perceptual development, the registering of the concurrent covariation from different organs. The pull of gravity, the push of the ground, and the sky-earth difference are correlated. The vestibular, haptic, and visual inputs are likewise correlated over time. Insofar as this linkage is invariant, the information is the same in all of them, that is, the systems are equivalent. Their inputs are associated, it is fair to say, but learning by association hardly need be assumed.

Covariation in time of differentiated inputs does not necessarily imply a one-to-one correspondence of sensory elements or qualities. Covariant but not coincident inputs from the statocyst and the skin will occur for an individual resting on a slope, as noted in Chapter 4 (Figure 4.3). The "calibration" of the ranges of inputs from different perceptual organs may well be a matter of learning, and it implies information of a higher order.

The learning of concurrent covariations in the external environment, of what goes with what, depends also on the pickup of concurrent covariation of neural input, but this requires that the exterospecific component of the input will have been isolated.

Isolating External Invariants

The perception of the color and layout of surfaces, of the distinctive features of objects, and of their real motions in space implies that the other-produced component of neural input is separated from the self-produced component. This separation is not difficult to explain if one supposes that relational inputs exist along with the anatomical inputs. The transformations of the anatomical pattern of excited receptors have subjective reference; the invariants of adjacent and successive order in the overall input specify the invariants of stimulation and thereby the invariants of the world.

This "constancy" of perception no doubt depends on development insofar as the invariants of input have to be differentiated from one another in the nervous system. But the registering of invariants is something that all nervous systems are geared to do, even those of the simplest animals. The visual perception of "depth," for example, is surely not dependent on a gradual process by which the brain learns to interpret local sensations of color. Constancy is learnable in some degree, but not by a process of associating, organizing, or remembering.

Consider the origin of the child's perception of the permanence of objects. Does it have to depend on some kind of intellectual understanding of the causes of the child's impermanent sensations? Piaget (1954) and many others have assumed so. David Hume asserted (1739) that the senses "are incapable of giving rise to the notion of the *continued* existence of objects after they no longer appear to the senses. For that would be a contradiction in terms" (Part IV, Sec. 2). Hume was quite right; the awareness of the continued existence of a thing after it has been hidden by the edge of something else cannot be derived from the visual sensation after it has been wiped out. But it *can* be explained by the detecting of stimulus information for occlusion, i.e., the property of the transformation that we call "wiping out," which is quite distinct from the transformation that we call "fading out" (Reynolds, 1966). This information was described in Chapter 10 (Figure 10.9). The child must distinguish, or learn to distinguish, between these two kinds of optical transformation in order to perceive when a thing merely goes out of sight and when it vanishes, but he does not have to "construct" reality out of impermanent sensations (Piaget, 1954). Nor does he have to associate tactual sensations with visual ones in order "to understand that the objects in his environment have a continuous and consistent identity entirely detached from himself" (Vernon, 1952, p. 10).

Learning the Affordances of Objects

When the constant properties of constant objects are perceived (the shape, size, color, texture, composition, motion, animation, and position relative to other objects), the observer can go on to detect their *affordances*. I have coined this word as a substitute for *values*, a term which carries an old burden of philosophical meaning. I mean simply what things furnish, for good or ill. What they *afford* the observer, after all, depends on their properties. The simplest affordances, as food, for example, or as a predatory enemy, may well be detected without learning by the young of some animals, but in general learning is all-important for this kind of perception. The child learns what things are manipulable and how they can be manipulated, what things are hurtful, what things are edible, what things can be put together with other things or put inside other things — and so on without limit. He also learns what objects can be used as the means to obtain a goal, or to make other desirable objects, or to make people do what he wants them to do. In short, the human observer learns to detect what have been called the values or meanings of things, perceiving their distinctive features, putting them into categories and subcategories, noticing their similarities and differences and even studying them for their own sakes, apart from learning what to do about them. All this discrimination, wonderful to say, has to be based entirely on the education of his attention to the subtleties of invariant stimulus information.

Detecting the Invariants in Events

Along with the discrimination of objects goes the developing discrimination of events. The child learns how things work as well as how they differ. He begins to perceive falling, rolling, colliding, breaking, pouring, tracing, and he ends by apprehending inertia, the lever, the train of gears, the chemical change, the electric current, and perhaps the concept of energy. The cause-and-effect relation in these observations becomes increasingly subtle. The simple perception of motion or of collision (Michotte, 1963) gives way more and more to what we call inference. Nevertheless there remains an element of perception in the appreciation of even the most abstract law. The physical scientist visualizes atoms or particles; the savage or the child sees spirits or magical rules behind a complex sequence of events (Piaget, 1951), but everyone perceives some kind of invariant over time and change. The information for the understanding of the law in such a case may be of staggeringly high order, but it is theoretically open to observation.

The Development of Selective Attention

Still another probable kind of perceptual development is the acquiring of what might be called *economical* perception. It is the ability to avoid distraction — to concentrate on one thing at a time in the face of everything going on in the environment — and yet to accomplish as much knowing as possible. To accomplish this, perceiving must be quick and efficient rather than slow and contemplative. As a result, the information registered about objects and events becomes only what is needed, not all that could be obtained. Those features of a thing are noticed which distinguish it from other things that it is not — but not *all* the features that distinguish it from *everything* that it is not.

This has been called the schematic tendency in perception, and it has been much studied in the psychological laboratory. The rule is, I suggest, that only the information required to identify a thing economically tends to be picked up from a complex of stimulus information. All the other available information that would be required to specify its unique and complete identity in the whole universe of things is not attended to.

This rule emphasizes economy in detecting the diagnostic features of things in the structure of stimulation. It does not refer to economy in a process of organization that is supposed to produce structure where none existed. The "minimum principle" in the organization of perception is one of the tenets of Gestalt theory; this is also a minimum principle, but the economy is in a process of selection, not one of organization.

XIV / The Causes of Deficient Perception

Any account of the facts of perceiving must include the facts of error —
the failures to notice as well as the noticing, the overlooking as well as the
looking. Actually, the deficiencies of perception are much more familiar
to us than its successes. We take the latter for granted, but we are naturally curious about the causes of our misperceptions, misjudgments, and
mistakes. We have a special curiosity about a class of inaccuracies that are
called illusions. They are usually not serious enough to be called misperceptions. Often we are aware of the illusion, as we are of the image in a
mirror, the bent stick in water, the circular coin that looks elliptical, and
the after-sensation "in front of the eyes". But these are still failures of
perception, to be exact, and they are very interesting.

How does a theory of information-based perception as distinguished
from the theories of sensation-based perception account for misperceptions
and illusions? Since the present theory is primarily a theory of correct
perception, it must explain incorrect perception by supplementary assumptions.

The classical theories of perception, on the contrary, explain both perception and misperception, both detection and illusion, with the *same* assumptions. The influence of past experience on sensory data, for example,
is supposed to be sometimes one of correcting the data and sometimes one
of distorting them. The effect of sensory organization in the brain on the
inputs of the nerves is supposed to be one that makes the forms in the
brain *like* the forms in the world, but also one that makes them *unlike* the
forms in the world. There is a lack of logic here. If misperception is the
opposite of perception, the law of association or the law of sensory organization cannot apply to both at the same time. The same principle should
not be used to explain why perceiving is so often correct and why it is so
often incorrect. A theory of perception should certainly *allow for* misperception, but it can hardly at the same time *be* a theory of misperception.

In the theory of information pickup, clearly, the pickup may fail when the available information is inadequate, or it may fail when the information is adequate but is not picked up. The former is no fault of the observer; the latter is. The two cases are theoretically separate, even if they are practically sometimes hard to distinguish. In this chapter the attempt is made to list the ecological inadequacies of information first and the psychological deficiencies of perception second. The perceptual systems, as we shall note, do the best they can with what they get, but in some circumstances they get very little to work on.

Inadequate Information

There are some natural circumstances in which the obvious information in light specifies a fact that is false. A straight stick looks bent (Figure 14.1) when part of it is submerged in water because its corresponding margins in the optic array are bent by the refraction of rays. A mirage of trees and buildings appears because of reflection from air layers. The green foliage of distant mountains appears blue because of the differential transmission of wavelengths through air. There can even be misinformation in mechanical stimulation, as when a jet of water feels solid instead of liquid because the information for an unyielding instead of a yielding surface is present. But these natural situations cannot be treated experimentally, and what the psychologist knows about perception comes largely from experiments. A large class of these are studies in which the stimulus information from objects or events has been artificially *reduced* by a curious investigator.

Experiments on perception with reduced information are very frequent in psychology. They have always been thought of, however, as experiments with reduced *stimulation*. It has been the hope of the investigators to cut back the sensory basis of perception so as to allow the perceptual process to come into its own — to reveal in relatively pure form the laws of its operation. We shall have to reinterpret the work in terms of reduced *information*.

In this chapter an attempt will be made to classify reduced stimulus information under seven headings: *minimal energy, blurring, masking, conflicting information, interval cutoff, narrowing down of an array,* and *operations on structure*. In some of these experiments, especially the last, the information may not have been reduced or diminished but only altered in form.

Minimal Energy and the Concept of Threshold

Photoreceptors, mechanoreceptors, and chemoreceptors require a certain amount of energy to be excited (Chapter 2), although the amount may be very small. Conceivably, a rod cell of the human retina when it is

Figure 14.1 An apparently bent stick. No matter how much experience one has had with straight sticks in water, and no matter how much knowledge one has about the laws of refraction, the edges still seem to be bent at an angle. This illusion must be one of the oldest experienced by man. A sophisticated modern observer, however, can see more than just bent edges — he can perceive *edges bent by refraction.*

dark-adapted can be discharged by one quantum of light energy (Pirenne, 1956). The absolute intensity thresholds for sensation of imposed stimulation, however, are not as simple as is implied by the theory of a receptor mosaic composed of cells, for the area of a stimulus combines with its intensity to determine the threshold and so does the short-term duration of a stimulus. The thresholds of the receptive units interspersed in the retina depend on the area stimulated and on the length of time. The size of the "goad," as it were, and the duration of its application, help to determine its effectiveness as a stimulus. All we can be sure of is this: a sufficiently distant lighthouse or a sufficiently distant star, or a sufficiently brief flash of either, will cease to be seen at night. If a source of vibration is far enough away, its pressure waves will cease to excite the ear; and if a contact with the body surface is sufficiently light, small, and brief, it will cease to affect the skin. Obviously no information can be obtained about the lighthouse, the star, the sounding object, or the touching thing if the stimulus in ineffective.

With respect to the ear and the skin, however, their mechanoreceptors are so sensitive that the absence of detected sound pretty well guarantees the absence of any vibrating object in the vicinity, and the absence of detected touch guarantees the presence only of air (or the medium) adjacent to the body. I have argued that these facts are themselves information, albeit of the most primitive sort.

The *obscuring* of the structural information in ambient light by a low level of illumination is a deficiency in the eye, not in the light. The obscuring of the information in sound waves by a low level of amplitude is a deficiency in the ear, not in the sound. The proof is that the information can be made available by operations of enhancement and amplification, e.g., by an image-magnifier or an audio-amplifier. The human eye declines in "acuity" as the light weakens, and the human ear fails to make out the words as the sound weakens, but the information is physically present, that is, theoretically available.

It is important to remember that the concept of a physiological *threshold* — a certain minimal amount of energy absorbed by a sensory surface over a given area during a given time — refers only to energy measurements and not to information, that is, not to the variables of higher order that contain information. Fixed thresholds apply to the theoretical sensitivity of passive receptors but not to the sensitivity of active organs, since the latter depends on the development and education of the perceptual system to which the organ belongs. The attempt to measure absolute thresholds, accordingly, can be carried out when sensory impressions are reported by a passive observer but not when he actively seeks to obtain perceptual information. Absolute thresholds of pure sensation, if they could be established, would probably not be lowered by learning. The trouble is that such fixed thresholds have not been established experimentally, for the notion of a wholly passive observer, an "ideal" observer as he is called by sensory physiologists, is a myth. Real observers in real experiments have to be motivated to observe, and their attention fluctuates with their degree of motivation. Consequently the idea of a *statistical* threshold has had to be substituted for the idea of a *physiological* threshold. But some theorists do not find this satisfactory and have suggested that a so-called threshold is actually the probability of detecting a *signal* in the presence of *noise* (see below). The very concept of a sensory threshold has become uncertain in recent years, although it is fundamental to the theory of sensations.

The attempt to measure intensities that will just excite neurons is a useful endeavor for physiologists. The attempt to measure intensities that will just arouse sensations is practically useful for such purposes as the design of lighthouses. But it is clear that the latter measures are not absolutes, and the former, although they set limits to the activity of perceptual systems, will never explain how they work.

. . . .

The Muddle of Subliminal Perception

An inconclusive controversy about social perception has recently arisen (Bevan, 1964) which illustrates the confusion into which we are led by assuming that information pickup must have a fixed threshold if supposedly basic sensation has a fixed threshold. Certain experiments purported to show that an observer could perceive meanings or suggestions unconsciously, or could discriminate them without awareness of the sensory difference between them. This seemed to imply unconscious defense mechanisms governing perception as well as motivated behavior — wishful perceiving. But to say that one can perceive in order *not* to perceive is a logical contradiction. Something is wrong somewhere.

When perception is conceived as the detection of information, the weakness of physical stimulation may cause it to be piecemeal, partial, and dependent on personal motivation. But this does not imply subthreshold perception or "subception"; it only suggests that a perceptual system may be sensitized to one level of information and not to another.

. . . .

The Blurring of Structure

The blurring of an optic array by fog, smoke, or haze should not be confused with the blurring of the retinal distribution by, say, myopia (nearsightedness). The loss of structure in the first case is incurable while that in the latter case can be corrected by eyeglasses. The blurring of an optic array by an imperfectly transparent medium can occur in varying degrees. The fine structure or texture of the array is the first to disappear. This yields what is called aerial perspective (Figure 14.2). Then, as the linear projection of the network of rays (Chapter 10) gives way to the dispersion or scattering of rays, the coarse structure may also disappear. In this situation the Londoner may ultimately complain that the fog is so thick he cannot see his hand in front of his face in full daylight. With fog in the air, the determinants of the features of environmental layout that do or do not remain visible (in accordance with the laws of size and distance) are extremely complex, as witness the difficulty of measuring visibility for the safe landing of airplanes. It is very hard for an observer in a control tower to tell whether or not there is enough structure in the manifold of perspectives in the air mass above an airport to enable a pilot to see what he needs to see. The structuring of light by the layout and reflectance of surfaces is itself complex, as we have noted. The fragile information with which we so confidently get about in the world is wholly at the mercy of atmospheric conditions. The nature of this information is such that it is physically weakened by *blur*. It is not, however, physically weakened by low intensity.

The ultimate degree of blur is found in a homogeneous optic array, that is, one with no structure at all. This is what the cloudless sky presents to

Figure 14.2 Aerial perspective. In this scene it can be observed that the farther away the buildings are, the more blurring occurs in the optic array from their edges, corners, and textures. In a moderately hazy atmosphere the fine structure of the array is increasingly lost with increasing distance of the surface. (Bahnsen from Monkmeyer)

an eye, or a fog of the highest density. This mode of stimulation is best achieved experimentally by covering the eyes of an observer with hemispheres of diffusing plastic. Halves of table-tennis balls serve nicely for this purpose, and I have repeatedly done this experiment (Gibson and Waddell, 1952; see also Cohen, 1957). The observer says he sees fog, or sometimes sky, or often "nothing." In a certain sense he is right. In the same sense that the absence of contact specifies nothing but air, the absence of optical texture specifies nothing but air. Under natural conditions a textureless sector within the total array of ambient light guarantees a space into which a bird can fly without danger of collision, into which one can proceed indefinitely, for no surface lies in that direction. So in a sense even the absence of structure conveys information as the alternative of *nothing* to *something*.

The appearance of sky is produced, as every theatergoer knows, by a finely textured curved surface at the back of a stage which can be flooded with illumination. It is called a cyclorama. The actual surface may be only a few feet behind the garden wall of a stage setting, but to the audience 50 feet away the illusion of depthless space will be compelling. There are other ways of causing a surface to look filmy and insubstantial (to be described later in this chapter), but making the grain of the optical texture too fine to be detected is one.

The occurrence of "whiteout" in the environment of a level snowplain under certain special weather conditions is instructive in this connection (see also Chapter 10, p. 212). It is analogous to a "blackout," in which case also nothing is visible. Blackout provides no information about the world because energy is absent; whiteout provides no information about the world because, although energy is present, structure is absent. It is said to be a very alarming experience for those who drive vehicles about in arctic regions. The undifferentiated light specifies an empty medium before the observer but this information is false; the snow-covered terrain with its potential obstacles exists although it seems to have vanished.

The Masking of Structure

In the study of auditory sensations a well-known effect is expressed by saying that one sound can *mask* another if the two are concurrent. Is this effect physical or physiological? It is widely assumed to be physiological because physical vibrations do not cancel one another out — or do they? For us the question is whether information can cancel out other information. In the study of auditory communication, where the notion of information is introduced, the fact is that a *signal* is progressively harder to detect as the level of *noise* is increased. Speech, for example, eventually becomes unintelligible in the presence of "static," or the hissing sound of a "white noise." On the assumption that the intelligible signal and the random noise are reciprocals of one another, the noise does objectively cancel the signal. This theory works very well for problems of communication by telephone or radio. There is some question, however, whether it should be applied to the broadcasting of information by natural events in a terrestrial environment.

It is a very interesting puzzle to decide whether, for example, the information broadcast by a bird call is present in the air at a station-point where a nearby waterfall fills the air with pressure waves of much higher amplitude. I am no expert in acoustics and may be wrong, but I am inclined to think that it is not present. However, in the "cocktail party phenomenon," where overlapping fields of speech sounds tend to make bedlam, it is possible that wave-front information as distinguished from wave-train information (Chapter 5) may help to sort out the vocal signals. In any event, whether the information is not available or is available but not registerable, one sound source can in effect mask another.

A rather similar kind of masking can occur in stationary optical structures. Examples are found in the hidden figures contained in line drawings, such as the one shown in Figure 14.3 (Gottschaldt, 1926; Metzger, 1953, Ch. 2). This masking has been compared to that which seems to occur in nature when animals "freeze" and presumably thereby reduce their visibility relative to the background, as for example, in Figure 14.4. Both kinds of masking have been compared to the art of military camouflage. In the drawings, the information for detecting the part figures is present in the optic array from the pictures, since they can in fact be perceived after considerable visual searching. So can the information for detecting the animals, but the question arises whether optical information can in other cases be so thoroughly imbedded in optical "noise" that it ceases to exist. For this puzzle, too, I have no certain solution. In any event, the information in the structure of pictorial optical stimulation, like that in acoustic stimulation, can become so intertwined with other information that observers cannot perceive it. Whether they can always be trained to do so is a theoretical question.

Visual masking as described is not the same thing as the "veiling" of contour and texture that occurs with high illumination. Presumably the latter is due to glare, so called, and this is a subjective phenomenon — that is, the failure to detect is a failure of the visual system, not of the structure of light. When the system is swamped by too much energy despite the moderating effect of the pupils, the situation can be remedied by wearing dark glasses.

Figure 14.3   Hidden figures. In each example the figure on the left is exactly replicated in the figure on the right. But it is difficult to *see* it in the figure on the right, and there may even be great difficulty in *finding* it. Demonstrations of this sort played an important role in the formulation of Gestalt theory, especially in the idea that a figure has to be "segregated" with respect to its surroundings. (From K. Koffka, *Principles of Gestalt Psychology,* Harcourt, Brace and World, Inc., 1935. Reprinted by permission of the publisher and Routledge and Kegan Paul Ltd.)

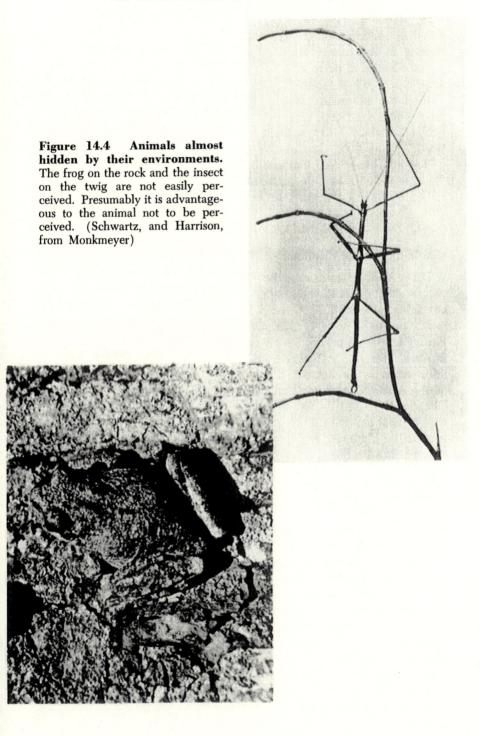

Figure 14.4   Animals almost hidden by their environments. The frog on the rock and the insect on the twig are not easily perceived. Presumably it is advantageous to the animal not to be perceived. (Schwartz, and Harrison, from Monkmeyer)

In Chapter 11 (Figure 11.7), four illustrations were given of the balanced opposition of stimulus information from a pictorial display, two causing an apparent reversal of figure-ground and the other two an apparent reversal of perspective. In one picture a goblet was seen to alternate with a pair of faces. The information for the goblet might be said to *mask* the information for the faces. This seems to me a more fundamental assertion than saying that the brain process corresponding to the goblet interferes with the brain process corresponding to the faces, as Gestalt theory does.

It should be recalled that in all such cases of equivocal percepts from the same frozen array, the ambiguity of edge and of depth would be resolved at once if the array underwent transformation. Static structure does not convey as much information as kinetic structure does. I believe that all cases of visual masking are confined to the static situation.

Conflicting or Contradictory Information

The reversible figures raise the question of conflicting stimulus information, or what is traditionally called "conflict of cues." In these figures the conflicting cues were both visual, but they need not be. Information is usually available to more than one perceptual system at the same time. Experimenters on perception have often devised situations where the information for one system, e.g., the visual, does not coincide with the information for another, e.g., the vestibular. An example is the perception of the vertical-horizontal framework of the environment, described in Chapter 4. Ordinarily, the main lines of the ambient array specify the true vertical and the pull of gravity on the weights of the inner ear also specifies it. Moreover, the upward pressure of the surface of support usually specifies it. But if a whole room is artificially tilted the visual and vestibular directions of up and down no longer coincide.

What exactly does this discrepancy or non-coincidence consist of? I would call it a discrepancy of information, not of sensations. Let us consider what this implies. A traditionalist would argue that the input of the hair cells of a statocyst organ (Chapter 4) and the input of a retinal image are mere arbitrary signals that must be associated before they have meaning. But this argument neglects what is important — namely, the *range* of inputs of a statocyst as the head goes from horizontal through vertical to horizontal again. A given input has meaning by virtue of its place in this range of inputs. Moreover, in ordinary life this is coincident with the range of inputs of the retina as one lies on the left side, sits up, and lies on the right side. The normal upright of haptic-somatic space coincides with the normal upright of visual space because the differentiated inputs of these two organ systems are covariant. Whatever one's posture, the line of the horizon as registered visually remains coupled with the line of gravity as registered by the body. These two kinds of perceptual development, differentiation and covariation, were described in the last chapter. The discrepancy introduced in the above experiments, therefore, means that a genuine biological invariant has been destroyed. The input of one system contradicts that of another. When the visual and the postural determinants of the phenomenal vertical disagree (see Figure 14.5), there is no longer any single unitary phenomenal vertical, I conclude, and this seems to fit the evidence (Gibson, 1952*b*). The observer in these experiments, e.g., a man seated in an artificially tilted room, must either accept the visual information and reject the postural, or accept the postural information and reject the visual, or alternate between the two, or compromise between the two. Of course, he may sometimes be just confused. All of these outcomes show up in the results of the experiment shown in Figure 14.5 (left).

The problem of conflicting cues in space perception has been studied

Man Upright, Room Tilted: a Discrepancy.　　　Man Tilted, Room Upright: No Discrepancy.

Figure 14.5　Discrepancy between the visual and postural vertical. In the experiment portrayed on the left, the lines of the optic array entering the man's eyes are not consistent with the direction of gravity as registered by his vestibular organ and by the pressure of the surface of support. This is an unnatural situation. In the experiment portrayed on the right, however, the lines of the array are coincident with the pull of gravity on his statoliths and the push of the surface of support on his skin. This is a natural situation, similar to what happens whenever the man inclines his body to one side. His perception of the true vertical is undisturbed in this situation.

in a great many experiments, by many investigators, but always with the aim of trying to solve the puzzle of how one sense could validate another, or provide criteria for another. The puzzle goes back to Bishop Berkeley, who maintained that visual sensations could only get spatial meaning from touch. Efforts to prove or disprove this hypothesis have continued up to the present. The issue disappears, however, on the assumption that any perceptual system can pick up information inasmuch as its inputs are differentiated with respect to its *possible* inputs. Usually this information is covariant, coincident, or correlated with the information got by another perceptual system, and it is therefore redundant or equivalent. It can be made contradictory, however, by an experimenter, with various interesting consequences for perception.

Interval Cutoff with a Tachistoscope

A favorite device for impoverishing visual stimulation is the tachistoscope, which presents a display for only a brief interval of time to a human eye fixated on the window. The effect of this device on the *information* available to the eye is complex, not simple. At very short intervals, measured in milliseconds, the energy needed for vision is minimized by virtue of the law of photosensitivity that trades intensity for duration. This reduces information perforce. At longer intervals, up to about a tenth of a second, the pickup of information is reduced to that obtained with a single fixation. Exploring or scanning is thus prevented, and the human eye, being highly foveated, unlike that of the horse, must explore in order to perceive fully. The eye is thus treated like a camera and its intake of information is unnaturally limited. The rationale of this experiment is that the tachistoscope, by limiting perception to what can be seen in a single glance, enables the experimenter to isolate a simpler and purer form of perception. The assumption that pictorial perception is simpler than transformational perception has already been discussed in Chapter 12. At still longer intervals, around half a second, applying the fovea to details of structure becomes possible, but the system is still frustrated to the degree that the sequence of fixations is cut short. Time is required for primate vision to reach its full scope. With the tachistoscope, therefore, available information is impoverished by limiting the time during which it is available.

It is instructive to contrast this method with another that is sometimes used by experimenters, one that reduces the ability to *register* the information instead of reducing the information. The subject may be required to fixate a mark on a screen and the display is then presented for a long interval at some angular distance peripheral to the clear center of the visual field. (The method demands a disciplined and practiced subject, for the urge to fixate on items of interest is very strong and must be inhibited.) In this situation the structural and temporal information from the display is fully available, but only the crudest features of it can be detected because the periphery of the human retina does not have the neural mechanisms for high acuity.

Narrowing Down of an Array

If the array entering an eye is reduced in angular scope to a few degrees by a tube or by a small aperture in a large screen, the surface reflecting the light within this narrow cone becomes invisible and the observer sees only a *film* at the end of the tube or in the aperture. Katz (1935) described it as a *film color* instead of a *surface color*, and thought of it as a "reduced" color. The experience seems to be the result of reducing the information for the detection of a surface. The area of optical texture projecting an area of surface texture has been so diminished that it no longer yields information about the layout of the surface. A certain minimum angular size of an array seems to be required for such detection. My observations suggest the following stages. When the angle is large one sees a surface extending behind the window at a certain orientation, of a certain color, and in a certain illumination. When the angle is reduced, these differential properties begin to be indefinite. When the angle is quite small, none of these properties is visible and the lack of *thingness* may be described by saying that it looks like a film stretched across the window. When the angle of the aperture in a screen is still smaller it may cease to look like an aperture and appear to be merely a spot on the surface of the screen. With the progressive narrowing of the array, what has been reduced is the structuring of the array, I suggest, and the supposed reduction of color from a perceptual mode to a sensory mode of appearance is only part of what happens.

The ultimate reduction of the optic array to a single point of light in a dark room is an even more familiar experiment in psychology. In that case not even the location of the point remains definite for long, and the "autokinetic" phenomenon is the result.

Experimental Operations on Structure

Finally, we should consider some of the various ways of modifying, altering, biasing, or distorting the spatial and temporal structure of stimulation that have been tried by experimenters. Operations on sound and light by electronic and optical means are easy because the energies are in the form of waves and rays outside the observer where the experimenter can intervene between the source and the impinging stimulus. This field of research is relatively new and therefore what can be said about it is provisional.

Electronic distortion of sound waves can now be achieved. Most of it has been done with speech sounds. Various sorts of "clipping" of the wave train have been tried. Interval clipping, for example, involves the introduction of short intervals of silence into the sound. Within limits, this can be done without affecting the intelligibility of the speech; beyond these limits the perception of speech suffers. In much the same way, intervals of darkness can be cut out of the changing optic array from a natural episode; the changing array from a motion-picture screen is clipped in this fashion with what seems no loss of information. As longer blank intervals are introduced into the continuous natural sequence, flicker appears and motion becomes jerky. This is what happens when the standard rate of 24 frames per second of the modern motion-picture projector is reduced to 10 or 12 per second. It is interesting to note, however, that even when the pictorial sequence is reduced to a few samples of still pictures, the major transformations of the episode may still be preserved. This is demonstrated by the fact of story-telling with a picture sequence, a so-called filmstrip, and by the success of comic strips.

Another sort of sound distortion is peak clipping, which alters the wave forms but not their sequence. This can also be imposed on speech sounds without affecting perception. Still other distortions are described in Cherry's book on human communication (1957). As he suggests, when the essential invariants are preserved under distortion, intelligibility remains. Some distortions destroy them; other do not. The "search for invariants," as he puts it, is the fundamental fact of perception (p. 297).

What can be done to the simultaneous structure of an optic array? Gaps can be introduced without much loss, as when one looks at a scene through a picket fence, or photographs such a scene. The half tone reproduction of a photograph is full of small gaps that do not affect perception. The natural optic array carries much more information than anyone is ever likely to pick up, and much of it can be sacrificed. It is highly redundant, in the terminology of information theory.

A similar introduction of gaps into the outlines of a representative drawing has been studied by the Gestalt psychologists and their followers. The interesting discovery here is that the information is destroyed if the gaps occur in certain critical locations but not if they occur in others. A classic example from Koffka (1935) of a drawing that contains barely enough information for a familiar percept is shown in Figure 14.6. What are the critical locations in a drawing that convey the essential information? That, of course, is the question. An answer is being sought by Hochberg (1964, Ch. 5).

The most interesting experimental operations on the structure of an optic array, however, come not from pictures but from what I call the spectacle-wearing experiments. These operations are imposed on the cone of rays entering an eye from the environment by means of optical distortion. The structure of this array can be wholly transformed in any of several ways by putting a refracting piece of glass, such as a prism or a lens, in front of the eye. Ordinary eyeglasses and contact lenses do not do this at all. These kinds of lenses, when properly fitted, are in effect merely adjuncts of the ocular system, correcting its anatomical defects and enabling it to register the finer details of an optic array. Experimental spectacles, on the contrary, alter the available information coming to each eye by introducing an inversion, reversal, or bias of its overall structure. A lens system will invert it; a wedge prism will bias it; a right-angle prism will reverse right and left (or up and down).

Figure 14.6 A drawing reduced to a few strokes of the brush. The essential information is present in these seemingly careless lines for perception of a highly distinctive entity — in Koffka's words, "a good-humored portly gentleman." But a great deal of unessential information has been left out. (After Hazlitt. From K. Koffka, *Principles of Gestalt Psychology*, Harcourt, Brace and World, Inc., 1935. Reprinted by permission of the publisher and Routledge and Kegan Paul Ltd.)

The first of the spectacle-wearing experiments was that of Stratton (1896, 1897), who inverted the field of view. The most comprehensive of them is the series of experiments at Innsbrück by Kohler (1964), who reversed or biased the field of view for long periods of time and tried other types of deformation. He also used colored spectacles, which bias the spectral structure of the array but not its geometrical structure. This kind of bias changes the colors of things at first, but as we know, the wearer soon adapts to the change. For spectacles altering geometrical structure, depending on the kind of optical alteration imposed, the perception of the environmental layout is correspondingly falsified. The information available in most of these experiments is not so much impoverished as deformed. It would be impoverished if the array were blurred by the spectacles, or if its adjacent order were permuted or disrupted as by transmission through pebbled glass, but the types of optical alteration so far used are not as radical as this. Wedge prisms, for example, introduce curvatures and compressions and spectral bands at the edges and corners of things, but the main features of the environment look the same as before.

The layout of surrounding surfaces is wrongly perceived in these experiments, and the acts of reaching and walking are accordingly made in the wrong direction. There is a conflict of information between the visual system and the haptic system. But the remarkable result is, first, that behavior soon adjusts to the altered information and, second, that the perception of layout gradually tends to become correct, at least with respect to certain variables of layout. The phenomenal curvatures of edges, the compressions of shape, the spectral bands, and the astonishing apparent motions of the world when one turns his head or walks about, weaken in the course of time. And at the end of the adaptation period, when the experimental spectacles are taken off and the observer looks around, the curvatures, compressions, color fringes, and non-rigid motions, all reappear as opposites of what he saw while wearing the spectacles.

The explanation of this adaptation, the correcting or *veridicalizing* of perceptual experience together with the readapting that must occur when the optical information returns to normal, is now being actively sought by a number of investigators. It is too soon to say what the final conclusions will be. The theory expounded in this book, however, implies a certain kind of explanation rather than other kinds. The theory was suggested, in part, by an effort to understand the early results of the spectacle-wearing experiments. There must be invariants over time in the flowing array of optical stimulation to *specify* the rectilinearity, the constancy, and the rigidity of the world. This assumption holds as much for vision without spectacles as for vision with spectacles. When they are first put on, the observer must learn what the new constants are in the stimulus flux. When they are taken off the observer must relearn the old constants again. The extraction of invariants by the perceptual system is taken to be the crux of the explanation of phenomenal adaptation.

· ·

The Adjustment of Visual Proprioception to Spectacle Wearing

The reason the apparent non-rigid motions of the world disappear during adaptation (and reappear as opposite motions when the spectacles are removed) is that the novel transformations, being in fact self-produced, come to be *taken* as self-produced, and therefore *cease* to be taken as specifying motions of the environment. The rule is that total optical transformations are propriospecific and that invariants under transformation are exterospecific, and this rule holds with or without spectacles. The altered transformations with spectacles demand a sort of relearning of what constitutes visual kinesthesis and what does not, but the visual system seems to be capable of this (Kohler, 1964; Held, 1965).

· ·

The Consequences of Inadequate Information

To conclude the first part of this chapter, we may ask, what happens to perception when the information is inadequate? In general, the answer seems to be that the perceptual system *hunts*. It tries to find meaning, to make sense from what little information it can get.

The observer keeps trying to see even in a dense fog, and he also does so at night in anything less than complete darkness. Similarly, he tries to hear even with little or no sound in the air. In darkness and silence, men and other diurnal animals may, of course, simply go to sleep and relax all attention, but so long as the individual stays awake and alert his exploratory attention persists.

In the complete darkness and utter silence of the so-called sensory deprivation experiments carried out recently with human subjects, the effort to see and hear is completely blocked. The subject cannot be deprived of *all* stimulation, however. He can always fall back on the haptic system, feeling the adjacent layout of surfaces. The information available to this system cannot be eliminated, for the subject is necessarily in touch with his surface of support even if not with more distant objects and events. But his "contact with the world" is much restricted. As a last resort he has only residual proprioception to keep his attention active; he can do exercises, feel himself, make noises, or talk to himself. But this is no longer perception; it is an egocentric or introverted kind of activity, and the ordinary person is dissatisfied by it. The subjects of experiments on perceptual deprivation have been paid large sums of money to persuade them to stay in their cubicles for more than a day or two. Despite the strong incentive, some of them report experiences so strange as to approximate hallucinations. Darkness, silence, and social isolation are highly frustrating. The perceptual systems seem to go on trying to function even without input, racing like a motor without a load. Perhaps this tendency explains the semi-hallucinations.

More typical of life than absence of stimulation, however, is the presence of stimulation with inadequate information — information that is conflicting, masked, equivocal, cut short, reduced, or even sometimes false. The effort of apprehension may then be strenuous. With conflicting or contradictory information the overall perceptual system alternates or compromises, as noted, but in lifelike situations a search for *additional* information begins, information that will reinforce one or the other alternative. When the information is masked or hidden in camouflage, a search is made over the whole array. If detection still fails, the system hunts more widely in space and longer in time. It tests for what remains invariant over time, trying out different perspectives. If the invariants still do not appear, a whole repertory of poorly understood processes variously called assumptions, inferences, or guesses come into play. Merely probable information, clues or cues, is not as satisfying for the perceptual system as the achieving of clarity, the insight that reveals the permanence underlying the change; but guessing does occur in highly complex situations and the individual may sometimes have to be content with it.

The above assertions are consistent with the results of many experiments on the effects of impoverished stimulation and inadequate information. The methods employed were described in the last section. The results have here been reinterpreted but the general formula of the *search for meaning* seems to fit them all fairly well.

The Deficiencies of the Perceptual Process

One can admire the efficiency of the perceptual process and at the same time study its failures and defects. If the available information about the world is theoretically unlimited, as I have assumed, perception at its best will always be deficient in some ultimate sense. For that matter, if potential scientific information is infinite, scientific knowledge will always be imperfect. From this cosmic and philosophic point of view we can never be absolutely sure of anything. But the point of view adopted in this book is more modest and less demanding. It is the point of view of a scientific psychologist concerned with the perceptual achievements of animals and men. He must formulate the findings of ecology and the physical sciences about the properties of the real environment and then ask why they are sometimes detected and sometimes not. It is a mistake for the psychologist to ask himself at this point how he *himself* perceives or knows the properties of the real environment. That is not his problem. If he does ask he is apt to find himself trapped in a circle of subjectivism. He can only properly ask *how one perceives,* not how *he* perceives. His role as an investigator of the perception of the world should not be confused with his other role of having to know what the world is like so that he can evaluate the process of perception. But the confusion of these roles is a common error, I believe, among psychologists.

Keeping in mind the above considerations, we can ask, what, then, are the deficiencies of the perceptual process commonly found in individuals? We know that perception is deficient in the lower animals as compared to the higher animals, and that it is less efficient in the human child than in the human adult, but let us confine the question to the last case only — to the supposedly normal observer. We exclude from consideration all deficiencies due to disease or injury.

The Failure of Organ Adjustment at High Intensity

The human retina does quite well at low levels of illumination but, as we have already noted, it is subject to the effect of glare at very high levels despite the adjusting of the pupil. Full sunlight on snow or water, or the direct rays of the sun itself, constitute an array whose differences of intensity cannot be registered because the intensities are too great. The capacity for adjustment of the system is then exceeded. The sensation of "dazzle," and even pain, accompanies this state of affairs.

The ear picks up the sequential structure of very weak sounds but it fails to do so for very loud sounds. There is a muscular mechanism in the middle ear that can alter the tension of the eardrum, which is thought to offer some protection against high-amplitude pressure waves, but it is not sufficient for the highest of them. Pain supplants perception in this event.

Intense mechanical encounters with objects are likewise painful. So is rapid absorption of heat. The haptic information is then not detectable. One cannot explore the shape of a nettle or finger a hot object. The pain is too obtrusive for that.

In all these cases the sensation of pain is no doubt useful biologically, inasmuch as it dictates the avoidance of injury, but it is nonetheless not a perception. It carries no information about the world, only about the body of the observer, and it interferes with perception.

Physiological After-effects

The way in which the semicircular canals of the vestibular organ presumably register turns of the head was described in Chapter 4. The stopping of a *prolonged* rotation, however, induces an illusion of being turned in the opposite direction, the experience called vertigo. It is probably caused by the off-center position of the flexible cupula after rotation has ceased. Under rather special conditions, especially those of passive locomotion in vehicles, the capability of the vestibular system to register starts and stops is exceeded. The after-sensation of rotation when real rotation has ceased is a consequence of the structure of the organ and of the way it works. When the cupula regains its null position, the illusion ceases. The purely perceptual illusion, of course, is mixed with motor disabilities of posture, of equilibrium, and of accurate pointing with the hand.

The illusion of the water which feels cold to a warm hand but warm to a cold hand was described in Chapter 7. It probably results from the fact that the information for the perception of warmness-coolness consists of the direction of heat flow at the skin, inward or outward, and from the fact that the skin tends to reach the same temperature as the medium in which it is maintained. The illusion is an after-effect of temperature adaptation. It is a consequence of the way the system works; the physiological zero between warm and cool being temporarily out of calibration.

The after-sensation of a patch of color in the visual field but not in the visual world, appearing in whatever direction one looks, is an illusion of visual perception that results from the way the retinal photoreceptors work. It is caused either by a high-intensity patch of light on the retina for a short time or a fixation of differential light for a long time. There are several types of this after-sensation, positive and negative, reflecting the complexity of the photoreceptive process. This statement does little justice to the careful study of these sensations and their implications for the photoreceptive theory of color vision, but it is sufficient for our present considerations of perceptual illusions.

In the usual course of events, these after-sensations do not seriously interfere with the getting of information by their respective perceptual systems. They only distract the attention from the registering of objective facts. When they are very strong, however, they can incapacitate the observer.

The Obtruding of Sensation on Perception

We may now consider some often-debated examples of phenomenal experience that seem to be midway between sensory impressions and percepts. They are called cases of incomplete perceptual constancy. One such case is the coin that is really circular but appears elliptical, and another is the railroad tracks that are really parallel but appear to converge. In the theories of sensation-based perception the explanation is offered that the conversion of the pictorial sensation into the tridimensional perception is incomplete, and that a compromise results. These cases of incomplete constancy seem to pose a very real difficulty for the present theory since they imply that objective facts cannot be fully registered by the perceptual system.

I have argued that the coin does *not* always look elliptical and that the tracks do *not* always seem to converge (surely not to the locomotive engineer!). But I do not seem to win this argument, for most people say they do, and the results of experiments on shape constancy and size constancy commonly bear them out. Must the conclusion be that the shape of objects at a slant and the size of objects receding in the distance is necessarily a compromise between visual sensation and perception? This would contradict the conclusion that perception can be independent of sensation, depending only on the pickup of invariants that specify shape and size. I would prefer, therefore, to interpret the facts of incomplete constancy in another way. I suggest that in certain conditions for the perception of the layout of things, visual sensations *obtrude themselves* on the perception of true layout and cause the illusions of seeing partially in perspective. Putting it another way, sometimes we attend to the pictorial projections in the visual field instead of exclusively to the ratios and other invariants in the optic array. The pictorial mode of perception (Chapter 11) then asserts itself, since pictorial attention interferes with attention to information. The compromise is not between the raw data and the complete processing of this data, but between two alternative kinds of attention.

Some sorts of visual sensation, especially linear perspective, are very obtrusive, the more so when attention has been educated to it by having learned to draw pictures. The result may be the illusory appearance of foreshortened surfaces and decreasing size with distance. When this attitude is adopted, the information for the *slant* of the coin becomes a sensation of elliptical shape and the information for the recession of distance becomes a sensation of angular convergence to a vanishing point. I do not know of any good evidence to show that animals or young children are subject to these illusions of perspective.

. . . .

Do young children see objects in perspective?

When Helmholtz was a grown man he wrote about an event in his childhood supporting his assumption that visual sensations are what the inexperienced eye and brain provide. Having been taken to Potsdam and seeing people high up in the belfry of the church tower, he had exclaimed that they were dolls. From this incident he concluded that the seeing of objects in the distance as small is unlearned; seeing in proper size comes only with learning the clues for distance. But I would draw precisely the opposite conclusion from this story. The infant Helmholtz had been naïvely perceiving the constant scale of things all along; what this precocious observer noticed for the first time was that men in the distance could be said to look small. Indeed they can to the sophisticated self-observer. Can we really believe that the young genius took the people to be dolls? Let us rather assume that he saw people but began to be aware of size perspective and of the puzzles of physiological optics. He later wrote a thousand-page treatise on the subject, so brilliant and convincing that his theory of "unconscious inference" still dominates the textbooks a century later.

. . . .

Another example of a sensory illusion is the finger which "looks double" when held close to the eye. The dual sensations are the consequence of disparity of the two optic arrays (Chapter 9) and they are usually called double "images." A finger held at the tip of the nose with the eyes converging at a considerable distance yields crossed disparity, a maximum degree of it, in fact. Crossed disparity is information for the visual system specifying the nearness of the finger. Usually it is registered simply as information, but if one attends to his retinal sensations, after being trained to do so, one gets the curious illusion of two fingers, knowing full well that there is only one.

The doubling of contours in the visual field can only be noticed when it is relatively strong. It is not usually obtrusive and it does not seem to interfere with the pickup of disparity information. In the present theory, the double sensations are an incidental symptom of binocular disparity. But the theories of sensation-based perception must assume a fusion of these double images in the brain, or the "sensorium," and this leads to all sorts of theoretical trouble.

After-effects of Habituation

One of the physiological after-effects described above was that in which a hand is immersed in warm water for a minute. The feeling of warmth diminishes. Then if the hand is put in water at room temperature it feels cold. This is said to be a result of physiological adaptation, but it is analogous to many other kinds of adaptation or habituation that are called *psychological*. The principle seems to be that whenever opposites can be judged, an experience on one side of the scale tends to shift the judgment of what is neutral toward that side of the scale. There are innumerable instances of this central tendency in perceiving, judging, rating, and evaluating, at various levels of perception. At one level, a moderate illumination seems bright after one has been in darkness but dark after one has been in bright light. At quite another level, ordinary conversation seems brilliant after talking to dull people, but dull after talking to bright people.

The principle applies not only to the qualities of objects that John Locke called *secondary*, but also to some that he called *primary*. The secondary qualities were colors, sounds, tastes, smells, and feelings of warmth and cold, and they were said to be only in us, not in the physical objects themselves. The primary qualities were shape, size, position, duration, motion, and solidity, and they were said to be in physical objects. Everything in this book, the reader will recognize, goes contrary to this doctrine of Locke's. It is plausible but pernicious, and the attempt to refute it was begun in the first chapters. The point of interest here is this: since after-effects in perception apply not only to colors, tastes, smells, and feelings of temperature, but also to shape, size, position, and motion, one reason for the doctrine breaks down.

Here are the facts. After looking at a curved edge for some time, a straight edge appears to be slightly curved the other way (Gibson, 1933). After looking at a surface slanted backward, a frontal surface appears slanted forward (Bergman and Gibson, 1959). After wearing prismatic spectacles yielding a whole family of abnormalities in surface perception, their opposites appear when the spectacles are removed (Kohler, 1964). The perceptual process for these supposedly objective qualities is not different in this respect from the perceptual process for the colors and the temperatures of surfaces.

The illusory negative after-effects in these cases are clearly the consequences of the adaptation or habituation. This might be a tendency to reset the neutral values of perceptual qualities to a running mean of environmental values. Something like this is suggested by Helson's theory of "adaptation level" (Helson, 1964). Whatever the process, it is a realistic one and the occasional errors of judgment are incidental to it.

Overselective Attention

It was said earlier in this chapter that the perceptual systems did not get enough information to work with in some circumstances, such as fog and darkness. In other circumstances, however, they get *too much* information to work with. In an eventful environment with sights and sounds and smells and touches all around, the individual cannot register everything at once and his perception must therefore be selective. The modes of selective attention, in fact, define the principal perceptual systems. The number of different identifiable objects in different directions may be enormous, and no one can look at them all. The world is often like a three-ring circus to a child — too many things happening too fast for him to comprehend them.

In the face of this situation, an expert perceiver develops a highly economical strategy of perception. This was described at the end of the last chapter. After things are discriminated and their properties abstracted, their number is reduced to a few categories of interest and the subcategories or cross-categories are neglected. At this stage only the information required to identify an object need be picked up and all the other information in the array, whatever makes it unique and special, can be neglected. Hence the percept of the object becomes a mere caricature or schema of what it would be if the perceiver took the time to scan the optical structure of the object. When he gives it only a glance, he *neglects* available information just as a tenth-second display of an object *reduces* available information. The tachistoscope forces observation at a glance.

There is great danger of error, we may now note, in this kind of economical perception. The object may in fact be unique or special, that is, an exceptional one that is not in one of the observer's categories of interest. An overselection of information has occurred. What the object really affords may be missed and what the observer perceives it as affording may be mistaken.

The danger of schematic perception is not so much that the percept is a caricature of the object and therefore an imperfect representation. A percept is never a representation in the first place. The danger is that the caricature may not be a *good* one. A clumsy caricature by a poor artist is not misleading because it is a distortion, but only because the information it conveys is wrong. The prejudgment involved in a skeletonized percept is a necessary result of the selective attunement of a perceptual system. If the prejudgments of conceptual attention are elaborate enough they will not get the observer into trouble. Prejudices and stereotypes are misleading when the interests of the observer are narrow or malicious. The prejudices of the open-minded observer are another matter.

A Classification of Illusions

When our early ancestors first noticed the images in a pool of water, or the shadows of things, and especially when they began to make pictures, we may fairly assume that they became puzzled about the problem of appearance and reality. For these appearances are not real things; they are ghost-like, as the simplest of tests show. They are illusions. Illusions, as the Latin root of the word suggests, mock us. There are many kinds, and some are difficult to explain. It is difficult even to decide just what an illusion is. How, for example, does an illusion differ from an hallucination? Can we now, on the basis of what has been said, define and classify illusions?

On the present theory, illusions, like misperceptions in general, should tend to fall into two major types, objective and subjective. I will suggest that those of the first type are caused by information from artificial sources, by the deflecting of light rays, by contradictory information from pictorial sources, and by obscure combinations of information in geometrical drawings. Those of the second type, on the other hand, arising from deficiencies of perception, seem to be caused by such factors as the after-effects of excitation, insufficient specialization of receptors, and internal excitation of the nervous system. These seven classes of illusions are probably not exhaustive. They illustrate the possibility, however, of a general theoretical approach to a difficult and confusing problem in the study of perception.

Artificial Sources

Perhaps the commonest illusions are representations or reproductions. These were defined in Chapter 11. The faithful picture, the painting, the wax flowers, the statue, and the model are examples. The rule is that if an artificial source of stimulation conveys information equivalent to a natural source, the perceptions will be to that extent equivalent.

For vision the same structure (or transformation) of an optic array, whatever its source, will always afford the same perception. The virtual object behind a mirror is also the result of this rule.

The motion picture is notoriously a case where the moving event is only apparent. Nothing in the window really moves, but insofar as the optical transformations in the light from the screen are the same as the transformations in the light from the event to the camera, an illusion will result. The virtual event may be highly convincing, as when the young child is distressed by the shadows of the hero and the villain knocking one another down with a display of violent gestures and facial expressions. He presumably has not learned to distinguish illusion from reality by spanning *all* the available information, including that outside the screen and that prior to or subsequent to the movie.

Onstage fighting, of course, may be even more frightening to the child than motion-picture fighting.

The optical motions produced by the gadgets used in psychological laboratories to isolate, control, and display them are also virtual but not real. The material rotation of a Plateau spiral (Figure 14.7) causes its optical array to undergo expansion or contraction. The device of a rotating spiral behind a slot causes an optical motion of linear translation. The motions of the apparatus are entirely distinct from the motions of the light. The rectangular room seen when a trapezoidal room is viewed from the proper peephole is another example. So are all the varieties of sound reproduction. If the fidelity of the system is high, there can be virtual orchestras, singers, speeches, or poetry readings.

The Bending of an Optic Array by Reflection or Refraction

The image of oneself in a pool or mirror, in fact the whole virtual scene, is caused by regular reflection of the pencil of rays comprising an array (Figure 10.15). The mirage of unreal trees and buildings in the desert is said to be due to regular reflection at a layer of heated air, following the same principle.

The apparent displacement of the visible environment and its objects by prisms in front of the eyes is due to refraction, which is another sort of bending of a pencil of rays. Apparent reversal of the world can be obtained by refraction and internal reflection in a right-angle prism. The straight stick that appears bent in water is due to refraction.

If the differential scattering of light of different wavelengths by particles in air is reduced to a multitude of reflections and refractions, then the apparent blueness of mountains (which are really green) in the distance is indirectly due to this cause.

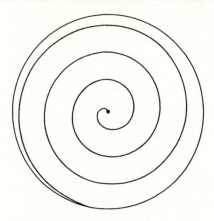

Figure 14.7   A Plateau spiral. If the spiral line is smooth and the surface of the disk is blank, a slow rotation will yield no optical information for rotation but only optical information for a motion of expansion. This occurs with a counterclockwise rotation of the disk; the opposite occurs with clockwise rotation. The continuous centrifugal flow of the optic array is similar to that of *approach,* except that its outer border does not participate in the motion. A strange experience of approach (or of recession) not embodied in an object is often reported when the disk is observed in rotation. And a reversed after-image of the motion is observed when the rotation stops. Plateau was a nineteenth-century Belgian scientist who made many discoveries about vision. (From Edwin G. Boring, *Sensation and Perception in the History of Experimental Psychology,* Figure 95. Copyright, 1942, by D. Appleton-Century Company, Inc. Reprinted by permission of Appleton-Century-Crofts, Division of Meredith Publishing Company.)

Contradictory Information from a Picture

The illusions that can be described as the seeing of two alternative things in the same place were explained in Chapter 11 as cases of equivocal information in the same array. The reversibility of figure and ground and of perspective depth were illustrated. Other examples of hidden representations and various sorts of puzzle pictures are familiar to painters and psychologists. The contradictions of optical structure that can be incorporated in a drawing or painting are endless, and it seems to be fashionable just now for artists to explore them.

The Geometrical Illusions

There is a large class of visual illusions, known to psychologists for a century, that do not involve representation but only the perception of the properties of lines, curves, and geometrical figures. They involve the judgment of apparent lengths, sizes, angles, and areas, and of rectilinearity, parallels, and the like. These are variables of optical structure, of structure *as such* in the present terminology, but they are variables of relatively low order. They come from plane geometry, not from the relational invariants of perspective or projective geometry, which, I argue, carry most of the information about the world. Length, size, and angle are basic variables for measurement, and it has been assumed that they must also be basic variables of visual sensation or perception, but that assumption has here been challenged.

According to Titchener (1906, Vol. I, Part 1), a geometrical illusion is "a perception which differs in some way from the perception which the nature of the visual stimuli would lead us to expect" (p. 151). The stimuli compared in the Müller-Lyer figure are essentially two lines of equal length. We would expect equal lengths to appear equal but they do not. Similarly, we would expect segments of the same line to appear co-linear, and parallels to appear parallel, for these are properties of the stimuli, and presumably of the corresponding sensations. These are illustrated in Figure 14.8.

But the *information* for length of line, I have argued, is not simply length of line. To suppose so is to confuse the picture considered as a surface with the optical information to the eye. A line drawn on paper is not a stimulus. The stimulus information for the length of a line is altered by combining it with other lines. We should never have expected equal lengths to appear equal when they are incorporated in different figures. Only if we can isolate the two line segments from the wings and arrowheads in the Müller-Lyer illusion should they appear equal, and this would require a very special kind of selective attention.

The question of why one line looks shorter than the other is no longer of major importance for the theory of perception if line segments as such are not components of perception. The answer depends on discovering combinations of information in line drawings. Of all the many theories of the Müller-Lyer illusion, the one most nearly consistent with our hypothesis is one of this sort: the left-hand figure contains information for the ridge of a roof seen from above, while the right-hand figure contains information for the ridge of a roof seen from below. The apparent sizes of the two ridge-lines depend on their apparent distances in accordance with the general principle of perception of size-at-a-distance illustrated in Figure 14.9.

If this hypothesis is valid, the geometrical illusions are not subjective phenomena as they have always been taken to be, but instead are special cases of the information in variables of optical structure as displayed in drawings.

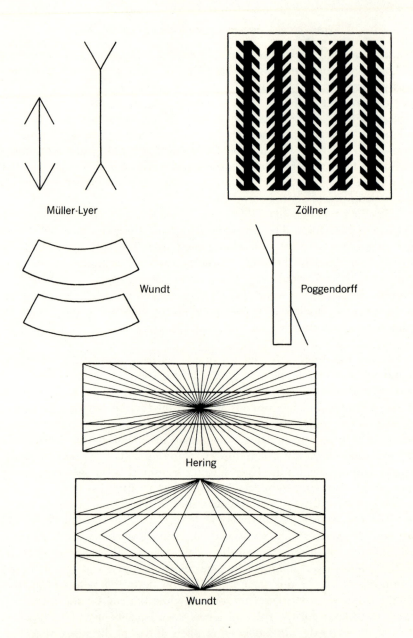

Müller-Lyer

Zöllner

Wundt

Poggendorff

Hering

Wundt

Figure 14.8   The better known geometrical illusions. Anomalies in the perception of the lengths of lines, the parallelism of lines, the sizes of outlines, the continuity of a line, and the rectilinearity or curvature of lines are illustrated. The illusions are named for their discoverers. (From E. B. Titchener, *Experimental Psychology*, Vol. I, *Qualitative Experiments*, Student's Manual. Copyright 1909, The Macmillan Company. Reprinted by permission of the publisher.)

Figure 14.9 The principle of the perception of size-at-a-distance. One kind of information for detecting the size of an object that is part of a terrestrial environment consists of the amount of environmental texture the object intercepts or hides. The far cylinder in this scene is more than twice as large as the near one because it intercepts more than twice as many units of texture. Hence, in a pictorial array, the length of a line on the picture-plane can scarcely be seen as such; there is a strong tendency for it to be perceived as the length of the object it represents in the virtual space of the picture. (From Gibson, 1950.)

After-effects of Excitation

We now come to those classes of illusions that are genuinely subjective phenomena. The after-sensations of light and color, of warmth and cold, and of rotation were described in the last section. As explained, they result from unusual conditions of stimulation, staring at a source, change of medium, and passive rotation, respectively. The neural input continues after stimulation has ceased.

The perceptual after-effects of habituation, the apparent curvatures and motions of the world described, are a little different. They are ultimately but not so obviously physiological in origin. Distortions of the shape and motion of things *look* as if they were external but they are just as dependent on neural processes as the patch of color that moves with the eye or the spots that sometimes appear with migraine.

Insufficient Specialization of Receptors

The so-called flashes of light that appear when the skull is severely jarred are a result of mechanical stimulation of the visual nervous system, that is, of cells that are supposed to respond only to light. Pressure on the eyeball can also excite the retina. This perceptual system is fairly well cushioned against bumps, but some are too much for it. Electrical stimulation, which fortunately is rare in life, will excite any receptor mosaic or any nervous tissue — eye, ear, skin, or muscle. Illusions of light, sound, touch, or action due to electric shock are not encountered unless one is the subject of an experiment. The photoreceptive equipment is well specialized for photoreception, but not perfectly so, and mechanical or electrical energy can touch it off.

None of the perceptual systems is perfectly specialized for the pickup of information. If there is no limit to potential information, perfection of discrimination is not to be expected. The tasting system, as noted in Chapter 8, is subject to a kind of illusion inasmuch as some harmful poisons do not arouse distaste, and conversely, some harmless emetics do arouse distaste. For an omnivorous species like man, not all environmental substances are differentiated with respect to their nutritive value. There are too many substances. Some things that are not nutritive are palatable, and some things that are nutritive are unpalatable.

Internal Excitation of the Nervous System

The false feeling of pain or other sensation in an amputated limb is an impressive demonstration of the fact that perception depends on impulses in nerve fibers and that nerve fibers fire in sequential chains. Where the excitation begins in the case of the feeling of a "phantom limb" is not known, but it is known that nerves are discharged by abnormal causes, especially after injury, and sometimes long after. Drugs can have a direct effect on nervous tissue, as in the false colors of things observed after taking mescaline. And with alcohol poisoning, or the new "psycho-mimetic" drugs, full hallucinations may arise as a result of direct action on the brain.

Hallucinations, it is said, are accompanied by a "feeling of reality," whereas illusions are not. Just what the feeling of reality consists of has not been established. Probably it is graded in degree. One clue to this gradation might be obtained by considering the continued efforts that have been made since the invention of photography to "add realism" to a picture, to make it lifelike, in short to make this classic type of illusion as much as possible like a perception (Chapter 11). The stationary, black-and-white screen picture produced by the early "magic lantern" was soon given color, and the fidelity of color representation has since been radically improved. The scope of the screen has been increased in the attempt to create a panorama. The stereoscopic picture was invented in the effort to enhance the perception of depth. The representation of sequence and transformation was achieved by cinematography. The sound film supplied auditory representation synchronized with the visual representation in recent times. We now have the panoramic motion picture in color with sound.

These developments have all made available *more information* to the main perceptual systems, vision and hearing. The perceiver does indeed get an approximation to first-hand experience nowadays, especially if the motion-picture camera takes the position of an actor in the scene.

Nevertheless, the modern motion picture is not an hallucination. It is still mere illusion. All proprioception is absent except for eye movements. The perceiver is passive. He sits in a chair. He is not fully surrounded by the environment represented on the screen. He cannot alter what will happen in the virtual world. Even though he may be given the experience of walking, approaching, inspecting, and riding in vehicles, it is not *his* experience for he did not get it for himself; most of it is imposed, not obtained. The perception of a real world cannot and never will be completely imitated, for in the real world the perceiver can always find out things for himself and the more he explores the more he will find.

The malfunctioning of the perceptual systems which leads to true hallucinations, as in serious mental diseases, is probably due to some kind of inhibition of perceptual exploration with a shutting off or rejection of the current input of perceptual information.

Summary

In this final chapter an attempt has been made to explain misperceptions and illusions as deficiencies in a process which usually comes out right but which for various reasons sometimes goes wrong. A tentative list of these reasons has been offered.

First, the available stimulus information for perception can be inadequate. The energy may be minimal, or the structure of an array may be blurred, or it can be masked, or the information in structure may be contradictory. The interval during which energy is available may be cut short, or the angular size of the optic array may be narrowed down. The spatial and temporal structure of light or sound can be displaced, or biased, or distorted. Mirrors, prisms, and lenses can alter the structure of light and modern electronic gadgetry can alter the structure of sound.

Second, the physiological process of information pickup can be deficient. Even normal perceptual organs fail to work at high intensities of energy. Their capacity can be overstrained. They get out of calibration after abnormal stimulation and the recovery process then yields aftersensations. The physiological action of the receptors as such may be so obtrusive as to distract the observer. The action of a whole system may be subject to perceptual adaptation followed by after-effects. And finally there are errors of attention due to false expectations.

These causes of misperception provide at least a systematic basis for the classification of what have been called illusions. Some illusions should be ascribed mainly to external conditions and some mainly to internal. Examples of the former are experiences aroused by artificial sources (images and reproductions, including motion pictures); experiences resulting from the bending of optic arrays by natural or artificial means; the ambiguous experiences from contradictory information in a picture; and the anomalies of the "geometrical" illusions. Examples of the latter are the after-sensations and perceptual after-effects, the sensations caused by inappropriate mechanical or electrical stimulation, and the little understood cases of purely internal excitation of the nervous system. The last-named include hallucinations.

Conclusion

Thomas Reid's assertion in 1785 is just as true as it ever was, that "the external senses have a double province; to make us feel and to make us perceive." They "furnish us with a variety of sensations" and they "give us a conception of external objects." Philosophers and psychologists have been fascinated by these feelings that accompany perceiving, and physiologists have discovered some of their causes. But animals and children and ordinary persons are not in the least concerned with how it feels to perceive. When the senses are considered as channels of sensations they are curious and interesting, but they are not the instruments of our contact with the world. The impressions of sense are incidental accompaniments of perceiving, not the data for perceiving. They are not entailed in perceiving. Sensations are not, as we have always taken for granted, the basis of perception.

When the senses are considered as perceptual systems, all theories of perception become at one stroke unnecessary. It is no longer a question of how the mind operates on the deliverances of sense, or how past experience can organize the data, or even how the brain can process the inputs of the nerves, but simply how information is picked up. This stimulus information is available in the everyday environment, as I have shown. The individual does not have to construct an awareness of the world from bare intensities and frequencies of energy; he has to detect the world from invariant properties in the flux of energy. Such invariants, the direction of gravity for instance, are registered even by primitive animals who do not have elaborate perceptual organs.

Mathematical complexities of stimulus energy seem to be the simplicities of stimulus information. Active perceptual systems, as contrasted with passive receptors, have so developed during evolution that they can resonate to this information. The mathematically simple and easily measurable variables of energy are bare of meaning, to be sure, but they

319

are only relevant to the action of mechanoreceptors, photoreceptors, and chemoreceptors.

When it is recognized that receptors, nerve bundles, and the corresponding modalities of sensory experience do not provide a fixed number of senses or permit a fixed inventory of sense impressions, we are free to study the redundant overlapping activity of perceptual systems unhindered by the old doctrines. Proprioception or self-sensitivity is seen to be an overall function, common to all systems, not a special sense. The activity of orienting and that of exploring and selecting — the commonsense faculty of attending — is seen to be one that extracts the external information from the stimulus flux while registering the change as subjective feeling. This feedback system also, of course, controls the performatory activity of the body, the executive systems of behavior proper as distinguished from perception, but that aspect of proprioception lies outside the scope of this book.

The puzzle of constant perception despite varying sensations disappears and a new question arises, how the invariant information is extracted. Perceptual development and perceptual learning are seen as a process of distinguishing the features of a rich input, not of enriching the data of a bare and meaningless input. A perceptual system hunts for a state of what we call "clarity." Whatever this state is physiologically, it has probably governed the evolution of perception in the species, the maturation of perception in the young, and the learning of perception in the adult.

The puzzle of depth perception disappears and the question becomes one of how animals detect the layout of their surroundings. The puzzle of form perception is no longer important (consisting only of the question of how men learned to see the perspectives of things from this or that point of view when they began to draw pictures) and the important question emerges of how animals and children detect those distinctive features of things that are invariant under changes of perspective.

The puzzle evaporates of the seemingly innate capacity of newborn animals and human infants to interpret certain sensations without prior experience. Instead, the question arises of how it is that vision, hearing, and smell are attuned to (or are rapidly imprinted by) certain sights, sounds, and odors.

Above all, the puzzle of meaning and value in perception takes an entirely new form. If what things afford is specified in the light, sound, and odor around them, and does not consist of the subjective memories of what they have afforded in the past, then the learning of new meanings is an education of attention rather than an accrual of associations.

The problem of the communication of information from one person to another also takes a new form. Pictures and words are now seen to be truly mediators of perception, of perception at second hand. Spoken and written words presuppose a code, and associative learning of the classical sort does come into the child's mastery of this code. But association is not the basis of learning as we have been taught. Discrimination has to precede association for language to be of any use. The ability to name and to predicate fixes the gains of perceiving but it does not explain perceiving. It fosters the education of attention to the facts of the world but cannot substitute for it.

The useful senses have been contrasted in this book with what might be called the useless senses. The fact is that, although different men do not all use their senses in the same way, they *can* all use their senses in the same way. The basis for agreement among men exists in the available stimulus information. Men often disagree but they are not fated to do so by their language or their culture. Disagreement is not caused by inherent differences in their habits of interpreting sensory experience — habits permanently fixed by the words they use. A man can always re-educate his attention. For that matter, a man can invent new words for something he has seen for himself. He can even get others to see what he has newly seen by describing it carefully, and this is a fortunate man.

Let us recognize the strength of the dead hand of habit on perception. Let us acknowledge that people — other people, of course — often perceive the world like silly sheep. But it is wrong to make a philosophy of this rather snobbish observation. The orthodox theories of perception have encouraged this fallacy and one purpose of this book has been to undermine them. This book is dedicated to all persons who want to look for themselves.

BIBLIOGRAPHY

Adey, W. R., The sense of smell, Chapter 21 in *Handbook of Physiology*, Vol. 1, *Neurophysiology*, American Physiological Society, 1959.

Allee, W. C., A. E. Emerson, O. Park, T. Park, and K. P. Schmidt, *Principles of Animal Ecology*, Saunders, 1949.

Ambrose, J A., The development of the smiling response in early infancy. In B. M. Foss (Ed.), *Determinants of Infant Behavior*, Wiley, 1961.

Arnheim, R., *Art and Visual Perception*, University of California Press, 1954.

Attneave, F., *Applications of Information Theory to Psychology*, Holt, 1959.

Ausubel, D. P., *Theory and Problems of Child Development*, Grune and Stratton, 1958.

Autrum, H., Nonphotic receptors in lower forms. Chapter 16 in *Handbook of Physiology*. Vol. 1, *Neurophysiology*, American Physiological Society, 1959.

Bergman R., and J. J. Gibson, The negative aftereffect of the perception of a surface slanted in the third dimension. *Amer. J. Psychol.*, 1959, 72, 364–374.

Berkeley, G., *An Essay Towards a New Theory of Vision*, 1709 (any modern edition).

Bevan, W., Subliminal stimulation: A pervasive problem for psychology. *Psychol. Bull.*, 1964, 61, 81–99.

Binns, H., Visual and tactual judgment as illustrated in a practical experiment. *Brit. J. Psychol.*, 1937, 27, 404–410.

Boring, E. G., *Sensation and Perception in the History of Experimental Psychology*, Appleton-Century, 1942.

Boring, E. G., Visual perception as invariance. *Psychol. Rev.*, 1952a, 59, 141–148.

Boring, E. G., The Gibsonian visual field. *Psychol. Rev.*, 1952b, 59, 246–247.

Bosma, J. F. (Ed.), *Symposium on Oral Sensation and Perception*, Thomas, 1966.

Broadbent, D. E., *Perception and Communication*, Pergamon Press, 1958.

Brunswik, E., *Systematic and Representative Design of Psychological Experiments*, University of California Press, 1949.

Brunswik, E., *Perception and the Representative Design of Psychological Experiments*, University of California Press, 1956.

Cannon, W. B., *Bodily Changes in Pain, Hunger, Fear, and Rage*, Appleton, 1929.

Carmichael, L., and W. F. Dearborn, *Reading and Visual Fatigue*, Houghton Mifflin, 1947.

Cherry, C., *On Human Communication*, Wiley, 1957.

Clifford, W. K., *The Common Sense of the Exact Sciences*, Knopf, 1946.

Cohen, W., Spatial and textural characteristics of the Ganzfeld. *Amer. J. Psychol.*, 1957, *70*, 403–410.

Daniel, G., *Lascaux and Carnac*, London: Lutterworth Press, 1955.

Davis, H., Excitation of auditory receptors. Chapter 23 in *Handbook of Physiology*. Vol. 1, *Neurophysiology*, American Physiological Society, 1959.

Eddington, A. S., *The Nature of the Physical World*, Macmillan, 1929.

Fantz, R. L., The origin of form perception. *Sci. Amer.*, 1961, *204*, 2–8.

Fieandt, K. von, and J. J. Gibson, The sensitivity of the eye to two kinds of continuous transformation of a shadow-pattern. *J. Exper. Psychol.*, 1959, *57*, 344–347.

Flock, H. R., A possible optical basis for monocular slant perception. *Psychol. Rev.*, 1964, *71*, 380–391.

Fraenkel, G. S., and D. L. Gunn, *The Orientation of Animals*, Oxford University Press, 1940 (Dover, 1961).

Frisch, K. von, *Bees: Their Vision, Chemical Senses, and Language*, Cornell University Press, 1960.

Fry, G. A., Review of Ronchi's *Optics*. *J. Opt. Soc. Amer.*, 1957, *47*, 977–978.

Garner, W. R., *Uncertainty and Structure as Psychological Concepts*, Wiley, 1962.

Geldard, F. A., *The Human Senses*, Wiley, 1953.

Gibson, Eleanor J., Improvement in perceptual judgments as a function of controlled practice or training. *Psychol. Bull.*, 1953, *50*, 401–431.

Gibson, Eleanor J., J. J. Gibson, O. W. Smith, and H. Flock, Motion parallax as a determinant of perceived depth. *J. Exper. Psychol.*, 1959, *58*, 40–51.

Gibson, J. J., Adaptation, aftereffect, and contrast in the perception of curved lines. *J. Exper. Psychol.*, 1933, *16*, 1–31.

Gibson, J. J., Adaptation with negative aftereffect. *Psychol. Rev.*, 1937, *44*, 222–244.

Gibson, J. J., A critical review of the concept of set in contemporary experimental psychology. *Psychol. Bull.*, 1941, *38*, 781–817.

Gibson, J. J., Studying Perceptual Phenomena. Chapter 6 in T. G. Andrews (Ed.), *Methods of Psychology*, Wiley, 1948.

Gibson, J. J., *The Perception of the Visual World*, Houghton Mifflin, 1950.

Gibson, J. J., The visual field and the visual world: A reply to Professor Boring. *Psychol. Rev.*, 1952a, *59*, 149–151.

Gibson, J. J., The relation between visual and postural determinants of the phenomenal vertical. *Psychol. Rev.*, 1952*b*, *59*, 370–375.

Gibson, J. J., A theory of pictorial perception. *Audiovisual Communic. Rev.*, 1954*a*, *1*, 3–23.

Gibson, J. J., The visual perception of objective motion and subjective movement. *Psychol. Rev.*, 1954*b*, *61*, 304–314.

Gibson, J. J., *Optical Motions and Transformations as Stimuli for Visual Perception* (motion picture). Psychological Cinema Register, State College, Pa., 1955.

Gibson, J. J., Optical motions and transformations as stimuli for visual perception. *Psychol. Rev.*, 1957, *64*, 288–295.

Gibson, J. J., Visually controlled locomotion and visual orientation in animals. *Brit. J. Psychol.*, 1958, *49*, 182–194.

Gibson, J. J., Perception as a function of stimulation. In S. Koch (Ed.), *Psychology: A Study of a Science*, Vol. 1, McGraw-Hill, 1959.

Gibson, J. J., The concept of the stimulus in psychology. *Amer. Psychol.*, 1960*a*, *15*, 694–703.

Gibson, J. J., Pictures, perspective, and perception. *Daedalus*, 1960*b*, *89*, 216–227.

Gibson, J. J., Ecological optics, *Vision Research*, 1961, *1*, 253–262.

Gibson, J. J., Observations on active touch. *Psychol. Rev.*, 1962, *69*, 477–491.

Gibson, J. J., The useful dimensions of sensitivity. *Amer. Psychol.*, 1963, *18*, 1–15.

Gibson, J. J., and Eleanor J. Gibson, Perceptual learning: differentiation or enrichment? *Psychol. Rev.*, 1955, *62*, 32–41.

Gibson, J. J., and Eleanor J. Gibson, Continuous perspective transformations and the perception of rigid motion. *J. Exper. Psychol.*, 1957, *54*, 129–138.

Gibson, J. J., and F. A. Backlund, An aftereffect in haptic space perception. *Quart. J. Exper. Psychol.*, 1963, *15*, 145–154.

Gibson, J. J., P. Olum, and F. Rosenblatt, Parallax and perspective during aircraft landings. *Amer. J. Psychol.*, 1955, *68*, 372–385.

Gibson, J. J., and Anne D. Pick, Perception of another person's looking behavior. *Amer. J. Psychol.*, 1963, *76*, 386–394.

Gibson, J. J., J. Purdy, and L. Lawrence, A method of controlling stimulation for the study of space perception: The optical tunnel. *J. Exper. Psychol.*, 1955, *50*, 1–14.

Gibson, J. J., and D. Waddell, Homogeneous retinal stimulation and visual perception. *Amer. J. Psychol.*, 1952, *65*, 263–270.

Goldscheider, A., *Gesammelte Abhandlungen von A. Goldscheider* (2 vols.), Leipzig: Barth, 1898.

Gombrich, E. H., *Art and Illusion: A Study in the Psychology of Pictorial Representation*, Pantheon, 1960.

Gottschaldt, K., Über den Einfluss der Erfahrung auf die Wahrnehmung von Figuren. *Psychol. Forsch.*, 1926, *8*, 261–317.

Graham, C. H., Color theory. In S. Koch (Ed.), *Psychology: A Study of a Science*, Vol. 1, *Sensory, Perceptual, and Physiological Formulations*, pp. 145–287, McGraw-Hill, 1959.

Gray, J. A. B., Initiation of impulses at receptors. Chapter 4 in *Handbook of Physiology*. Vol. 1, *Neurophysiology*, American Physiological Society, 1959.

Harlow, H. F., The nature of love. *Amer. Psychol.*, 1958, *13*, 673–685.

Harper, R., Physiological and psychological aspects of studies of craftsmanship in dairying. *Brit. J. Psychol. Monogr. Suppl.*, 1952, *28*, 1–63.

Harper, R., and S. S. Stevens, Subjective hardness of compliant materials. *Quart. J. Exper. Psychol.*, 1964, *16*, 204–215.

Harris, C. S., Adaptation to displaced vision: visual, motor, or proprioceptive change? *Science*, 1963, *40*, 812–813.

Hasler, A. D., and W. J. Wisby, Discrimination of stream odors by fishes and its relation to parent stream behavior. *Amer. Naturalist*, 1951, *85*, 223–238.

Hebb, D. O., *The Organization of Behavior*, Wiley, 1949.

Heider, F., Ding und Medium, *Symposion*, 1926, *1*, 109–157. Translated as "Thing and medium," in F. Heider, *On Perception, Event Structure, and Psychological Environment*, International Universities Press, 1959 (*Psychological Issues*, 1959, Vol. 1, No. 3).

Held, R., Plasticity in sensory-motor systems. *Sci. Amer.*, 1965, *213*, 84–94.

Helmholtz, H., *Physiological Optics*, Vol. 3 (J. P. C. Southall, Ed.), Optical Society of America, 1925.

Helson, H., *Adaptation-Level Theory*, Harper and Row, 1964.

Hochberg, J. E., *Perception*, Prentice-Hall, 1964.

Hochberg, J. E., and J. Beck, Apparent spatial arrangement and perceived brightness. *J. Exper. Psychol.*, 1954, *47*, 263–266.

Hockett, C. F., and R. Ascher, The human revolution. *Current Anthropol.*, 1964, *5*, 135–168.

Holst, E. von, Relations between the central nervous system and the peripheral organs. *Brit. J. Anim. Behav.*, 1954, *2*, 89–94.

Holst, E. von, and H. Mittelstädt, Das reafferenzprinzip. *Naturwiss*, 1950, *37*, 464–476.

Hornbostel, E. M. von, The unity of the senses. *Psyche*, 1927, *7*, 83–89. Reprinted in W. D. Ellis, *A Source Book of Gestalt Psychology*, Harcourt Brace, 1938.

Hull, C. L., *Principles of Behavior*, Appleton-Century, 1943.

Hume, D., *A Treatise of Human Nature*, 1739 (any modern edition).

Humphrey, G., *Thinking, An Introduction to its Experimental Psychology*, London: Methuen, 1951.

Hurvich, L. M., and Dorothea Jameson, *The Perception of Brightness and Darkness*, Allyn & Bacon, 1966.

Hutchinson, Ann, *Labanotation*, New Directions, 1954.

Jakobson, R., and M. Halle, *Fundamentals of Language*, The Hague: Mouton and Co., 1956.

James, W., *The Principles of Psychology*, Holt, 1890.

Jennings, H. S., *Behavior of the Lower Organisms*, Macmillan, 1906.

Johansson, G., *Configurations in Event Perception*, Uppsala: Almkvist and Wiksell, 1950.

Kalmus, H., The discrimination by the nose of the dog of individual human odors and in particular of the odors of twins. *Brit. J. Anim. Behav.*, 1955, 3, 25–31.

Kalmus, H., The chemical senses. *Sci. Amer.*, 1958, *198*, 97–106.

Kare, M., and M. S. Ficken, Comparative studies on the sense of taste. In Y. Zotterman (Ed.), *Olfaction and Taste*, Macmillan, 1963.

Katz, D., *Der Aufbau der Tastwelt*, Leipzig: Barth, 1925.

Katz, D., *The World of Colour* (Tr. by R. B. MacLeod and C. W. Fox), London: Kegan Paul, Trench, Trubner and Co., 1935.

Katz, D., A sense of touch. The techniques of percussion, palpation, and massage. *Brit. J. Phys. Med.*, 1936, 2, 35ff.

Katz, D., and W. Stephenson, Experiments on elasticity. *Brit. J. Psychol.*, 1937, 28, 190–194.

Katz, D., and R. B. MacLeod, The mandible principle in muscular action. *Acta Psychol.*, 1949, 6, 33–39.

Kelvin, R. P., Discrimination of size by sight and touch. *Quart. J. Exper. Psychol.*, 1954, 6, 23–34.

Kepes, G., *The Language of Vision*, Geo. Theobald, 1944.

Klüver, H., *Behavior Mechanisms in Monkeys*, University of Chicago Press, 1933.

Koffka, H., *Principles of Gestalt Psychology*, Harcourt Brace, 1935.

Kohler, I., *The Formation and Transformation of the Perceptual World* (Tr. by H. Fiss), International Universities Press, 1964 (*Psychological Issues*, 1964, Vol. 3, No. 4). Originally *Über Aufbau und Wandlungen der Wahrnehmungswelt*, Vienna: R. M. Rohrer, 1951.

Köhler, W., *The Mentality of Apes* (Tr. by E. Winter), London: Routledge and Kegan Paul, 1925.

Köhler, W., *Gestalt Psychology*, Liveright, 1929.

Köhler, W., and D. Dinnerstein, Figural after-effects in kinesthesis. In *Miscellanea Psychologica Albert Michotte*, Louvain: Editions de l'Institut Superieur de Philosophie, 1949, pp. 196–220.

Lashley, K. S., *Brain Mechanisms and Intelligence*, University of Chicago Press, 1929.

Lashley, K. S., In search of the engram. In *Physiological Mechanisms in Animal Behaviour* (Symposium No. 4, Soc. Exper. Biol.), Academic Press, 1950.

Lashley, K. S., The problem of serial order in behavior. In L. A. Jeffress (Ed.), *Cerebral Mechanisms in Behavior: The Hixon Symposium*, Wiley, 1951.

LeBarre, W., *The Human Animal*, University of Chicago Press, 1954.

Lewin, K., *Dynamic Theory of Personality*, McGraw-Hill, 1935.

Lewin, K., *Principles of Topological Psychology*, McGraw-Hill, 1936.

Liberman, A., K. S. Harris, P. Eimas, L. Lisker, and J. Bastian, An effect of learning on speech perception: The discrimination of durations of silence with and without phonemic significance. *Language and Speech*, 1961, 4, 175–195.

Licklider, J. C. R., Basic correlates of the auditory stimulus. Chapter 25 in S. S. Stevens (Ed.), *Handbook of Experimental Psychology*, Wiley, 1951.

Luckiesh, M., *Visual Illusions,* Van Nostrand, 1922.

MacLeod, R. B., An experimental investigation of brightness constancy. *Arch. Psychol.,* 1932, No. 135.

Matthews, L. H., and M. Knight, *The Senses of Animals,* Philosophical Library, 1963.

Metzger, W., *Gesetze des Sehens,* Frankfort am Main: Waldemar Kramer, 1953.

Michotte, A., *The Perception of Causality* (Tr. by T. R. Miles and E. Miles), London: Methuen, 1963.

Michotte, A., G. Thinès, and G. Crabbé, Les complements amodaux des structures perceptives. *Studia Psychologica,* Louvain: Publ. Univ. de Louvain, 1964.

Mill, J. S., *An examination of Sir William Hamilton's Philosophy.* London, 1865.

Milne, L. J., and M. Milne, Photosensitivity in invertebrates. Chapter 26 in *Handbook of Physiology.* Vol. 1, *Neurophysiology,* American Physiological Society, 1959.

Milne, L. J., and M. Milne, *The Senses of Animals and Men,* Atheneum, 1962.

Montessori, M. *Montessori Method* (Tr. by A. S. George), Stokes, 1912.

Moorhouse, A. C., *The Triumph of the Alphabet,* Henry Schuman, 1953.

Nafe, J. P., The pressure, pain, and temperature senses. Chapter 20 in C. Murchison (Ed.), *Handbook of General Experimental Psychology,* Clark University Press, 1934.

Ogden, C. K., and I. A. Richards, *The Meaning of Meaning,* 3rd ed., London: Kegan Paul, 1930.

Pavlov, I. P., *Conditional Reflexes* (Tr. by G. V. Anrep), Oxford University Press, 1927.

Pfaffman, C., The sense of taste. Chapter 20 in *Handbook of Physiology.* Vol. 1, *Neurophysiology,* American Physiological Society, 1959.

Piaget, J., *The Construction and Thought of the Child* (Tr. by M. Gabain), Humanities Press, 1951.

Piaget, J., *The Construction of Reality in the Child* (Tr. by M. Cook), Basic Books, 1954.

Piaget, J., and B. Inhelder, *The Child's Conception of Space* (Tr. by F. J. Langdon and J. L. Lunzer), Humanities Press, 1956.

Piéron, H., *The Sensations* (Tr. by M. H. Pirenne and B. C. Abbott), London: J. Garnet Miller, 1952.

Pirenne, M. H., Physiological mechanisms of vision and the quantum nature of light. *Biol. Rev.,* 1956, *31,* 194–241.

Polyak, S. L., *The Vertebrate Visual System,* University of Chicago Press, 1957.

Prince, J. H., *Comparative Anatomy of the Eye,* C. C. Thomas, 1956.

Purdy, W. C., The hypothesis of psychophysical correspondence in space perception. Doctoral dissertation, Cornell University. Ann Arbor: University Microfilms, 1958, No. 58–5594. Reproduced in part as Report No. R60ELC56 of the General Electric Technical Information Series.

Reid, T., *Essays on the Intellectual Powers of Man*, 1785 (any modern edition).

Revesz, G., *Psychology and Art of the Blind*, Longmans, Green, 1950.

Reynolds, H., Factors affecting the accuracy of visual tracking of a moving object when it has disappeared from sight (Thesis). Cornell University Library, 1966.

Ronchi, V., *Optics: The Science of Vision* (Tr. by E. Rosen), New York University Press, 1957.

Rose, J. E., and V. B. Mountcastle, Touch and kinesthesis. Chapter 17 in *Handbook of Physiology*. Vol. 1, *Neurophysiology*, American Physiological Society, 1959.

Schiff, W., Perception of impending collision: A study of visually directed avoidant behavior. *Psychol. Monogr.* 1965, 79, Whole No. 604.

Schiff, W., J. A. Caviness, and J. J. Gibson, Persistent fear responses in Rhesus monkeys to the optical stimulus of "looming." *Science*, 1962, *136*, 982–983.

Schlosberg, H., Stereoscopic depth from single pictures. *Amer. J. Psychol.*, 1941, *54*, 601–605.

Senden, M. von, *Space and Sight* (Tr. by P. Heath), London: Methuen, 1960.

Sheppard, D., The sensory basis of the cheese-grader's skill. *Occup. Psychol.*, 1955, *29*, 150–163.

Sherrington, C. S., *The Integrative Action of the Nervous System*, Cambridge University Press, 1906.

Singer, C., E. J. Holmyard, and A. R. Hall, *A History of Technology*, Oxford University Press, 1954.

Skinner, B. F., *The Behavior of Organisms*, Appleton-Century, 1938.

Stebbing, L. S., *Philosophy and the Physicists*, London: Methuen, 1937.

Stevens, S. S. (Ed.), *Handbook of Experimental Psychology*, Wiley, 1951.

Stevens, S. S., and Judith R. Harris, The scaling of subjective roughness and smoothness. *J. Exper. Psychol.*, 1962, *64*, 489–494.

Stratton, G. M., Some preliminary experiments on vision without inversion of the retinal image. *Psychol. Rev.*, 1896, *3*, 611–617.

Stratton, G. M., Vision without inversion of the retinal image. *Psychol. Rev.*, 1897, *4*, 341–360, 463–481.

Taylor, B., *Linear Perspective*, London, 1715 (rev. ed., 1719).

Thorpe, W. H., *Learning and Instinct in Animals*, Harvard University Press, 1956.

Tinbergen, N., *The Study of Instinct*, Oxford University Press, 1951.

Tolman, E. C., *Purposive Behavior in Animals and Men*, Century, 1932.

Titchener, E. B., *Experimental Psychology*, 4 vols., Macmillan, 1906.

Titchener, E. B., *Textbook of Psychology*, Macmillan, 1910.

Troland, L. T., *The Principles of Psychophysiology*. Vol. 1, *Problems of Psychology and Perception*, 1929; Vol. 2, *Sensation*, 1930; Vol. 3, *Cerebration and Action*, 1932; Van Nostrand.

Vernon, Magdalen D., *A Further Study of Visual Perception*, Cambridge University Press, 1952.

Walk, R. D., and Eleanor J. Gibson, A comparative and analytical study of visual depth perception. *Psychol. Monogr.*, 1961, 75, Whole no. 519.

Wallach, H., The role of head movements and vestibular and visual cues in sound localization. *J. Exper. Psychol.*, 1940, 27, 339–368. Reprinted in D. C. Beardslee and M. Wertheimer, *Readings in Perception*, Van Nostrand, 1958.

Wallach, H., On sound localization. *J. Acoust. Soc. Amer.*, 1939, 10, 270–274. Reprinted in D. C. Beardslee and M. Wertheimer, *Readings in Perception*, Van Nostrand, 1958

Walls, G. L., *The Vertebrate Eye and its Adaptive Radiation*, Cranbrook Institute of Science, 1942.

Ware, W. R., *Modern Perspective*, Macmillan, 1900.

Wertheimer, M., *Productive Thinking*, Harper, 1945.

Wever, E. G., *Theory of Hearing*, Wiley, 1949.

Wever, E. G., and M. Lawrence, *Physiological Acoustics*, Princeton University Press, 1954.

Whorf, B. L., *Language, Thought, and Reality* (Ed. by J. B. Carroll), Wiley, 1956.

Woodworth, R. S., *Experimental Psychology*, Holt, 1938.

Woodworth, R. S., Reinforcement of perception. *Amer. J. Psychol.*, 1947, 60, 119–124.

Index

In general the items included in this Index do not include the topics listed systematically in the Table of Contents. Instead, the more traditional terms and facts of sense perception are here included. Authors are included when their contributions are important for the text but not when the references are merely supportive. For the full list of references, see the Bibliography.

ISBN 0-313-23961-4

90000>

HARDCOVER BAR CODE